ESSENTIALS OF

BUSINESS

COMMUNICATION

THIRD EDITION

Mary Ellen Guffey

Los Angeles Pierce College

South-Western College Publishing

An International Thomson Publishing Company

Sponsoring Editor: *Randy G. Haubner*
Production Editor: *Crystal Chapin*
Production House: *Robin Lockwood & Associates*
Compositor: *GTS Graphics*
Cover and Interior Designer: *Paula Goldstein*
Cover Photographer: *Comstock, Inc.*
Marketing Manager: *Steve Momper*

IP

International Thomson Publishing

South-Western is an ITP Company. The ITP trademark is used under license.

BRIEF CONTENTS

DETAILED CONTENTS

CHAPTER 3   TONE, STYLE, AND ETHICS   38

CHAPTER 4   EFFECTIVE SENTENCES, PARAGRAPHS, AND MESSAGES   56

UNIT III

COMMUNICATING ROUTINE MESSAGES   77

CHAPTER 5   MEMORANDUMS THAT INFORM, REQUEST, AND RESPOND   79

PREFACE

Tell me, I forget. Show me, I remember. Involve me, I understand.

—Chinese proverb

Essentials of Business Communication, Third Edition, is founded on this proverb. This book involves students in the learning process so that they *understand* what's being taught. As one instructor said, "This is a hands-on book." Writing skills receive particular emphasis because these skills are in great demand and because such skills are difficult to acquire.

This textbook will be especially helpful to postsecondary, college, and adult students with outdated, inadequate, or weak language arts training. Numerous features facilitate the teaching/learning process.

TEXT-WORKBOOK FORMAT

The convenient text-workbook format presents an all-in-one teaching/learning package that includes concepts, workbook application exercises, writing problems, and a combination handbook/reference manual. Readers need to purchase only one volume.

FOUR-STAGE PLAN

Essentials of Business Communication, Third Edition, develops communication skills in a carefully designed four-stage plan. Stage 1 lays a foundation by presenting communication theory and by providing an optional review of basic grammar, punctuation, usage, and style. Stage 2 introduces writing techniques, including "tricks of the trade" for writers. Stage 3 teaches writing strategies and helps students apply these strategies in composing business letters and memos. Stage 4 adapts basic communication strategies and techniques to a range of communication problems.

GRAMMAR/MECHANICS EMPHASIS

Each chapter includes instructions for a systematic review of the Grammar/Mechanics Handbook, along with a short quiz. In this way students receive continual review and reinforcement of the fundamentals of correct writing. New to the Third Edition are Grammar/Mechanics Challenge exercises that provide documents to be revised and edited.

WRITING IMPROVEMENT EXERCISES AND CASES

Two unique features help readers develop writing skills. First, writing improvement exercises break down the total writing process into simple components. Second, many writing improvement cases enable students to rewrite realistic business messages, thereby helping them concentrate on applying strategies and solving writing problems rather than struggling to provide unknown details to unfamiliar, hypothetical writing cases.

LETTERS AND MEMORANDUM WRITING

Students learn to write letters and memos that request information, order goods, make claims, respond to inquiries, respond to claims, refuse requests, and refuse credit. They also learn to apply practical psychology in persuasion and sales, as well as to develop goodwill with letters of appreciation, congratulations, sympathy, and recommendation.

REPORT WRITING

Two chapters develop functional report-writing skills. Chapter 11 concentrates on informal, short reports. Chapter 12 covers formal, long reports and includes a model long report.

LISTENING AND SPEAKING SKILLS

Students learn to reduce barriers to effective listening, as well as to become more active listeners. They also study methods of organizing and delivering oral presentations; and they refine telephone, voice mail, and meeting skills.

EMPLOYMENT SKILLS

Successful résumés, letters of application, and other employment documents are among the most important topics in a good business communication course. The Third Edition includes a completely new chapter with more information on the job search and more model résumés.

DIAGNOSTIC TEST

The optional grammar/mechanics diagnostic test helps students and instructors systematically pinpoint specific student writing weaknesses. Students may be directed to the Grammar/Mechanics Handbook for remediation.

GRAMMAR/MECHANICS HANDBOOK

The comprehensive Grammar/Mechanics Handbook supplies a thorough review of English grammar, punctuation, capitalization style, and number usage. Its self-teaching exercises may be used for classroom instruction or for supplementary assignments. The handbook also serves as a convenient reference throughout the course.

NEW IN THE THIRD EDITION

- *Cross-cultural and international communication.* A new section in Chapter 1 helps prepare students for expanding global markets as well as for increasingly diverse local work environments.
- *Ethics issues and tools.* New to Chapter 3 is a discussion of the goals of ethical business communicators along with a set of questions that serve as tools for doing the right thing. Students also learn to recognize and avoid five common ethical traps.
- *New employment chapter.* A completely new employment communication chapter presents up-to-date résumés reflecting today's emphasis on aggressive job search tactics. The Third Edition now provides more model résumés than any other book in the field.
- *New grammar/mechanics exercises.* To provide more challenging and realistic grammar reviews, each chapter now includes a letter, memo, or short report that reviews and tests basic language skills. Instructors have transparency keys for easy, immediate reinforcement. Additional reinforcement exercises have also been added to the Grammar/Mechanics Handbook.
- *New correction symbols keyed to Grammar/Mechanics Handbook.* This new list of correction symbols includes page and paragraph references to guide students to clarifying concepts and examples in the Grammar/Mechanics Handbook.
- *Updated letters of recommendation and credit refusals.* New guidelines teach business writers how to avoid letters of recommendation and credit refusals that might cause lawsuits.
- *Electronic mail and voice mail.* Guidelines and tips are provided for businesspeople who will be communicating electronically.
- *Improved document formatting.* Many letters, memos, and reports appear in framed boxes showing realistic margins and spacing.
- *Expanded document reference section.* Appendix A now provides a complete reference guide to document formats, with models of letter, memo, and fax styles, along with helpful formatting tips.
- *Expanded transparency coverage.* In addition to 150 transparency acetates, we now provide to adopters additional transparency masters showing the solutions to all writing improvement exercises and case problems.

INSTRUCTOR SUPPORT

One reason for the continuing success of *Essentials of Business Communication* is its comprehensive support materials, such as the following:

- *Annotated Instructor's Edition.* The Instructor's Edition includes a key so that instructors have an easy-to-read, all-in-one manual from which to teach.
- *Transparencies.* A packet of approximately 150 acetates and 30 masters provides lecture summaries, additional examples, enrichment ideas, and solutions.
- *Solutions.* Nearly every chapter case and writing improvement exercise has a prepared solution.

- *Testing materials.* New to the Third Edition are expanded test banks with 40 questions for each chapter, available in hard copy and computerized versions. Greater emphasis is placed on evaluating writing applications. Completely new printed unit tests are also available to adopters.
- *Software.* A diskette for IBM-compatible computers contains all writing improvement exercises and selected cases from the textbook.
- *Newsletter.* The author's twice-a-year newsletter brings news and teaching tips in addition to free teaching materials to adopters.
- *Chapter teaching plans.* The expanded *Instructor's Resource Manual and Testing Materials* details a complete lesson plan for presenting each chapter.
- *Textbook coordination.* The principles of grammar and usage incorporated in *Essentials of Business Communication* coordinate with and reinforce those presented in Guffey's *Business English*, Fourth Edition, and Clark and Clark's *HOW 7: Handbook for Office Workers*, Seventh Edition.

ACKNOWLEDGMENTS

Sincere thanks are extended to the reviewers whose excellent advice and constructive suggestions helped shape the Third Edition of *Essentials of Business Communication*. I am grateful for the consultation of the following professors:

Jean Bush-Bacelis
  Eastern Michigan University

Judith Graham
  Holyoke Community College

Rovena L. Hillsman
  California State University,
  Sacramento

Diana K. Kanoy
  Central Florida Community College

Lydia Keuser
  San Jose City College

Linda Kissler
  Westmoreland County Community
  College

Richard B. Larsen
  Francis Marion University

Karen McFarland
  Salt Lake Community College

Margarita Maestas-Flores
  Evergreen Valley College

Diana S. McKowen
  Indiana University at Bloomington

Carolyn A. Quantrille
  Spokane Falls Community College

Marilyn St. Clair
  Weatherford College

James Calvert Scott
  Utah State University

Lance Shaw
  Blake Business School

Ruth D. Richardson
  University of North Alabama

William Wells
  Lima Technical College

For their contributions to previous editions, I warmly thank the following professionals:

Patricia Beagle
  Bryant & Stratton Business Institute

Karen Bounds
  Boise State University

Jeanette Dostourian
  Cypress College

Nancy J. Dubino
  Greenfield Community College

Cecile Earle
  Heald College

Valerie Evans
  Cuesta College

Pat Fountain
  Coastal Carolina Community College

Marlene Frederich
  New Mexico State University–
  Carlsbad

Margaret E. Gorman
  Cayuga Community College

Jackie Ohlson
  University of Alaska–Anchorage

Vilera Rood
  Concordia College

L. P. Helstrom
  Rochester Community College

Edna Jellesed
  Lane Community College

Edwina Jordan
  Illinois Central College

Ron Kapper
  College of DuPage

Keith Kroll
  Kalamazoo Valley Community
  College

Nedra Lowe
  Marshall University

Jane Mangrum
  Miami-Dade Community College

Bonnie Miller
  Los Medanos College

Willie Minor
  Phoenix College

Nancy Moody
  Sinclair Community College

Nancy Mulder
  Grand Rapids Junior College

Carl Perrin
  Casco Bay College

Jeanette Purdy
  Mercer County College

Carlita Robertson
  Northern Oklahoma College

Joseph Schaffner
  SUNY College of Technology
  at Alfred

Cinda Skelton
  Central Texas College

Clara Smith
  North Seattle Community College

Judy Sunayama
  Los Medanos College

Marilyn Theissman
  Rochester Community College

Lois A. Wagner
  Southwest Wisconsin Technical
  College

Linda Weavil
  Elan College

Beverly Wickersham
  Central Texas College

Leopold Wilkins
  Anson Community College

Almeda Wilmarth
  State University of New York–Delhi

Barbara Young
  Skyline College

Finally, for his inestimable counsel and support, I salute my husband, Dr. George R. Guffey, professor of English, University of California, Los Angeles.

INSTRUCTOR NETWORKING

Each year I develop and distribute new classroom teaching materials for business communication instructors. To ensure that you receive notice of these materials, please send me your name and address—and any comments about your course and this book.

Dr. Mary Ellen Guffey
23715 West Malibu Road
Suite 307
Malibu, CA 90265

LAYING

COMMUNICATION

FOUNDATIONS

1

COMMUNICATION IN

BUSINESS TODAY

IN THIS CHAPTER YOU WILL LEARN TO DO THE FOLLOWING:

- Explain why communication skills are valuable both to employers and to employees.
- Analyze the process of communication.
- Describe five key dimensions of North American culture.
- List ten or more ways to improve cross-cultural communication.
- Describe how communication skills can be developed in four stages.

Instructor: See p. 13 for author's suggested lesson plan for Chapter 1.

Where do you see yourself professionally in five years? Think about it for a moment. This question, a favorite during employment interviews, forces us to look into the future.

Although you can't project precisely what you'll be doing, you can be fairly certain about the following changes in your employment environment. You can expect to work in an ethnically diverse culture, as our country continues to assimilate immigrants from around the world. You can count on more women not only in the work force but also in management. You can expect to do business across the country, across the continent, and across the world as markets continue to expand. And you will undoubtedly be working with technology and information—government estimates suggest that 95 percent of all new jobs will be service- or information-related.

Your future employment environment will probably include ethnic diversity, global interactions, and working with information.

Your life and your job will probably revolve around information—its development, management, manipulation, processing, and exchange. To exchange information, we must communicate. This book is about understanding how we communicate and learning how to improve our communication skills.

Some things about ourselves we can't change—our height, our complexion, our disposition, even our native intelligence. But other characteristics we can change, and proficiency in communication is one of them.

You can improve your communication skills through instruction and practice.

Frank Carey, former board chair of IBM, once said that the four qualities of truly successful top executives are intelligence, integrity, empathy, and the ability to communicate. Some of these traits can be learned, and certainly communication ranks high among learnable skills. Aspiring employees, as well as top executives, can learn to communicate well through instruction and practice.

This chapter takes a broad look at communication today. First, it discusses the importance of communication skills in the workplace. Next, it examines communication theory and discusses communicating across cultures. Finally, it outlines a plan to help you improve your skills.

WANTED: GOOD COMMUNICATION SKILLS

Transparency 1.1

Individuals who possess effective communication skills are highly regarded in the business world. Employers, aware of the dollar-and-cents value of clear expression, increasingly identify and require oral and writing skills in job announcements.[1] Examine the following excerpts from employment advertisements taken from two of the nation's largest newspapers, *The New York Times* and the *Los Angeles Times.* Notice how these ads for diverse positions in professional, managerial, technical, and secretarial fields specifically designate good communication skills.

DIRECTOR OF PERSONNEL
400-bed metropolitan New York hospital seeks highly motivated, sensitive, results-oriented personnel generalist. Must be a hands-on self-starter with *effective communication skills.*

MANAGEMENT TRAINEE
Leading, innovative financial organization seeks energetic, organized, detail-oriented individual to monitor . . . programs. Candidates must have initiative, *excellent written and verbal skills,* and strong analytical ability.

Classified ads reflect a growing concern for good verbal and writing skills.

MANAGER, BUSINESS SYSTEMS
National organization seeks project manager to develop, coordinate, and provide automated tracking and control systems. . . . An outgoing, congenial personality and *exceptional communication skills* essential.

WORD PROCESSING SPECIALISTS
Immediate openings for operators with Word, WordPerfect, or Windows experience. *Communication skills tested.*

EXECUTIVE SECRETARY
Expanding engineering firm. Applicant must have 5 years of secretarial experience and excellent keyboarding and *communication skills.*

EXECUTIVE SECRETARY
Beverly Hills cosmetic firm seeks capable administrative assistant to work with our dynamic team. Requirements include keyboarding, software, and *excellent communication skills.*

WHY EMPLOYERS VALUE GOOD COMMUNICATORS

Business needs good communicators because these employees stimulate additional business. They are persuasive. They are able to sell ideas, services, and products. They know how to analyze, organize, and clarify information. They keep administrative costs down because their messages are not misunderstood and do not have to be repeated. And, because they feel positive about themselves and about their organizations, good communicators produce goodwill for their companies.

Executive Warren Yerks warns that employees have little chance in industry if they can't process and present information in writing. Everyone in his organization must be able to write: engineers, secretaries, managers, production personnel, and equipment operators. Employees who cannot write effectively probably wouldn't be hired in the first place; but if they are, according to Yerks, they often end up in a "professional eddy." These unproductive employees are frustrated and unhappy, locked out of the corporate mainstream, and going nowhere professionally.[2]

In locating individuals with good communication skills, organizations use various techniques. Some companies ask prospective employees to give presentations, prepare reports, or process in-baskets filled with memos and problem documents to be answered.[3] Other employers administer grammar and writing tests. And all recruiters judge an applicant's performance in the interview. How well you answer questions, communicate your ideas, explain your qualifications, and promote yourself will determine whether you are hired. A survey of employers who hired recent college graduates revealed that the two characteristics in which employers were most interested were poise and communication skills.

Many companies find ways to test communication skills before hiring.

COMMUNICATING ON THE JOB

Once you have been hired, you'll need good speaking, listening, and writing skills to get your work done. How much communication skill you will need depends on the field you enter and on the stage of your career. Jobs such as selling insurance and managing investments demand excellent communication skills for entry-level positions. Other positions initially may not require exceptional writing and speaking skills.

However, as one advances into supervisory and management roles, the demand for communication skills increases. Studies show, as you might expect, that supervisors, managers, and executives spend a much higher percentage of their time writing memos, letters, and reports than do their employees. Promotions are often given to those employees who demonstrate that they are effective communicators. In a national study of vice presidents selected from Fortune 500 corporations, 98 percent reported that effective communication skills had positively affected their advancement to top executive positions.[4]

Individuals who are promoted into supervisory and managerial positions generally require better communication skills than do entry-level employees.

BUT NOT FOR ACCOUNTANTS?

"But," you may protest, "I'm going to be an accountant (or computer specialist or financial analyst or health care specialist). In my field, language skills are unimportant."

Even in business activities that center on technical concepts, skill in communicating ideas rates highly among employers. In a study of accounting academics and professionals, an average of 70 percent of professional accountants reported that the written communication skills of the typical newly graduated accountant were inadequate. One employer in this study made the following revealing comment:

Workers in technical areas must be able to communicate their ideas to both technical and nontechnical colleagues.

The most neglected skill apparent in entry-level accountants is the ability to write effectively. For the most part, these "new" accountants have excellent technical preparation. However, they are unable to communicate the results of their technical procedures in a clear and concise manner.[5]

Promotion from technical jobs into supervisory or managerial positions brings increased administrative responsibilities. Consider the duties of the director of budgets and controls for a major American airline. In addition to working with figures, this individual is responsible for the "preparation, consolidation, and distribution of budgets; the analysis and interpretation of results; and the preparation of financial and operating statistical reports to provide a basis of management planning and operating controls." In other words, the budget director must be proficient in writing financial reports that other managers can understand.

ON THE PERSONAL SIDE

Aside from professional considerations, good communication skills benefit us personally. Since we spend the better part of our waking existence communicating with others, it is reasonable to assume that individuals who express ideas easily and clearly are better understood and experience greater satisfaction in interpersonal relationships than do those with weak skills.

The impressions you make on others are largely determined by the way you communicate.

Moreover, good communicators create favorable impressions. For better or worse, we all make judgments about others based on a number of factors, including the way they speak and the way they write. Our judgments, then, are influenced to a great extent by communication skills. Individuals who speak and write well convey the impression of intelligence, education, and success. They command respect, whether deserved or not. They are also happier because they are productive.

UNDERSTANDING THE COMMUNICATION PROCESS

Transparency 1.2

Communication skills play an important part in our personal lives and in our business careers. Before we begin our plan for improving those skills, it would be wise to explore briefly the process of communication. Only in comparatively recent times has the communication process been studied. In the past fifty years, theories of communication have been developed. Theories, by the way, seldom solve immediate problems; rather, they help us view our experiences in a fresh way. Theories and models enable us to organize experiences so that relationships are simplified and more easily comprehended.

Effective communication is a cyclic rather than a linear process.

The model shown in Figure 1.1 breaks down the process of communication into its component parts and illustrates its cycle. Because communication is the *exchange* of information, feedback is an important part of the process. Let's look more carefully at each part of the communication process.

FIGURE 1.1 Communication Process

Communication barriers and noise may cause the communication process to break down.

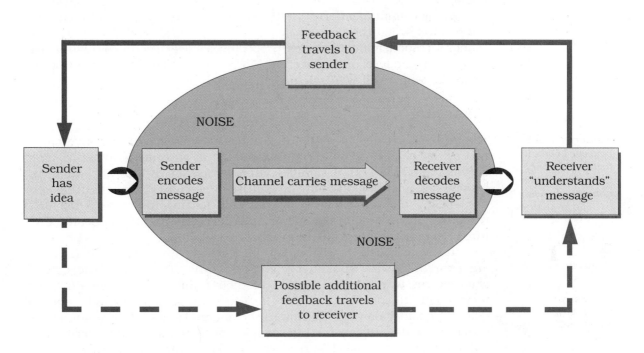

SENDER

The communication process begins with a sender who has an idea to transmit to another individual. How can the sender shape that idea into a message that the receiver will understand? The sender must make choices regarding the length, emphasis, tone, and organization of the message. The words the sender selects to convert, or *encode,* the idea into an appropriate form require careful thought. The sender must consider the purpose, the subject, and the intended receiver of the message.

Messages are shaped by the sender's objective, audience, communication skills, attitudes, and culture.

The message that the sender encodes will be influenced by the communication skills, attitudes, experiences, and culture of the sender. The goal of a good communicator is to create a message that is understood as he or she intended.

To ensure understanding, the sender chooses words and concepts that are not beyond the receiver's knowledge and experience. For example, a telecommunication software sales representative presenting a new product to an office manager with little knowledge of computer networks would be wise to avoid descriptions like "it's a file-transfer-level protocol designed

Source: Reprinted by permission of Johnny Hart and Creators Syndicate, Inc.

for dial-up asynchronous transmission." Even though such language may make perfect sense to the sales rep, it's less likely to do so to the office manager.

In the communication cycle the sender may fail to communicate with the receiver when the code or symbols are not understood by both. The sender's responsibility includes preparing a message that is within the comprehension level of the receiver. Moreover, the sender should strive for feedback, which will be discussed shortly.

MESSAGE

Messages may be conveyed verbally (with spoken or written words) or nonverbally (with actions or pictures).

Transparency 1.3

↺ *Instructor: See p. 17 for supplementary lecture, "Nonverbal Communication."*

The message created to represent an idea may be verbal or nonverbal. A nod of the head delivers a simple message of agreement. When a smile accompanies that nod, it signifies approval as well. Nonverbal communication is often subtle and may be culture-dependent. Throughout most of the world, shaking one's head from side to side indicates a negative response, but in certain regions of India it means just the opposite. Culture affects both nonverbal and verbal messages.

In this textbook we will be most concerned with verbal messages that are expressed with spoken or written words. The words the sender chooses, the way they are arranged, their number, their meaning, and their length all contribute to the effect a message has on the listener or reader. Consider Howard Hightower, the national sales manager for a publisher. He must inform all salespeople that declining sales necessitate reducing their commissions; however, he also wants to encourage them to increase their sales. He could make this announcement in a blunt 15-word statement. But if he desires comprehension, compliance, and cooperation, he will probably create a lengthier message with well-considered words organized into an effective strategy. The same information delivered by a Japanese sales manager to salespeople in his or her firm might be presented quite differently. Messages, then, are determined by the sender's objective, audience, subject, communication skills, attitudes, and culture.

CHANNEL

The selection of an appropriate channel for a message is determined by its complexity, importance, expected response, immediacy, degree of formality, audience, and cost.

The medium over which the message is physically transmitted is the channel. Messages may be delivered by computer, telephone, letter, memorandum, report, announcement, picture, face-to-face exchange, or fax, or through some other channel.

How should a message be sent? Several factors determine the choice of channel, the most important of which are these:

- *Complexity of the message.* Is the information so detailed that the receiver will need to read and study it?
- *Importance of the message.* Is the content of this message such that it requires a permanent record?
- *Anticipated reaction.* Will this message generate a positive or negative receiver response?
- *Immediacy of the situation.* Is a quick response needed?
- *Degree of formality.* Does a personal relationship exist between the sender and the receiver?
- *Size and location of the audience.* Is the message intended for a single receiver nearby or for hundreds of distant receivers?
- *Comparative costs.* Does the message warrant a costly channel in terms of time, equipment, and people?

Let's say, for example, that you are an executive in a large company and you are announcing a profit-sharing plan to employees. The best channel for your message would probably be a memo rather than a personal interview with or a telephone call to each employee. If, however, you wish to convince a director of the company that certain options in the profit-sharing plan should be revised, then a personal conference, along with a factual report, would be most effective. If you were inviting a colleague to lunch, the most appropriate communication channel would be the telephone.

Physical transmission of a message can affect the receiver's perception of that message. If you receive a letter addressed to "Occupant," you may dismiss it as junk mail. The same message, however, addressed to you by name and delivered on quality stationery may command your attention. You perceive the message as important; you have a favorable mind-set toward it.

Method of transmission can affect the receiver's perception of a message.

RECEIVER

The receiver's reaction to a message is determined by a number of external and internal factors, including the following:

- *Form and appearance of the message.* Is the channel appropriate? Is the message attractive and clear?
- *Subject of the message.* How much does the receiver know about the subject?
- *Attitude toward the message.* Does the receiver have an open, closed, or neutral attitude toward the message? Is the receiver in a receptive mood?
- *Communication skills.* Does the receiver possess sufficient communication skills to comprehend the message?
- *Physical conditions.* Is the receiver free of physical distractions so that it is possible to concentrate on the message?

Successful communication results when a receiver understands a message as the sender intended and responds as expected. To do this, the receiver must decode the symbols and ascribe to them the same general meanings as the sender ascribes.

FEEDBACK

The verbal or nonverbal response of the receiver is feedback, a vital part of the communication process. Feedback helps the sender know that the message was received and understood. If as a receiver you hear the message "How are you," your feedback might consist of words ("I'm fine") or body language (a smile or a wave of the hand). Although the receiver may respond with additional feedback to the sender (thus creating a new act of communication), we'll concentrate here on the initial message flowing to the receiver and the resulting feedback.

To ensure that receivers comprehend their messages, skilled communicators provide opportunities for feedback during and after the delivery of their messages.

Senders can encourage feedback by asking questions such as "Am I making myself clear?" and "Is there anything you don't understand?" Senders can further improve feedback by timing the delivery appropriately and by providing only as much information as the receiver can handle. Receivers can improve the process by paraphrasing the sender's message with comments like "Let me try to explain that in my own words" or "My understanding of your comment is . . ." In concluding documents, skilled communicators solicit feedback by asking for a specific action that indicates comprehension of the idea communicated.

BARRIERS

Communication barriers and noise prevent effective communication.

Transparency 1.4

⊃ *Instructor: See p. 14 for supplementary lecture, "Barriers to Effective Communication."*

For an infinite number of reasons, the communication process is not always successful. Barriers may cause the breakdown of communication in any of the encoding, transmitting, decoding, and responding stages of the process. A message sender who lacks awareness of the receiver or who possesses poor communication skills will have difficulty sending clear messages.

Barriers in transmitting messages are created by physical distractions and by long communication chains. Messages become distorted when too many people must process them. In the decoding stage communication is disrupted if the receiver lacks interest in or knowledge of the topic. Emotional distractions may interfere with both the encoding and the decoding of messages. These disruptions, sometimes called "noise," can cause failure at any stage of the communication process.

COMMUNICATING ACROSS CULTURES[6]

Transparency 1.5

Communication is further complicated when people do not share the same culture. Think of how you show embarrassment, for example. Chances are that you blush or lower your head. By contrast, when embarrassed, Japanese generally laugh or giggle, while Arabs stick out their tongues slightly.

Understanding the meaning of a message requires special sensitivity and skills when business communicators are from different cultures. Negotiators for an American company learned this lesson when they were in Japan looking for a trading partner in the Far East. The Americans were quite pleased after their first meeting with representatives of a major Japanese firm. The Japanese had nodded assent throughout the meeting and had not objected to a single proposal. The next day, however, the Americans were stunned to learn that the Japanese had rejected the entire plan. In decoding the nonverbal behavioral messages, the Americans made a typical mistake. They assumed the Japanese were nodding in agreement, as fellow Americans would. In this case, however, the nods of assent indicated comprehension—not approval.

Every country has a unique common heritage, joint experience, and shared learning that produces its culture. This background gives members of that culture a complex system of shared values, traits, morals, and customs. It teaches them how to behave; it conditions their reactions. Comparing traditional North American values with those in other cultures will broaden your worldview and help you develop the proper attitude for successful intercultural communication.

Improving intercultural communication skills is important because global markets are expanding and because the workplace is becoming more ethnically diverse.

We need to improve our intercultural communication skills for two reasons. First, world markets and economies are becoming increasingly intertwined. This trend means that Americans at home and abroad will be doing business with more people from other countries. A second, equally important factor, however, is that America's own population and workforce are rapidly becoming more ethnically diverse. You may find that your future employers, fellow workers, or clients are from other countries or cultures. And learning about the powerful effect that culture has on behavior will help you minimize misunderstandings in your dealings with colleagues, customers, and friends from other cultures.

COMPREHENDING CULTURAL DIVERSITY

A typical North American has habits and beliefs similar to those of other members of Western, technologically advanced societies. In this limited space it's impossible to cover fully the infinite facets of Western culture. But we can outline some key North American habits and values[7] and briefly contrast them with other cultural views. Remember, though, that these are generalizations, intended to help us form a broad perspective. They may not describe you or members of other cultures personally.

Understanding key North American beliefs helps you contrast them with values in other cultures.

Individualism.   North Americans value individualism, an attitude of independence and freedom from control. They think that initiative and self-assertion result in personal achievement. They believe in individual action and personal responsibility, and they desire a large degree of freedom in their personal lives.

Other cultures emphasize membership in organizations, groups, and teams; they encourage acceptance of group values, duties, and decisions. Members of these cultures typically resist independence because it fosters competition and confrontation instead of consensus. In group-oriented cultures like that of Japan, for example, self-assertion and individual decision making are discouraged. "The nail that sticks up gets pounded down" is a common Japanese saying.[8] Business decisions are often made by all who have competence in the matter under discussion. Similarly, in China managers focus on the group rather than on the individual, preferring a "consultative" management style over an autocratic style.[9]

While North Americans value individualism and personal responsibility, other cultures emphasize group- and team-oriented values.

Formality.   Americans place less emphasis on tradition, ceremony, and social rules than do people in some other cultures. They dress casually and are soon on a first-name basis with others. Their lack of formality is often characterized by directness. In business dealings Americans come to the point immediately; indirectness, they feel, wastes time, a valuable commodity.

This informality and directness may be confusing abroad. In Mexico, for example, a typical business meeting begins with handshakes, coffee, and an expansive conversation about the weather, sports, and other light topics. An invitation to "get down to business" might offend a Mexican executive.[10] In Japan signing documents and exchanging business cards are important rituals. In Europe first names are never used without invitation. In Arab, South American, and Asian cultures, a feeling of friendship and kinship must be established before business can be transacted.[11]

While North Americans value informality and straightforwardness, other cultures may value tradition and ceremony.

Communication Style.   North Americans value straightforwardness, are suspicious of evasiveness, and distrust people who might have a "hidden agenda" or who "play their cards too close to the chest."[12] North Americans also tend to be uncomfortable with silence and impatient with delays. Some Asian businesspeople have learned that the longer they drag out negotiations, the more concessions impatient North Americans are likely to make.

North Americans also tend to use and understand words literally. Latins, on the other hand, enjoy plays on words; and Arabs and South

North Americans tend to be direct and to understand words literally.

Americans sometimes speak with extravagant or poetic figures of speech (such as "the Mother of all battles"). Nigerians prefer a quiet, clear form of expression; and Germans tend to be direct but understated.[13]

North Americans may place different values on change and time orientation than do people in other cultures.

Change.　In cultures shaped by Western religious values, change is a phenomenon that can be influenced and even controlled. Change is accepted and planned for.

In other cultures change is perceived as inevitable, the natural evolution of people and society. Thus, the future cannot be altered; it is predetermined. To devout Moslems, for example, planning for the future is sacrilegious because such plans might circumvent the will of Allah. Managers of an American electronics company sent to Iran to establish a telephone switching station were aware of this belief. As a result, they trained Iranian employees in extensive troubleshooting techniques so that equipment problems would not be attributed to Allah.[14]

Time Orientation.　North Americans consider time a precious commodity to be conserved. They correlate time with productivity, efficiency, and money. Keeping people waiting for business appointments wastes time and is also rude.

In other cultures time may be perceived as an unlimited and never-ending resource to be enjoyed. An American businessperson, for example, was kept waiting two hours past a scheduled appointment time in Latin America. She wasn't offended, though, because she was familiar with Hispanics' more relaxed concept of time.[15]

Although Asians are punctual, their need for deliberation and contemplation sometimes clashes with North Americans' desire for speedy decisions. They do not like to be rushed. A Japanese businessperson considering the purchase of American appliances, for example, asked for five minutes to consider the salesperson's proposal. The potential buyer crossed his arms, sat back, and closed his eyes in concentration. A scant 18 seconds later, the American resumed his sales pitch—to the obvious bewilderment of the Japanese.[16]

CULTIVATING THE RIGHT ATTITUDE

Learning about other cultures and respecting other cultural values helps you avoid ethnocentrism.

Being aware of your own culture and how it contrasts with others is an important first step in preventing intercultural misunderstanding. Avoiding ethnocentrism and stereotyping, while at the same time developing tolerance, are additional steps to help business communicators overcome cultural barriers.

Avoiding Ethnocentrism.　The belief in the superiority of one's own race is known as *ethnocentrism,* a natural attitude inherent in all cultures. If you were raised in North America, the values described previously probably seem "right" to you, and you might wonder why the rest of the world doesn't function in the same sensible fashion. An American businessperson in an Arab or Asian country might feel irritated at time spent over coffee or other social rituals before any "real" business is transacted. In these cultures, however, personal relationships must be established and nurtured before credible negotiations may proceed.

Ethnocentrism causes us to judge others by our own values. We expect others to react as we would, and they expect us to behave as they would. Misunderstandings naturally result. An American who wants to set a deadline for completion of negotiations is considered pushy by an Arab.

That same Arab, who prefers a handshake to a written contract, is seen as naive and possibly untrustworthy by an American. These ethnocentric reactions can be reduced through knowledge of other cultures and development of flexible, tolerant attitudes.

Developing Tolerance. Working among people from different cultures demands tolerance and acceptance of diversity. Close-minded people cannot look beyond their own ethnocentrism. But as global markets expand and as our own society becomes increasingly multiethnic, tolerance becomes especially critical. Some current job descriptions now include statements such as "Must be able to interact with ethnically diverse personnel."

One of the best ways to develop tolerance is by practicing empathy. This means trying to see the world through another's eyes. It means being nonjudgmental, recognizing things as they are rather than as they "should be." It includes the ability to accept others' contributions in solving problems in a culturally appropriate manner. When Kal Kan Foods began courting the pets of Japan, for example, an Asian advisor suggested that the meat chunks in its Pedigree dog food be cut into perfect little squares. Why? Japanese pet owners feed their dogs piece by piece with chopsticks. Instead of insisting on what "should be" (feeding dogs chunky meat morsels), Kal Kan solved the problem by looking at it from another cultural point of view (providing neat small squares).[17]

Developing intercultural tolerance means practicing empathy, being nonjudgmental, and being patient.

In business transactions North Americans usually assume that economic factors are the primary motivators of people. It's wise to remember, though, that strong cultural influences are also at work. Saving face, for example, is important in many parts of the world. Because Americans value honesty and directness, they come right to the point and "tell it like it is." Mexicans and Asians, on the other hand, are more concerned with preserving social harmony and saving face. They are indirect and go to great lengths to avoid giving offense by saying no. The Japanese, in fact, have 16 different ways to avoid an outright no. The empathic listener recognizes the language of refusal and pushes no further.

While North Americans value directness, people from other cultures may strive for harmony and face-saving.

Being tolerant also involves patience. If a foreigner is struggling to express as idea in English, Americans must avoid the temptation to finish the sentence and provide the word that they presume is wanted. When we put words in their mouths, our foreign friends often smile and agree out of politeness, but our words may in fact not express their thoughts. Thus, our impatience may prevent us from learning the communicator's true thoughts. Remaining silent is another means of exhibiting tolerance. Instead of filling every lapse in conversation, for example, Americans should recognize that in Asian cultures people deliberately use periods of silence for reflection and contemplation.

Moving Beyond Stereotypes. Our perceptions of other cultures sometimes cause us to form stereotypes about groups of people. A *stereotype* is an oversimplified behavioral pattern applied uncritically to groups. For example, the Swiss are hard-working, efficient, and neat; Germans are formal, reserved, and blunt; Americans are loud, friendly, and impatient; Asians are gracious, humble, and inscrutable. These attributes may or may not accurately describe cultural norms, but when applied to individual business communicators, such stereotypes create misconceptions and cause misunderstandings. As an American, are you loud, friendly, and impatient? Probably not, and you resent being lumped into this category.

Looking beyond stereotypes means seeing individual qualities.

When you meet and work with people from other cultures, remember that they, too, resent being stereotyped. Look beneath surface stereotypes and labels to discover individual personal qualities.

RESPONDING TO INTERCULTURAL AUDIENCES

Working successfully with people from other cultures requires a certain amount of sensitivity and adjustment. The following suggestions provide specific tips for minimizing oral and written miscommunication.

Communicating Orally. Although it's best to speak a foreign language fluently, many of us lack that skill. Fortunately, global business trans- actions are often conducted in English, though the level of proficiency may be limited among those for whom it is a second language. An executive with Ford-Europe said that North Americans abroad make a big mistake in thinking that people who speak English always understand what is being said. "Comprehension can be fairly superficial," he warns. The fol- lowing suggestions may help you better understand and be understood in English:

- *Learn foreign phrases.* Even if English is used, foreign nationals appre- ciate it when you learn greetings and a few phrases in their language. To be understood, practice the phrases phonetically.
- *Use simple English.* Use simple words, and speak in short sentences (under 15 words). Eliminate puns, sports and military references, slang, jargon (special business terms), and any words that can't be translated.
- *Observe eye messages.* Be alert to a glazed expression or wandering eyes—these tell you the listener is lost.
- *Encourage accurate feedback.* Ask probing questions, and encourage the listener to paraphrase what you say. Don't assume that a yes, a nod, or a smile indicates comprehension.
- *Check frequently for comprehension.* Avoid waiting until you finish a long explanation to request feedback. Instead, make one point at a time, pausing to check for comprehension, and don't proceed to B until A has been grasped.
- *Speak slowly and enunciate clearly.* However, don't raise your voice. Also, overpunctuate with pauses and full stops, and always write num- bers for all to see.
- *Accept blame.* If a misunderstanding results, graciously accept the blame for not making your meaning clear.
- *Listen without interrupting.* Curb your inclination to finish sentences or to fill out ideas for the speaker. Keep in mind that North Americans abroad are often accused of listening too little and talking too much.

After conversations or oral negotiations, confirm the results and agreements with follow-up letters. For proposals and contracts, engage a translator to prepare copies in the local language. Roger Axtell, interna- tional behavior expert, offers three other important pieces of advice: smile, smile, smile. He calls the smile the single most understood and most use- ful form of communication in either personal or business transactions.[18]

Communicating in Writing. Many of the suggestions for oral communi- cation hold true for written documents as well. In addition, you may find it helpful to do some research to learn how documents are formatted and how letters are addressed and developed in the intended reader's country.

Engage a translator if (1) your document is important, (2) your document will be distributed to many readers, or (3) you must be persuasive. As one international executive says, "You can buy in English, but you have to sell in the other person's language."[19]

In writing documents some simple guidelines will help you communicate effectively. Use short sentences and short paragraphs (under five lines). Include relative pronouns *(that, which, who)* for clarity in introducing clauses. Stay away from contractions (especially ones like *Here's the problem)*. Use precise, simple words *(end* instead of *terminate, use* instead of *implement)*. Avoid idioms *(once in a blue moon)*, slang *(my presentation really bombed)*, acronyms *(ASAP* for *as soon as possible)*, abbreviations *(DBA* for *doing business as)*, and jargon *(input, output, bottom line)*. You'll learn more about words and specific writing techniques in succeeding chapters.

Numbers can be particularly problematic in cross-cultural communication. For international trade it's a good idea to learn and use the metric system. In citing numbers for figures *(15)* instead of spelling them out *(fifteen)*. Always convert dollar figures into local currency. Moreover, avoid using figures to express the month of the year. In North America, for example, March 5, 1996, might be written as 3/5/96, while in Europe the same date might appear as 5.3.96. For clarity, always spell the month out.

Making the effort to communicate with sensitivity across cultures pays big dividends. "Much of the world wants to like us," says businessman and international consultant Kevin Chambers. "When we take the time to learn about others, many will bend over backward to do business with us."[20] Another dividend is improved harmony on the job with fellow workers and increased productivity through greater cooperation.

Tranlsate your message into the receiver's language if the document is important, if it will have many readers, of if you must be persuasive.

DEVELOPING YOUR COMMUNICATION SKILLS

Thus far in this chapter you've learned that communication skills are vital both in the business world and in your personal life. You've become familiar with the communication process, and you've taken a look at communication across cultures.

What does all this mean to you? It means that career success in a rapidly changing world requires well-developed communication skills. But the ability to communicate effectively is not a universal trait. Most of us require instruction, practice, supervision, and feedback to develop and improve these communication skills.

Effective communication includes oral, listening, and writing skills. All these topics will be presented in this book, along with numerous opportunities to apply the concepts presented. In addition to techniques, you will learn to think critically in solving typical communication problems. Many of the suggestions intended for analyzing business communication problems are equally helpful in resolving personal problems.

The process of "putting it in writing" can be painful. Writing is not easy, especially if the writer has little instruction or supervised practice. Effective writing techniques, however, can be learned, and real skill can be developed.

Good writers are not born with their writing skills; they develop such skills through training and practice.

FOUR STAGES OF DEVELOPMENT

Good writers learn the craft of writing in much the same way that other skilled artisans or professionals learn their trades. Each of them typically follows a four-stage plan.

The first stage involves learning how to use the *tools of the trade.* For the writer, these tools are the basic rules of language, including grammar, punctuation, and capitalization, as well as number, spelling, and syntax conventions.

In the second stage the writer learns the *proper techniques* for efficient and coherent combination of these basic tools. These techniques involve learning how to use words skillfully and precisely, how to write effective sentences and paragraphs, and how to develop appropriate style and tone.

After learning these techniques, the writer needs a *plan of action.* For example, what procedures or strategies are known to be effective in writing a business letter? The third stage, then, involves learning and applying strategies for producing the desired result.

Finally, in the fourth stage, the writer practices *applying the tools, techniques, and strategies* in varying situations. In this way writers improve their skills in producing satisfactory results.

TEXTBOOK PARALLEL

This textbook is organized to parallel and amplify these four stages of skill development. Stage 1 (Chapter 1 and the Grammar/Mechanics Handbook) lays a foundation for communication by introducing communication theory and concepts. Some students will need to review the basic tools in language. Your instructor may assign the Grammar/Mechanics Diagnostic Test so that you can assess your strengths and weaknesses. The Grammar/Mechanics Handbook, following the diagnostic test, provides a review of grammar and punctuation, as well as exercises to enable you to sharpen your basic skills.

Stage 2 (Chapters 2–4) presents writing techniques, the "tricks of the trade" for authors. Stage 3 (Chapters 5–9) develops communication strategies. Stage 4 (Chapters 10–14) applies and adapts these techniques and strategies in varying communication situations.

Throughout this volume you'll find that we practice what we preach: concise, simple expression and straightforward organization. This "no-frills" book concentrates on *essential* communication concepts so that you can develop quickly and efficiently the functional career skills you need.

APPLICATION AND PRACTICE—1

Discussion

1. How do communication skills affect promotion to and within management?
2. Discuss the notion that today's advanced computer programs make it unnecessary for anyone to worry about developing good communication skills.
3. Describe the communication process. Why should it be considered cyclic rather than linear?

4. Why are North Americans increasingly concerned about intercultural communication skills?

5. Discuss the following statement in terms of North American and Japanese cultures: "The nail that sticks up gets pounded down."

Short Answers

6. Name three jobs in which good communication skills would be important for entry-level positions.
   1. *Salesperson*
   2. *Counselor (investment, loan, social)*
   3. *Receptionist*

7. Name three positions to which an employee with good communication skills could be promoted.
   1. *Manager (of sales)*
   2. *Supervisor (of word processing)*
   3. *Vice president (of personnel)*

8. Name two or more ways in which an individual with good communication skills could be valuable to an organization.
   1. *A good communicator creates and promotes business.*
   2. *A good communicator saves administrative costs.*

9. Name two reasons for putting a business message in writing.
   1. *To make a permanent record*
   2. *To make the document legal*

10. Give a brief definition or explanation of the following words:
    a. Encode   *Selecting and organizing symbols to represent a message*
    b. Channel   *The method by which a message is sent*
    c. Decode   *Deciphering or interpreting a message at its destination*

11. Name six or more channels over which messages may be transmitted. What factors determine the selection of an appropriate channel?

    Channels over which messages may be transmitted:
    1. *Computer*
    2. *Telephone*
    3. *Letter*
    4. *Memo*
    5. *Report*
    6. *Announcement*
    7. *Picture*
    8. *Face-to-face exchange*
    9. *Fax*

    Factors that determine selection:
    1. *Complexity of message*
    2. *Importance of message*
    3. *Anticipated reaction*
    4. *Immediacy of situation*
    5. *Degree of formality*
    6. *Size and location of audience*
    7. *Comparative costs*

12. Describe the concept of North American individualism. How does this concept set North Americans apart from some other cultures?
    Individualism suggests an attitude of independence and freedom from control. People act individually and take personal responsibility. Other cultures emphasize belonging to groups and teams; they encourage acceptance of group values, duties, and decisions. They resist independence because it encourages competition and confrontation, rather than consensus.

13. What is *ethnocentrism*, and how can it be reduced?
    Ethnocentrism is the belief in the superiority of one's own race. It can be reduced by learning more about other cultures and by developing flexible, tolerant attitudes.

14. List eight suggestions for enhancing comprehension when you are communicating with people for whom English is a second language. Be prepared to discuss each.
    1. *Learn foreign phrases.*
    2. *Use simple English.*
    3. *Observe eye messages.*
    4. *Encourage accurate feedback.*
    5. *Check frequently for comprehension.*
    6. *Speak slowly and enunciate clearly.*
    7. *Accept blame.*
    8. *Listen without interrupting.*

15. Name six guidelines for communicators who are writing to receivers for whom English is a second language.

    1. *Use a translator for important, persuasive documents and for those with many receivers.*
    2. *Use short sentences and short paragraphs.*
    3. *Include relative pronouns* (that, which, who) *for clarity in introducing clauses.*
    4. *Avoid contractions (especially like* There's a report*).*
    5. *Use precise, simple words.*
    6. *Avoid idioms, slang, acronyms, abbreviations, and jargon.*
    7. *Use the figure form for numbers.*
    8. *Convert dollar figures into local currency.*

Activities

16. Get to know your classmates. Since a successful communication class begins with open lines of communication among class members, learn something about your classmates. Your instructor may choose one of the following two techniques.

    a. For larger classes your instructor may divide the class into groups of four or five. Take one minute to introduce yourself briefly (name, major academic interest, hobbies, goals). Spend five minutes in the first group session. Record the first name of each individual you meet. Then informally regroup. In new groups, again spend five minutes on introductions. After three or four sessions, study your name list. How many names can you associate with faces?

    b. For smaller classes your instructor may ask each student to introduce himself or herself in a two-minute oral presentation while standing before the class at the rostrum. Where are you from? What are your educational goals? What are your interests? This informal presentation can serve as the first of two or three oral presentations correlated with Chapter 14, "Listening and Speaking."

17. From the Sunday classified section of your local newspaper (or the newspaper of a larger city nearby), select five or more advertisements for positions that require good communication skills. Bring them to class for discussion.

18. Analyze the communication process for a vice president of sales who must send an announcement to the sales staff regarding a new product. Using the communication model on page 7, discuss the components of the process. How might noise interfere with successful communication? How could the vice president reduce or prevent such noise? How could he or she ensure feedback?

19. Imagine a business in which you have been employed or an organization in which you have participated. Suggest five specific ways in which this organization could improve its communication with employees or members. Your instructor may ask you to present your suggestions in memo form. See Appendix B for information on memo formatting.

20. Imagine that classmates of yours are unconvinced of the need for good communication skills in your major. They believe that such skills are unnecessary in this field. Moreover, they claim that they will have secretaries or word processors to clean up weak writing. Do you agree or disagree?

21. Begin reading articles in business magazines and newspapers. Some possibilities are *Business Week, Consumer Reports, Entrepreneur, Forbes, Fortune, Money, The Economist, The Monthly Labor Review, U.S. News & World Report,* and *Venture.* Two good newspapers are *The*

Wall Street Journal and *Barron's National Business and Financial Weekly.* Consult the *Business Periodicals Index* for articles listed by subject. Reading well-written articles will not only help you improve your vocabulary and provide examples of good writing but will also expand your knowledge of events in the business world. Your instructor may direct you to write a memo summarizing each article. Your memo should introduce the topic, summarize main points, describe weaknesses and strengths, identify the audience for whom the article was intended, and conclude with your reactions to what you have learned. See Appendix B for information on memo formatting.

22. Make an informal study of technology in your field. Talk with two or more individuals who are familiar with your career field. Ask them which, if any, of the new communication and decision-making technologies they are using. What reactions do they have to the effectiveness of these technologies? What recommendations do they have for individuals training to enter the field? Be prepared to present your findings in an oral or written report.

23. Conduct a panel discussion about intercultural issues. Find two or three students from other countries (possibly members of your class) who could report on differences between their cultures and North American culture. Ask student travelers to report on their experiences abroad. In addition to individualism, formality, communication style, change, and time, consider such topics as importance of family, gender roles, and attitudes toward education, clothing, leisure time, and work.

GRAMMAR/MECHANICS CHECKUP—1

NOUNS

These checkups are designed to improve your control of grammar and mechanics. They systematically review all sections of the Grammar/ Mechanics Handbook. Answers are given for odd-numbered statements; answers to even-numbered statements will be provided by your instructor.

Review Sections 1.01–1.06 in the Grammar/Mechanics Handbook. Then study each of the following statements. Underscore any inappropriate form, and write a correction in the space provided. Also record the appropriate G/M section and letter to illustrate the principle involved. If a sentence is correct, write *C.* When you finish, compare your responses with those provided. If your answers differ, study carefully the principles shown in parentheses.

Example: Two surveys revealed that many <u>companys</u> will move to the new industrial park.   *companies*   *(1.05e)*

1. Several <u>attornies</u> investigated the case and presented their opinions.   *attorneys*   *(1.05d)*
2. At the counter we are busier on <u>Saturday's,</u> but telephone business is greater on Sundays.   *Saturdays*   *(1.05a)*
3. Some of the <u>citys</u> in Mr. Graham's report offer excellent opportunities.   *cities*   *(1.05e)*
4. Frozen chickens and <u>turkies</u> are kept in the company's basement lockers.   *turkeys*   *(1.05d)*
5. All secretaries were asked to check supplies and other <u>inventorys</u> immediately.   *inventories*   *(1.05e)*
6. Both the <u>Finchs</u> and the Lopezes agreed to attend the business meeting.   *Finches*   *(1.05b)*

1990s	*(1.05g)*

7. In the 1980s profits slowly grew; in the <u>1990's</u> we anticipate greater growth.

fathers-in-law	
	(1.05f)

8. The two <u>father-in-laws</u> kept silent during the civil and religious ceremonies.

complexes	*(1.05b)*

9. Luxury residential <u>complexs</u> are part of the architect's overall plan.

counties	*(1.05e)*

10. Voters in three <u>countys</u> are likely to approve increasing gas taxes.

Jennifers	*(1.05a)*

11. The instructor was surprised to find three <u>Jennifer's</u> in one class.

C	*(1.05d)*

12. California's interior valleys become quite warm in August.

secretaries	*(1.05e)*

13. All of the bosses of the <u>secretarys</u> attended the luncheon.

C	*(1.05h)*

14. The sign was difficult to read because one could not distinguish between its *o's* and *a's.*

runners-up	*(1.05f)*

15. Two <u>runner-ups</u> complained that they should have won the contest.

---

1. attorneys (*1.05d*) 3. cities (*1.05e*) 5. inventories (*1.05e*) 7. 1990s (*1.05g*)
9. complexes (*1.05b*) 11. Jennifers (*1.05a*) 13. secretaries (*1.05e*) 15. runners-up (*1.05f*)

GRAMMAR/MECHANICS CHALLENGE—1
· ·

DOCUMENT FOR REVISION

Transparency 1.6

The following memo has many faults in grammar, spelling, punctuation, capitalization, word use, and number form. Use standard proofreading marks (see Appendix B) to correct the errors. Study the guidelines in the Grammar/Mechanics Handbook to sharpen your skills. When you finish, your instructor can show you the revised version of this memo.

Poor Memo

TO: Tran Nguyen   DATE: May 14, 199X

FROM: Rachel Stivers, Manager

Ineffective Writing

SUBJECT: WORK AT HOME GUIDELINES

Since you will be completeing most of your work at home for the next 2 months. Follow these guidelines;

1. Check your message bored daily and respond promptly, to those who are trying to reach you.

2. Call the office at least twice a week to pick up any telephone messages, return these calls promply.

3. Transmit any work you do, on the computer to Jerry Gonzalez in our computer services department, he will analyze each weeks accounts, and send it to the proper Departments.

4. Provide me with monthly reports' of your progress.

I know you will work satisfactory at home Tran. Following these basic guidelines should help you accomplish your work, and provide the office with adequate contact with you.

· ·

UNIT

II

Developing

Basic

Communication

Skills

2

SKILLFUL WORD USE

IN THIS CHAPTER YOU WILL LEARN TO DO THE FOLLOWING:

- Make your writing more readable by substituting familiar words for unfamiliar words.
- Recognize and avoid unnecessary jargon, legalese, foreign expressions, and slang.
- Achieve a forceful style by using precise verbs, concrete nouns, vivid adjectives, and other specific forms.
- Avoid clichés, buzz words, repetitious words, and redundancies.
- Identify and employ idiomatic expressions.

Instructor: See p. 21 for author's suggested lesson plan for Chapter 2.

We usually take the words we use for granted, seldom thinking consciously about choosing them carefully. We use whatever words come to mind. In this chapter you will learn to become more aware of the words that you write.

We seldom choose our words carefully enough.

Writers are totally dependent on their words to convey meaning. If the speaker's words are not understood in conversation, the listener will signal verbally or nonverbally that more information is needed to clarify an idea being expressed. If a writer's words are unclear, the reader cannot immediately seek clarification.

Because words commonly have different meanings for different individuals, the communicator must be judicious in word selection and usage. We can never be certain that our words will have the exact effect intended. We can, however, improve our chances for successful communication by following specific word selection and writing techniques. The techniques presented in this chapter include practical suggestions encouraging the use of familiar and vivid words. This chapter will also show you how to avoid overworked, redundant, and improper words.

FAMILIAR WORDS

Familiar words are more meaningful to readers.

Clear messages contain words that are familiar and meaningful to the reader. How can we know what is meaningful to a given reader? Although we can't know with certainty, we can avoid long or unfamiliar words that have simpler synonyms. Whenever possible in business communication, substitute short, common, simple words. Don't, however, give up precise words if they say exactly what you mean.

Transparency 2.1

LESS FAMILIAR WORDS	SIMPLE ALTERNATIVES
ascertain	find out
conceptualize	see
encompass	include
hypothesize	guess
monitor	check
operational	working
option	choice
perpetuate	continue
perplexing	troubling
reciprocate	return
stipulate	require
terminate	end
utilize	use

JARGON

Jargon, which is terminology unique to a certain profession, should be reserved for individuals who understand it.

Except in certain specialized contexts, you should avoid jargon and unnecessary technical terms. Jargon is special terminology that is peculiar to a particular activity or profession. For example, geologists speak knowingly of *exfoliation, calcareous ooze,* and *siliceous particles.* Engineers are familiar with phrases like *infrared processing flags, output latches,* and *movable symbology.* Telecommunication experts use such words and phrases as *protocol, mode,* and *asynchronous transmission.*

Every field has its own special vocabulary. Using that vocabulary within the field is acceptable and even necessary for accurate communication. Don't use specialized terms, however, if you have reason to believe that your reader may misunderstand them.

Transparency 2.2

Inflated, unnatural writing that is intended to impress readers more often confuses them.

PLAIN LANGUAGE

Good writers use plain language to express clear meaning. They do not use showy words and ambiguous expressions in an effort to dazzle or confuse readers. They write to express ideas, not to impress others.

Some business, legal, and government documents are written in an inflated style that obscures meaning. This style of writing has been given various terms, such as *legalese, federalese, bureaucratese, doublespeak,* and the *official style.* It may be used intentionally to mask meaning, or it may simply be an attempt to show off the writer's intelligence and education. What do you think the manager's intention was in writing the following message?

> Personnel assigned vehicular space in the adjacent areas are hereby advised that utilization will be suspended temporarily Friday morning.

Inflated language often results in obfuscation (confusion).

Employees would probably have to read that sentence several times before they understood that they were being advised not to park in the lot next door Friday morning.

Legal documents and contracts often suffer from this same inflated, ambiguous style. In response some state governments have passed "plain English" laws. These laws require that consumer contracts be written in a clear and coherent style using everyday words. One New York firm specializes in producing "dejargonized" forms for banks, government offices, insurance companies, and real estate firms.

Instructor: See p. 22 for supplementary lecture, "Doublespeak."

What does plain English mean? Although it's difficult to define precisely, it generally means writing that is clear, simple, and understandable. It suggests writing that is easy to follow, well organized, and appropriately divided. A plain English document should include many of the writing techniques you are about to study (active voice, positive form, parallel construction, use of headings).

Don't be impressed by high-sounding language and legalese, such as *herein, thereafter, hereinafter, whereas,* and similar expressions. Your writing will be better understood if you use plain language.

FOREIGN EXPRESSIONS

To many readers, foreign expressions are like a code; they hold secret meanings known only to the select few. Writers who use foreign expressions risk offending readers who cannot decipher the code. Although such expressions as *crème de la crème* may flavor the prose of world travelers, they are inappropriate in business writing.

Avoid unfamiliar foreign expressions in business communication.

SIX STEPS TO INCREASE YOUR VOCABULARY

Success in your education, career, and personal life is enhanced by possessing a precise vocabulary. The number one learning deficiency among college students is vocabulary. Word skills are also important in the workplace. A direct correlation exists between vocabulary and success in employment. Studies show that managers and executives have larger vocabularies than the employees they direct. Often individuals are hired or promoted because they are able to express their ideas persuasively and precisely. If you are serious about improving your vocabulary, here are six steps that research shows are most effective in helping adults increase their knowledge of words.[1]

- *Make a commitment.* Decide that you want to increase your vocabulary and that you are willing to work toward that goal. Without a goal or a commitment, little is achieved. Vague feelings regarding self-improvement and half-hearted attempts seldom produce significant change.
- *Select your own material.* Research with post-secondary students shows that long-term vocabulary gains are greatest when learners choose the target words themselves instead of attempting to memorize isolated words on lists developed by others. Moreover, words drawn from a unifying content, such as your major subject area, allow you to integrate your previous knowledge and provide a framework in which to use the new words.
- *Choose five good words.* From your assigned homework reading in any course, select five good words each week. The words should be ones that you feel are important in your field and ones whose meanings you do not know. Record the words in a vocabulary journal, following this format: word, source, pronunciation, sentence in which you found the word (underline the word), and dictionary definition. Use a journal or keep the same information on 3 × 5 cards.

SLANG

Slang sounds fashionable, but it lacks precise meaning and should be avoided in business writing.

Like foreign expressions, slang usually has precise meaning for only a favored few. Slang is composed of informal words with arbitrary and extravagantly changed meanings. Slang words quickly go out of fashion because they are no longer appealing when everyone begins to understand them. Consider the following statement, quoted in the *Los Angeles Times,* by a government official. He had been asked why his department was dropping a proposal to lease offshore oil lands, and he responded: "The Administration has an awful lot of other things in the pipeline, and this has more wiggle room so they just moved it down the totem pole." He added, however, that the proposal might be offered again since "there is no pulling back because of hot-potato factors."

The meaning here, if the speaker really intended to impart any, is considerably obscured by the use of slang. Good communicators, of course, aim at clarity and avoid unintelligible slang.

FORCEFUL WORDS

Effective writing creates meaningful images in the mind of the reader. Such writing is sparked by robust, concrete, and descriptive words. Ineffective writing is often dulled by insipid, abstract, and generalized words.

- *Use the key image method.* Research with learners of all ages reveals that we can remember a new word better if we form a mental picture of its definition or an image of some part of the word that will relate to the definition. For example, the word *acrophobia* has two parts: *acro* means "height" and *phobia* means "fear." Imagine the word *acrobat*, which starts with the same letters and could suggest a performer high in the air, a performer who conquered his or her fear of height. Form a mental picture of the acrobat. Make a sentence using this picture and the new word: *The acrobat performed skillfully on the high wire showing absolutely no acrophobia, a fear of heights.* Close your eyes; recall the picture and the sentence.
- *Make concept cards.* If no key image comes to mind, try another strategy. Record the targeted word in bold letters on the front of a 3 × 5 card. In the upper right-hand corner, record the topic or category into which the word could be classified. For example, the word *boilerplate* would be classified under the concept of *word processing.* On the back of the card, record the definition in your own words. Then show examples of the word, if possible: *Examples—form letter paragraphs used by insurance companies—one kind of boilerplate.* Add any other personal associations or clues that will help you remember this word.
- *Practice your words.* Study and pronounce your five weekly words. Look for other occurrences of these words in your assignments. Use the words in sentences. Review your vocabulary journal and/or cards several times a week.

College students and other adults using these steps are much more successful in increasing their vocabularies than are those who simply memorize word lists. Remember, though, that nothing substantial is achieved without effort.

To be able to choose forceful words, of course, you must have a large and precise vocabulary. Success in your education, your career, and even your personal life is enhanced by a powerful vocabulary. That's why you'll probably want to work to increase your vocabulary while you are in this class focused on word use. Increasing your vocabulary is largely a matter of commitment, as described in the accompanying box. Among the vocabulary words you'll find most useful for business messages are precise verbs, concrete nouns, and vivid adjectives.

PRECISE VERBS

The most direct way to improve lifeless writing is through effective use of verbs. Verbs not only indicate the action of the subject but also deliver the force of the sentence. Select verbs carefully so that the reader can visualize precisely what is happening.

Precise verbs make your writing forceful and intelligible.

GENERAL: Our salesperson will *contact* you next month.
PRECISE: Our salesperson will *(telephone, write, visit)* . . .

GENERAL: The vice president *said* that we should contribute.
PRECISE: The vice president *(urged, pleaded, demanded)* . . .

GENERAL: We must *consider* this problem.
PRECISE: We must *(clarify, remedy, rectify)* . . .

GENERAL: The newspaper was *affected* by the strike.
PRECISE: The newspaper was *(crippled, silenced, demoralized)* . . .

The power of a verb is diminished when it is needlessly converted into a noun. This happens when verbs such as *acquire, establish,* and *develop* are made into nouns (*acquisition, establishment,* and *development*). These nouns then receive the central emphasis in the sentence. In the following pairs of sentences, observe how forceful the original verbs are as compared with their noun forms.

VERB: The city *acquired* park lands recently.
NOUN: *Acquisition* of park lands was made recently by the city.

VERB: Mr. Miller and Mrs. Lopez *discussed* credit card billing.
NOUN: Mr. Miller and Mrs. Lopez had a *discussion* concerning credit card billing.

VERB: Both companies must *approve* the merger.
NOUN: Both companies must grant *approval* of the merger.

Transparency 2.3
Concrete nouns help readers visualize the meanings of words.

CONCRETE NOUNS

Nouns name persons, places, and things. Abstract nouns name concepts that are difficult to visualize, such as *automation, function, justice, institution, integrity, form, judgment,* and *environment.* Concrete nouns name objects that are more easily imagined, such as *desk, car,* and *light bulb.* Nouns describing a given object can range from the very abstract to the very concrete—for example, *object, motor vehicle, car, convertible, Mustang.* All of these words or phrases can be used to describe a Mustang convertible. However, a reader would have difficulty envisioning a Mustang convertible when given just the word *object* or even *motor vehicle* or *car.*

In business writing, help your reader "see" what you mean by using concrete language.

GENERAL	CONCRETE
a *change* in our budget	a *10 percent reduction* in our budget
that company's product	*Panasonic's Sensicolor videotape*
a person called	*Mrs. Swain, the administrative assistant,* called
we *improved* the assembly line	we *installed 26 advanced Unimate robots* on the assembly line

VIVID ADJECTIVES

Including highly descriptive, dynamic adjectives is the easiest way to make writing more vivid and concrete. Be careful, though, not to overuse them nor to lose objectivity in selecting them.

GENERAL: The report was on time.
VIVID: The *detailed 12-page* report was submitted on time.

GENERAL: John needs a better truck.
VIVID: John needs a *rugged, four-wheel-drive Dodge* truck.

GENERAL: We enjoyed the movie.
VIVID: We enjoyed the *entertaining* and *absorbing* movie.
OVERKILL: We enjoyed the *gutsy, exciting, captivating,* and *thoroughly marvelous* movie.

A thesaurus (on your computer or in a book) helps you select precise words and also increases your vocabulary.

A good writer combines precise verbs, concrete nouns, and vivid adjectives with other carefully selected words to give the reader specific facts rather than flabby generalizations. Notice how much more meaningful the concrete version is in each of the following sentence pairs:

GENERAL: One of the company's officers has proved unworthy of corporate trust.
CONCRETE: Don DeSoto, treasurer, embezzled $25,000 of Datacom's funds.

GENERAL: The computer is portable and handy.
CONCRETE: The 5-pound, notebook-sized MicroOffice "RoadRunner" portable computer uses removable, reusable cartridges.

GENERAL: The implementation of improved operations may change company vitality soon.
CONCRETE: By improving packaging, shipping, and distribution procedures, we expect to increase gross profits by 14 percent within three months.

GENERAL: A new management official was recently hired to improve the division.
CONCRETE: Appointed senior vice president of marketing on August 27, Jeffrey Bamford launched a comprehensive program to retrain sales representatives in his Market Services Division.

By describing facts with precise verbs, concrete nouns, and vivid adjectives, you can make sure your readers understand your message.

CLICHÉS

Clichés are expressions that have become exhausted by overuse. These expressions not only lack freshness but also frequently lack clarity for some individuals who misunderstand their meaning. The following partial list contains representative clichés you should avoid in business writing.

Clichés are dull and sometimes ambiguous.

Transparency 2.4

below the belt
better than new
beyond the shadow of a doubt
easier said than done
exception to the rule
fill the bill
first and foremost
hard facts

keep your nose to the grindstone
last but not least
make a bundle
pass with flying colors
quick as a flash
shoot from the hip
stand your ground
true to form

Can you think of any clichés to add to this list? How about, *it goes without saying*—(and it probably should)?

BUZZ WORDS

Another category of overworked expressions is that of so-called buzz words. These expressions, often borrowed from industry or government, are words and phrases of fashion. Buzz words like the following seem to be used more often to impress the reader than to express the user's meaning.

Buzz words are overworked expressions taken from industry or government.

commonality
configuration
dysfunction
impact on
incremental
interface
interrelationships
logistical
orientate

parameter
productionwise (profitwise, budgetwise, and other -*wise* words)
prioritize
scenario
state of the art
subsystem
systematized
unilateral

REPETITIOUS WORDS

The unconscious repetition of words creates monotonous and boring reading.

Good communicators vary their words to avoid unintentional repetition. Observe how leaden and monotonous the following personnel announcement seems:

> Employees will be able to elect an additional six employees to serve with the four previously elected employees who currently comprise the employees' board of directors. To ensure representation, swing-shift employees will be electing one swing-shift employee as their sole representative.

The preceding version uses the word *employee* six times. In addition, the last sentence begins with the word *representation* and ends with the similar word *representative.* An easier-to-read version follows:

> Employees will be able to elect an additional six representatives to serve with the four previously elected members of the employees' board of directors. To ensure representation, swing-shift workers will elect their own board member.

In the second version synonyms *(representatives, members, workers)* replaced *employee.* The last sentence was reworked by using a pronoun *(their)* and by substituting *board member* for the repetitious *representative.* Variety of expression can be achieved by searching for appropriate synonyms and by substituting pronouns.

Good writers are also alert to the overuse of the articles *a, an,* and particularly *the.* Often the word *the* can simply be omitted. Articles can also be eliminated by changing singular constructions to plurals. In the following revision, for example, *a change in the price of gas* becomes *changes in gas prices*:

WORDY: The deregulation of the natural gas industry has caused a change in the price of gas.

IMPROVED: Deregulation of the natural gas industry caused changes in gas prices.

Notice the efficiency of the second sentence.

REDUNDANT WORDS

Redundant expressions (such as combined together) needlessly repeat their meanings.

Transparency 2.5

Repetition of words to achieve emphasis or effective transition is an important writing technique we'll discuss in forthcoming chapters. The needless repetition, however, of words whose meanings are clearly implied by other words is a writing fault called *redundancy.* For example, in the expression *final outcome,* the word *final* is redundant and should be omitted, since *outcome* implies finality. Learn to avoid redundant expressions such as the following:

absolutely essential
adequate *enough*
advance warning
basic fundamentals
big *in size*
combined *together*
consensus *of opinion*
continue *on*
each *and every*
exactly identical
few *in number*

final outcome
grateful thanks
mutual cooperation
necessary prerequisite
new beginning
past history
reason *why*
red *in color*
refer *back*
repeat *again*
true facts

IDIOMATIC WORDS

Every language has its own *idiom*, that is, its own special way of combining words. In English, as in any language, it's important to use combinations of words that "sound right" to the typical native speaker. Particularly important is the use of the right prepositions with certain words. Study the following examples:

acquainted *with* (not *on* or *about*)
agree *to* (not *with*) a proposal
agree *with* a person
angry *at* (not *with*) a thing
angry *with* a person
authority *on* (not *about* or *in*)
buy *from* (not *off of*)
capable *of*

guard *against* (not *from*)
in accordance *with* (not *to*)
independent *of* (not *from*)
interest *in* (not *about*)
plan *to* (not *on*)
retroactive *to*
sensitive *to*
try *to* (not *and*)

APPLICATION AND PRACTICE—2

Discussion
1. Should writers always use familiar words?
2. Because legal documents are written to be extremely precise, everyone should write like an attorney. Discuss.
3. How can dull, lifeless writing be made forceful?
4. Because clichés are familiar and have stood the test of time, do they help clarify writing?
5. Why is idiom one of the hardest elements of language for foreign speakers to master?

Short Answers
6. Define *jargon.*
   Jargon is special terminology that is unique to a particular profession.

7. Provide at least three examples of jargon from your chosen field of specialization.
   Word processing, for example: menu, data disk, boilerplate

8. Define *slang.*
   Slang words are fashionable, informal words with arbitrary and often extravagantly changed meanings.

9. Give at least three examples of current slang.
   1. He "pigged out" on pizza.
   2. He was a real "low-life."
   3. Why don't you "chill out" (cool off)?

10. Verbs are the most important words in sentences because they do what?
    Verbs indicate the action of the subject and deliver the force of the sentence.

11. What happens when verbs are converted to nouns (for example, when *acquire* becomes *to make an acquisition*)?
    The power of the verb is decreased. The central emphasis in the sentence is shifted to the noun.

12. Define *cliché* and provide at least one example (other than those shown in the chapter) that you have heard frequently.
    A cliché is an overworked expression. Example: She has eyes like a hawk.

13. What are articles, and what problem do they present to writers?
    The adjectives a, an, *and* the *are articles. Writers should not overuse them.*

14. Define *redundant* and provide an example.
    A redundant expression needlessly repeats its meaning. Example: uniquely original

15. Define *idiom* and provide an illustration.
    Idiom refers to a combination of words that is unique to a given language. Example: to guard against

Writing Improvement Exercises

⊃ *Instructor: Writing Improvement Exercises are available on diskette.*

Transparency Master 2.1

Familiar Words.   Revise the following sentences using simpler language for unfamiliar terms. Assume that you are writing at a level appropriate for typical business communication. Use a dictionary if necessary.

EXAMPLE: Please ascertain the extent of our fiscal liability.

REVISION: Please find how much we owe.

16. Profits are declining because our sales staff is insufficiently cognizant of our competitor's products.
    Profits are declining (or falling) because our sales staff is unaware of our competitor's products.

17. He hypothesized that the vehicle was not operational because of a malfunctioning gasket.
    He guessed that the car (or truck) was not working because of a broken gasket.

18. It may be necessary to terminate the employment of Mr. Sims.
    We may have to fire Mr. Sims.

19. The contract stipulates that management must perpetuate the present profit-sharing plan.
    The contract requires that management continue the present profit-sharing plan.

20. Numerous employee options are encompassed in the recently revised benefit package.
    Many employee choices are included (or provided) in the recently revised benefit package.

Jargon, Slang.   Revise the following sentences using simpler language that would be clear to an average reader. Avoid jargon, foreign expressions, and slang.

EXAMPLE: Because of a glitch in the program, the printout appears *sans* statistics.

REVISION: Because of an error in the program, the printout appears without statistics.

21. This contract contains a caveat stipulating that vendors must utilize *bona fide* parts.
    This contract contains a warning that vendors (sellers) must use genuine parts.

22. Quality products had heretofore helped this organization perpetuate its central market position.
    Quality products had in the past helped this organization maintain its central market position.

23. Although there is little wiggle room in our budget, by keeping a tight ship we should have this project operational right on target.
    Although there is little room for flexibility, by practicing economy we should complete this project within its budget.

24. In regard to our advertising budget, Mr. Hargrove says that TV is going down the tubes because audiences are being fractionalized into special interest groups.
    With regard to our advertising budget, Mr. Hargrove says that TV is no longer effective because audiences are being split into special interest groups.

25. This half-price promotional campaign sounds real gutsy, but I don't think we should touch it with a 10-foot pole.
    This half-price promotional campaign sounds daring, but I don't think we should even consider it.

Precise Verbs.   Rewrite these sentences, centering the action in the verbs.

EXAMPLE: Mrs. Kinski gave an appraisal of the equipment.

REVISION: Mrs. Kinski appraised the equipment.

Transparency Master 2.2

26. The engineer made a description of the project.
    The engineer described the project.

27. Can you bring about a change in our company travel policy?
    Can you change our company travel policy?

28. In writing this proposal, we must make application of the new government regulations.
    In writing this proposal, we must apply the new government regulations.

29. Streamlined procedures will produce the effect of reduction in labor costs.
    Streamlined procedures will reduce labor costs.

30. The board of directors made a recommendation affirming abandonment of the pilot project.
    The board of directors recommended abandoning the pilot project.

31. An investigator made a determination of the fire damages.
    An investigator determined the fire damages.

32. We hope to have production of our new line of products by January.
    We hope to produce our new line of products by January.

33. The duty of the comptroller is verification of departmental budgets.
    The comptroller verifies departmental budgets.

34. Please make a correction in my account to reflect my late payment.
    Please correct my account to reflect my late payment.

35. The compilation of tax returns is the function of our accountant.
    Our accountant compiles tax returns.

Vivid Words.   Revise the following sentences to include vivid and concrete language. Add appropriate words.

EXAMPLE: They said it was a long way off.

REVISION: Management officials announced that the merger would not take place for two years.

36. Our new copier is fast.
    Our new Minex Model XL copier prints ten copies a second.

37. Mr. Grant's record indicates that he is a good worker.
    Mr. Grant's personnel record indicates that he is an industrious worker.

38. An employee from that company called about our new computer.
    The chief operations officer at Becker Products telephoned about our new Lang Super ST computer.

39. Please contact them soon.
    Please telephone DataCom by September 20.

40. They said that the movie they saw was very interesting.
    Sherry and Alan reported that Monsters from the Deep *was convincing and frightening.*

Clichés, Buzz Words, Repetition.   Revise the following sentences to avoid clichés, buzz words, and unnecessary repetition.

EXAMPLE: The president said that it was the president's job to spearhead the drive for energy conservation.

REVISION: The president said that it was his job to lead the drive for energy conservation.

41. The production manager arrived just in the nick of time to prevent the oil damage from damaging the floor.
    The production manager arrived just in time to prevent oil damage to the floor.

42. New corporate taxes will impact on corporations in the course of events.
    New taxes will affect corporations in time.

43. The contract will be considered a valid contract if the terms of said contract are configured to meet with the approval of all parties who will sign the contract.
    The contract is valid if its terms are approved by all signers.

44. Employees receive employee raises in orderly incremental step raises.
    Employees receive incremental raises.

45. Without rhyme or reason Sales Manager Shimada refused to interface or have personal conferences with any sales reps face to face.
    Without reason Sales Manager Shimada refused to face any sales reps.

Redundant Words, Idiomatic Expressions.   Rewrite the following sentences to correct the use of redundant words and unidiomatic expressions.

Transparency Master 2.3

EXAMPLE: In accordance to your wishes, we have completely eliminated tipping.

REVISION: In accordance with your wishes, we have eliminated tipping.

46. First and foremost, we plan on emphasizing an instructional training program.
First, we plan to emphasize a training (or instructional) program.

47. If you will refer back to her file, you will see that the reason why Carmen Campis was chosen is that she has experience on many different fields.
If you refer to her file, you will see that Carmen Campis was chosen because she has experience in many different fields.

48. It was the consensus of opinion of the committee that it should meet at 11 a.m. in the morning.
It was the consensus of the committee that it should meet at 11 a.m.

49. Although she was angry with the report, Lucy Williams collected together her facts to make a last and final effort.
Although she was angry at the report, Lucy Williams collected her facts to make a final effort.

50. One local resident asked for all the important essentials regarding small business loans.
One resident asked for the essentials regarding small business loans.

Activity

Legalese, Bureaucratese, Jargon. Find examples of legalese, bureaucratese, or jargon in newspapers, magazines, or other documents. Bring them to class for discussion. Continue to search for such examples as your course continues.

GRAMMAR/MECHANICS CHECKUP—2

PRONOUNS

Review Sections 1.07–1.09 in the Grammar/Mechanics Handbook. Then study each of the following statements. In the space provided, write the word that completes the statement correctly and the number of the G/M principle illustrated. When you finish, compare your responses with those shown below. If your responses differ, study carefully the principles in parentheses.

Example: The Recreation and Benefits Committee will be submitting (*its, their*) report soon. — *its*   *(1.09d)*

1. I was expecting Mr. Marks to call. Was it (*he, him*) who left the message? — *he*   *(1.08b)*

2. Every one of the members of the men's bowling team had to move (*his car, their cars*) before the tournament could begin. — *his car*   *(1.09b)*

3. A serious disagreement between management and (*he, him*) caused his resignation. — *him*   *(1.08c)*

4. Does anyone in the office know for (*who, whom*) this paper was ordered? — *whom*   *(1.08j)*

5. It looks as if (*her's, hers*) is the only report that contains the sales figures. — *hers*   *(1.08d)*

me	(1.08c)

6. Mrs. Simmons asked my friend and *(I, me, myself)* to help her complete the work.

I	(1.08a)
yours	(1.08d)

7. My friend and *(I, me, myself)* were also asked to work on Saturday.

8. We sent both printers in for repair, but *(yours, your's)* should be returned shortly.

whoever	(1.08j)
me	(1.08i)

9. Give the budget figures to *(whoever, whomever)* asked for them.

10. Everyone except the broker and *(I, me, myself)* claimed a share of the commission.

he	(1.08f)
us	(1.08g)

11. No one knows that problem better than *(he, him, himself)*.

12. Investment brochures and information were sent to *(we, us)* shareholders.

her	(1.09c)

13. If any one of the women tourists has lost *(their, her)* scarf, please see the driver.

its	(1.09g)

14. Neither the glamour nor the excitement of the position had lost *(its, it's, their)* appeal.

his or her	(1.09b)

15. Any new subscriber may cancel *(their, his or her)* subscription within the first month.*

---

1. he *(1.08b)*   3. him *(1.08c)*   5. hers *(1.08d)*   7. I *(1.08a)*   9. whoever *(1.08j)*
11. he *(1.08f)*   13. her *(1.09c)*   15. his or her *(1.09b)*

GRAMMAR/MECHANICS CHALLENGE—2

DOCUMENT FOR REVISION

Transparency 2.5

The following memo has many faults in grammar, spelling, punctuation, capitalization, word use, and number form. Use standard proofreading marks (see Appendix B) to correct the errors. Study the guidelines in the Grammar/Mechanics Handbook to sharpen your skills. When you finish, your instructor can show you the revised version of this memo.

Ineffective Writing

Poor Memo

TO: Jamal Wilkerson, Vice President   DATE: July 24, 199x

FROM: Roxanne Crosley, Manager, Payroll

SUBJECT: Departmental Error

Last month our central accounting department changed it's computer program for payroll processing. When this computer change was operationalized some of the stored information was not transfered to the new information database. As a consequence of this maneuver several errors occured in employee paychecks (1) medical benifits were not deducted (2) annuity deductions were not made and (3) errors occured in Federal witholding calculations.

Note: How could the last statement be reworded to avoid the awkward *his-or-her* construction? See 1.09b.

Each and every one of the employees effected has been contacted; and this error has been elucidated. My staff and me has been working overtime to replace all the missing data; so that corrections can be made about the August 30th payroll run.

Had I made a verification of the information before the paychecks were ran this slip-up would not have materialized. To prevent such an error in the future I decided to take the bull by the horns and implemented a rigorous new verification system.

. . . .

3

TONE, STYLE,

AND ETHICS

⊃ *Instructor: See p. 25 for author's suggested lesson plan for Chapter 3.*

IN THIS CHAPTER YOU WILL LEARN TO DO THE FOLLOWING:

- Appreciate how writing tone and style affect goodwill.
- Distinguish between formal and conversational language.
- Use positive language.
- Recognize and develop reader benefits.
- Avoid outdated expressions.
- Develop a concise writing style.
- Replace sexist terms with appropriate alternatives.
- Communicate ethically.

In addition to using words skillfully, good writers and communicators pay attention to tone and style to make their communication successful. This chapter discusses ways to use conversational language, highlight reader benefits, and say things positively in order to improve tone and at the same time develop goodwill. In this chapter you'll also learn to control your writing style by eliminating outdated, wordy, and sexist language. Finally, you'll study the goals and techniques of ethical business communicators.

TONE

The tone of a message conveys the sender's attitude toward the receiver.

Tone in a business message describes its mood; it reflects the sender's attitude toward the receiver. The tone of a letter may be constructive or destructive, casual or formal, patronizing or sincere, arrogant or helpful, objective or subjective, pompous or humble, subtle or blunt, demeaning or conciliatory, old-fashioned or contemporary. Notice how harsh and patronizing the following sentence sounds. Although the writer may not have intended to project a hostile tone, the reader definitely feels it.

If you would take the time to read your operator's manual, you will see that your car should have received full servicing at 20,000 miles.

You've already learned some techniques for developing appropriate tone (using familiar words and plain language, and avoiding jargon, slang, clichés, and redundant words). Now you'll study how conversational language, positive expression, and emphasis on reader benefits further improve message tone.

CONVERSATIONAL LANGUAGE

Business letters, memos, and reports replace conversation. Therefore, they are most effective when they convey an informal, conversational tone instead of a formal, artificial tone.

Transparency 3.1

Big words, complex sentences, abstractions, and depersonalized expressions (such as the writer believes) make writing sound formal and distant.

A casual, conversational tone in letters is harder to achieve than it may appear. Many writers tend to become formal, unnatural, and distant when they put words on paper. They seem to undergo a personality change when they pick up a pencil or approach a keyboard. Perhaps this is a result of composition training in schools. Many students learned to develop a writing style that impressed the instructor. They were rewarded when they used big words, complex sentences, and abstractions, even if their ideas were not altogether clear. After leaving school, some writers continue to use words that inflate ideas, making them sound important and intellectual. Instead of writing as they would speak in conversation, they construct long and complex sentences, and expression of their thoughts becomes confusing. Rather than using familiar pronouns such as *I, we,* and *you,* they depersonalize their writing by relying on third-person constructions such as *the undersigned, the writer,* and *the affected party.*

To develop a warm, friendly tone in your letters, imagine that you are sitting next to the reader. *Talk* to the reader with words that sound comfortable to you. Don't be afraid to use an occasional contraction such as *we're* or *I'll.* Avoid legal terminology, technical words, and formal constructions. Your writing will be easier to read and understand if it sounds like the following conversational examples:

You can develop a conversational tone in your written messages by using familiar words, an occasional contraction, and first-person pronouns instead of third-person expressions.

FORMAL: All employees are herewith instructed to return the appropriately designated contracts to the undersigned.
CONVERSATIONAL: Please return your contracts to me.

FORMAL: Pertaining to your order, we must verify the sizes that your organization requires prior to consignment of your order to our shipper.
CONVERSATIONAL: We'll send your order as soon as we confirm the sizes you need.

⊃ *Instructor: See p. 26 for supplementary lecture, "Levels of Style in Language."*

FORMAL: The writer wishes to inform the above-referenced individual that subsequent payments may henceforth be sent to the address cited below.
CONVERSATIONAL: Your payments should now be sent to us in Lakewood.

Transparencies 3.4 and 3.5

FORMAL: To facilitate ratification of this agreement, your negotiators urge that the membership respond in the affirmative.
CONVERSATIONAL: We urge you to approve the agreement by voting yes.

Business letters can be warm and friendly without becoming familiar and intimate.

The preceding examples illustrate effective conversational style. Although friendly, the tone of these messages is businesslike and objective. Successful letter writers are able to make their business letters conversational without becoming chatty, friendly without becoming familiar, and warm without becoming intimate. Strive to achieve a balance between objectivity and friendliness.

POSITIVE LANGUAGE

Transparencies 3.1 and 3.5

Readers learn more when you write positively.

⊃ *Instructor: See p. 27 for supplementary lecture, "Negative Expressions."*

The tone of a letter is considerably improved if you use positive rather than negative language. It's uplifting and pleasant to focus on the positive. Moreover, positive language generally conveys more information than negative language does. Positive wording tells what *is* and what *can be done* rather than what *isn't* and what *can't be done*. For example, *Your order cannot be shipped by January 10,* is not nearly so informative as *Your order will be shipped January 20.*

Analyze what you have to say, and then present it in positive language. Here are examples of statements in which the negative tone can be revised to reflect a positive impression.

NEGATIVE: We are unable to send your shipment until we receive proof of your payment.
POSITIVE: We are happy to have your business and look forward to sending your shipment as soon as we receive your payment.

NEGATIVE: We are sorry that we must reject your application for credit at this time.
POSITIVE: At this time we can serve you on a cash basis only.

NEGATIVE: You will never regret opening a charge account with us.
POSITIVE: Your new charge account will enable you to purchase executive suits at reasonable prices.

NEGATIVE: We cannot use this computer keyboard efficiently until we receive the proper template.
POSITIVE: After we receive the proper computer template, we will be able to use this computer keyboard efficiently.

NEGATIVE: Although I've never had a paid position before, I have worked as an intern in an attorney's office while completing my degree requirements.
POSITIVE: My experience in an attorney's office and my recent training in legal procedures and office automation can be assets to your organization.

EMPHASIS ON READER BENEFITS

Smart communicators know that the tone of any message, as well as its chance for success, is greatly improved by emphasizing reader benefits. This means making the reader see how the message affects and benefits her or him.

It is human nature for individuals to be most concerned with matters that relate directly to themselves. This is a natural and necessary condition of existence. If we weren't interested in attending to our own needs, we could not survive.

Transparencies 3.2 and 3.4

Most of us are also concerned with others. We are interested in their lives, and we care about their feelings. Individuals who are successful in the business world—and in their personal lives—often possess a trait called *empathy*. *Empathy* is the capacity to put yourself into another's position and experience that person's feelings.

Look at your message from the reader's position.

Empathic business writers care about readers and express that concern in their communication. They try to see the reader's viewpoint. Place yourself in the reader's position. How would you react? How would you feel? When you read a message, you're very likely thinking, consciously or unconsciously, "What's in it for me?" When you write a message, say to yourself, "What's in it for the reader?" In what aspect of your message would the reader be most interested? How will it benefit the reader? Once you've answered these questions, write your message so that it emphasizes the benefits to the reader.

Be especially alert to the overuse of first-person pronouns like *I, my, we,* and *our.* These words indicate that the writer is most interested in only one narrow view—the writer's. On the other hand, you should not sacrifice fluency, brevity, and directness to avoid an occasional *I* or *me.*

Overemphasis of the pronouns I and me reflect the writer's interests instead of the reader's.

Compare the following sets of statements. Notice how first-person pronouns are deemphasized and second-person pronouns (*you, your*) become more obvious when the focus shifts to benefits to and interests of the reader. Some authorities refer to this technique as the *you* attitude.

I/WE ATTITUDE: I am very pleased that I am able to offer my customers a new investment program.

YOU ATTITUDE: You are the first of our customers to be offered our new investment program.

I/WE ATTITUDE: We are happy to announce the opening of our new bank branch in Newton to meet all banking needs.

YOU ATTITUDE: You will now be able to use our new Newton branch for all your banking needs.

I/WE ATTITUDE: All new employees are required to complete and return the attached parking application if they want to park in our lot.

YOU ATTITUDE: You may begin enjoying company parking privileges as soon as you complete and return the attached card.

I/WE ATTITUDE: Before we can allow you to write checks on your account, we request that you sign the enclosed signature card.

YOU ATTITUDE: For your protection please sign the enclosed signature card before you begin to write checks on your account.

Develop the you attitude by emphasizing reader benefits.

STYLE

Writing style is influenced greatly by the personality of the author, the organization's goals and environment, the message, and the audience. In our discussion, which focuses on essential elements that you can apply immediately in your writing, we'll be most concerned with outdated expressions, concise wording, and sexist terms.

OUTDATED EXPRESSIONS

The world of business has changed greatly in the past century or two. Yet, some business writers continue to use antiquated phrases and expressions borrowed from a period when the "language of business" was exceedingly formal and flowery. In the 1800s, letter writers "begged to state" and "trusted to be favored with" and assured their readers that they "remained their humble servants." Such language suggests quill pens, sealing wax, tall stools, powdered wigs, green eyeshades, and sleeve guards.

Transparency 3.2

Compare these two versions of a letter acknowledging an order. The first uses old-fashioned, flowery language that was appropriate a century ago. The second represents a modern, efficient style.

Outdated, flowery style

Dear Sirs,

Your esteemed favor of the 10th has been received and contents duly noted. Please be advised that your shipment is forthcoming. Trusting to be favored by future orders and assuring you of my cooperation,

I remain, Dear Sirs,
Yours respectfully,

The same message today might sound like this:

Modern, efficient style

Dear Mr. Sims:

Your order for 75 Datacom Desk Planners should reach you by July 1. Call me at 800-757-7008 to place future orders. We appreciate your business.

Sincerely,

Few modern letters sound as dated as the first example shown here, yet some time-worn, stale expressions linger from the past and should be avoided. Replace outdated expressions such as those shown here with more modern phrasing:

Outdated expressions sound stale and insincere to readers.

Transparency 3.2

OUTDATED EXPRESSIONS	MODERN PHRASING
are in receipt of	have received
as per your request	at your request
attached hereto	attached
enclosed please find	enclosed
kindly advise	please write
pursuant to your request	at your request
thanking you in advance	thank you
I trust that	I think, I believe
under separate cover	separately

Source: Duffy. Copyright 1985 Universal Press Syndicate. Reprinted with permission. All rights reserved.

CONCISE WORDING

Improve your writing by imagining that you will be fined $5 for every unnecessary word.

In business, time is indeed money. Translated into writing, this means that concise messages save reading time and, thus, money. In addition, messages that are written directly and efficiently are easier to read and comprehend. Say what you have to say and then stop.

Developing a concise writing style requires conscious effort. The scientist and philosopher Blaise Pascal once apologized for the length of a letter, explaining to his correspondent that the letter would have been shorter if he had more time.

Taking the time to make your writing concise means that you look for other—shorter—ways to say what you intend. Examine every sentence that you write. Could the thought be conveyed in fewer words? In addition to eliminating repetitious words (see Chapter 2), you should concentrate on shortening flabby phrases, eliminating expletives, deleting excessive prepositions, revising negatives, avoiding long lead-ins, and omitting needless adverbs. All these techniques improve your writing style.

Shortening Flabby Phrases.   Eliminate wasted words by boiling a phrase down to its essence. Compare the flabby expressions and the more concise forms shown here:

Transparency 3.2

FLABBY	CONCISE	FLABBY	CONCISE
at a later date	later	in addition to the above	also
at this point in time	now	in spite of the fact that	even though
afford an opportunity	allow	in the event that	if
are of the opinion that	believe	in the amount of	for
at the present time	now, presently	in the near future	soon
despite the fact that	though	in view of the fact that	because
due to the fact that	because, since	inasmuch as	since
during the time	while	more or less	about
feel free to	please	until such time as	until
for the period of	for		
fully cognizant of	aware		

Rewrite sentences with flabby expressions, omitting the wasted words.

WORDY: Inasmuch as you have had an excellent credit history previous to your illness, we are willing to extend your due date until a later date.

CONCISE: Since you had an excellent credit history before your illness, we are willing to extend your due date.

WORDY: In regard to your request for a parking decal, we would like to tell you that first of all we must see your motor vehicle registration.

CONCISE: We can issue a parking decal after we see your registration.

Eliminating Expletives.   Expletives are sentence fillers such as *there* and occasionally *it*. Avoid expletives that fatten sentences with excess words.

An expletive is a word such as there *or* it *that is used to fill in a sentence.*

WORDY: There are three vice presidents who report directly to the president.

CONCISE: Three vice presidents report directly to the president.

WORDY: It was the federal government that protected the health of workers.

CONCISE: The federal government protected the health of workers.

Transparency 3.3

Deleting Excessive Prepositions.   Some wordy prepositional phrases may be replaced by single adverbs. For example, *in the normal course of events* becomes *normally* and *as a general rule* becomes *generally.*

WORDY: Datatech approached the merger *in a careful manner.*
CONCISE: Datatech approached the merger *carefully.*

WORDY: The merger will *in all probability* be effected.
CONCISE: The merger will *probably* be effected.

WORDY: We have taken this action *in very few cases.*
CONCISE: We have *seldom* taken this action.

Thomas Jefferson said, "The most valuable of all talents is that of never using two words when one will do."

Revising Wordy Negatives.   Shorten negative expressions by using the prefixes *un-* and *dis-* (for example, *unclear* for *not clear* and *dissatisfied* for *not satisfied*), or shorten negative constructions by using a positive construction (for example, *didn't have any excuse* becomes *had no excuse*).

WORDY: James was *not happy* with his bonus.
CONCISE: James was *unhappy* with his bonus.

WORDY: Dr. Francisco did *not agree* with the report.
CONCISE: Dr. Francisco *disagreed* with the report.

WORDY: Although he *did not have* a parking permit, he entered the lot.
CONCISE: Although he *had no* parking permit, he entered the lot.

Avoiding Long Lead-ins.   Delete unnecessary introductory words. The meat of the sentence often follows the words *that* or *because.*

WORDY: *I am sending you this announcement to let you all know that* the office will be closed Monday.
CONCISE: The office will be closed Monday.

WORDY: *You will be interested to learn that* you may now use the automatic teller at our Lynwood branch.
CONCISE: You may now use the automatic teller at our Lynwood branch.

WORDY: *I am writing this letter because* Professor Lydia Brunton suggested that your organization was hiring trainees.
CONCISE: Professor Lydia Brunton suggested that your organization was hiring trainees.

Omitting Needless Adverbs.   Eliminating adverbs like *very, definitely, quite, completely, extremely, really, actually, somewhat,* and *rather* streamlines your writing and makes the tone more businesslike.

WORDY: We *actually* did not *really* give his plan a *very* fair trial.
CONCISE: We did not give his plan a fair trial.

WORDY: Professor Larsen offered an *extremely* fine course that students *definitely* appreciated.
CONCISE: Professor Larsen offered a fine course that students appreciated.

SEXIST TERMS

Sexist words suggest prejudice or discrimination based on sex. For example, notice the use of the masculine pronouns *he* and *his* in the following sentences:

If a physician is needed, *he* will be called.
Every homeowner must read *his* insurance policy carefully.

These sentences illustrate an age-old grammatical rule called "common gender." When a speaker or writer did not know the gender (sex) of an individual, masculine pronouns (such as *he* or *his*) were used. Masculine pronouns were understood to indicate both men and women.

Today, however, sensitive writers and speakers replace common-gender pronouns with alternate nonsexist constructions.

SEXIST: Every attorney has ten minutes for *his* summation.
NONSEXIST: All *attorneys* have ten minutes for *their* summations. (Use a plural noun and plural pronoun.)
NONSEXIST: Attorneys have ten minutes for summations. (Omit the pronoun entirely.)
NONSEXIST: Every attorney has ten minutes for *a* summation. (Use an article instead of a pronoun.)
NONSEXIST: Every attorney has ten minutes for *his or her* summation. (Use both a masculine and a feminine pronoun.)

Sensitive writers today try to use sex-neutral terms, such as letter carrier instead of mailman.

Note, however, that the last alternative, which includes a masculine and a feminine pronoun, is wordy and awkward. Don't use it too frequently.

Other words are considered sexist because they suggest stereotypes. For example, the nouns *fireman* and *mailman* suggest that only men hold these positions. Avoid offending your listener or reader by using nonsexist job titles or functions such as the following: *firefighter, letter carrier, salesperson, flight attendant, department head, committee chair, technician,* and *police officer.*

A stereotype is a standardized, usually oversimplified opinion.

Transparency 3.6

ETHICS

Communicators have many goals in communicating business messages.[1] Most of the techniques presented thus far focused on creating clear and sensitive messages. Naturally, communicators strive to use those methods that will make their words most persuasive. But how far can a communicator go in getting a point across? Laws prohibit the most harmful behavior, such as false claims about products, misleading advertising, and mail fraud. Still, much borderline behavior is not covered by laws.

Businesspeople in the 1990s are increasingly concerned with ethics. An estimated 95 percent of Fortune 500 corporations, as well as many smaller companies, have now adopted ethics statements or codes of conduct.[2] Moreover, business organizations are sponsoring ethics workshops, conducting ethics simulations, and hiring ethics counselors/facilitators. Why this sudden interest in ethics? Many businesses are becoming more aware of social responsibilities. Beyond earning profits, they feel obligated to act as good corporate citizens. Companies also recognize that ethical practices make good business sense. Ethical companies endure less litigation, less resentment, and less government regulation.[3] Equally important, ethical business managers and businesses "tend to be more trusted and better treated by employees, suppliers, stockholders, and consumers."[4]

Ethical business practices make good business sense.

GOALS OF ETHICAL BUSINESS COMMUNICATION

Just what is ethical behavior? Ethics author Mary E. Guy defines it as "that behavior which is the *right* thing to do, given the circumstances."[5]

Transparency 3.7

FIVE COMMON ETHICAL TRAPS

Making ethical decisions is usually difficult because the issues and alternatives are not always clear. Further complicating a decision are conflicting loyalties—to yourself, your organization, your family, and your friends. In deciding the right thing to do, you'll especially want to avoid the following five traps, which can lead you astray unless you recognize them.[8]

- *The false necessity trap.* People act from the belief that they're doing what they *must* do. They convince themselves that they have no other choice, when in fact it's generally a matter of convenience or comfort. Consider the Beech-Nut Corporation's actions when it discovered that its supplier was providing artificial apple juice. Beech-Nut canceled its contracts but continued to advertise and sell the adulterated "apple" juice as a 100 percent natural product in its baby food line. Apparently falling into the false necessity trap, Beech-Nut felt it had no choice but to continue the deception.
- *The doctrine-of-relative-filth trap.* Unethical actions sometimes look good when compared with the worse behavior of others. What's a little fudging on an expense account compared with the pleasure cruise the boss wrote off as a business trip? On Wall Street many stockbrokers probably considered their minor deviations from ethical sales techniques to be insignificant, and therefore, acceptable, when compared to the major crimes of junk-bond king Michael Milken and others.
- *The rationalization trap.* In falling into the rationalization trap, people try to explain away unethical actions by justifying them with excuses. Con-

---

Ethical behavior is doing the "right" thing under the circumstances.

Identifying the right thing to do, of course, is not always easy. The accompanying box describes five common ethical traps into which anyone can accidentally fall. Recognizing such pitfalls is one way to avoid unethical behavior. But most communicators need additional ethical guidance. Thus, the following five goals are provided as a framework to guide you in creating ethical messages.

Telling the Truth.   Ethical business communicators do not intentionally make statements that are untrue or deceptive. We become aware of dishonesty in business when violators break laws, notably in advertising, packaging, and marketing. The Federal Trade Commission, for example, ordered Kraft Foods to cancel a deceptive advertisement claiming that each Kraft Singles processed cheese slice contained as much calcium as five ounces of milk, an untrue statement.[6]

Ethical business communicators tell the truth, label opinions, remain objective, write clearly, and give credit when using the ideas of others.

Half-truths, exaggerations, and deceptions constitute unethical communication. But conflicting loyalties sometimes blur the line between right and wrong for businesspeople. Let's say you helped the marketing director, who is both your boss and your friend, conduct consumer research about a new company product. When you see the final report, you are astonished at how the findings have been distorted to show a highly favorable product approval rating. You are torn between loyalty to your boss (and friend) and loyalty to the company. Tools for helping you solve such ethical dilemmas will be discussed shortly.

Labeling Opinions.   Sensitive communicators know the difference between facts and opinions. *Facts* are verifiable and often are quantifiable;

sider employees who "steal" time from their employers—taking long lunch and coffee breaks, claiming sick leave when not ill, and completing their own tasks on company time. It's easy to rationalize such actions: "I deserve an extra-long lunch break because I can't get all my shopping done on such a short lunch hour" or "I'll just write my class report at the office because the computer printer is much better than mine, and they aren't paying me what I'm worth anyway."

- *The self-deception trap.* Applicants for jobs often fall into the self-deception trap. They are all too willing to inflate grade-point averages or exaggerate past accomplishments to impress prospective employers. One applicant, for example, claimed experience as a broker's assistant at a prestigious securities firm. A background check revealed that he had interviewed for the securities job but was never offered it.[9] Another applicant claimed that in his summer job he was "responsible for cross-corporate transferral of multidimensional client receivables." In other words, he moved boxes from sales to shipping. Self-deception can lead to unethical and possible illegal behavior.
- *The ends-justify-the-means trap.* Taking unethical actions to accomplish a desirable goal is a common trap. Consider a manager in a Medicare claims division of a large health insurance company who coerced clerical staff into working overtime without pay. The goal was the reduction of a backlog of unprocessed claims. Despite the worthy goal, the means of reaching it was unethical.

Being aware of these five traps can help you avoid falling into them when you are weighing the alternatives in difficult ethical decisions.

opinions are beliefs held with confidence but without substantiation. It's a fact, for example, that women are starting new businesses at twice the rate of men.[7] It's an opinion, though, that increasing numbers of women are abandoning the corporate employment arena to start these businesses. Such a statement can't be verified. Stating opinions as if they were facts is unethical.

Being Objective.   Ethical business communicators recognize their own biases and strive to keep them from distorting a message. Suppose you are asked to investigate microcomputers and write a report recommending a brand for your office. As you visit stores and watch computer demonstrations, you discover that an old high school friend is selling Brand X. Because you always liked this person and have faith in his judgment, you may be inclined to tilt your recommendation in his direction. However, it's unethical to misrepresent the facts in your report or to put a spin on your arguments based on friendship. To be ethical, you could note in your report that you have known the person for ten years and that you respect his opinion. In this way, you have disclosed your relationship as well as the reasons for your decision. Honest reporting means presenting the whole picture and relating all facts fairly.

Writing Clearly.   The ethical business communicator feels an obligation to write clearly so that the reader understands easily and quickly. Many states have passed "Plain English" laws, discussed earlier, that require businesses to write policies, warranties, and contracts in language comprehensible to average readers. Plain English means short sentences, simple words, and clear organization. Writers who intentionally obscure the meaning with long sentences and difficult words are being unethical.

A thin line separates unethical composition from inefficient composition. Some might argue that writers who send wordy, imprecise messages requiring additional correspondence to clarify the meaning are acting unethically. However, the problem may be one of experience and skill rather than ethics. Although such messages waste the time and resources of both senders and receivers, they are not unethical unless the *intent* is to deceive.

Giving Credit.   As you probably know, using the written ideas of others without credit is called *plagiarism.* Ethical communicators give credit for ideas by (1) referring to originators' names within the text, (2) using quotation marks, and (3) documenting sources with endnotes, footnotes, or internal references. (See Appendix C for more information about documentation.) One student writer explained his reasons for plagiarizing material in his report by rationalizing, "But the encyclopedia said it so much better than I could!" This may be so, yet such an argument is no justification for appropriating the words of others. Quotation marks and footnotes could have saved the student. In school or on the job, stealing ideas or words from others is unethical.

TOOLS FOR DOING THE RIGHT THING

In composing messages or engaging in other activities on the job, business communicators can't help being torn by conflicting loyalties. Do we tell the truth and risk our jobs? Do we show loyalty to friends even if it means bending the rules? Should we be tactful or totally honest? Is it our duty to make a profit or to be socially responsible? Again, to paraphrase Mary Guy, acting ethically means doing the right thing *given the circumstances.* Each set of circumstances requires analyzing issues, evaluating choices, and acting responsibly.

Resolving ethical issues is never easy, but the task can be made less difficult if you know how to identify key issues. The following questions may be helpful.

- *Is the action you are considering legal?* No matter who asks you to do it or how important you feel the result will be, avoid anything that is prohibited by law. Giving a kickback to a buyer for a large order is illegal, even if you suspect that others in your field do it and you know that without the kickback you will lose the sale.
- *How would you see the problem if you were on the opposite side?* Looking at all sides of an issue helps you gain perspective. Consider the issue of mandatory drug testing among employees. From management's viewpoint such testing could stop drug abuse, improve job performance, and lower health insurance premiums. From the employees' viewpoint mandatory testing reflects a lack of trust of employees and constitutes an invasion of privacy. By weighing both sides of an issue, you can arrive at a more equitable solution.
- *What are alternate solutions?* Consider all dimensions of other options. Would the alternative be more ethical? Under the circumstances, is the alternative feasible? Can an alternate solution be implemented with a minimum of disruption and with a high degree of probable success? In the situation involving your boss's distortion of consumer product research, you could go to the head of the company and tell what you

know. A more tactful alternative, however, would be to approach your boss and ask if you misunderstood the report's findings or if an error might have been made.

- *Can you discuss the problem with someone whose opinion you value?* Suppose you feel ethically bound to report accurate information to a client—even though your boss has ordered you not to do so. Talking about your dilemma with a co-worker or with a colleague in your field might give you helpful insights and lead to possible alternatives.
- *How would you feel if your family, friends, employer, or co-workers learned of your action?* If the thought of revealing your action publicly produces cold sweats, your choice is probably not a wise one. Losing the faith of your friends or the confidence of your customers is not worth whatever short-term gains might be realized.

Perhaps the best advice in ethical matters is contained in the Golden Rule: Do unto others as you would have others do unto you. The ultimate solution to all ethics problems is treating others fairly.

APPLICATION AND PRACTICE—3

Discussion
1. What is tone in a business message, and how is it established?
2. Why is the flowery, formal language once used in business communication no longer appropriate?
3. Explain why and how empathic business writers try to see the reader's viewpoint.
4. Why is a conversational tone in business writing hard to achieve?
5. Why are businesses increasingly concerned with ethics?

Short Answers
6. List three techniques for developing a warm, friendly, and conversational tone in business messages.
   1. *Imagine that you are sitting next to the reader and talk to that person with words that sound comfortable to you.*
   2. *Use occasional contractions, such as we're or I'll.*
   3. *Avoid legal terminology, technical words, and formal constructions (such as the undersigned and the writer).*

7. Why does positive language usually tell more than negative language? Give an original example.
   Positive wording tells what is and what can be done rather than what isn't and what can't be done.
   Example: We refund your full purchase price within seven days, instead of Absolutely no refunds after seven days.

8. Define *empathy.*
   Empathy is the capacity to put yourself into another's position and experience that person's feelings.

9. What is meant by *reader benefit?* Give an original example.
   Reader benefit means writing a message so that it is seen from the reader's viewpoint. It means showing how the information relates to the receiver.
   Example: This new computer program saves you time in preparing your income tax return.

10. Name some outdated expressions that you have heard in business. Why do you suppose they remain in use?
    Examples: As per your request, attached hereto please find, *and* enclosed please find. *People go on using these dated expressions because they think they sound "businesslike" and because other businesspeople still use them.*

11. List six ways to make writing more concise.
    1. Shorten flabby phrases.
    2. Eliminate expletives.
    3. Delete excessive prepositions.
    4. Revise wordy negatives.
    5. Avoid long lead-ins.
    6. Omit needless adverbs.

12. List five examples of sexist pronouns and nouns.
    1. he, him, his
    2. she, her
    3. fireman
    4. salesman
    5. foreman

13. Supply shorter words for the following expressions:
    a. in addition to the above   *also*
    b. in view of the fact that   *because*
    c. until such time as   *until*

14. Explain five goals of ethical business communicators.
    1. Telling the truth
    2. Labeling opinions
    3. Being objective
    4. Writing clearly
    5. Giving credit

15. What are five questions to ask in resolving an ethical dilemma?
    1. Is the action you are considering legal?
    2. How would you see the problem if you were on the opposite side?
    3. What are alternate solutions?
    4. Can you discuss the problem with someone whose opinion you value?
    5. How would you feel if your family, friends, employer, or co-workers learned of your action?

Writing Improvement Exercises

Conversational Language. Revise the following sentences to make the tone more conversational.

Instructor: Writing Improvement Exercises are available on diskette.

Transparency Master 3.1

EXAMPLE: As per your recent request, the undersigned is happy to inform you that we are sending you forthwith the brochures you requested.
REVISION: I'm happy to send you the brochures you requested.

16. Kindly inform the undersigned whether or not your representative will be making a visitation in the near future.
    Please tell me if your representative will be visiting before June 1.

17. Pursuant to your letter of the 12th, please be advised that your shipment was sent June 9.
    Your shipment was sent June 9.

18. Kindly be informed that your vehicle has been determined to require corrective work.
    Your car needs repair.

19. As per your recent request, attached herewith please find our quotation for the three-board computer set.

Attached is our quotation for the three-board computer set.

20. The undersigned respectfully reminds affected individuals that employees desirous of changing health plans must do so before December 30.

Employees changing health plans must do so before December 30.

Positive Language. Revise the following sentences to use positive language. Add information if needed.

21. We regret to inform you that your order did not reach us immediately, so we cannot ship your electrical conduits until August 1.

We are shipping your electrical conduits August 1.

22. Parking is not permitted in any lot other than South Lot D.

Parking is permitted only in South Lot D.

23. We are sorry to inform you that you do not qualify for a charge account at this time.

We will be happy to serve you on a cash basis.

24. Because your name was overlooked, you will not receive our introductory packet until we make our second mailing.

You will receive your introductory packet with our June 25 mailing.

25. You will never be sorry that you applied for a federally insured student loan at Pacific Bank.

You can enjoy the benefits of a federally insured student loan at Pacific Bank.

Transparency Master 3.2

Reader Benefit. Revise the following sentences to emphasize benefits to the reader.

EXAMPLE: We have just designed an amazing computer program that automatically computes income tax.

REVISION: You will be amazed by our computer program that automatically computes your income tax.

26. To prevent us from possibly losing large sums of money, our bank now requires verification of any large check presented for immediate payment.

To protect your deposits and those of other customers, we now verify any large checks presented for immediate payment.

27. Our extensive experience in investments enables us to find our customers the most profitable programs.

You can benefit from our extensive investment experience by letting us set up a profitable program for you.

28. Our company policy demands that individuals who rent power equipment must demonstrate a proficiency in its use.

For your safety, you must be proficient in the use of power equipment before you can rent it.

29. We are offering a new series of short-term loans that may be used for carrying accounts receivable and for stocking inventory.

You may use our new series of short-term loans to help carry your accounts receivable and to stock your inventory.

30. For just $250 per person, we have arranged a three-day trip to Las Vegas that includes deluxe accommodations, the "City Lights" show, and selected meals.

    For just $250 each, you can spend three days in Las Vegas, where you will enjoy deluxe accommodations, the "City Lights" show, and selected meals.

Outdated Expressions. Revise the following sentences to eliminate outdated expressions and to improve tone.

EXAMPLE: This is to inform you that we are sending you under separate cover one dozen toner cartridges as per your request.

REVISION: We're sending you one dozen toner cartridges.

31. We are in receipt of your letter of October 3, and as per your request, we are sending to you two complimentary passes to Expo 2000.

    We are sending you two complimentary passes to Expo 2000.

32. Attached please find instructions for completing the above-referenced claim.

    Instructions are attached for completing this claim.

33. Please allow the writer to take the liberty of offering his congratulations on your recent promotion.

    Congratulations on your recent promotion.

34. Thanking you in advance, we genuinely hope that you can accept this invitation to address our organization.

    We genuinely hope that you can address our organization.

35. We trust that our letter under date of July 17 reached you and that its contents were duly noted.

    We hope you received our July 17 letter.

Transparency Master 3.3

Flabby Phrases. Revise the following sentences to eliminate flabby phrases. Be particularly alert to negative constructions, long lead-ins, imprecise words, and needless adverbs like *very* and *quite.*

EXAMPLE: This is to notify you that our accountant actually couldn't find anything wrong with your report.

REVISION: Our accountant could find no fault with your report.

36. This memorandum is to inform you that all books and magazines must be taken back to the library by June 1.

    All library books and magazines must be returned by June 1.

37. This is to let you know that you should feel free to use your credit card for the purpose of purchasing household items for a period of 60 days.

    Please use your credit card to purchase household items for 60 days.

38. You may be interested to learn that there are a number of references in medical literature citing support for higher-dose aspirin.

    A number of references in medical literature support higher-dose aspirin.

39. As you may possibly be aware, Nordstrom is opening a discount fashion center in the Fallbrook area December 1.

    Nordstrom is opening a discount fashion center in the Fallbrook area December 1.

40. Filling out an application is not really necessary unless you are basically interested in that position.
Interested individuals may complete an application.

Expletives. Revise the following sentences to avoid wordy expressions using the expletives *there* and *it.*

EXAMPLE: There are four major fields in accounting. They are public accounting, private accounting, government accounting, and auditing.
REVISION: The four major fields in accounting are public accounting, private accounting, government accounting, and auditing.

41. There are at least five advantages that computers have over the human decision maker.
Computers have at least five advantages over the human decision maker.

42. The report shows that there are numerous employers looking for qualified job applicants.
The report shows that numerous employers are looking for qualified job applicants.

43. As a result of our research, we learned that there is no single factor causing the decline of interest in our product.
As a result of our research, we learned that no single factor caused the decline of interest in our product.

44. There are specialized areas one can branch off into, such as tax accounting, teaching, management advisory services, and investment banking.
One can branch off into specialized areas such as tax accounting, teaching, management advisory services, and investment banking.

45. There is a great demand for legal secretaries because of the growing number of attorneys beginning law practices.
Legal secretaries are in great demand because of the growing number of attorneys beginning law practices.

Prepositional Phrases, Wordy Phrases. Revise the following sentences to eliminate flabby expressions. Be alert to prepositional phrases that could be reduced to an adverb or adjective, and watch for wordy expletives.

EXAMPLE: Under ordinary circumstances, there are two technicians to repair appliances.
REVISION: Ordinarily, two technicians repair appliances.

Transparency Master 3.4

46. There are two sources of funding that we have available for your business.
Two funding sources are available for your business.

47. At an early date you may be sure that Mr. Benson will see you in regard to providing supplies for your office.
Mr. Benson will see you soon about providing office supplies.

48. In very few cases do we revoke the privileges of our credit cards.
We seldom revoke credit-card privileges.

49. During our spring sale there is a week of private previews that may be enjoyed by our preferred customers.
   During our spring sale preferred customers enjoy a private-preview week.

50. If the form is filled out in a satisfactory manner, we can process it with immediacy.
   If the form is filled out satisfactorily, we can process it immediately.

Sexist Language. Revise the following sentences to avoid sexist expressions.

51. Every employee has the right to examine his personnel file under recent federal regulations.
   Employees have the right to examine their personnel files under recent federal regulations.

52. Any applicant for the position of fireman must submit a medical report signed by his physician.
   Applicants for firefighter positions must submit medical reports signed by their physicians.

53. At most hospitals in this area a nurse provides her own uniform.
   At most hospitals in this area nurses must provide their own uniforms.

Activities

Outside Reading. Bring in three to five examples of writing that demonstrates (or fails to demonstrate) concepts from this chapter: conversational language, positive expression, reader benefit, outdated expressions, flabby phrases, and so forth.

Ethical Dilemma. What advice would you give in this situation? Lisa is serving as interim editor of the company newsletter. She receives an article written by the company president describing, in wordy and pompous language, the company's goals for the coming year. Lisa thinks the article will need considerable revising to make it readable. Attached to the president's article are complimentary comments by two of the company vice presidents. What action should Lisa take?

GRAMMAR/MECHANICS CHALLENGE—3

DOCUMENT FOR REVISION

Transparency 3.8

The following letter has faults in grammar, punctuation, tone, conversational language, outdated expressions, concise wording, long lead-ins, and many other problems. Use standard proofreading marks (see Appendix B) to correct the errors. Study the guidelines in the Grammar/Mechanics Handbook to sharpen your skills. When you finish, your instructor can show you the revised version of this letter.

Poor Letter

Ineffective Writing

October 4, 199X

Ms. Kay Bradley

Title Guaranty & Abstract Company

2430 Providence Avenue

Anchorage, AK 99508

Dear Kay:

Pursuant to our telephone conversation this morning, this is to advise that two (2) agent's packages will be delivered to you next week. Due to the fact that new forms had to be printed; we do not have them immediately available.

Although we cannot offer a 50/50 commission split, we are able to offer new agents a 60/40 commission split. There are two new agreement forms that show this commission ratio. When you get ready to sign up a new agent have her fill in both forms.

When you send me an executed agency agreement please make every effort to tell me what agency package was assigned to the agent. On the last form that you sent you overlooked this information. We need this data to distribute commissions in an expeditious manner.

If you have any questions, don't hesitate to call on me.

Yours very truly,

. . . .

4

···

EFFECTIVE SENTENCES,

PARAGRAPHS, AND

MESSAGES

IN THIS CHAPTER YOU WILL LEARN TO DO THE FOLLOWING:

- Avoid three basic sentence faults.
- Vary the length and structure of sentences.
- Emphasize important ideas.
- Match sentence parts in achieving parallelism.
- Use active- and passive-voice verbs appropriately.
- Develop clear, unified, and coherent paragraphs.
- Organize the process of writing.

Instructor: See p. 29 for author's suggested lesson plan for Chapter 4.

Successful writers employ numerous techniques as their "tricks of the trade."

Good writers have mastered a number of effective techniques regarding sentence and paragraph formation. These techniques are some of the "tricks of the trade" that can be acquired through study and practice. In this chapter you will practice techniques that help you achieve variety, emphasis, and unity in your writing. You will learn how to make effective use of parallelism and active- and passive-voice verbs. In addition, you will study how to compose unified and coherent paragraphs developed deductively and inductively. Finally, you will examine the total process of writing. A logical place to start is with a review of sentence components.

PHRASES AND CLAUSES

Clauses have subjects and verbs; phrases do not.

The construction of effective sentences begins with an understanding of the role of phrases and clauses. A *phrase* is a group of related words without a subject and a verb. Study the phrases in the following example:

56

We will be making a decision about the case in two weeks.

verb phrase   prepositional   prepositional
                        phrase   phrase

A group of related words including a subject and a verb is a *clause.*

Mr. Lee is our shipping manager, and he will call you.

clause   clause

An *independent clause* makes sense and is complete in itself. A *dependent clause,* although it has a subject and a verb, depends for its meaning upon an independent clause.

If you are able to attend, the meeting is next Tuesday.

dependent clause   independent clause

Understanding the difference between phrases and clauses will help you avoid writing unclear, faulty sentences.

THREE BASIC SENTENCE FAULTS

Beginning or careless writers sometimes produce sentences with one or more of the following three glaring faults.

- *Fragment.* A fragment is a part of a sentence, usually a phrase or dependent clause, punctuated as if it were an independent clause. Notice how the following fragments do not make sense by themselves.

    FRAGMENT: *Persuading employees to support the United Fund, to learn how to program a computer, or to prepare for an assignment in a new department.* These activities all require human change. (The italicized fragment is a series of phrases.)

    FRAGMENT: Federal regulations in the financial field have been changed. *Which explains why savings and loans, thrifts, and other financial institutions are now more competitive.* (The italicized fragment is a dependent clause.)

    FRAGMENT: Most attempts at change are likely to meet some resistance. *Change that brings about doubt and that may be seen as a threat to a worker's security and salary.* (The italicized fragment is an incomplete sentence.)

    Do not capitalize and punctuate a broken-off portion of a sentence as if it were complete.

- *Run-on sentence.* When one independent clause follows another without appropriate punctuation, a run-on sentence results.

    RUN-ON: The Intel Corporation makes computer chips *it serves a large portion of the computer industry.* (The clause beginning with *it* should be capitalized to form a new sentence, and a period should follow *chips.*)

- *Comma splice.* When two independent clauses are joined together inappropriately with a comma, a comma splice results.

Three common sentence faults are (1) fragments, (2) run-on sentences, and (3) comma splices.

Transparencies 4.1 and 4.2

COMMA SPLICE: We are sorry that your order was delayed, your shipment will be sent out this afternoon.

COMMA SPLICE: The titles of the jobs were quite similar, the duties of the jobs were substantially different.

Sentences with comma splices can be revised in several ways, as you see here.

COMMA SPLICE: The workshops for the managers start on Tuesday, the sessions for representatives begin Wednesday.

REVISION: The workshops for managers start on Tuesday. The sessions for representatives begin Wednesday.

REVISION: The workshops for managers start on Tuesday; the sessions for representatives begin Wednesday.

REVISION: The workshops for managers start on Tuesday, and the sessions for representatives begin Wednesday.

SENTENCE VARIETY AND LENGTH

⮌ *Instructor: See p. 30 for supplementary lecture, "Types of Sentences."*

Transparency 4.9

Good writers vary the length and structure of their sentences. Messages composed of sentences that sound the same are monotonous to read. Such messages may also divert the reader's attention from what is being said to how it is being said. Compare these two versions of the same paragraph:

LACKS VARIETY: We congratulate you on the purchase of your new home. It will be a source of pride and enjoyment for many years. It will increase in value. It can provide a valuable hedge against inflation. We encourage you to protect that investment.

SHOWS VARIETY: Congratulations on the purchase of your new home. We know that it will be a source of pride and enjoyment for many years. As it increases in value, it can provide a valuable hedge against inflation. We encourage you to protect that investment.

Sentences with varied structures are interesting to readers.

The first paragraph bores the reader because it relies solely on simple sentences of about the same length with the same subject-verb-object structure. The second paragraph is more interesting because it includes both short, emphatic sentences and longer sentences with dependent clauses. As a result of its varied sentence structures, the second paragraph is less choppy and more fluent.

Generally, it's best to write short sentences since they are more easily understood. What happens to comprehension as a sentence length increases? The American Press Institute makes the following estimates:

SENTENCE LENGTH	PERCENT OF PEOPLE WHO UNDERSTAND
0–8 words	100%
9–15 words	90%
16–19 words	80%
20–28 words	50%

The average sentence contains between 15 and 20 words.

The average sentence length is between 15 and 20 words. This doesn't mean that all sentences should be 15 or 20 words long, however. Effective paragraphs contain a mixture of sentences, some shorter and some longer.

EMPHASIS

Speakers can emphasize main ideas by saying them loudly or by repeating them slowly or by pounding the table as they speak. They can signal the relative importance of an idea by raising their eyebrows or shaking their head or whispering in a low voice. Writers, however, must rely on other means to tell their readers which ideas are more important than others. Emphasis in writing can be achieved primarily in two ways: mechanically or stylistically.

Writers may empha-size their ideas by using mechanical or stylistic devices.

EMPHASIS THROUGH MECHANICS

To emphasize an idea in print, a writer may use any of the following devices:

UNDERLINING:　Underlining draws the eye to a word.
TYPEFACE:　Using a different typeface, such as **boldface,** is like shouting a word.
ALL CAPS:　Words stand out when typed in ALL CAPS.
DASHES:　Dashes—if used sparingly—can be effective in capturing attention.
TABULATION:　Listing items vertically makes them stand out:
　　　1. First item
　　　2. Second item
　　　3. Third item

Transparency 4.3

　Other means of achieving mechanical emphasis include the arrangement of space, color, lines, boxes, columns, titles, headings, and subheadings to set off ideas.

EMPHASIS THROUGH STYLE

Although mechanical means are occasionally appropriate, more often a writer achieves emphasis stylistically. That is, the writer chooses words carefully and constructs sentences skillfully to emphasize main ideas and deemphasize minor or negative ideas. Here are four suggestions for emphasizing ideas stylistically:

Transparency 4.4

- *Use vivid words.* Vivid words, as you recall from Chapter 2, are emphatic because the reader can picture ideas clearly.

  GENERAL:　　　　　*One business* uses *personal* selling techniques.
  VIVID AND EMPHATIC:　*Avon* uses *face-to-face* selling techniques.

  GENERAL:　　　　　A *customer said* that he wanted the contract returned *soon.*
  VIVID AND EMPHATIC:　*Mr. Santos insisted* that the contract be returned *July 1.*

- *Label the main idea.* If an idea is significant, tell the reader.

  UNLABELED:　Explore the possibility of leasing a site, but *also* hire a business consultant.
  LABELED:　　Explore the possibility of leasing a site; but *most important,* hire a business consultant.

- *Place the important idea first or last in the sentence.* Ideas have less competition from surrounding words when they appear first or last in a sentence. Observe how the concept of *productivity* is emphasized in the first and second examples:

  EMPHATIC:　*Productivity* is more likely to be increased when profit-sharing plans are linked to individual performance rather than to group performance.

EMPHATIC: Profit-sharing plans that are linked to individual performance rather than to group performance are more effective in increasing *productivity.*

UNEMPHATIC: Profit-sharing plans are more effective in increasing *productivity* when they are linked to individual performance rather than to group performance.

- *Place the important idea in a simple sentence or in an independent clause.* Don't dilute the effect of the idea by making it share the spotlight with other words and clauses.

EMPHATIC: You are the first trainee that we have hired for this program. (Use a simple sentence for emphasis.)

EMPHATIC: Although we considered many candidates, you are the first trainee that we have hired for this program. (Independent clause contains main idea.)

UNEMPHATIC: Although you are the first trainee that we have hired for this program, we had many candidates and expect to expand the program in the future. (Main idea is lost in a dependent clause.)

DEEMPHASIS

The word stylistic refers to literary or artistic style as opposed to content.

To deemphasize an idea, such as bad news, try one of the following stylistic devices:

- *Use general words.* Just as vivid words emphasize, the use of general words can soften an unpleasant point when necessary.

VIVID: Our records indicate that *you recently were fired.*
GENERAL: Our records indicate that *your employment status has changed.*

Bad news can be made less painful by deemphasizing its presentation.

- *Bury the bad news in the middle of a sentence or in a dependent clause.* Instead of placing a negative point where it is conspicuous and perhaps painful to the reader, include it in a dependent clause.

EMPHASIZES BAD NEWS: We cannot issue you credit at this time, but we do have a plan that will allow you to fill your immediate needs on a cash basis.

DEEMPHASIZES BAD NEWS: We have a plan that will allow you to fill your immediate needs on a cash basis since we cannot issue you credit at this time.

Additional tips and strategies for announcing bad news will be provided in Chapter 8.

UNITY

Unified sentences contain only related ideas.

Unified sentences contain thoughts that are related to only one main idea. The following sentence lacks unity because the first clause has little or no relationship to the second clause:

LACKS UNITY: Our insurance plan is available in all states, and you may name anyone as a beneficiary for your coverage.

Three factors that destroy sentence unity are zigzag writing, mixed constructions, and misplaced modifiers. Let's consider each of these faults.

ZIGZAG WRITING

Sentences that twist or turn unexpectedly away from the main thought are examples of zigzag writing. Such confusing writing may result when too many thoughts are included in one sentence or when one thought does not relate to another. To rectify a zigzag sentence, revise it so that the reader understands the relationship between the thoughts. If that is impossible, move the unrelated thoughts to a new sentence.

ZIGZAG SENTENCE: I appreciate the time you spent with me last week, and I have purchased a personal computer that generates graphics.

REVISION: I appreciate the time you spent with me last week. As a result of your advice, I have purchased a personal computer that generates graphics.

ZIGZAG SENTENCE: The stockholders of a corporation elect a board of directors, although the chief executive officer is appointed by the board and the CEO is not directly responsible to the stockholders.

REVISION: The stockholders of a corporation elect a board of directors, who in turn appoints the chief executive officer. The CEO is not directly responsible to the stockholders.

Zigzag sentences often should be broken into two sentences.

MIXED CONSTRUCTIONS

Writers who fuse two different grammatical constructions destroy sentence unity and meaning.

MIXED CONSTRUCTION: The reason I am late is *because* my car battery is dead.

REVISION: The reason I am late is *that* my car battery is dead. (The construction introduced by *the reason is* should be a noun clause beginning with *that*, not an adverbial clause beginning with *because*.)

MIXED CONSTRUCTION: When the stock market index rose five points was our signal to sell.

REVISION: When the stock market index rose five points, we were prepared to sell. *Or,* Our signal to sell was an increase of five points in the stock market index.

MISPLACED MODIFIERS

Sentence unity can also be destroyed by the separation of phrases or clauses from the words that they modify.

MISPLACED MODIFIER: We will be happy to send a park map for all motorists reduced to a 1-inch scale.

REVISION: We will be happy to send all motorists a park map reduced to a 1-inch scale.

MISPLACED MODIFIER: Whether you travel for business or for pleasure, charge everything to your credit card in the United States.

REVISION: Whether you travel for business or for pleasure in the United States, charge everything to your credit card.

Keep phrases and clauses close to the words they describe.

Transparency 4.5

In each of the preceding sentences, the sentence made sense once the misplaced phrase was moved closer to the words it modified.

    Another modifier fault called a *dangling modifier* results when an introductory verbal phrase is not followed immediately by a word that it can logically modify. Notice in each of the following revisions of dangling modifiers that the sentence makes sense once we place the logical modifier after the introductory phrase.

Beware of introductory verbal phrases that are not immediately followed by the words they describe.

DANGLING MODIFIER: To receive a degree, 120 credits are required. (This sentence reads as if *120 credits* are receiving a degree.)

REVISION: To receive a degree, a student must earn 120 credits.

DANGLING MODIFIER: When filling out an employment application, the personnel manager expects each applicant to use ink. (The personnel manager is not filling out the application.)

REVISION: When filling out an employment application, each applicant is expected to use ink.

PARALLELISM

Balanced wording helps the reader anticipate your meaning.

Parallelism is a skillful writing technique that involves balanced writing. Sentences written so that their parts are balanced or parallel are easy to read and understand. To achieve parallel construction, use similar structures to express similar ideas. For example, the words *computing, coding, recording,* and *storing* are parallel because the words all end in *-ing.* To express the list as *computing, coding, recording,* and *storage* is disturbing because the last item is not what the reader expects. Try to match nouns with nouns, verbs with verbs, phrases with phrases, and clauses with clauses. Avoid mixing active-voice verbs with passive-voice verbs. Keep the wording balanced in expressing similar ideas.

Transparency 4.6

LACKS PARALLELISM: The market for industrial goods includes manufacturers, contractors, wholesalers, and *those concerned with the retail function.*

REVISION: The market for industrial goods includes manufacturers, contractors, wholesalers, and *retailers.* (Parallel construction matches nouns.)

LACKS PARALLELISM: Our primary goals are to increase productivity, reduce costs, and *the improvement of product quality.*

REVISION: Our primary goals are to increase productivity, reduce costs, and *improve product quality.* (Parallel construction matches verbs.)

LACKS PARALLELISM: We are scheduled to meet in Dallas on January 5, *we are meeting in Houston on the 15th of March,* and in Austin on June 3.

REVISION: We are scheduled to meet in Dallas on January 5, *in Houston on March 15,* and in Austin on June 3. (Parallel construction matches phrases.)

LACKS PARALLELISM: Mrs. Horne audits all accounts lettered A through L; accounts lettered M through Z are audited by Mr. Shapiro.

REVISION: Mrs. Horne audits all accounts lettered A through L; Mr. Shapiro audits accounts lettered M through Z. (Parallel construction matches active-voice verbs in balanced clauses.)

In presenting lists of data, whether shown horizontally or tabulated vertically, be certain to express all the items in parallel form. Which item in the following tabulated list is not parallel?

All items in a list should be expressed in balanced constructions.

LACKS PARALLELISM: Three primary objectives of advertising are as follows:
1. Increase frequency of product use
2. Introduce complementary products
3. Enhancement of the corporate image

ACTIVE AND PASSIVE VOICE

In sentences with active-voice verbs, the subject is the doer of the action. In passive-voice sentences, the subject is acted upon.

ACTIVE VERB: Mr. Johnson *completed* the tax return before the April 15 deadline. (The subject, *Mr. Johnson,* is the doer of the action.)

PASSIVE VERB: The tax return *was completed* before the April 15 deadline. (The subject, *tax return,* is acted upon.)

Transparency 4.7

In the first sentence, the active-voice verb emphasizes Mr. Johnson. In the second sentence, the passive-voice verb emphasizes the tax return. In sentences with passive-voice verbs, the doer of the action may be revealed or left unknown.

Most writers prefer active verbs because such verbs tell the reader clearly what the action is and who or what is performing that action.

On the other hand, passive verbs can be employed to perform certain necessary functions. They are helpful in (1) emphasizing an action or the recipient of the action (*You have been selected to represent us*), (2) deemphasizing negative news (*Your watch has not been repaired*), and (3) concealing the doer of an action (*A major error was made in the estimate*). In business writing, as well as in our personal relations, some situations demand tact and sensitivity. Instead of using a direct approach with active verbs, we may prefer the indirectness that passive verbs allow. Rather than making a blunt announcement with an active verb (*Mr. Sullivan made a major error in the estimate*), we can soften the sentence with a passive construction (*A major error has been made in the estimate*).

Although active-voice verbs are preferred in business writing, passive-voice verbs perform useful functions.

How can you tell if a verb is active or passive? Identify the subject of the sentence and decide if the subject is doing the acting or if it is being acted upon. For example, in the sentence *An appointment was made for January 1,* the subject is *appointment.* The subject is being acted upon; therefore, the verb (*was made*) is passive. Another clue in identifying passive-voice verbs is this: they always have a *to be* helping verb, such as *is, are, was, were, being,* or *been.*

PARAGRAPHS

We have thus far concentrated on the basic unit of writing, the sentence. The next unit of writing is the paragraph. A paragraph is a group of sentences with a controlling idea, usually stated first. Paragraphs package ideas into meaningful groups for readers. Often when you're writing the first draft of a message, the idea units are not immediately clear. In revising, though, you see that similar ideas should be placed together. You recognize ways to improve the sequencing of thoughts so that the reader better understands. Here are suggestions for working with paragraph unity, coherence, length, and organization.

PARAGRAPH UNITY

Just as sentences require unity, so do paragraphs. When is a paragraph unified? A paragraph is unified when all its sentences focus on just one topic or idea. Any sentence that treats a new topic should fall in a new paragraph or be revised to relate to the current paragraph topic.

PARAGRAPH COHERENCE

Three ways to create paragraph coherence are (1) repetition of key ideas, (2) use of pronouns, and (3) use of transitional expressions.

Effective paragraphs are coherent; that is, they hold together. Coherence is a quality of good writing that does not happen accidentally. It is consciously achieved through effective organization and through skillful use of three devices:

- *Repetition of key ideas or key words.* Repeating a word or key thought from a preceding sentence helps guide a reader from one thought to the next. This redundancy is necessary to build cohesiveness into writing.

  EFFECTIVE REPETITION: Quality control problems in production are often the result of poor-quality raw materials. Some companies have strong programs for ensuring the *quality of incoming production materials and supplies.*

Transparency 4.8

The second sentence of the preceding paragraph repeats the key idea of *quality.* Moreover, the words *incoming production materials and supplies* refer to *raw materials* mentioned in the preceding sentence. Good writers find other words to describe the same idea, thus using repetition to clarify a topic for the reader.

- *Use of pronouns.* Pronouns such as *this, that, they, these,* and *those* promote coherence by connecting the thoughts in one sentence to the thoughts in a previous sentence. To make sure that the pronoun reference is clear, consider joining the pronoun with the word to which it refers, thus making the pronoun into an adjective.

  PRONOUN REPETITION: Xerox has a four-point program to assist suppliers. *This program* includes written specifications for production materials and components.

Be very careful in using pronouns. A pronoun without a clear antecedent can be most annoying. The reader doesn't know precisely to what the pronoun refers.

  FAULTY: When company profits increased, employees were given a bonus, either a cash payment or company stock. *This* became a real incentive to employees.

IMPROVED: When company profits increased, employees were given a bonus, either a cash payment or company stock. *This profit-sharing plan* became a real incentive to employees.

- *Use of transitional expressions.* One of the most effective ways to achieve paragraph coherence is through the use of transitional expressions. These expressions act as road signs: they indicate where the message is headed, and they help the reader anticipate what is coming. Here are transitional expressions grouped according to uses:

TIME ASSOCIATION	CONTRAST	ILLUSTRATION
before, after	although	for example
first, second	but	in this way
meanwhile	however	
next	instead	
until	nevertheless	
when, whenever	on the other hand	

CAUSE, EFFECT	ADDITIONAL IDEA
consequently	furthermore
for this reason	in addition
hence	likewise
therefore	moreover

Used appropriately, transitional expressions help the reader see how ideas and sentences are related, thus achieving paragraph coherence.

PARAGRAPH LENGTH

Have you ever avoided reading a document because the paragraphs were forbiddingly long? If so, you're like most readers, who find short paragraphs more inviting than long ones. As a writer, you can make your messages more attractive by controlling paragraph length. In business letters, first and last paragraphs are often very short (one to four typed lines). Other paragraphs in letters and most paragraphs in reports should average about six lines, with ten lines being the maximum.

PARAGRAPH ORGANIZATION

Sentences within paragraphs are usually arranged either deductively (directly) or inductively (indirectly).

Deductive Method.   In this arrangement a topic sentence stating the main idea appears first, followed by other information. A topic sentence serves to orient readers so that they know what this paragraph is going to be about. It may be a summarizing statement followed by explanation and amplification of the main idea. This orienting sentence provides an introduction so that readers can better understand the following sentences. Without a topic sentence, readers must guess at why the paragraph is being written. Readers need a frame of reference provided by a topic sentence. Notice how the topic sentence in the following paragraph provides an overview:

> Personnel administrators for large companies are changing their preferences for items included in résumés of prospective employees. Recent surveys show that today's companies want to see evidence of achievement such as grade-point average, work experience, and college activities. They are less interested in personal items such as birth date, marital status, health, and number of dependents. A new category that many personnel officers said they would like to see is a summary of qualifications.

SEVEN WAYS COMPUTERS CAN MAKE YOU A BETTER BUSINESS WRITER

Although computers and software programs cannot actually do the writing for you, they provide powerful tools for making the writing process easier and more efficient. Here are some of the ways your computer can help you with your writing.

- *Fighting writer's block.* Because word processors enable ideas to flow almost effortlessly from your brain to a screen, you can expect fewer delays resulting from writer's block. You can compose rapidly, and you can experiment with structure and phrasing, later retaining and polishing the most promising thoughts. Many writers "sprint" write, recording unedited ideas quickly, to start the writing process and also to brainstorm for ideas on a project. Then they tag important ideas and use computer outlining programs to organize those ideas into logical sequences.
- *Collecting information electronically.* Much of the world's information is now stored in databases accessible by computer. If, for example, your company were introducing a new exercise bicycle, you could use an electronic directory to locate sporting goods stores, ranking them by total revenue and zip code to facilitate your sales strategy. Specialized databases store vast libraries of computerized financial, marketing, economic, government, and current events information. All you need is a computer, a modem, a telephone line, and a credit card to deliver mountains of data to your computer screen.
- *Composing and revising.* By freeing writers from tiresome typing and retyping, computers have become the favored composition medium among business communicators and other writers. Word processing features that especially appeal to business writers are *insert* (separates text and allows words to be added), *move* (shifts text to different positions), *undo* (rescues and returns deleted text), *search* (locates targeted words quickly), *math* (calculates rows and columns of figures), and *sort* (alphabetizes items).

Inductive Method.   The inductive (indirect) plan supplies examples and reasons first and then draws conclusions from them. Paragraphs or entire messages may be arranged inductively. This technique is especially useful when bad news is being presented or when persuasion is necessary. Instead of bluntly announcing the primary idea in the first sentence of a paragraph, the author delays the big idea. The topic sentence comes at the end of the paragraph. If you were a student about to ask your parents for a new car, would you make the request immediately? Or would you first build a case by discussing the many solid reasons why you deserve and need a new car, followed by the big idea? Clever individuals have learned that indirectness has value in certain instances. In the following paragraph notice that the topic sentence comes last. It is a conclusion drawn from the previous sentences.

Employees have rightfully complained recently of a lack of parking space in our company lots. As more employees are needed and hiring escalates, it's more difficult for us to provide guaranteed parking for everyone. *For this reason, we've purchased two company vans that will be used in a carpooling plan.*

Footnoting, indexing, thesaurus, and other features further ease the writing task.

- *Detecting and correcting errors.* Nearly all word processing programs today provide features that catch and correct spelling and typographical errors. Poor spellers and weak typists universally bless their spell checkers for repeatedly saving them from humiliation. Still, writers must recognize that misused words (*effect/affect*) and confusing words (*its/it's*) will escape spell-check detection. Other writing tools include grammar and style checkers. These programs make suggestions about word usage, readability, jargon, and other writing problems.

- *Designing and producing professional-looking documents.* Gone are the days when writers were forced to take their copy to printers for special typographical features. With most high-end word processing programs today, scalable font (for different character sizes and styles), italics, and boldface enable you to produce professional-looking titles, subheadings, captions, and footnotes. In addition, you can use bullets, circles, lines, boxes, arrows, and many other features to highlight ideas.

- *Adding graphics for emphasis.* Your letters, memos, and reports may be improved by the addition of graphs and artwork to clarify and illustrate data. Instead of cutting and pasting these items into a report and then photocopying the page, you can now create a diagram exactly where you want it. You can also import graphs, charts, or diagrams created in database, spreadsheet, graphics, and draw-and-paint programs. Moreover, ready-made pictures, called "clip art," can be used to symbolize or illustrate ideas.

- *Using collaborative software for team writing.* Assume you are part of a group preparing a lengthy proposal to secure a government contract. You expect to write one segment of the proposal yourself and help revise parts written by others. Special word processing programs with commenting and strikeout features allow you to revise easily and to identify each team member's editing. These collaborative programs, called "groupware," also include decision-support tools to help groups generate, organize, and analyze ideas more efficiently than in traditional meetings.

Most paragraphs and most business messages are organized deductively with primary ideas presented first. However, when tactfulness or persuasion is necessary, inductive organization is appropriate. You'll learn more about these strategies in forthcoming chapters.

PROCESS OF WRITING

Now that we've considered using words skillfully, developing effective sentences, and organizing unified paragraphs, let's look at the total process of writing. Experienced business writers generally follow a series of five steps in producing messages and documents. These five steps, which we'll call the POWER plan, include Planning, Organizing, Writing, Editing, and Reexamining. While learning the details of the POWER plan, remember that a computer can ease the entire writing process. See the accompanying box for seven specific ways your computer can make you a better business writer.

The POWER writing process includes five steps: Planning, Organizing, Writing, Editing, and Reexamining.

- *Planning.* Every successful document begins with planning. Examine your message in relation to the communication cycle. What is your purpose, and what effect do you hope to achieve? Consider your audience, and anticipate reader reaction to the message. Decide on the medium for your message, considering noise and feedback. Decide what ideas to emphasize and which to deemphasize or omit. This planning process should take place whether you are responding to another message or initiating communication. In its simplest form planning occurs when the writer reads an incoming letter and underlines significant points or makes marginal notes regarding the response. In a more complex form planning may involve research to solve a problem.

- *Organizing.* The next step in the process of writing is organizing the message. Follow a deductive (direct) strategy, shown more fully in Chapter 5, for good news and for neutral messages. Use an inductive (indirect) strategy, presented in Chapter 8, for negative messages and persuasion. Novice writers often need help in organizing messages effectively. To give you practice in developing this skill, we will provide writing plans and organizational tips for a variety of business writing situations in forthcoming chapters. As you develop your skills, though, fewer organizational suggestions are provided. Learn to jot down a brief outline or list of points to be covered before you begin to write any message.

- *Writing.* Once you have planned a document and organized its content, begin writing. Some writers compose a rough draft at a typewriter; others prefer pencil and paper. Increasingly, writers are learning the joys of word processing for ease in composition and revision. Your first version should be considered a rough draft only. If you have time and if the document is significant, put it aside for a day before revising it. Fresh insights may help you see the subject differently—perhaps more clearly. Apply the principles you have learned in writing effective sentences and paragraphs.

- *Editing.* Read over your rough draft critically. Is the tone appropriate? Will the reader understand what you have said? Will this message achieve your purpose? Edit your message by crossing out awkward and unclear sections. Replace dull or meaningless words with precise, vivid ones. Look for ways to polish the content and structure of your message. Many experts consider the editing phase the most important step in the process of writing. After prudent editing, prepare the final copy.

- *Reexamining.* The final step is a careful reexamination of the message. Proofread the final copy not only for meaning and expression but also for typographical as well as spelling, grammar, capitalization, and other errors. Also consider the document's appearance. Is it attractive and neat? Is it balanced on the page? Are names, addresses, and numbers expressed accurately?

As you start writing business documents in the next chapter, apply this POWER formula. Too often, inexperienced writers begin writing a document immediately, without preparing and without aiming toward a goal.

APPLICATION AND PRACTICE—4

Discussion

1. How are speakers and writers different in the manner in which they emphasize ideas?
2. Why is parallelism an important technique for writers to master?

3. Why are active-voice verbs preferred in business writing?
4. How does a writer achieve paragraph unity?
5. Differentiate between the deductive and inductive methods for organizing paragraphs.

Short Answers

6. Write definitions for these words.
   a. Phrase   *A phrase is a group of related words without a subject and a verb.*
   b. Clause   *A clause is a group of related words with a subject and a verb.*

7. What is the difference between an independent and a dependent clause?
   An independent clause makes sense and is complete. A dependent clause depends for its meaning on an independent clause.

8. Write definitions for these sentence faults.
   a. Fragment   *A fragment is a broken-off part of a sentence.*
   b. Run-on sentence   *A run-on sentence contains two independent clauses without appropriate punctuation.*
   c. Comma splice   *A comma splice results when two independent clauses are joined by a comma*

9. Name the five steps in the POWER formula that describe the process of writing.
   1. Planning
   2. Organizing
   3. Writing
   4. Editing
   5. Reexamining

10. What is the average length of a sentence?
    Between 15 and 20 words

11. List five techniques for achieving emphasis through mechanics.
    1. Underlining
    2. Typeface
    3. All caps
    4. Dashes
    5. Tabulation

12. List four techniques for achieving emphasis through style.
    1. Use vivid words.
    2. Label the main idea.
    3. Place the important idea first or last in the sentence.
    4. Place the important idea in a simple sentence or in an independent clause.

13. List two stylistic techniques for deemphasizing an idea.
    1. Use general words.
    2. Bury the idea in the middle of a sentence or in a dependent clause.

14. Define zigzag writing.
    Zigzag writing twists and turns unexpectedly away from the main thought.

15. How can a writer achieve parallelism? Give an example.
    Parallelism is achieved through the use of similar grammatical construction.
    Example: to sit, to walk, and to jog

Transparency
Master 4.1

⊃ *Instructor: Writing Improvement Exercises are available on diskette.*

Writing Improvement Exercises

Sentence Structure.   Each of the following groups of words could be classified as a fragment, comma splice, or run-on sentence. In the space provided, name the fault. Be prepared to discuss how to remedy sentence faults.

fragment   **Example:**   Since the trip originates in Los Angeles and makes one stop in Chicago.

comma splice   16. We would like to inspect your car, please contact your authorized dealer immediately.

fragment   17. If the necessary work has already been done or if you no longer own your Volkswagen.

run-on   18. We would very much appreciate your completing the enclosed questionnaire return it in the postage-paid envelope.

fragment   19. Because they know they can save money and time when they shop with us.

comma splice   20. Bills are mailed on the 16th of each month, they are payable by the 10th of the next month.

run-on   21. We are happy to grant your request for a credit account with us we welcome you as a charge customer.

fragment   22. Accounts that are payable by the 10th of each month and subject to a finance charge of 1.5 percent if unpaid.

comma splice   23. Your credit record, Mr. Deckman, is excellent, therefore, we are happy to welcome you as a charge customer.

run-on   24. A service representative was dispatched immediately he found that the computer had been programmed incorrectly.

fragment   25. As long as you are able to make a rush delivery of pottery to arrive before February 28.

Emphasis.   For each of the following sentences, circle (a) or (b).

26. Which is more emphatic?
   (a) It is a good idea that we advertise more.
   (b) It is critical that we advertise heavily.
27. Which is more emphatic?
   (a) The committee was powerless to act.
   (b) The committee was unable to take action.
28. Which sentence places more emphasis on *product loyalty*?
   (a) Product loyalty is the primary motivation for advertising.
   (b) The primary motivation for advertising is loyalty to the product, although other purposes are served also.
29. Which is more emphatic?
   (a) We need a faster, more efficient distribution system.
   (b) We need a better distribution system.
30. Which sentence places more emphasis on the seminar?
   (a) An executive training seminar that starts June 1 will include four candidates.
   (b) Four candidates will be able to participate in an executive training seminar that we feel will provide a valuable learning experience.
31. Which sentence places more emphasis on the date?
   (a) The deadline is December 30 for applications for overseas assignments.
   (b) December 30 is the deadline for applications for overseas assignments.

32. Which is *less* emphatic?
    (a) Miss Curtis said that her financial status had worsened.
    (b) Miss Curtis said that she had lost her job and owed $2,000.

33. Which sentence *deemphasizes* the credit refusal?
    (a) We are unable to grant you credit at this time, but we will reconsider your application later.
    (b) Although we welcome your cash business, we are unable to offer you credit at this time; but we will be happy to reconsider your application later.

34. Which sentence gives more emphasis to *judgment*?
    (a) He has many admirable qualities, but most important is his good judgment.
    (b) He has many admirable qualities, including good judgment and patience.

35. Which is more emphatic?
    (a) Three departments are involved: (1) Legal, (2) Accounting, and (3) Distribution.
    (b) Three departments are involved:
        (1) Legal
        (2) Accounting
        (3) Distribution

Sentence Unity.   The following sentences lack unity. Rewrite, correcting the identified fault.

Example: (Dangling modifier) By advertising extensively, all the open jobs were filled quickly.

Revision: By advertising extensively, we were able to fill all the open jobs quickly.

36. (Dangling modifier) To open a money market account, a deposit of $3,000 is required.
    To open a money market account, a customer (or you) must deposit $3,000.

37. (Mixed construction) The reason why Mrs. Harris is unable to travel extensively is because she has family responsibilities.
    The reason Mrs. Harris is unable to travel extensively is that she has family responsibilities.

38. (Misplaced modifier) Identification passes must be worn at all times in offices and production facilities showing the employee's picture.
    Identification passes showing the employee's picture must be worn at all times in offices and production facilities.

39. (Misplaced modifier) The editor in chief's rules were to be observed by all staff members, no matter how silly they seemed.
    The editor in chief's rules, no matter how silly they seemed, were to be observed by all staff members.

40. (Zigzag sentence) The business was started by two engineers, and these owners worked in a garage, which eventually grew into a million-dollar operation.
    The million-dollar operation was started in a garage by two engineers.

Parallelism.   Revise the following sentences so that their parts are balanced.

41. (Hint: Match verbs.) Some of our priorities include linking employee compensation to performance, keeping administrative costs down, The expansion of computer use, and the improvement of performance-review skills of supervisors.
    Some of our priorities include linking employee compensation to performance, keeping administrative costs down, expanding computer use, and improving performance-review skills of supervisors.

42. (Hint: Match active voice of verbs.) Sally Strehlke, of the Newport office, will now supervise our Western Division; and the Eastern Division will be supervised by our Baltimore office manager, James McFee.
    Sally Strehlke, of the Newport office, will now supervise our Western Division; and James McFee, of the Baltimore office, will supervise the Eastern Division.

43. (Hint: Match nouns.) Word processing is being used in the fields of health care, by attorneys, by secretaries in insurance firms, for scripts in the entertainment industry, in the banking field, and in many other places.
    Word processing is being used in the fields of health care, law, insurance, entertainment, banking, and in many other areas.

44. If you have decided to cancel our service, please cut your credit card in half, and the card pieces should be returned to us.
    If you have decided to cancel our service, please cut your credit card in half and return the pieces to us.

45. We need more laboratory space, additional personnel is required, and we also need much more capital.
    We need more laboratory space, additional personnel, and much more capital.

46. The application for a grant asks for this information: funds required for employee salaries, how much we expect to spend on equipment, and what is the length of the project.
    The grant application requires this information: employee salaries, equipment funding, and project length.

47. To lease an automobile is more expensive than buying one.
    To lease an automobile is more expensive than to buy one. Or, *Leasing an automobile is more expensive than buying one.*

48. Mr. Claiborne's attorney said that a will should contain three elements: distribution of property, some way for an executor to be appointed, and you must provide for administration of the will.
    Mr. Claiborne's attorney said that a will should contain three elements: distribution of property, appointment of an executor, and provision for administration.

49. To use the copier, insert your meter, the paper trays must be loaded, indicate the number of copies needed, and your original sheet should be inserted through the feeder.
    To use the copier, insert your meter, load the paper trays, indicate the number of copies needed, and insert your original sheet through the feeder.

50. The new teleconferencing service allows on-line users to send data, data can be received by users, they can discuss it, and data is clarified.

    The new teleconferencing service allows on-line users to send, receive, discuss, and clarify data.

Active-Voice Verbs. Business writing is more forceful if it uses active-voice verbs. Revise the following sentences so that verbs are in the active voice. Put the emphasis on the doer of the action. Add subjects if necessary.

Transparency Master 4.4

Example: The computers were powered up each day at 7 a.m.
Revision: Kevin powered up the computers each day at 7 a.m.

51. Initial figures for the bid were submitted before the June 1 deadline.

    The company submitted initial figures for the bid before the June 1 deadline.

52. A separate bill from AT&T will be sent to customers who continue to lease their equipment from AT&T.

    AT&T will send a separate bill to customers who continue to lease their equipment from AT&T.

53. Substantial sums of money were saved by customers who enrolled early in our stock option plan.

    Customers who enrolled early in our stock option plan saved substantial sums of money.

54. A significant financial commitment has been made by us to ensure that our customers will be able to take advantage of our discount pricing.

    We have made a significant financial commitment to ensure that our customers will be able to take advantage of our discount pricing.

55. Smaller-sized automated equipment was ordered so that each manager could have an individual computer.

    Our Purchasing Department ordered smaller-sized automated equipment so that each manager could have an individual computer.

Passive-Voice Verbs. When indirectness or tact is required, use passive-voice verbs. Revise the following sentences so that they are in the passive voice.

Example: Mrs. Murdock did not turn in the accounting statement on time.
Revision: The accounting statement was not turned in one time.

56. Mr. Kelly made a computational error in the report.

    A computational error was made in the report.

57. We cannot ship your order for 50 motors until June 15.

    Your order for 50 motors cannot be shipped until June 15. Or, Your order for 50 motors will be shipped June 15.

58. The government first issued a warning regarding the use of this pesticide over 15 months ago.

    A warning regarding the use of this pesticide was first issued by the government over 15 months ago. Or, A warning regarding the use of this pesticide was first issued over 15 months ago.

59. The private laboratory rated products primarily on the basis of their performance.
Products were rated by the private laboratory primarily on the basis of their performance. Or, Products were rated on the basis of their performance.

60. We will notify you immediately if we make any changes in your travel arrangements.
You will be notified immediately if any changes are made in your travel arrangements.

Inductive/Deductive Organization.   Read the lettered statements below and answer the following questions. Be prepared to justify your responses.

d _____

61. If you were organizing the lettered ideas in a deductive strategy, with which statement would you logically begin?

d _____

62. If you were organizing the lettered ideas in an inductive memo, with which statement would you conclude?
  (a) The Los Angeles Convention Center has facilities to accommodate over 250 exhibitors and thousands of visitors.
  (b) Los Angeles is a large metropolitan center that will attract a sizable audience for the conference.
  (c) The Los Angeles Convention Center has excellent parking facilities and better-than-average transportation connections.
  (d) The conference planning committee recommends that the next National Automation Conference be held in Los Angeles.

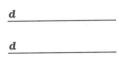

C A S E   4 - 1

PARAGRAPH UNITY

↻ *Instructor: See p. 31 in the Instructor's Manual for solutions to 4–1 and 4–2.*

Transparency Master 4.5

The following paragraph is poorly organized and lacks unity and coherence. On a separate sheet of paper, revise the paragraph following the suggestions provided in the text. Add or delete information as necessary. Pay attention to the use of transitions to connect thoughts coherently.

> We are pleased to welcome you to First National. Our family of banking customers is satisfied with First National. Group term life insurance is offered. This is one of the services we make available to our customers. This group term life insurance program has many benefits. It is low in cost. No medical examination is necessary to qualify for this program. The cost of living is steadily rising, and our premium rates remain reasonable. Take a look at the enclosed outline describing our group term life insurance.

C A S E   4 - 2

PARAGRAPH ORGANIZATION

The following material is part of a letter of application. It lacks organization, emphasis, and coherence. Its unity could be improved by including only relevant information. Revise this paragraph to remedy its faults. (Do not write the entire letter.)

You will see that I have wide variety in the field of communications in course work, and I have some work experience. My résumé that is enclosed shows this. I had a course in media analysis, one in business writing, one in communications law, and television ethics. I was active in the Scouts, 4-H, the Band Club, and my church. I worked with a newspaper for a while, television special events, and did a radio show. I have studied reporting, how to edit, and public relations.

CASE 4-3

PARAGRAPH ORGANIZATION

Select *one* of the topics below to write a well-organized, unified 100- to 150-word paragraph. Identify your topic sentence and method of organization.

1. Explain to a professor why you feel a grade you received should be changed.
2. Explain to an employer why you feel you should work different hours or be given a different assignment.

GRAMMAR/MECHANICS CHECKUP—4

ADJECTIVES AND ADVERBS

Review Sections 1.16 and 1.17 of the Grammar/Mechanics Handbook. Then study each of the following statements. Underscore any inappropriate forms. In the space provided write the correct form and the number of the G/M principle illustrated. You may need to consult your dictionary for current practice regarding some compound adjectives. When you finish, compare your responses with those shown below. If your answers differ, study carefully the principles in parentheses.

Example: He was one of those individuals with a <u>live and let live</u> attitude.   *live-and-let-live* (1.17e)

1. Most large corporations do not rely upon one source of <u>long term</u> financing only.   *long-term* (1.17e)
2. Many subscribers considered the <u>$25 per year</u> charge to be a bargain.   *$25-per-year* (1.17e)
3. Other subscribers complained that <u>$25 per year</u> was exorbitant.   *C* (1.17e)
4. The computer supplied the answer so <u>quick</u> that we were all amazed.   *quickly* (1.17d)
5. He <u>only had</u> $1 in his pocket.   *had only* (1.17f)
6. If you expect <u>double digit</u> inflation to return, look for safe investments.   *double-digit* (1.17e)
7. Jeremy found <u>a once in a lifetime</u> opportunity when he vacationed in the seacoast village.   *once-in-a-lifetime* (1.17e)
8. Although the house was four years old, it was in good condition.   *C* (1.17e)
9. Of the two sample colors shown in the brochure, which do you think is <u>best</u>?   *better* (1.17a)
10. Professor Roberts is very <u>well-known</u> in his field.   *C* (1.17e)
11. Channel 12 presents <u>up to the minute</u> news broadcasts for viewers around the world.   *up-to-the-minute* (1.17e)
12. Lower tax brackets would lessen the <u>after tax</u> yield of some bonds.   *after-tax* (1.17e)
13. The conclusion drawn from the statistics couldn't have been <u>more clearer</u>.   *have been clearer* (1.17b)

fifty-fifty   *(1.17e)*   14. The new investment fund has a better than <u>fifty fifty</u> chance of out-performing the older fund.

bad   *(1.17c)*   15. If you feel <u>badly</u> about the transaction, contact your portfolio manager.

---

1. long-term *(1.17e)*   3. C *(1.17e)*   5. had only *(1.17)*   7. once-in-a-lifetime *(1.17e)*   9. better *(1.17a)*   11. up-to-the-minute *(1.17e)*   13. have been clearer *(1.17b)*   15. bad *(1.17c)*

GRAMMAR/MECHANICS CHALLENGE—4

DOCUMENT FOR REVISION

Transparency 4.10

The following letter has faults in grammar, punctuation, spelling, number form, lead-ins, and other areas. Use standard proofreading marks (see Appendix B) to correct the errors. When you finish, your instructor can show you the revised version of this letter.

Poor Letter

Ineffective Writing

November 4, 199x

Mr. Sam Watson, Manager

Village Home Center

Dayton, OH 45420

Dear Mr. Watson:

This is to inform you that we will definitely credit your account for five hundred fifty dollars for the 2 no. 115 Electric Motors that arrived in damaged condition.

According to our records you received 9 electric motors. Please keep in mind that you are still elligible for the 10% discount on the 6 remaining motors. If you pay within 30 days. Remember too that the 10 percent discount is applicable on your reorder; should you wish us to replace the damaged motors.

We are happy to learn that the 9 batteries and 3 drills arrived in good condition. If your like our other customers you'll be particularly pleased with the results of the No. 118 drill. Nearly 100 customers have wrote to tell us of it's superiority over other drills on the market.

Please return the damaged electric motors to our St. Louis distribution center, if you wish us to replace them, just complete the enclosed authorization.

Sincerely yours,

COMMUNICATING

ROUTINE

MESSAGES

5

MEMORANDUMS

THAT INFORM, REQUEST,

AND RESPOND

Instructor: See p. 33 for author's suggested lesson plan for Chapter 5.

IN THIS CHAPTER YOU WILL LEARN TO DO THE FOLLOWING:

- Distinguish between direct and indirect writing strategies.
- Recognize functions, characteristics, and kinds of memorandums.
- Write memorandums that deliver information.
- Write memorandums that make requests.
- Write memorandums that respond to other documents.

Memorandums (memos) are forms of internal communication; that is, they deliver information within an organization. In many organizations more internal memos and E-mail messages are written than messages addressed to outsiders. Studies of executives, managers, and clerical personnel indicate that the memo is actually the workhorse of the office.[1] In fact, one expert reports that executives spend 22 percent of their time writing and reading memos.[2]

Memos deliver messages within organizations.

A WORD ABOUT STRATEGIES

Before we continue our discussion of memos, we need to consider plans or strategies. Business writing usually follows one of two strategies: the direct (deductive) plan or the indirect (inductive) plan. In Chapter 4 you learned to organize paragraphs inductively and deductively. Now we'll apply those same strategies to complete messages. How do you know which strategy to use? By analyzing your message and the anticipated reader reaction to that message, you can determine whether to use the direct or the indirect strategy. Most messages can be divided into three categories:

- *Positive or neutral messages.* Expect the reader to be pleased or at least not displeased.
- *Negative messages.* Expect the reader to be displeased.
- *Persuasive messages.* Expect the reader to be initially uninterested.

The anticipated reader reaction determines whether a message should be written directly or indirectly.

For positive or neutral messages, the direct strategy is most effective. You will learn to apply the direct strategy in writing informational memos in this chapter. In Chapters 6 and 7 you will use the direct strategy for routine request letters and for routine replies. In Chapters 8 and 9 you will learn to use the indirect strategy for negative messages and for persuasive messages.

FUNCTIONS OF MEMOS

Memos can save time and provide a written record.

Memos are a vital means of conducting business within an organization. They explain policies, procedures, and guidelines. They make announcements, request information, and follow up conversations. They provide a written record of decisions, telephone conversations, and meetings. They save time by relaying information to many people without the need for a meeting. Moreover, they ensure that all concerned individuals receive the *same* message, which would be unlikely if the message were transmitted orally.

When used judiciously, memos serve useful functions. When misused, however, they waste time, energy, and resources. A memo should not be written if a telephone call or a short note would function equally well. Memos should not be written as self-serving attention-getters. Some individuals churn out lengthy memos on the slightest pretense, such as the need for additional wastepaper baskets or catered coffee service or assigned parking spaces. Moreover, copies of memos should be sent only to concerned individuals. The fact that the office has an excellent copy machine or electronic mail network does not justify sending copies of memos to all employees.

Memos should be used for producing a permanent record, for gathering information, and for transmitting information when a personal meeting is impossible or unnecessary.

Most memos can be classified into four groups: (1) memos that inform, (2) memos that request, (3) memos that respond, and (4) memos that persuade. In this chapter we will be concerned with the first three groups because they use the direct strategy. The fourth group, persuasive memos, uses the indirect strategy and will be discussed in Chapters 8 and 9.

CHARACTERISTICS OF MEMOS

Transparency 5.1

Well-considered memos

- Begin with *To, From, Date,* and *Subject*
- Cover just one topic
- Are informal
- Are concise

FIGURE 5.1   Sample Memorandum

Laser Enterprises
Internal Memorandum

TO: Carlita Robertson

FROM: Edwina Jordan *EJ*

DATE: February 6, 199x

SUBJECT: FORMATTING COMPUTER MEMORANDUMS

Here is the information you requested regarding appropriate formatting for memorandums keyed at computers and printed on plain paper.

Use 1 to 1 1/4-inch side margins.

Leave a top margin of 1 to 2 inches.

Type in all caps the headings TO, FROM, DATE, and SUBJECT.

Single-space within paragraphs but double-space between them.

We prefer to make a master memo document with all the format settings. Then we read that command file into any new memo. This method is fast and accurate.

If you'd like to discuss formatting computer memos further, please call me at Ext. 606.

Writers of memos usually place their initials here.

Notice that memos do not end with a closing such as Sincerely.

Memos use an efficient standardized format, as shown in Figure 5.1 (See Appendix A for more information about formatting memos.) Use of the headings *To, From, Date,* and *Subject* has two benefits. First, headings force senders to organize their thoughts in order to compose the subject of the message. Second, headings are invaluable aids for filing and retrieving memos.

A memo normally covers only one topic. This facilitates action and filing. If an executive, for example, discusses in the same memo both the faulty exhaust system on the company car and the approaching company banquet, the reader may place the memo in a stack of paper relating to company cars and forget the details of the company banquet.

To facilitate action and filing, memos should cover a single topic only.

Memos may be written somewhat more informally than letters addressed outside the organization. Because you usually know and work with the reader, you do not have to build goodwill or strive to create a favorable image. Like business letters, memos should sound like conversation. For example, *Please be informed that* is much more formal than *I'd like you to know that.* Which would you be more likely to say in conversation?

Although informality is appropriate in memos, the degree of informality depends on the relationship between the employees. When a close working relationship exists between the sender and the receiver, a warm personal tone is fitting.

The techniques that you learned in Chapters 2, 3, and 4 for writing concisely will help make your memos succinct. Remember, memos are more likely to be read and acted on if they are just long enough to say what is necessary.

Frustrated business-people, sinking under piles of paper-work, appreciate concise, easy-to-read documents.

FORMS OF MEMOS

Memos in today's offices may appear in two forms: (1) hard-copy standard memos (printed on paper) or (2) electronic mail (E-mail) memos (sent over computer networks). Although many larger companies are rapidly installing E-mail networks, smaller organizations still rely on standard memos printed and distributed on paper.

Standard memos include TO, FROM, SUBJECT, and DATE and are printed on paper.

Standard Memos.   Some organizations provide stationery printed with the guide words *To, From, Date,* and *Subject.* Aligning the text that follows the guide words, however, can be difficult on today's computers and printers. Thus, individuals using computers may prefer to skip the printed memo stationery and type in the guide words themselves. An alternative is storing a master form to be recalled any time a memo is started.

The position of the date varies; it could appear at the top, in the middle, or after the subject line. Some memos, especially in large organizations, include additional guide words, such as *Routing, Department, Floor,* or *Reference File.* When memos are addressed to groups of people, their names may be listed under the word *Distribution* in the heading or in the lower left corner.

Unlike business letters, memos are usually unsigned. Instead, writers initial the *From* line. Close friends may add salutations *(Dear Andre)* and signatures to personalize their memos, but generally memos do not include these items. Senders of E-mail memos are encouraged to key their names at the ends of their messages because personal identification (usually supplied automatically) may be lost when messages travel from one system to another.

Electronic mail memos are transmitted over networks.

Electronic Mail Memos.   Instead of using paper to send memos, increasing numbers of businesspeople are turning to E-mail. E-mail requires computers, modems, and software to send messages electronically over networks connected by telephone lines and satellites. Almost instantaneously, a keyboarded memo travels to another computer—at the next desk or halfway around the world—and is stored in the recipient's mailbox until accessed. These messages may be printed, edited, stored, deleted, or forwarded—and all without paper!

Currently, E-mail is most effective in delivering simple messages; complex data should probably be sent in hard-copy documents. Because your future will probably include E-mail, the following tips will be helpful:

- *Upload your message.* Whenever possible, compose your message on a word processor and upload it to the E-mail network. Most E-mail text editors are primitive; therefore, you'll be able to produce better messages with your familiar word processing program.
- *Provide a descriptive subject line.* Nearly all E-mail systems include a prompt for a subject. This subject often determines *whether* a message will be read and *when* it will be read. Thus, you'll want to make subject lines interesting, accurate, and informative. For example, instead of *Meeting,* try *Meeting About Department Budget Cuts.*
- *Keep lines and paragraphs short.* Because computer monitors are small, lines under 65 characters in length are most readable. Paragraphs of no more than eight lines, with a blank line preceding a new paragraph, also enhance readability.
- *Care about correctness.* Senders and receivers of E-mail tend to be casual about spelling, grammar, and usage. However, people are still judged by their writing, whether electronic or paper-based. Some businesspeople have been passed over for promotions as a result of sloppy E-mail messages. And some E-mail memos never intended for mass distribution have been downloaded into print and distributed through entire organizations. Correctness still counts.
- *Avoid sensitive messages.* Because E-mail is far from private, do not send sensitive, confidential, or potentially embarrassing messages. Moreover, think twice before transmitting inflammatory messages that you may later regret. An employment attorney says, "A lot of people are getting into trouble. They feel a message is private. They press a button and think it's gone, but it's not."[3] E-mail creates a permanent record; even deleting it does not always remove it, so be careful about what you write.

Direct Memos

Whether you send hard-copy or electronic memos, you'll want to use the direct strategy for neutral or positive messages.

Transparency 5.2

Direct Strategy
- Main idea first
- Details or explanation
- Closing thought

The direct strategy gets right down to business quickly, with the main idea first. If your memo has a new procedure to announce, summarize that announcement in the first sentence. Don't explain why the new procedure is being introduced or what employee reactions to the new procedure might be. Save explanations and details for later.

Stating the main idea first has several advantages:

- *It saves time for readers.* They don't have to skim the first part of the message quickly to find a key sentence telling what the message is about.

The direct strategy starts with the main idea.

- *It enables readers to develop the proper mind-set.* After they learn the main idea, the following explanations and details make sense. Readers comprehend more quickly because they anticipate what is coming.
- *It helps the writer organize the message logically.* Once the writer has stated the main idea, the rest of the message is easier to write.

Remember, however, that the direct strategy is useful only if you expect that the reader will not be displeased by the content of the message. If the announcement of a new procedure might generate resistance, then persuasion is necessary and the indirect strategy (see Chapter 9) would be more effective.

DEVELOPING A MEMO-WRITING PLAN

A writing plan helps you organize a complete message.

Once you have decided on the strategy for your message, proceed to a writing plan. In this book you will be shown a number of writing plans appropriate for different messages. These plans provide a skeleton; they are the bones of a message. Writers provide the flesh. Simply plugging in phrases or someone else's words won't work. Good writers provide details and link together their ideas with transitions to create fluent and meaningful messages. However, a writing plan helps you get started and gives you ideas about what to include. At first, you will probably rely on these plans considerably. As you progress, they will become less important. Later in the book no plans are provided. Here is the writing plan for a memo that is not expected to create displeasure or resistance.

Transparency 5.3

WRITING PLAN FOR MEMOS
- *Subject line*—summarizes memo contents.
- *First sentence*—states the main idea.
- *Body*—provides background data and explains the main idea.
- *Closing*—requests action or summarizes the message.

WRITING THE SUBJECT LINE

A subject line must be concise but meaningful.

Probably the most important part of a memo is the subject line, which summarizes its contents in concise language. It should be brief, but not so brief that it makes no sense. The subject line *Revised Procedures* is probably meaningless to a reader. An improved subject line might read, *Revised Procedures for Scheduling Vacations.* For memos addressed to busy executives, subject lines must also entice them to read further. If they don't see something that snags their attention, they may not go beyond the subject line.

A subject line is like a newspaper headline. It should attract attention, create a clear picture, and present an accurate summary. It should not be a complete sentence and should rarely occupy more than one line. Cramming comprehensive information into one dense line is a challenge that many writers enjoy because it tests their word and organizational skills.

BEGINNING WITH THE MAIN IDEA

Although an explanation occasionally must precede the main idea, the first sentence usually states the primary idea of the memo. An appropriate opening sentence for a memo that announces a new vacation procedure is as follows:

Here are new guidelines for employees taking two- or three-week vacations between June and September.

Don't open a memo by asking the reader to refer to another memo. Attach a copy of that document if necessary. Or provide a brief review of the relevant points. Asking the reader to dig out previous correspondence is inefficient and inconsiderate.

It's better to attach a copy of previous correspondence than to ask the reader to find it.

The first sentence may constitute the entire first paragraph. If more information is needed to present the main idea, write a unified paragraph using the techniques suggested in Chapter 4. In many memos, however, the first paragraph consists of a single sentence.

EXPLAINING CLEARLY IN THE BODY

In the body of the memo, explain the main idea. If you are asking for detailed information, arrange the questions in logical order. If you are providing information, group similar information together. When considerable data are involved, use a separate paragraph for each topic. Work for effective transitions between paragraphs. Above all, use clear words. You don't want to leave your readers scratching their heads wondering what you are saying.

"... and contrary to the previously described permutations, which were unquestionably too abrupt and obviate any chance for ..."

Reprinted with special permission of Glenn Bernhardt.

The tone of memos is informal. Don't be self-conscious about using contractions *(won't, didn't, couldn't)*, conversational language, and occasional personal pronouns *(I, me, we)*. Make an effort, though, to deemphasize first-person pronouns. Concentrate on developing the *you* attitude.

Memos are most effective when they are concise. For this reason lists often appear in memos. Lists condense information into readable and understandable form. See the accompanying box for tips about writing effective lists.

CLOSING THE MEMO

End the memo with a request for action, a summary of the contents of the memo, or a closing thought. If action on the part of the reader is sought, spell out that action clearly. A vague request such as *Drop by to see this customer sometime* is ineffective because the reader may not understand exactly what is to be done. A better request might be worded as follows: *Please make an appointment to see John Ayers before August 5.* Another

End a memo with a request for action, a summary, or a closing remark.

HOW TO WRITE WINNING LISTS

A list is a group or series of related items, usually three or more. Business and professional writers have learned that presenting similar information in list form improves readability and emphasis. Because lists require fewer words than complete sentences, they can be read and understood more quickly and easily. Listed information stands out; therefore, it's swiftly located and quickly reviewed.

How can you write good lists? Concentrate on two concepts: (1) the list itself, and (2) the paragraph or sentence that introduces it.

ITEMS IN LIST

Use lists only if the items that are related can be shown in the same form. If one item is a single word but the next item requires a paragraph of explanation, the items are not suitable for listing.

Items in a list must be balanced, or parallel, in construction. Use similar grammatical form.

INSTEAD OF THIS	TRY THIS
Her primary pastimes are sleeping, eating, and work.	Her primary pastimes are sleeping, eating, and working.
We are hiring the following: sales clerks, managers who will function as supervisors, and people to work in offices.	We are hiring the following: sales clerks, supervising managers, and office personnel.
Some of the most pressing problems are refunds that are missing, payments directed to the wrong place, and lost documents.	These are the most pressing problems: missing refunds, misdirected payments, and lost documents.

A list of instructions snaps to attention if each item is a command starting with a verb. Bullets (periods) can also emphasize items.

Here are instructions for using the copy machine:

- Insert the departmental meter in the slot.
- Load paper, curved upward, in the upper tray.
- Feed flat copies through the feed chute.

Some items are most efficiently shown with headings:

DATE	CITY	SPEAKER
September 16	Portland	Dr. Roietta Fulgham
October 30	Seattle	Dr. Iva Upchurch

way to close a memo is by summarizing its major points. This is particularly helpful if the memo is complicated.

If no action request is made and a closing summary is unnecessary, the writer may prefer to end the memo with a simple closing thought. Although it is unnecessary to conclude memos with goodwill statements such as those found in letters to customers, some closing statement is useful to prevent a feeling of abruptness. For example, a memo might end with *I'll appreciate your assistance* or *What do you think of this proposal?*

Items may be listed vertically or horizontally. Items shown vertically, obviously, stand out more—but they require more space. To use less space and to show less separation from the surrounding paragraph, arrange items horizontally. In horizontal lists items are usually part of one sentence. Notice that each item is followed by a comma and that the word *and* precedes the last item in the series. If the items are too long for incorporation in one sentence, use a vertical list or rewrite the material without a list. Using letters or numbers for listed items gives them more importance and separation.

> Many individuals backslide on their resolutions regarding fitness. To keep exercising, you should (a) make a written commitment to yourself, (b) set realistic goals for each day's workout, and (c) enlist the support of your spouse or a friend.

> The health club has four sign-up months: January, May, August, and October.

INTRODUCTORY WORDS

The introductory words to a list must make sense in relation to each item in the list. The introduction should be as complete as possible so that the same words do not have to be repeated in each item.

INSTEAD OF THIS	TRY THIS
Our goal	Our goal is to recruit sales reps who are
• Is to recruit intensely competitive sales reps	• Intensely competitive
• Is to use reps who are familiar with our products	• Familiar with our products
• Recruit intelligent reps who learn quickly	• Intelligent and learn quickly

PUNCTUATING AND CAPITALIZING LISTS

Although some flexibility exists, most writers follow similar guidelines in punctuating and capitalizing words in lists.

- *Use a colon following the introduction to most lists.* However, do *not* use a colon if (1) the listed items follow a verb or preposition *(the colors are red, yellow, and blue)* or (2) another sentence precedes the list.
- *Omit punctuation after any item listed vertically.* Use a period *only* if the item is a complete sentence.
- *Capitalize the initial letter of any item listed vertically.*

USING LISTS

Information in memos often lends itself to listing. Because all of us would rather read listed information than blocky paragraphs, skilled writers make frequent use of lists. But you can't make a good list unless the information is similar in content and is arranged in parallel (balanced) statements. You can learn more about how to itemize, introduce, punctuate, and capitalize listed information by studying the above box.

MEMOS THAT INFORM

Transparencies 5.4 and 5.5

The memo format is useful to explain organization policies, procedures, and guidelines. As policy-making documents, memos that inform should be particularly clear and concise.

The memo shown in Figure 5.2 informs department managers of a change in job-hiring procedures. It begins directly by telling readers immediately what the memo is about. The next paragraph explains why the change is necessary. A list enumerates step-by-step procedures for clear reading and quick reference. The final paragraph restates the primary benefits of the new procedure and tells how more information may be obtained if necessary.

FIGURE 5.2   Memo That Informs

DATE: January 15, 199x

TO: Pat Walker, Cecille Cabanne, Don Deonne, Gil Sweeney, and
             Kathy Pedroza
                              PWL
FROM: Phyllis W. Livingston, Director, Human Resources

SUBJECT: CHANGE IN JOB ADVERTISING PROCEDURES

Summarizes main idea.

Effective today, all advertisements for departmental job openings should be routed through the Human Resources Department.

Explains why change in procedures is necessary.

A major problem resulted from the change in hiring procedures implemented last month. Each department is placing newspaper advertisements for new-hires individually, when all such requests should be centralized in this office. To process applications more efficiently and quickly, please follow this procedure:

Lists new procedures in parallel form, starting each with a verb.

1. Write an advertisement for a position in your department.

2. Take the ad to the Human Resources Department and discuss it with one of our counselors.

3. Let Human Resources place the ad in an appropriate local newspaper or other publication.

4. Pick up applicant folders from Human Resources the day following the closing date provided in the ad.

Closes by repeating benefits.

Following these guidelines will save you work and will also enable Human Resources to help you fill your openings more quickly. Call Ann Edmonds at Ext. 2505 if you have questions about this procedure.

PWL:edr

MEMOS THAT REQUEST

Memos that make requests are most effective when they use the direct approach. The reader learns immediately what is being requested. However, if you have any reason to suspect that the reader may resist the request, then an indirect approach would probably be more successful.

Requests should be courteous and respectful (see Figure 5.3), not demanding or dictatorial. The tone of the following request would likely antagonize its recipient:

> I want you to find out why the Davis account was not included in this report, and I want this information before you do anything else.

So that the intent of the memo is not misunderstood, requests should be considered carefully and written clearly. What may seem clear to the

Transparency 5.6

The tone of a request memo should encourage cooperation.

FIGURE 5.3 **Memo That Requests**

TO: All Department Heads   DATE: February 20, 199x

FROM: Joseph Ferguson, Vice President, Operations   *JF*

SUBJECT: SURVEY OF COMPUTER EQUIPMENT AND PROGRAMS

Please answer the questions below about the kinds of computers and software your department is now using.

Because many of our departments find it difficult to exchange data electronically, we are considering the purchase of networking hardware and software to make our equipment and data more compatible. Your answers to the following questions will help us understand our needs more completely.

1. How many and what kinds of computers does your department currently use?

2. What software programs do you use?

3. Are you anticipating the purchase of additional computer equipment in the near future? If so, what kind?

4. Do you expect to be adding new software in the near future?

I'll appreciate your answers by March 7 so that we can analyze your responses before our budget requests are due March 15.

States request courteously.

Lists questions for improved readability and comprehension.

Provides end date and reason.

End dating includes a deadline and, if possible, a reason explaining the deadline.

writer may not always be clear to a reader. Therefore, it's wise to have a fellow worker read important memos for clarity before they are sent out.

Whenever possible, the closing paragraph of a request memo should be *end dated.* An end date sets a deadline for the requested action and gives a reason for this action to be completed by the deadline. Such end dating prevents procrastination and allows the reader to plan a course of action to ensure completion by the date given. For example, a request that an employee order mailing labels might conclude with the following:

> Please submit your order by December 1 so that sufficient labels will be on hand for mailing the year-end reports January 15.

Many requests within organizations relate to the collection of information necessary for decision making. The memo shown in Figure 5.3 requests data about personal computers.

MEMOS THAT RESPOND

Much office correspondence reacts or responds to other memos or documents. When responding to a document, follow these preparatory steps: (1) collect whatever information is necessary, (2) organize your thoughts, and (3) make a brief outline of the points you plan to cover. You may wish to make your outline or notes right on the document you are answering.

Begin the memo with a clear statement of the main idea, which often is a summary of the contents of the memo. Avoid wordy and dated openings such as *Pursuant to your request of January 20, I am herewith including the information you wanted.* Although many business messages actually sound like this, they waste time and say little. Notice in Figure 5.4 that Lois Jones, manager of Legal Support Services, uses a straightforward opening in responding to her boss's request for information. She refers to his request, announces the information to follow, and identifies her department.

The body of a response memo provides the information requested. Its organization generally follows the sequence of the request. In Figure 5.4 Lois answers the questions as her boss presented them. However, she further clarifies the information by providing summarizing headings in bold type. These headings (*Computers, Software,* and so forth) emphasize the groupings and help the reader see immediately what information is covered. The memo closes with a summarizing and reassuring statement.

Memorandums serve as vital channels of information within business offices. They use a standardized format to request and deliver information. In this chapter you learned to apply the direct strategy in writing informational memos. In the next chapter you will extend the direct strategy to writing letters that make requests.

FIGURE 5.4   Memo That Responds

TO: Joseph Ferguson   DATE: March 5, 199x
             Vice President, Operations

FROM: Lois R. Jones, Manager *LRJ*
             Legal Support Services

SUBJECT: SURVEY OF COMPUTER EQUIPMENT AND SOFTWARE IN
          LEGAL SUPPORT SERVICES

Here is the information you requested February 20 about computer
equipment and software in Legal Support Services.

1. **Computers.** Our staff members are now using three Compaq Model
   500s, one Astro XR 6000, one Dell-Quattro, and one Apple SX350.

2. **Software.** Our work concentrates on word processing; hence, our
   software programs include Microsoft Word for Windows and
   Powerpoint for Windows. We need both DOS and Apple versions of
   Word.

3. **New Hardware.** Since many new programs require more memory
   than our current PCs provide, we are investigating adding memory to
   our existing computers. If that proves impossible or uneconomical, we
   may purchase entirely new systems. Under consideration are Zeos,
   ProAstro, and Inmac.

4. **New Software.** We are considering improving our presentation
   graphics programs as well as adding some form of integrated office
   applications. Specific programs have not been selected.

We, too, are interested in making our data and programs compatible with
those in other departments. Let me know if I may offer additional
information.

Opens directly with reference to previous request.

Provides headings to emphasize and clarify information groupings.

Closes with reassuring remark.

APPLICATION AND PRACTICE—5

Discussion
1. Explain the functions of memos within organizations.
2. Distinguish between the direct and indirect strategies.
3. How can memos waste time, money, and resources?
4. What are the differences between internal and external correspondence for an organization?
5. Name four groups of memos and explain what strategy each should follow.

Short Answers

6. List three categories into which most messages can be divided.
   1. *Positive or neutral messages*
   2. *Negative messages*
   3. *Persuasive messages*

7. Explain what reader reaction you might expect for each of the three categories of messages you listed above.
   1. *For positive or neutral messages, the reader will be pleased or at least not displeased.*
   2. *For negative messages, the reader probably will be displeased.*
   3. *For persuasive messages, the reader may be initially uninterested.*

8. What are the four guide words that appear at the top of most printed memo forms?
   To, From, Subject, Date

9. The use of a standardized memo format benefits whom?
   Both the sender and the receiver

10. Why should a memo cover only one topic?
    To facilitate action and filing

11. List three ways to close a memo.
    1. *Request action*
    2. *Summarize the contents of the memo*
    3. *Express a closing thought*

12. How do electronic mail and standard memos differ?
    Electronic mail memos are transmitted over networks; they are not printed. Standard memos include TO, FROM, SUBJECT, and DATE lines; they are printed on paper and circulated through office mail.

13. List and describe briefly four parts of the writing plan for a memo.
    1. *Subject line—summarizes the message*
    2. *First sentence—states the main idea of the memo*
    3. *Body—explains and amplifies the main idea of the memo*
    4. *Closing—ends with a request for action, a summary of the memo, or a closing thought*

14. What is *end dating*?
    An end date sets a deadline for a requested action to be completed.

15. Most memos will use which strategy?
    Direct

Writing Improvement Exercises

⊃ *Instructor: Writing Improvement Exercises available on diskette.*

Memo Openers and Organizations.   Compare the sets of memo openers below. Circle the letter of the opener that illustrates a direct opening. Be prepared to discuss the weaknesses and strengths of each opener shown.

16. a. For some time now we have been thinking about the possibility of developing an in-service training program for some of our employees.

b. Employees interested in acquiring and improving computer skills are invited to an in-service training program beginning October 4.

17. a. I am asking our Customer Relations Department to conduct a study and make recommendations regarding the gradual but steady decline of customer checking accounts.

   b. We have noticed recently a gradual but steady decline in the number of customer checking accounts. We are disturbed by this trend, and for this reason I am asking our Customer Relations Department to conduct a study and make recommendations regarding this important problem.

18. a. Some of the customer representatives in the field have suggested that they would like to dictate their reports from the field instead of coming back to the office to dictate them here. For this reason, we're going to make some changes.

   b. Customer representatives may now dictate their field reports using the following procedures.

Opening Paragraphs.   The following opening paragraphs to memos are wordy and indirect. After reading each paragraph, identify the main idea. Then, write an opening sentence that illustrates a more direct opening. Use a separate sheet if necessary.

Transparency Masters 5.1 and 5.2

19. Some of our staff members are interested in computer software that might lessen our work here in Accounting. Several staff members asked if they could attend a seminar February 11. This seminar previews accounting software that might be effective in our department. I am allowing the following employees to attend the seminar: Artie Miller, Ethel Martin, and Aurelia Gomez.
   Artie Miller, Ethel Martin, and Aurelia Gomez will attend an accounting software seminar February 11.

20. Your TechData Employees Association has secured for you discounts on auto repair, carpet purchases, travel arrangements, and many other services. These services are available to you if you have a Buying Power Card. All TechData employees are eligible for their own private Buying Power Cards.
   As a TechData employee, you are eligible for a Buying Power Card that entitles you to discounts on auto repair, carpet purchases, travel arrangements, and many other services.

Lists

21. Use the following information to compose a horizontal list with an introductory statement.

   Please follow in the plant at all times the following rules and restrictions. Hard hats should be worn at all times. Refrain from horseplay please. Smoking is prohibited for the good of all.
   Please observe the following plant restrictions at all times: (a) wear hard hats, (b) refrain from horseplay, and (c) don't smoke.

22. Use the following information to compose a vertical list with an introductory statement.

    Traditional employee suggestion programs often fail—for a number of reasons. To make them more successful, participation must be increased. Try to get more people to participate. For one thing, invitations should be extended to managers, part-timers, temporary workers, and even representatives of suppliers. But the rules must be simple—so simple that anyone may suggest anything at any time. And when they do submit a suggestion, they should be rewarded immediately. It's easy to give a simple reward, such as a button or a coffee mug, to anyone as soon as a suggestion is made.

    Improve participation in traditional employee suggestion programs by trying these ideas:
    1. *Invite managers, part-timers, temporary workers, and even supplier representatives to submit suggestions.*
    2. *Keep the rules simple so that anyone may suggest anything at any time.*
    3. *Give immediate rewards, such as a button or a coffee mug, to anyone making a suggestion.*

23. Use the following information to compose a horizontal list with an introductory statement.

    Your lease is about to mature. When it does, you must make a decision. Three options are available to you. If you like, you may purchase the equipment at fair market value. Or the existing lease may be extended, again at fair market value. Finally, if neither of these options is appealing, the equipment could be sent back to the lessor.

    When your lease matures next month, you may choose one of three options: (1) purchase the equipment at fair market value, (2) extend the existing lease at fair market value, or (3) return the equipment to the lessor.

Memo Format.   Study memo formatting and parts in Appendix A (p. 350). Then answer these questions:

24. Are memos usually single- or double-spaced?
    Single-spaced

25. How many inches should you leave for side margins when typing a memo?
    1 or $1\frac{1}{4}$ inches

⊃ *Instructor: See pp. 35–37 in the Instructor's Manual for solutions to 5-1, 5-2, and 5-3.*

26. Where does an author sign a memo?
    No signature appears on a memo; however, the author may place his or her initials after the typed name following From. *Writers of E-mail memos should key their names at the ends of messages.*

27. If you have no printed stationery on which to type a memo, on what line should you begin typing?
    Line 7 or 13 depending on your preference.

CASE 5-1

···

MEMO THAT REQUESTS

Play the part of Gordon Burns, president of Alloy Products. You must send a memo to Stacy Stafford, assistant personnel director, asking her to write a report comparing group health insurance plans. The Board of Directors of Alloy Products has authorized this study in preparation for the eventual adoption of a plan for your employees. The board has specific key factors to consider in the comparison: the cost to the company for each employee covered; kinds of illnesses and/or injuries covered; total annual health benefits allowed per employee; the costs to employees; and the coverage for hospital, outpatient, and home visits. You want Stacy to make a thorough investigation of the plans offered by seven or eight companies in your area. You need the report by July 1. In her report she should recommend three plans that are most appropriate. The board will make the final selection.

> *Instructor: See p. 12 for evaluation form for grading student assignments.*

Transparency Master 5.3

　　To help you organize your memo according to the principles you have learned in this chapter, read the options suggested here. Circle appropriate responses.

1. From the point of view of the person receiving the memo, what is the big idea in this memo?
   a. The Board of Directors is considering a health plan for employees.
   b. Stacy is to make a comparative study of group health plans.
   c. The Board of Directors has certain key factors to consider.
   d. Stacy's report must be submitted by July 1.
2. An effective opening sentence for your memo might be
   a. At its last meeting the Board of Directors considered adopting an employee group health insurance plan.
   b. We are very interested in employee group health insurance plans.
   c. Please make a comparative study of employee group health insurance plans as a preliminary step in selecting a suitable program for our employees.
   d. I have been authorized by the Board of Directors to begin an investigation of employee group health insurance plans.
3. The body of your memo should include
   a. An explanation of what the Board of Directors has authorized.
   b. A description of the Board of Directors' meeting.
   c. An inquiry about the personnel file of Jack Hays, which you gave her last week.
   d. References to complaints from employees regarding the lack of health benefits.
4. An effective closing for this memo might be
   a. Thanks for your assistance in this matter, Stacy.
   b. Please submit your comparison report to me by July 1.
   c. If I may be of assistance to you, please do not hesitate to call on me.
   d. I wonder, Stacy, if you would be able to speak to a group of high school students who asked us to supply a speaker on the topic of high-tech employment.

Use this memo for class discussion or use it as a writing assignment. If your instructor so directs, write the entire memo to Stacy on a separate sheet. Begin with an appropriate subject line. You may wish to incorporate some of the sentences you selected here. Add other information and join your thoughts with logical transitions. Be sure that your list of key factors is concise and parallel.

CASE 5-2 ....

MEMO THAT REQUESTS

Analyze the following poorly written memo. List its faults in the space provided. Outline an appropriate plan for a memo that requests. Then, on a separate sheet, write an improved version of this memo, rectifying its faults.

TO: Susan Richardson   DATE: April 3, 199x
         Community Relations Coordinator

FROM: H. W. Rosenblum
         President

SUBJECT: SUMMER INTERNSHIP PROGRAM

As you know, Susan, we at TechData have not been altogether pleased with the quality of the new employees we attract each year. We do not feel that we are getting the crème de la crème of the college graduates on the market, so to speak.

Our Management Council has suggested that we make a consideration of the possibility of adding a summer internship program for the express purpose of attracting superior college students to our company.

A number of questions arise. Accordingly, this memo is to make a request that you do some research on this possibility. Here are some things I want you to find out about. How much would such a program cost? I would like this question and the others answered in a report that you submit to me by June 15. Has this kind of program been tried in other companies? Do you think colleges and universities would participate? And if so, which ones would participate? We need to know if such a plan is likely to improve our present situation. We're also wondering if the company would be obligated to offer permanent positions to these summer interns.

If you'd like to talk with me about this project, Susan, just give me a jingle.

1. List at least five faults:
   1. *Subject line is ineffective.*
   2. *Main idea (the report) is lost in body of memo.*
   3. *Language is wordy throughout.*
   4. *List of questions is disorganized.*
   5. *Questions are not parallel.*
   6. *Ending does not request specific action.*

2. Outline a writing plan for this memo.
   Subject line: Summarize memo contents.
   Body: Provide background data and explain the main idea.
   Closing: Request action, summarize the message, or express a concluding remark.

CASE 5-3

MEMO THAT RESPONDS

Cynthia Chomsky, secretary of the Management Council of DataTech, wrote a first draft of the following memo. Then she attended a company workshop on improving communication techniques. She wrote comments to herself based on some of the things she learned. Revise the memo using her suggestions.

Transparency Master 5.5

TO: Martin Reid, Sal Alvarez, Kim Rockenrader

FROM: Cynthia Chomsky

DATE: February 3, 199x

SUBJECT: Reminder

really vague must improve

Long-winded memo... wastes everyone's time!

this first ¶ is a real drag !!

As we discussed, the Management Council is very concerned about our employee hiring techniques. This has become a problem in our company. I heard many of you say at our last meeting in January that you felt we had to improve our selection of employees. I understand that some new employees are hired for positions for which they are unsuited, and we don't seem to learn about the problem until it's too late. We really need to improve the entire personnel selection process, beginning with the writing of job specifications to the interviewing process. One area where we have been particularly lax is the checking of applicants' references.

they already know this stuff ... condense or leave out

I was asked at our last meeting in January to find speakers. I spent a lot of time finding individuals who I thought would bring us valuable information about improving our interviewing and other hiring techniques. I think you're all really going to benefit from the programs I've arranged. Please be reminded that the Management Council meets at 2:30 p.m. in Conference Room C.

too much "I" — not enough "you"

move to end

need this?

add end date

what a dictator I sound like!

If for some reason you cannot attend any of these meetings, you must call me. We also voted, if you will recall, to include outside guests at these last three sessions. So, if you would like to invite anyone, tell me his name so I can send him an invitation.

should come last

sexist!

by when?

Here are the three speakers I have arranged. The first is Norman J. Withers, from ABC Consultants. He will speak February 20 on the topic of "Job Specifications." Ann D. Seaman, Ph.D., Weber State University, is the next speaker. She will speak on the topic of "The Interviewing Process," and her date is March 28. Last but not least is Erick Basil, from Smith & Burney, Inc. The title of his talk is "Reference Checking" set for April 30.

check spelling of names arrange in list ... use headings?

cliché

shorten entire memo !

CASE 5-4

PERSONAL WRITING SITUATION

Write the following memo based on your own work or personal experience. Some employees have remarked to the boss that they are working more than other employees. Your boss has decided to study the matter by collecting memos from everyone and asks you to write a memo describing your current duties and the skills required for your position. If some jobs are found to be overly demanding, your boss may redistribute job tasks or hire additional employees. Write a well-organized memo describing your duties, the time you spend on each task, and the skills needed for what you do. Provide enough details to make a clear record of your job. Use actual names and describe actual tasks. If you have no work experience, use experience from an organization or institution to which you belong. Report to the head of the organization, describing the duties of an officer or of a committee. Your boss or organization head appreciates brevity. Keep your memo under one page.

Additional Problems

1. Assume you are Stephanie Adams and you work for Petro Products, Inc. The office manager, Sharon Chambers, asks you to go to a U.S. Post Office to gather information about current formatting of envelopes. Ms. Chambers wants to know how envelopes should be prepared and why they are no longer prepared the way they were twenty years ago. Get the information, and write a memo summarizing your findings. Your memo should be no more than one page.

2. You have been asked to draft a memo to the office staff about the company's Christmas party. Include information about where the party will be held, when it is, what the cost will be, a description of the food to be served, whether guests are allowed, and whom to make reservations with.

3. Assume you are Pamela Haas, marketing director, United Foods, Inc. Write a memo to V. A. McFee, vice president, informing him about the following advertising program. You have just completed the planning stages of a promotion campaign for your pasta product, Creamettes. Together with Sunkist Growers, Inc., you have worked out an agreement to launch a joint campaign aimed at combining the use of Creamettes with Sunkist lemons. The details for the planned campaign were formulated by your advertising agency, McFarlaine and Becker, over the past two months. The promotion will concentrate on light recipes for summer consumption. Along with the recipes, discount coupons on Creamettes will be offered. The coupons and recipes will be published in appropriate magazines and in the Thursday food sections of 48 daily newspapers in the Western states. The campaign will be concentrated in June, July, and August. You expect this campaign to cost $190,000 for advertising in newspapers and magazines, $90,000 for redeemed coupons (300,000 coupons at 30 cents each), and $37,000 to McFarlaine and Becker. Sunkist will provide one fifth of these costs. Mr. McFee has no prior knowledge of this promotion; he'll need all the details you can provide.

4. As director of employee relations of United Foods, write a memo to all employees informing them of new banking services soon to be avail-

able. You have arranged with First National Bank of your city to install an automated teller machine (ATM) in your lobby. It will operate from 6 a.m. to 9 p.m., six days a week, beginning next week. Describe the advantages of ATMs. Tell employees that a representative from First National will be present in the lobby for the next two weeks. This representative will be able to open accounts for employees who want to take advantage of their banking services, including a range of combination checking and savings accounts. NOW (negotiable order of withdrawal) accounts, CDs (certificates of deposit), and time deposits are available. The company has also arranged with First National to enable employees to deposit their paychecks directly to the bank. Describe the advantages of direct deposits. Encourage employees to visit the First National representatives in the next two weeks.

5. As Sanford Henry, vice president for personnel at United Foods, write a memo to Kathleene Basil, director of information services. Tell her that you have attended a conference on ergonomic office environments. You learned of employee complaints in some organizations where automated information processing equipment has been introduced. Ask her if she is aware of any dissatisfaction among word processing specialists regarding muscular discomfort or eyestrain. Has she noticed increased absenteeism among word processors? Have operators expressed unhappiness with their jobs? Is there a high turnover rate? Have any steps been taken to reduce job discomfort and dissatisfaction? You are very concerned about the health and happiness of employees. Ask Ms. Basil to give this matter her immediate consideration. You want a quick response. You don't expect her to conduct an elaborate investigation.

6. As Kathleene Basil, director of information services, respond to Mr. Henry's memo request described in No. 5 above. You don't know of any employee complaints about aching necks and shoulders. Only one employee, Edith Yen, the chief editor/proofreader, complained of eye trouble. You tried to solve that problem by rotating the task of editing among all word processing operators. You are concerned, too, about providing an ergonomically satisfactory work environment. You encourage employees who are performing eye-straining tasks to take 10-minute breaks every hour. You make sure that furniture is adjusted to the body size of users. You've checked on the absenteeism of your division compared with other divisions, and you find that your is lower. You have also installed glare-resistant screens on your monitors to reduce eyestrain. You admit that you have had a higher turnover rate than you would like, but employees seem to be leaving for better-paying word processing positions elsewhere. You are also experimenting with job-enrichment tasks to try to reduce any employee dissatisfaction in the Information Services Division. If Mr. Henry has any suggestions for you, you'd be glad to hear them. Encourage him to come to visit your division.

7. Again as Sanford Henry, vice president for personnel, write a memo to all department managers of United Foods. The city of Milwaukee has mandated that employees "shall adopt, implement, and maintain a written smoking policy which shall contain a prohibition against smoking in restrooms and infirmaries." Employers must also "maintain a nonsmoking area of not less than two thirds of the seating capacity in cafeterias, lunchrooms, and employee lounges, and

make efforts to work out disputes between smokers and nonsmokers." Make this announcement to your department managers. Tell the managers that you want them to set up departmental committees to mediate any smoking conflicts before the complaints surface. Explain why this is a good policy.

8. You are Mike O'Dell, manager of accounting services for United Foods, responding to Mr. Henry's memo in No. 7. You could have called Mr. Henry, but you prefer to have this problem in writing. The problem is the difficulty you are experiencing in enforcing the smoking ban in restrooms. Only one men's room serves your floor, and 15 of your 27 male employees are smokers. You have already received complaints, and you see no way to enforce the ban in the restrooms. You have also noticed that smokers are taking longer breaks than other employees. Smokers complain that they need more time because they must walk to an outside area. Smokers are especially unhappy when the weather is cold, rainy, or snowy. Moreover, smokers huddle near the building entrances, thus creating a negative impression for customers and visitors. Your committee members can find no solutions; in fact, they have become polarized in their meetings to date. You need help from a higher authority. Appeal to Mr. Henry for solutions. Perhaps he should visit your department.

GRAMMAR/MECHANICS CHECKUP—5

PREPOSITIONS AND CONJUNCTIONS

Review Sections 1.18 and 1.19 in the Grammar/Mechanics Handbook. Then study each of the following statements. Write *a* or *b* to indicate the sentence that is expressed more effectively. Also record the number of the G/M principle illustrated. When you finish, compare your responses with those provided below. If your answers differ, study carefully the principles shown in parentheses.

b   *(1.18a)*   **Example:** (a) Tiffany will graduate college this spring.
                            (b) Tiffany will graduate from college this spring.

b   *(1.19d)*   1. (a) DataTech enjoyed greater profits this year then it expected.
                            (b) DataTech enjoyed greater profits this year than it expected.

a   *(1.19c)*   2. (a) I hate it when we have to work overtime.
                            (b) I hate when we have to work overtime.

b   *(1.18e)*   3. (a) Dr. Simon has a great interest and appreciation for the study of robotics.
                            (b) Dr. Simon has a great interest in and appreciation for the study of robotics.

b   *(1.19c)*   4. (a) Gross profit is where you compute the difference between total sales and the cost of goods sold.
                            (b) Gross profit is computed by finding the difference between total sales and the cost of goods sold.

a   *(1.19a)*   5. (a) We advertise to increase the frequency of product use, to introduce complementary products, and to enhance our corporate image.
                            (b) We advertise to have our products used more often, when we have complementary products to introduce, and we are interested in making our corporation look better to the public.

b   *(1.18a)*   6. (a) What type computers do you prefer?
                            (b) What type of computers do you prefer?

7. (a) Many of our new products are selling better then we anticipated.   *b*   *(1.19d)*
   (b) Many of our new products are selling better than we anticipated.

8. (a) The sale of our San Antonio branch office last year should improve   *a*   *(1.18c)*
   this year's profits.
   (b) The sale of our branch office in San Antonio during last year
   should improve the profits for this year.

9. (a) Do you know where the meeting is at?   *b*   *(1.18b)*
   (b) Do you know where the meeting is?

10. (a) The cooling-off rule is an FTC rule that protects consumers from   *a*   *(1.19c)*
   making unwise purchases at home.
   (b) The cooling-off rule is where the FTC has made a rule that protects consumers from making unwise purchases at home.

11. (a) Meetings can be more meaningful if the agenda is stuck to, the   *b*   *(1.19a)*
   time frame is followed, and if someone keeps follow-up notes.
   (b) Meetings can be more meaningful if you stick to the agenda, follow
   the time frame, and keep follow-up notes.

12. (a) They printed the newsletter on yellow paper like we asked them to   *b*   *(1.19b)*
   do.
   (b) They printed the newsletter on yellow paper as we asked them to
   do.

13. (a) A code of ethics is a set of rules spelling out appropriate standards   *a*   *(1.19c)*
   of behavior.
   (b) A code of ethics is where a set of rules spells out appropriate standards of behavior.

14. (a) We need an individual with an understanding and serious interest   *b*   *(1.18e)*
   in black-and-white photography.
   (b) We need an individual with an understanding of and serious interest in black-and-white photography.

15. (a) The most dangerous situation is when employees ignore the safety   *b*   *(1.19c)*
   rules.
   (b) The most dangerous situation occurs when employees ignore the
   safety rules.

---

1. b (*1.19d*)   3. b (*1.18e*)   5. a (*1.19a*)   7. b (*1.19d*)   9. b (*1.18b*)   11. b (*1.19a*)
13. a (*1.19c*)   15. b (*1.19c*)

GRAMMAR/MECHANICS CHALLENGE—5

DOCUMENT FOR REVISION

The following memo has faults in grammar, punctuation, spelling, number
form, repetition, wordiness, and other areas. Use standard proofreading
marks (see Appendix B) to correct the errors. When you finish, your
instructor can show you the revised version of this memo.

Transparency 5.8

Poor Memo

TO: Amy MacKenzie   DATE: June 25, 199x

FROM: Ira White

SUBJECT: COLLECTING DATA FOR ANNUAL REPORT

Ineffective Writing

You have been assigned a special project, to collect information for next years annual report. You'll probably need to visit each department head personally to collect this information individually from them.

The Corporate Communications division which oversee the production of the annual report is of the opinion that you should concentrate on the following departmental data;

1. specific accomplishments of each department for the past year.

2. you must find out about goals of each department for the coming year.

3. in each department get names of interesting employees and events to be featured.

In view of the fact that this is a big assignment Maria Marquez has been assigned to offer assistance to you. Inasmuch as the annual report must be completed by September first; please submit your data in concise narrative form to me by August fifth.

· ·

6

LETTERS THAT MAKE

ROUTINE REQUESTS

IN THIS CHAPTER YOU WILL LEARN TO DO THE FOLLOWING:

- Analyze letter content and select an appropriate writing strategy.
- Write letters that request information concisely.
- Order merchandise clearly and efficiently.
- Write letters that make justified claims.

Instructor: See p. 39 for author's suggested lesson plan for Chapter 6.

Written communication outside an organization is conducted largely by letters. Executives, managers, and supervisors at all levels of management, as well as nonmanagement employees, typically are called upon daily to exchange information with customers and other organizations. Although information is also exchanged verbally, written communication in the form of letters is essential to provide a convenient, well-considered, and permanent communication record. This chapter examines letters that make routine requests, such as those requesting information, ordering merchandise, and making claims.

Like memos, letters are easiest to write when you have a strategy or plan to follow. The plan for letters, just as for memos, is determined by the content of the message and its anticipated effect on the receiver. Letters delivering bad news require an indirect approach (Chapter 8). Most letters, however, carry good or neutral news. Because such letters will not produce a negative effect on their readers, they follow the deductive or direct strategy. You will recall that the main idea comes first in the direct strategy.

The content of a message and its anticipated effect on the reader determine the strategy you choose.

INFORMATION REQUESTS

The first kind of letter to be described in this chapter is the information request. Although the specific subject of each inquiry may differ, the similarity of purpose in routine requests enables writers to use the following writing plan.

WRITING PLAN FOR AN INFORMATION REQUEST

- *Opening*—asks the most important question first, or expresses a polite command.
- *Body*—explains the request logically and courteously and asks other questions.
- *Closing*—requests a specific action with an end date, if appropriate, and shows appreciation.

OPENING DIRECTLY

The most emphatic positions in a letter are the first and last sentences. Readers tend to look at them first. The writer, then, should capitalize on this tendency by putting the most significant statement first. The first sentence of an information request is usually a question or a polite command. It should not be an explanation or justification, unless resistance to the request is expected. When the information requested is likely to be forthcoming, immediately tell the reader what you want. This saves the reader's time and may ensure that the message is read. A busy executive who skims the mail, quickly reading subject lines and first sentences only, may grasp your request rapidly and act on it. A request that follows a lengthy explanation, on the other hand, may never be found. This inquiry about a computer program gets off to a slow start:

> I read about the A-plusTax program in the June 5 issue of *The Wall Street Journal.* Because I have a business preparing tax returns primarily for construction contractors, I am very interested in this program. Would you please send me information about it.

The same request with the main idea first, expressed as a polite command, is far more effective because the reader knows immediately what is being requested:

> Please send me information about your A-plusTax program that was advertised in *The Wall Street Journal* on June 5.

When a request seeks specific information, the first sentence of the inquiry letter will probably be a question:

> Will the A-plusTax preparation program advertised in *The Wall Street Journal* run on my Astro computer?

If several questions must be asked, use one of two approaches: ask the most important question first, or introduce the questions with a summary statement. The following example poses the most important question first, followed by other questions:

> Will the Dunn & Bradstreet seminar at the Hyatt Regency in San Francisco July 30 offer college credit?
> How much of the total expense for this seminar is tax deductible?
> If I make a reservation and then must cancel, may I receive a refund?

If you want to ask many questions that are equally important, begin with a summarizing statement:

> Will you please answer the following questions about the Dunn & Bradstreet seminar in San Francisco.

Notice that the summarizing statement sounds like a question but has no question mark. That's because it's really a command disguised as a question. Rather than bluntly demanding information *(Answer the following questions)*, we often prefer to soften commands by posing them as questions. Such statements (some authorities call them rhetorical questions) should not be punctuated as questions because they do not require answers.

DETAILS IN THE BODY

The body of a letter that requests information should provide necessary details. For example, if you want information about the type of printer that is appropriate for your personal computer, you must explain what kind of computer you have and what your requirements are. Requesting general information without pinpointing your exact demands may produce a general response that requires a second inquiry.

The body of a request letter may contain an explanation or a list of questions.

If a summarizing statement opens the letter, the body of your request may consist of a list of specific questions. Compare the two following methods of requesting information. The first is generalized and ineffective:

> I am interested in the cash value of my insurance policy. I am also thinking of borrowing against this policy. How do I do this? Too, a friend told me that if I didn't pay the premium, it would be automatically paid from the cash value of the policy. Is this true?

This second request asks the same questions but enumerates them:

Items enumerated in a list are much easier to read than items bunched in a paragraph.

> 1. What is the current cash value of my insurance policy?
> 2. What is the current loan value of this policy?
> 3. What is the procedure for borrowing against this policy?
> 4. If I do not pay the policy premium, is it automatically paid from the policy's cash value?

The enumerated request is more effective for these reasons: (1) each question stands by itself and is numbered, (2) each request is phrased as a question that requires a specific answer, and (3) each item is structured in parallel form so that the reader may anticipate and grasp its meaning quickly.

The quality of the information obtained from a request letter depends on the clarity of the inquiry. If you analyze your needs, organize your ideas, and frame your request logically, you are likely to receive a meaningful answer.

CLOSING WITH AN ACTION REQUEST

Use the final paragraph to ask for specific action, to set an end date if appropriate, and to express appreciation.

The ending of a request letter should tell the reader what you want done and when.

As you learned in working with memos, a request for action is most effective when an end date and reason for that date are supplied. If it's appropriate, use this kind of end dating:

> Please have your accountant fill out the enclosed survey and return it to me by February 15. In this way we may update your file before you come in for your tax preparation.

It's always appropriate to end a request letter with appreciation for the action taken. However, don't fall into a cliché trap, such as *Thanking*

Transparency 6.3

FIGURE 6.1   Letter That Requests Information—Block Style

Letterhead

GEOTECH

770 Stewart Avenue
Garden City, New Jersey 11530

Dateline

August 20, 199x

Inside Address

Ms. Jane Mangrum, Manager
Scottsdale Hilton Hotel
6333 North Scottsdale Road
Scottsdale, AZ 85253-4310

Salutation

Dear Ms. Mangrum:

Body

Can the Scottsdale Hilton provide meeting rooms and accommodations for about 250 Geotech sales representatives from May 25 through May 29?

It is my responsibility to locate a hotel that offers both resort and conference facilities appropriate for the spring sales meeting of my company. Please answer these additional questions regarding the Scottsdale Hilton:

1. Does the hotel have a banquet room that can seat 250?

2. Do you have at least four smaller meeting rooms, each to accommodate a maximum of 75?

3. Do you provide public address systems, audio-visual equipment, and ice water in each meeting room?

4. Do you offer special room rates for conferees?

5. What is the nearest airport, and do you provide transportation to and from it?

I will be most grateful for answers to these questions and for any other information you can provide about your resort facilities. May I please have your response by September 1 so that I can meet with our planning committee September 4.

Sincerely yours,

Complimentary close

Marlene Frederick

Author's name Identification

Marlene Frederick
Corporate Travel Department

Reference initials

MF: gdr

you in advance, I remain . . . or the familiar *Thank you for any information you can send me.* Your appreciation will sound most sincere if you avoid mechanical, tired expressions. Here's a simple but sincere closing to a request for insurance information:

I'll be most appreciative if you will send me this information by July 10, when I will be reevaluating my entire insurance program.

Transparencies 6.4 and 6.5

ILLUSTRATING THE PLAN

The letter shown in Figure 6.1 requests information about conference accommodations and illustrates the writing plan you have learned. The writer has many questions to ask and begins with the most important one. (Appendix A shows letter formats and styles.)

The letter also illustrates block style, the most popular letter style.

THE WALL STREET JOURNAL

BUSINESS MACHINES

"It's a combination word processor and food processor, in case you have to eat your words."

Source: From *The Wall Street Journal.* Reprinted with permission of the Cartoon Features Syndicate, Inc.

ORDER REQUESTS

The second category of letter to be presented in this chapter is the order request. Orders for merchandise are usually made by telephone, by fax, or by filling out an order form. On occasion, though, you may find it necessary to write a letter ordering merchandise. For example, if you had a merchandise catalog but couldn't find its order forms, or if you were responding to an advertisement in a magazine, you'd have to write a letter to place an order.

Order requests use the direct strategy, beginning with the main idea.

To order merchandise, you may occasionally have to write a letter.

WRITING PLAN FOR AN ORDER REQUEST

- *Opening*—authorizes purchase, and suggests method of shipping.
- *Body*—lists items vertically; provides quantity, order number, description, and unit price; and shows total price of order.
- *Closing*—requests shipment by a specific date, tells method of payment, and expresses appreciation.

Transparency 6.6

EFFECTIVE AND INEFFECTIVE ORDER LETTERS

A vague and confusing order letter, such as that shown at the top of Figure 6.2, is frustrating because it forces the reader to request additional information. Jeffrey wrote this letter in response to an advertisement featuring bargain prices for computer games. But the ad provided no toll-free number or order blank.

Transparency 6.7

FIGURE 6.2   Order Letters

Ineffective

Dear Sirs:

I am writing this letter in response to your advertisement in which you show close-out prices on computer games including Dracula in London, Duke of Nukem, Hugo's Horror House, and perhaps Robomaze II, which are now $10.95 and $12.95 each. Because you did not include an order blank or a toll-free number, I'm writing to you. Your prices really blew me away! I hope these items are for sale by mail.

I would be interested in two sets of each—one set for me and the others for gifts. Please send these as soon as possible.

Sincerely,

Outdated salutation.

Unfocused, long opening fails to identify this message as an order.

Confusing instructions. Omits method of payment.

Improved

1302 North Plum Street
Hutchinson, KS 67501
November 23, 199x

Discount Computer Sales
3981 East 53 Street
New York, NY 11205

MAIL ORDER FOR CLOSED-OUT COMPUTER GAMES

Please send by UPS the following items shown on page 38 in the December issue of *Video News:*

2	RVGA4.3	Dracula in London	$10.95	$ 21.90
2	TVGA2.3	Duke of Nukem	12.95	25.90
2	EVGA4.2	Hugo's Horror House	10.95	21.90
2	WVGA3.2	Robomaze II	8.50	17.00
	Total			$ 86.70

Because some of these games will be used as Christmas gifts, I would appreciate receiving them before December 15. Please charge my Master-Card account 4301-3390-8893-3201. Should you need to discuss any of these items, call me at (735) 420-3219.

Jeffrey M. Cicero

JEFFREY M. CICERO

Simplified style includes subject line but omits salutation.

Authorizes order.

Lists items clearly.

Establishes end date and identifies method of payment.

Omits complimentary close.

SOLVING THE SALUTATION DILEMMA

Letters usually begin with a salutation, a greeting to the reader. This greeting is included to personalize a letter. If the name of the individual receiving the letter is known, the salutation is easy: *Dear Kevin* or *Dear Mr. Roberts* or *Dear Ms. Hayden*. But what should be used when no name is known? Grammar hotline services all across the country report that one of their most frequent inquiries concerns proper salutations.

In the past we used *Dear Sirs* or *Gentlemen* to address an organization and *Dear Sir* for anonymous individuals. With increasing numbers of women entering the workplace and a new sensitivity to the power of language, writers are reconsidering these familiar business letter salutations. Although no perfect all-purpose salutation has emerged, the clear trend today is to avoid the totally masculine salutations of the past.

In this state of flux, probably the best alternatives for business communicators are these:

- Use the name of an individual whenever possible in addressing letters.
- When no name is available, use the simplified letter style (Figure 6.4), thus omitting a salutation.
- When no name is available and you cannot use simplified style, rely on *Ladies and Gentlemen*.

For more information about salutations, see Figure A.2 in Appendix A.

His first version is faulty for many reasons. Notice that the opening doesn't establish the message as an order. Moreover, the first sentence is 42 words long, making its meaning difficult to comprehend. Most sentences should average 15 to 20 words. Finally, this letter does not sufficiently describe the items being ordered, and it fails to mention a method of payment. The reader probably wonders if this is really an order.

An improved version of the order letter, also shown in Figure 6.2, begins with specific order language, itemizes and describes the goods clearly, includes shipping and payment information, and closes with an end date.

This letter illustrates simplified letter style, a wise choice when writing to companies or individuals whom you cannot address individually. By using this style, Jeffrey does not have to search for a suitable salutation. Notice that a subject line replaces the salutation, and the complimentary close is omitted. To learn more about the simplified style, see Figure A.4 in Appendix A.

SIMPLE CLAIM REQUESTS

The third category of letters to be presented in this chapter is the simple claim request. A claim is a demand for something that is due or is believed to be due. A simple claim is one to which the writer believes the reader will

The direct strategy is best for simple claims that require no persuasion.

Transparency 6.8

agree—or *should* agree. For example, a purchaser has a legitimate claim for warrantied products that fail, for goods that are promised but not delivered, for damaged products, or for poor service. When the writer feels that the claim is justified and that persuasion is not required, a claim request should follow the direct strategy.

WRITING PLAN FOR A SIMPLE CLAIM

- *Opening*—describes clearly the desired action.
- *Body*—explains the nature of the claim, tells why the claim is justified, and provides details regarding the action requested.
- *Closing*—ends pleasantly with a goodwill statement, and includes end dating if appropriate.

OPENING WITH ACTION

Start with a clear statement of the action you want taken.

In a simple claim request, tell the reader immediately what action you would like taken. Such directness may appear to be blunt, but actually it's businesslike and efficient. Don't begin a claim letter with an attempt to establish goodwill or an explanation:

> We've used Pentack tools for years and have always appreciated the quality product that you produce and the prompt service that we have received when we placed our orders.

Save the explanation for the body and the goodwill for the closing. Tell the reader what you want in the opening sentence:

> Please send us two ½-inch socket sets to replace the two ⅜-inch sets sent with our order shipped October 23.

With this direct opening, the reader knows what you want and can read the remainder of the letter in the proper context.

JUSTIFYING IN THE BODY

Explain the reasons that justify your claim without becoming angry or emotional.

Here's where you explain why you feel your claim is justified. Provide the necessary details so that the problem can be rectified without misunderstanding. Avoid the tendency to fix blame. Instead of saying *You failed to send the items we ordered*, describe the situation objectively. Omit negative or angry words that offend the reader and may prevent compliance with your claim.

An objective explanation of the reason for replacing merchandise could read as follows:

> On October 10 we placed a telephone order requesting, among other things, two ½-inch socket sets. However, when the order arrived yesterday, we noted that two ⅜-inch socket sets had been sent. Because we cannot use that size, we are returning the ⅜-inch sets by UPS.

This unemotional presentation of the facts is more effective in achieving the writer's goal than an angry complaint.

After you have presented the circumstances of your claim objectively, you may wish to suggest alternatives to solving the problem; for example, *If it is impossible to send ½-inch socket sets, please credit our account.* When goods are being returned, you should inquire about the proper procedure. Some companies allow returns only with prior authorization.

CLOSING PLEASANTLY

End the claim letter pleasantly with an effort toward maintaining goodwill. If appropriate, include a date by which you want the claim satisfied.

> We realize that mistakes in ordering and shipping sometimes occur. Because we've been impressed by your prompt delivery in the past, we hope that you will be able to send the ½-inch socket sets to us by November 1.

EFFECTIVE AND INEFFECTIVE CLAIM LETTERS

Transparencies 6.9 and 6.10

The claim letter shown in Figure 6.3 is unlikely to achieve its goal. In demanding that a tire warranty be honored, the writer failed to provide sufficient information. The account of what happened to the tire is incoherent, and the reader will be uncertain as to what action the writer wants. In addition, the tone of the letter is angry and harsh.

The improved version of the irritating letter, shown in Figure 6.4, takes a different tone and approach. In the first sentence this improved letter forthrightly asks for a refund under the tire warranty. The letter includes an unemotional, logical explanation of the problem. Its rational tone and sensible expression are more appealing to the reader, who needs to understand the problem before the organization can resolve it.

The improved version illustrates modified block style and mixed punctuation. Notice that the date is centered (although it may also be placed to end at the right margin), and the closing lines start at the center of the page. Paragraphs may be blocked, as shown here, or indented five spaces. This letter also shows the company name in the closing lines. If included, it should appear in all-capital letters two lines below the complimentary close. Leave enough space after it for the writer to sign the letter.

The claim letter shown in Figure 6.5 seeks permission to return a microcomputer to the manufacturer for repair. Normally, repairs are made locally, but this computer defies diagnosis. The letter writer does not angrily blame the local dealer for ineptness nor criticize the manufacturer for producing a faulty product. Instead, the letter cleverly invites the man-

FIGURE 6.3   Angry, Ineffective Claim Letter

Dear Goodday Tires:

What good is a warranty if it's not honored? I don't agree with your dealer that the damage to my tire was caused by "road hazards." This tire was defective, and I am entitled to a refund.

Begins with emotional, illogical, unclear demand.

My company purchased a GasSaver tire September 5, and it had been driven only 14,000 miles when a big bubble developed in its side. The gas station attendant said that its tread had separated from its body. But the dealer where my company bought it (Harbor Tire Company) refused to give us a refund. The dealer said that the damage was caused by "road hazards." They also said that they never make refunds, only replacements.

Provides inadequate explanation of what happened.

My company has always purchased GasSaver tires, but you can be sure that this is our last. Unless we get the refund to which we are rightfully entitled, I intend to spread the word about how we were treated.

Ends with threat instead of an attempt to establish goodwill.

Yours truly,

FIGURE 6.4   **Simple Claim Letter—Modified Block Style**

Smith, Klein Industries

255 Cherry Street
Milford, Connecticut 06460-6301

March 4, 199x

Ms. Michelle N. Jameson
Director, Customer Service
Goodday Tire Manufacturers
8401 Broad Street
Newark, NJ 07101-5210

Dear Ms. Jameson:

SUBJECT: WARRANTY REFUND ON GASSAVER TIRE

Opens with direct request

Please honor the warranty and issue a refund for one GasSaver radial tire that was purchased for my company car at Alliance Tire Center on September 5.

Provides coherent, unemotional explanation.

This whitewall tire cost $139.13 and carried a warranty for 42,000 miles. It had only 14,000 miles of wear when trouble developed. On a business trip to Albany recently, I noticed that the tire made a strange sound. When I stopped the car and inspected the tire, it had an ugly bulge protruding from its rim. A service station attendant said that the tread had separated from the tire body. I was forced to purchase a replacement tire at considerably more than the price we paid for the GasSaver tire.

When I returned the GasSaver tire to Alliance, it would not honor the warranty. Alliance said the tire was damaged by "road hazards" and that refunds could not be made.

Ends courteously with specific request for action.

My company generally purchases GasSaver tires, and we have been pleased with their quality and durability. Enclosed are copies of the sales invoice and the tire warranty for the tire in question. Also enclosed is a receipt showing that the defective tire was returned to Alliance Tire Company.

I am confident that you will honor my request for a refund of the purchase price of $139.13 prorated for 14,000 miles of wear.

Sincerely yours,

SMITH, KLEIN INDUSTRIES

Includes optional company name in capital letters above signature.

Jeffrey M. Dailey
Vice President

JMD:prw
Enclosures

---

ufacturer to help solve a "mystery." Notice that the letter opens by asking for *instructions on how* to return the computer rather than for *permission* to return the computer. The request for shipping instructions suggests the writer's confidence that the manufacturer will want to do the right thing and repair the malfunctioning computer.

This personal letter is shown with the return address typed above the date. Use this style when typing on paper without a printed letterhead.

In summary, the three types of letters presented in this chapter (information requests, order letters, and claim letters) all use the direct strategy. They open directly with the main idea first followed by details and explanations. In the next chapter you will learn how to use the direct strategy in responding to these same kinds of letters.

FIGURE 6.5   Effective Claim Letter—Modified Block Style

23956 Hamlin Street
Canoga Park, CA 91307
August 14, 199x

CompuCap, Inc.
2308 Borregas Avenue
Sunnyvale, CA 94088-3565

Ladies and Gentlemen:

SUBJECT: RETURN OF MALFUNCTIONING COMPUCAP 2-X.

Please tell me how I may return my malfunctioning CompuCap 2-X microcomputer to you for repair.

I am sure you can solve a problem that puzzles my local dealer. After about
45 minutes of normal activity, the screen on my 2-X computer suddenly fills
with a jumble of meaningless letters, numbers, and symbols. Computers For
You, the dealer from whom I purchased my 2-X, seems to be unable to
locate or correct the malfunction.

Although I am expected to have my computer serviced locally, my dealer
has been unable to repair it. I am confident that you can solve the mystery
and that you will repair my 2-X quickly.

Sincerely yours,

Carole Eustice

(Mrs.) Carole Eustice

*Return address
appears above date.*

*Opens confidently,
requesting instruc-
tions for return of
computer.*

*Describes malfunc-
tion coherently.*

*Closes pleasantly
with assurance that
manufacturer will
want to do the right
thing.*

APPLICATION AND PRACTICE—6

Discussion

1. How are letters like memos? How are they different?
2. Why should routine letters, such as inquiries and orders, follow the direct strategy?
3. Which is more effective in claim letters—anger or objectivity? Defend your position.
4. Why should the writer of a claim letter offer alternatives for solving the problem?
5. The quality of the information obtained from a request depends on the clarity of the inquiry. Discuss.

Short Answers

6. List three reasons for exchanging business information in letter form rather than in oral form.
   1. Letters are convenient.
   2. They provide a permanent record.
   3. They allow the writer to consider his or her communication clearly.

7. When a request seeks specific information, the first sentence of the inquiry letter will probably be what?
   A question

8. Consider the following situations. Which strategy would be more effective? Write *Direct* or *Indirect* to indicate your choice.

   Direct
   a. You need information about skiing equipment advertised in a magazine.

   Indirect
   b. You want to convince your boss to change your assigned work schedule.

   Direct
   c. You want a replacement for a defective cassette tape recorder, still under warranty, that you ordered by mail.

   Direct
   d. You want to find out how much it costs to rent a houseboat in the Mississippi Delta region for you and your family.

   Indirect
   e. As credit manager of a department store, you must deny a customer credit.

   Direct
   f. You wish to order merchandise from a catalog.

9. What are the two most emphatic positions in a letter?
   The first and last sentences

10. What is the most popular letter style?
    Block style

11. List two ways that you could begin an inquiry letter that asks many questions.
    1. Ask the most important question first.
    2. Introduce the questions with a summary statement.

12. What is an enumerated request?
    Numbered items

13. What three elements are appropriate in the closing of a request for information?
    1. A request for specific action
    2. An end date
    3. An expression of appreciation

14. The first sentence of an order letter should include what information?
    Purchase authorization and suggested shipping method

15. The closing of an order letter should include what information?
    Method of payment, desired shipment date, and expression of appreciation

⊃ *Instructor: Writing Improvement Exercises are available on diskette.*

Writing Improvement Exercises

Routine Request Openers. Revise the following openers from routine request letters so that they are more direct.

16. I am interested in your rental rates for a three-bedroom cabin on Devil's Lake in August.
    What is the rental rate for a three-bedroom cabin on Devil's Lake in August?

17. Recently I purchased a Country Manor linen tablecloth at Robinson's. I haven't been pleased with it, and I am interested in a replacement.
    Please replace the Country Manor linen tablecloth I purchased recently at Robinson's.

18. The Hi-Sound stereo set that I ordered from you has arrived, and it seems to have a problem in the amplifier. I'm wondering if you can tell me where I may take it for repair.
    Where may I take my Hi-Sound stereo set for repair of its amplifier?

19. Your spring sale catalog shows a number of items in which I am interested. I would like the following items.
    Please send the following items from your spring sale catalog to me by UPS.

Order Request Letter.   Analyze the following poorly written order letter and respond to the questions following it.

Ineffective Writing

> Ladies and Gentlemen:
>
> We are interested in a number of items for our office overhead projectors used by our sales staff. Some of these items were shown in your fall catalog. The primary item we need is four Overhead Projection Lamps (Order No. 108-559) priced at $25.99 each. I'm also interested in 3M Scotch Laser Printer Film (Order No. 172-822) at $20.79 a pack. We need five packs. Because we have many permanent transparencies, we want to try your frames that mount transparencies. I believe the 3M mounting frames (Order No. 179-392) are listed at $21.99 for a pack of 50. Send just one pack for us to try. While I'm at it, I might as well order six sets of Stabilo Marker Sets (Order No. 329-010), listed at $4.16 each. Please be sure that these are the water-soluble kind. I'll pay for this with MasterCard, and I need everything by September 1.
>
>   Sincerely,

20. What does the opening lack?
    Clear language identifying the letter as an order

21. Write an appropriate opening for this order letter.
    Please send me by UPS the following items from your fall catalog.

22. How would you group the order information so that it is orderly and logical? Name five headings you could use.
    1. *Quantity*
    2. *Order number*
    3. *Description*
    4. *Unit price*
    5. *Total price*

23. Write an appropriate closing for this order request.
    You may charge these items to my MasterCard account, No 4004 3991 5679. I am hoping to receive this order by September 1.

Letter Format.   Read about letter formats and parts in Appendix A. Then answer the following questions.

24. If you are typing a letter for yourself on plain paper, what items appear above the date?
    1. *Your street address*
    2. *Your city, state, and zip code*

25. How is simplified letter style different from block style, and why do some writers prefer simplified style?
    Simplified style omits the salutation and complimentary close. The subject line and writer's name are typed in all caps. Writers like this style because it eliminates the problem of choosing an appropriate salutation.

26. In what two places could an attention line be typed?
    Two lines below the inside address or immediately below the organization name within the address block

27. If you write a letter to Data General Corp., what salutation would be appropriate?
    Although it's always best to address letters to specific individuals, if you must write to a company in general, you have two options. Use Ladies and Gentlemen *as the salutation, or use the simplified letter style that omits a salutation.*

⊃ *Instructor: See pp. 41–43 in the Instructor's Manual for solutions to 6-1, 6-2, and 6-3.*

28. When letters are addressed to individuals, should their names always contain a courtesy title, such as *Mr., Ms., Miss,* or *Mrs.*?
    Yes

CASE 6-1

INFORMATION REQUEST

Assume that you are Mrs. Stephanie Jones. Based on an ad that you saw in a magazine, you wish to write to Mary Powell, Manager, Garden Court Rentals, Carmel-by-the-Sea, CA 93921. You want information about renting a two-bedroom condominium with an ocean view. You'd like to be there from July 17 through July 25, which is the time of the Carmel Bach Festival. You'll need accommodations for three (you, your husband, and your daughter). You're interested in having kitchen utensils, dishes, and bedding. Your husband is interested in nearby golf courses, and your daughter wants to know how close the beach is. You'll need to know what time you can arrive July 17 and how much the rental fee is. You'd like this information by April 1 so that you can complete your summer plans.

Before writing the letter, answer the following questions:

1. What should you include in the opening of an information request?
   Ask the most important question first or express a polite command.

2. What should the body of your letter contain?
   Other questions and logical explanations

3. How should you close the letter?
   Request specific action by a specific date and show appreciation.

4. What is the most important question Mrs. Jones has to ask?
   Is a condominium with an ocean view available for the week of July 17–25?

5. How can the other questions be handled effectively?
   Arrange them vertically in a list and write them in balanced constructions.

On a separate sheet, write the letter. Use modified block style, and write on plain paper. Be sure to include your return address above the date. (See Appendix A.)

CASE 6-2 ....

CLAIM REQUEST

Play the role of Joseph Albanese. On June 24 your company had the basement walls of its office building sealed with Modac II, an acrylic coating. This sealant was applied to reduce moisture in the basement so that you could store company files in this area. The contractor, Peter Muscarelli, promised that this product would effectively seal the walls and prevent moisture penetration, as well as prevent peeling, chalking, and color fading for many years. He said that if you had any trouble, he might have to give it a second coat. After the first rain in September, the walls of the basement leaked, making it necessary for you to remove the files stored there. Write a claim letter to Mr. Muscarelli asking that he correct the situation. Let him know that you want the basement effectively sealed by October 30 because heavy seasonal rains usually begin in November.

To help you organize your letter according to the principles you studied in this chapter, read the following suggestions and circle the most appropriate responses. Be prepared to discuss each of the possible responses that follow.

1. To open this letter directly, you might
   a. Remind Mr. Muscarelli that he recommended Modac II and that it just wasn't doing the job.
   b. Describe your disappointment in the ineffectiveness of Modac II and angrily demand that Mr. Muscarelli repeat this job and do it right this time.
   c. Ask Mr. Muscarelli to apply a second coat of Modac II to the basement walls of your company to prevent moisture penetration.
   d. Review chronologically the beginning of this project and your initial dealings with Mr. Muscarelli.
2. The body of this letter would probably
   a. Review the sealing process and your understanding of how you expected Modac II to make your walls moisture-proof.
   b. Threaten to sue if Mr. Muscarelli doesn't rectify this matter immediately.
   c. Explain that the June 24 coat was ineffective and that he promised to apply a second coat if necessary.
   d. Blame Mr. Muscarelli for doing a poor job and specify clearly what he must do to satisfy your claim.

⊃ Instructor: Case 6-2 is available on diskette.

Transparency Master 6.4

3. The closing of this letter should
   (a.) Explain when and why you want the second coat applied, and express appreciation for Mr. Muscarelli's efforts to keep your basement dry.
   b. Summarize all your dealings with Mr. Muscarelli and reiterate your dissatisfaction with Modac II and with his workmanship as well.
   c. Tell Mr. Muscarelli that you need this storage space badly and that you'd like to use it as soon as possible.
   d. Thank Mr. Muscarelli for his past work and express confidence that he will do the right thing for your company.

If your instructor directs, write the entire letter on a separate sheet to Mr. Peter Muscarelli, 5807 Redwood Highway, Grants Pass, OR 97526–5807. Add any information that you feel is necessary. Assume that you are writing this letter on letterhead stationery. Use block style. (See Appendix A.)

C A S E 6 - 3

Transparency Master 6.5

ORDER REQUEST

Analyze the following ineffective request for merchandise, and list its faults. Outline a writing plan for an order request. Then, on a separate sheet, rewrite this request. Use modified block style, and place your return address above the date. Send the letter to Cameratone, Inc., 140 Northern Boulevard, Flushing, NY 11354–1400. Add any necessary information.

Ineffective Writing

Dear Sir:

I saw a number of items in your summer/fall catalog that would fit my Lentax ME camera. I am particularly interested in your Super Zoom 55-200mm lens. Its number is SF39971, and it costs $139.95. To go with this lens I will need a polarizing filter. Its number is SF29032 and costs $22.95 and should fit a 52mm lens. Also include a 05CC magenta filter for a 52mm lens. That number is SF29036 and it costs $9.95. Please send also a Hikemaster camera case for $24.95. Its number is SF28355.

I am interested in having these items charged to my credit card. I'd sure like to get them quickly because my vacation starts soon.

Sincerely,

1. List at least five faults in this letter.
   1. *Fails to authorize purchase in first sentence*
   2. *Does not list items vertically*
   3. *Omits total amount of order*
   4. *Fails to provide credit card number*
   5. *Lacks end date*
   6. *Expresses appreciation perfunctorily*

2. Outline a writing plan for an order.

Opening: *Authorize purchase of items and suggest method of shipping.*

Body: *List items vertically; provide quantity, order number, description, and unit prices; and show total price of order.*

Closing: *Request shipment by specific date, tell method of payment, and express appreciation.*

CASE 6-4

PERSONAL ORDER

Write a letter ordering items advertised in a magazine, newspaper, or catalog. Assume that no order form is available. Attach the advertisement to your letter. Be sure to use an appropriate letter style for a personal business letter.

CASE 6-5

PERSONAL ROUTINE CLAIM

Write a routine claim letter for a product or service you have purchased. Assume that the product or service required a claim to the dealer or manufacturer because the product was defective or the service was not what you expected. Use a situation in which you can reasonably expect the manufacturer to honor your claim.

Additional Problems

1. Assume that you are Marc Vannault, manager of a health spa and also an ardent backpacker. You are organizing a group of hikers for a wilderness trip to Canada. One item that must be provided is freeze-dried food for the three-week trip. You are unhappy with the taste and quality of backpacking food products currently available. You expect to have a group of hikers who are older, affluent, and natural-food enthusiasts. Some are concerned about products containing preservatives, sugar, and additives. Others are on diets restricting cholesterol, fat, and salt. You heard that Oregon High, Box 51, McMinnville, OR 97128, offers a new line of freeze-dried products. You want to know what they offer and if they have sufficient variety to serve all the needs of your group. You need to know where their products can be purchased and what the cost range is. You'd also like to try a few of their items before placing a large order. You are interested in how they produce the food products and what kinds of ingredients they use. If you have any items left over, you wonder how long they can be kept and still be usable. Write an inquiry letter to Oregon High.

2. Play the role of Edith Sterling, assistant vice president, Bank of Virginia. You have been given the responsibility of developing an

employee suggestion program for the bank, which employs over 15,000 workers in the state. You have done some research and have collected helpful ideas, but now you'd like to gather reactions from an organization with first-hand experience. A friend suggested that you write Clifford Bianchi, director, Employee Development Division, Pratt and Whitney, P.O. Box 25438, Minneapolis, MN 55424. Pratt and Whitney implemented a suggestion program three years ago, and Mr. Bianchi has indicated that he would be happy to share details of how successful the Pratt and Whitney employee suggestion program has been. You are interested in the "nuts and bolts" of the program. You need to know how employees are encouraged to participate, how they submit their suggestions, who evaluates them, and what kinds of awards are made. Should suggestions go to supervisors or local administrators first, or should they go directly to an evaluation committee? Are there potential legal problems? Also, should you have minimum and maximum awards? Must you respond to every suggestion? What if an employee protests the decisions of the evaluation committee? You have many questions, but you realize that you can't burden Mr. Bianchi with all of them. However, he was reported to be quite enthusiastic about employee suggestion programs. Write an inquiry letter to him.

3. You are Greg Fontecilla, manager, Datatronics, Inc. You want to order some items from an office supply catalog, but your catalog is one year old and you have lost the order form. You're in a hurry. Rather than write for a new catalog, you decide to take a chance and order items from the old catalog (Fall 1994), realizing that prices may be somewhat different. You want three Panasonic electric pencil sharpeners, Item 22-A, at $19.95 each. You want one steel desktop organizer, 60 inches long, Item No. 23-K. Its price is $117.50. Order two Roll-a-Flex files for 2- by 4-inch cards at $14.50 each. This is Item 23-G. The next item is No. 29-H, file folders, box of 100, letter size, at $5.29. You need ten boxes. You would like to be invoiced for this purchase, and you prefer UPS delivery. Even though the prices may be somewhat higher, you decide to list the prices shown in your catalog so that you have an idea of what the total order will cost. Write a letter to Blackfield's Discount Office Furniture, 2890 Post Road, Warwick, RI 02886.

4. Play the part of Susan Lee, who lives at 845 Wainee Street, Lahaina, Maui, HI 96761. When you were in California recently, you saw an unusual toy (use your imagination to describe it) at Toys-R-Us in San Dimas. Now that you're back on Maui, you'd like to have that toy as a present for your nephew, but you have not been able to locate it. Write to Toys-R-Us and describe the toy. To save time, you want to order it and have it charged to your Visa credit card (supply the number and expiration date). You expect the toy to cost about $30, but you would go as high as $40 to purchase it. You would like to receive the toy within three weeks, so they should ship it by whatever method will ensure a timely delivery. If they can't ship it immediately, you would appreciate hearing from them so that you can purchase a present locally. Write to Toys-R-Us, 194 West Terrace Avenue, San Dimas, CA 91773, ordering the toy.

5. Assume that you are Sandra Fenwick, president of Fenwick Consulting Services. Since your consulting firm was doing very well, you decided to splurge and purchase a fine executive desk for your own

office. You ordered an expensive desk described as "North American white oak embellished with hand-inlaid walnut cross-banding." Although you would not ordinarily purchase large, expensive items by mail, you were impressed by the description of this desk and by the money-back guarantee promised in the catalog. When the desk arrived, you knew that you had made a mistake. The wood finish was rough, the grain looked splotchy, and many of the drawers would not pull out easily. The advertisement had promised "full suspension, silent ball-bearing drawer slides." You are disappointed with the desk and decide to send it back, taking advantage of the money-back guarantee. You want your money refunded. You're not sure whether they will refund the freight charges, but it's worth a try. Supply any details needed. Write a letter to Idaho Wood Products, P.O. Box 488, Sandpoint, ID 83864.

6. Assume that you are Paul Friedman, purchase manager, Datatronics, Inc., 2569 Missouri Street, Mesa, AZ 85016. You purchased for your company two Ever-Cool window air conditioners, Model D-2, Serial Nos. 38920 and 38921. One of the units, Serial No. 38920, is not working properly. It worked when it first arrived, but after two weeks it is malfunctioning. The compressor comes on and off from time to time, but the room does not cool down. Perhaps the thermostat is the problem. The control knob is also defective. You would not normally mention such a small matter, but since the entire unit needs repair, it seems worth mentioning the control knob, too. No service representative is convenient to you in Mesa. You have a six-month warranty. How can this unit be repaired? It's very warm in Mesa at this time of the year, and employees are complaining about the lack of air conditioning. Write a claim letter and send a copy of your sales invoice and warranty to Ever-Cool Manufacturing Company, 951 Lawrence Drive, Newbury Park, CA 91320.

GRAMMAR/MECHANICS CHECKUP—6

COMMAS 1

Review the Grammar/Mechanics Handbook Sections 2.01–2.04. Then study each of the following statements and insert necessary commas. In the space provided write the number of commas that you add; write *0* if no commas are needed. Also record the number of the G/M principle illustrated. When you finish, compare your responses with those shown below. If your answers differ, study carefully the principles shown in parentheses.

Example: In this class students learn to write business letters, memos, and reports clearly and concisely.   *2*   *(2.01)*

1. We do not, as a rule, allow employees to take time off for dental appointments.   *2*   *(2.03)*
2. You may be sure, Mrs. Schwartz, that your car will be ready by 4 p.m.   *2*   *(2.02)*
3. Anyone who is reliable, conscientious, and honest should be very successful.   *2*   *(2.01)*
4. A conference on sales motivation is scheduled for May 5 at the Anaheim Marriott Hotel beginning at 2 p.m.   *0*
5. As a matter of fact, I just called your office this morning.   *1*   *(2.03)*
6. We are relocating our distribution center from Memphis, Tennessee, to Des Moines, Iowa.   *3*   *(2.04c)*

1   *(2.03)*   7. In the meantime, please continue to address your orders to your regional office.

2   *(2.04a)*   8. The last meeting recorded in the minutes is shown on February 4, 1990, in Chicago.

2   *(2.01)*   9. Mr. Silver, Mrs. Adams, and Ms. Horne have been selected as our representatives.

4   *(2.04b)* 10. The package mailed to Ms. Leslie Holmes, 3430 Larkspur Lane, San Diego, CA 92110, arrived three weeks after it was mailed.

2   *(2.03)*   11. The manager feels, needless to say, that the support of all employees is critical.

2   *(2.01)*   12. Eric was assigned three jobs: checking supplies, replacing inventories, and distributing delivered goods.

1   *(2.02)*   13. We will work diligently to retain your business, Mr. Lopez.

2   *(2.03)*   14. The vice president feels, however, that all sales representatives need training.

0   15. The name selected for a product should be right for that product and should emphasize its major attributes.

---

1. (2) not, rule, *(2.03)*   3. (2) reliable, conscientious, *(2.01)*   5. (1) fact, *(2.03)*   7. (1) meantime, *(2.03)*   9. (2) Silver, Adams, *(2.01)*   11. (2) feels, say, *(2.03)*   13. (1) business, *(2.02)*   15. (0)

GRAMMAR/MECHANICS CHALLENGE—6

Transparency 6.11

DOCUMENT FOR REVISION

The following letter has faults in grammar, punctuation, spelling, number form, and wordiness. Use standard proofreading marks (see Appendix B) to correct the errors. When you finish, your instructor can show you the revised version of this letter.

Ineffective Writing

Poor Letter

March 3, 199x

FAX TRANSMISSION

Ms. Susan Petty, Manager

Customer Service Department

Steel Cabinets, Inc.

Flint, MI 48433

Dear Ms. Petty:

Please rush a shipment of twenty-three No. 36-440 verticle file cabinets to us, to replace those

damaged in transit recently.

We appreciate you filling our order for 100 of these file cabinets as shown on the accompanying Invoice. Twenty-three of them however were damaged in transit and cannot be sold in there present condition. Because of the fact that 2 transit companies handled the shipment of the file cabinets we cannot determine whom is responsable for the damage.

These verticle files were featured in our newspaper add and we expect to sell a good many in our presale which is scheduled to begin 3/15. Therefore we would appreciate you rushing these cabinets by Red Dog Freight before 3/12. Moreover please let us know what should be done with the damaged cabinets.

Sincerely,

. . . .

7

LETTERS THAT RESPOND

POSITIVELY

⊃ *Instructor:*
*Please see p. 45 for
author's suggested
lesson plan for
Chapter 7.*

IN THIS CHAPTER YOU WILL LEARN TO DO THE FOLLOWING:

- Apply the direct strategy in letters that respond positively.
- Write clear and efficient letters and memos that deliver information.
- Promote goodwill in acknowledging order requests.
- Grant claims efficiently and effectively.

*Deliver good news
early in a response
letter.*

L etters that respond positively bring good news to the reader. They answer requests for information and action, they acknowledge orders, and they agree to claims. These letters deliver positive news that the reader expects and wants. Therefore, they follow the direct strategy with the main idea first. In this chapter you will practice techniques for crafting effective positive letters of response.

RESPONDING TO INFORMATION REQUESTS

Transparency 7.1

Applying the direct strategy to replies for information results in the following writing plan:

WRITING PLAN FOR AN INFORMATION RESPONSE

- *Subject line*—identifies previous correspondence
- *Opening*—delivers the most important information first
- *Body*—arranges information in a logical sequence, explains and clarifies, provides additional information, and builds goodwill
- *Closing*—ends pleasantly

SUBJECT LINE EFFICIENCY

*Use the subject line
to refer to previous
correspondence.*

Although it's not mandatory, a subject line is useful in responding to requests. It allows the writer to identify quickly and efficiently the previous correspondence, and it jogs the reader's memory regarding the request. By putting identifying information in a subject line, the writer reserves the first sentence (one of the most important spots in a letter) for the main idea. Here's an effective subject line that responds to a request for information:

> SUBJECT: YOUR NOVEMBER 3 LETTER ABOUT INTERNSHIPS AT LIZ CLAIBORNE, INC.

OPENING STRENGTH

Transparency 7.2

As the most emphatic position in the letter, the first sentence should carry the most important information. A response to a student's inquiry about cooperative education and internships at a large garment manufacturer should reveal the most important information immediately:

> Internships are available at Liz Claiborne, Inc., for business administration and other majors who are enrolled for course credits in school work programs.

Compare the preceding direct opening with the following indirect, wordy, and ineffective opening:

> We have received your letter of November 3 requesting information regarding our college cooperative education/internship program here at Liz Claiborne, Inc., and I am happy to respond to your inquiry.

If you are answering a number of questions, use one of two approaches. The most direct approach is to answer the most important question in the first sentence. Other answers may be supplied in the body of the letter. For example, the following response to a request from an airline customer with many questions begins directly:

> On flights within the U.S. and between the U.S. and Canada, passengers are entitled to a total of three pieces of baggage, whether all are checked or one or two are carried on board.

A less direct approach starts with a summary statement that shows the reader you are complying with the request:

> Here is the information you requested about passenger baggage aboard Atlantic Airlines.

This opening is followed by answers to the questions contained in the body of the letter.

Either of these two approaches is superior to the familiar openings *Thank you for your letter of . . .* or *I have received your letter asking for . . .* These openings are indirect, overworked, and obvious. Stating that you received the customer's letter is obviously unnecessary, since you are answering it.

LOGIC IN THE BODY

Give explanations and additional information in the body of a letter that responds to an information request. If you are answering a number of questions or providing considerable data, arrange your information logically. It may be possible to enumerate information, as shown in this response to the inquiry about customer baggage. Notice that the writer offers a brief explanation of each restriction.

1. The largest and heaviest piece of baggage can weigh up to 70 pounds. This restriction is based on the total capacity of our aircraft.

2. The length plus width plus height of the largest bag can total no more than 62 inches. These dimensions are based on what our people can physically handle in the confined work space of an aircraft belly.

3. Certain sporting equipment is carried free, when that equipment is counted as the largest bag. This category includes skis, fishing equipment, golf clubs, boogie boards, and other sporting items.

If your response requires more information, devote an entire paragraph to each.

In answering request letters from customers, you have an opportunity to build goodwill toward yourself and your organization by offering additional advice or data. Don't confine your response to the questions presented. If you recognize that other facts would be helpful, present them. For example, in the inquiry about Liz Claiborne internships, the writer could describe the full-time internship program, which releases a student from classroom study for a semester (3–6 months), as well as the part-time program (usually 20 hours per week). The writer also could offer helpful information about eligibility, application, deadlines, and rewards— information about which the student writer may not have known to inquire.

TAILOR-MADE CLOSING

To avoid abruptness, include a pleasant closing remark that shows your willingness to help the reader. Tailor your remarks to fit this letter and this reader. Since everyone appreciates being recognized as an individual, avoid form-letter closings such as *If we may be of any further assistance, do not hesitate to call upon us.* Improved closings are personalized:

> We appreciate your interest, Ms. Sullivan, in Liz Claiborne's cooperative education/internship programs. The enclosed brochure describes the many departments within our organization that sponsor internships. Should you be interested in joining us, we would welcome your application.

"I liked it better when it listed all of our names!"

Source: From *The Wall Street Journal.* Reprinted with permission of the Cartoon Features Syndicate, Inc.

ILLUSTRATIONS OF INFORMATION RESPONSES

The letter in Figure 7.1 responds to an inquiry from a reporter for information about a credit-reporting agency. Most consumers are surprised to learn that their credit records may be examined before they are hired for certain jobs. This letter answers a number of frequently asked questions, including one about the role of credit-reporting agencies in employment decisions.

Transparency 7.3

In responding to the reporter's inquiry, the writer uses a personalized salutation *(Dear Ms. Roper)* and a time-saving subject line. Although the first sentence does not begin directly with an answer to a specific question, it does offer a summary statement introducing the responses. The body of the letter enumerates logically and in parallel form the information requested. Because the letter writer understands the reporter's need for complete explanations, she provides more than basic facts. Notice that the writer even answers a question the reporter did not ask (how consumers may receive free credit reports). This letter builds goodwill by anticipating the needs of the inquirer, providing complete answers, and offering additional information. The cordial but concise closing avoids the usual clichés.

In contrast to this well-written letter, the information response in Figure 7.2 suffers from a number of faults.

The first sentence of this ineffective letter uses dated language *(pursuant to)*, a wordy expression *(this is to advise you about)*, and needless repetition *[two (2)]*. In addition, the first sentence does not deliver the information requested. The second paragraph opens with *the writer*, a formal expression, instead of the more conversational *I*. Moreover, the tone of the body of the letter is rather harsh and negative, and the closing sounds insincere.

The information conveyed in the preceding message could be more effectively delivered by using the direct strategy and by improving the tone of the letter. Notice how the letter shown in Figure 7.3 achieves its objective.

RESPONDING TO ORDER REQUESTS

Many companies acknowledge orders by sending a printed postcard that merely informs the customer that the order has been received. Other companies take advantage of this opportunity to build goodwill and to promote new products and services. A personalized letter responding to an order is good business, particularly for new accounts, large accounts, and customers who haven't placed orders recently. An individualized letter is also necessary if the order involves irregularities, such as delivery delays, back-ordered items, or missing items.

Letters that follow up orders create excellent opportunities to improve the company image and to sell products.

Letters that respond to orders should deliver the news immediately; therefore, the direct strategy is most effective. Here's a writing plan that will achieve the results you want in acknowledging orders.

Transparency 7.4

WRITING PLAN FOR AN ORDER RESPONSE

- *Opening*—tells when and how shipment will be sent.
- *Body*—explains details of shipment, discusses any irregularities in the order, includes resale information, and promotes other products and services if appropriate.
- *Closing*—builds goodwill and uses friendly, personalized closing.

FIGURE 7.1 **Information Response Letter—Block Style**

TRG Credit Service
301 N. International Parkway
Richardson, TX 75081

February 6, 199x

Ms. Hillary A. Roper
The Houston Post
4980 Washington Avenue
Houston, TX 77048

Dear Ms. Roper:

SUBJECT: YOUR FEBRUARY 1 LETTER ABOUT TRG SERVICES

I'm pleased to answer your questions about our credit-reporting agency in preparation for the newspaper article you are writing for *The Houston Post.* Naturally, we are eager to publish accurate information about our services.

1. TRG is a credit-reporting agency that stores information about the credit history of consumers. Such agencies are necessary to help credit grantors evaluate the credit history of consumers in a timely manner so that creditworthy people can have ready access to credit. Without credit-reporting agencies, banks and other credit grantors would have to check an individual's payment history with each individual creditor, significantly delaying the decision process.

2. We do not collect or maintain information about race, religion, gender, salary, personal assets, checking or savings accounts, medical history, personal background, lifestyle, or criminal record.

3. The Fair Credit Reporting Act allows employers to access an applicant's credit report for employment purposes. We do not, however, make decisions about hiring applicants or denying employment. Individuals must check with employers to determine why they were denied employment.

4. A "risk score" is a numerical summary of the information in a consumer's file. It provides a credit grantor a nonjudgmental, empirically derived, and statistically correct tool to be used as part of the credit-evaluation process.

Although you didn't ask, most individuals want to know how they may receive copies of their credit reports. To receive a free credit report, an individual should send us her or his full name, spouse's name (if married), current home address, previous addresses for the past five years, Social Security number, and year of birth.

You'll find additional information in the enclosed booklet, "Understanding TRG's Credit-Reporting Service." To speak with me personally, just call (414) 598-2300. We look forward to seeing your article in print.

Sincerely,

Debbie Wills-Garcia

Debbie Wills-Garcia
Consumer Services Division

DWG:rio
Enclosure

Identifies previous correspondence.

Answers each inquiry fully and logically in list form.

Builds goodwill by providing extra information.

Ends cordially without clichés.

FIGURE 7.2 **Poor Information Response Letter**

Dear Mr. Meyers:

Pursuant to our telephone conversation of yesterday morning, this is to advise you about the two (2) NEC computer/monitors in which you are interested.

Ineffective Writing

Opens indirectly and uses legalese.

The writer has been in contact with Mike Waldon, our office manager, and he has no record of these monitors. These monitors are not now on our premises nor have they been on our premises for almost two years. He is convinced that someone from your organization (he knows not who) picked these monitors up some time ago.

Sounds harsh and needlessly formal.

It is my hope that this answers your question. If I may be of further assistance, please let me know.

Uses tired, insincere-sounding closing.

Sincerely,

FIGURE 7.3 **Effective Information Response Letter**

Dear Mr. Meyers:

Apparently the two NEC computer monitors about which you called yesterday are not on our premises.

Gives requested information immediately.

I checked with Mike Waldon, our office manager, and he feels that these two monitors were picked up by your organization nearly two years ago. It is possible, however, that the monitors were transferred to our Peachtree Park facility without Mike's knowledge. I suggest that you call Barbara Merton, our Peachtree Park office manager, at (404) 582-8902 to make further inquiries.

Explains courteously and informally.

You know that I'll be happy to help if I can.

Ends cordially.

Sincerely,

GIVING DELIVERY INFORMATION IN THE OPENING

Customers want to know when and how their orders will be sent. Since that news is most important, put it in the first sentence. It is unnecessary to say that you have received an order. An inefficient opener such as *We have received your order dated June 20* wastes words and the reader's time by providing information that could be inferred from more effective openers. Even a seemingly courteous opening like *Thank you for your recent order* does not really tell readers what they want to know. Instead of stating that an order has been received, imply it in a first sentence that provides delivery details. Here's an example:

The first sentence should tell when and how an order will be sent.

> We are sending your computer checks and invoice forms by Z Express air freight service, and these forms should arrive by February 8.

This opening sentence provides delivery information, and it is certainly superior to the two perfunctory openers shown above. However, it could still be improved. Notice that it emphasizes "we" instead of "you." Because this letter is primarily a goodwill effort, its effect can be enhanced by presenting its message from the viewpoint of the reader. Notice how the following version suggests reader benefits and emphasizes the *you* attitude:

A perfunctory opening is routine, superficial, and mechanical.

Your computer checks and invoice forms were sent by Z Express air freight service. They should reach you by February 8—two days ahead of your deadline.

PUTTING DETAILS IN THE BODY

You should include details relating to an order in the body of a letter that acknowledges the order. You will also want to discuss any irregularities about the order. If, for example, part of the order will be sent from a different location or prices have changed or items must be back-ordered, present this information.

When a sales clerk tells you how good you look in the new suit you just purchased, the clerk is practicing "resale."

The body of an order response is also the appropriate place to include resale information. *Resale* refers to the process of reassuring customers that their choices were good ones. You can use resale in an order letter by describing the product favorably. You might mention its features or attributes, its popularity among customers, and its successful use in certain applications. Perhaps your competitive price recommends it. Resale information confirms the discrimination and good judgment of your customers and encourages repeat business. After an opening statement describing delivery information, resale information such as the following is appropriate:

> The multipurpose checks you have ordered allow you to produce several different check formats, including accounts payable and payroll. Customers tell us that these computerized checks are the answer to their check-writing problems.

Resale emphasizes a product already sold; promotion emphasizes additional products to be sold.

Order acknowledgment letters are also suitable vehicles for sales promotion material. An organization often has other products or services that it wishes to highlight and promote. For example, a computer supply house might include the following sales feature:

> Another good buy from Quill is our popular 3½-inch disk available in our "mini" bulk pack of 25 disks at only 99 cents each. And we will send you free a desk storage tray for your disks.

Use sales promotion material, however, in moderation. Too much can be a burden to read and therefore irritating.

SHOWING APPRECIATION IN THE CLOSING

The best closings are personalized; they relate to one particular letter.

The closing should be pleasant, forward-looking, and appreciative. Above all, it should be personalized. That is, it should relate to one particular letter. Don't use all-purpose form-letter closing such as *We appreciate your interest in our company* or *Thank you for your order* or *We look forward to your continued business.*

Notice that the following personalized closings refer to the customers personally and to their current orders:

> You may be certain that your checks and invoice forms will reach you before your February 10 deadline. We genuinely appreciate your business and look forward to serving you again.

> We appreciate the payment you enclosed with your order. It is always a pleasure to do business with your organization.

> You have our appreciation for this order and our assurance, Ms. Johnson, that your future orders will be processed as efficiently and as promptly as this one.

We are confident that you will be pleased with the quality and durability of your Super-Grip 4-ply tires. Your satisfaction with our products and our service, Mr. Steiner, is our primary concern. We hope it will be our privilege to serve you again.

SKILLFUL AND FAULTY RESPONSES TO ORDERS

Transparency 7.5

The letter shown in Figure 7.4 reflects a wordy and inefficient style that some businesspeople still use. This letter has many faults. Can you spot them all?

You're right if you said that this order letter starts out poorly with an impersonal salutation. It continues to progress slowly in the first sentence by stating obvious information that could be implied. It also gives the reader no hint of when the books will arrive. The second paragraph of the letter is unnecessarily negative. Instead of capitalizing on the popularity of the books ordered, the writer uses negative language *(sorry to report, we will be forced)*, implying that the shipment might be delayed. The letter contains a number of outdated and wordy expressions *(pursuant to your request, every effort will be made, attached please find)*. The writer does not use resale or sales promotion to encourage repeat orders. Finally, the closing is wordy and overly formal.

The improved version of this letter shown in Figure 7.5 is written in an upbeat style that promotes good feelings between the writer and the customer. Notice that the letter contains a personal salutation and the first sentence reveals immediately when the books should arrive. The body of the letter confirms the wise selection of the reader by mentioning the successful sales of the books ordered. To promote future sales, this letter includes sales promotion information. It closes with sincere appreciation that ties in directly with the content of the letter. Notice throughout the letter the emphasis on the *you* attitude and benefits to the reader.

Ineffective Writing

FIGURE 7.4   Faulty Order Acknowledgment Letter

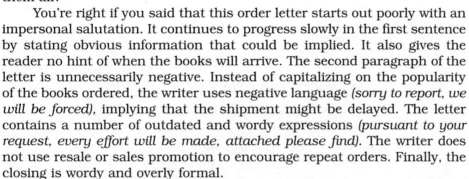

Fails to address receiver by name. Opens with obvious statement.

Uses negative language.

Misses chance to promote products.

RESPONDING TO CLAIMS

A claim is usually bad news to the organization receiving it. A claim means that something went wrong—goods were not delivered, a product failed to perform, a shipment was late, service was poor, or billing was fouled up.

FIGURE 7.5   **Effective Order Acknowledgment Letter—
Block Style**

*Addresses receiver
by name.*

*Opens with informa-
tion the reader
wants most.*

*Includes resale by
reassuring reader of
wise selections and
also promotes
future business.*

*Ties in appreciation
for order with con-
tent of letter.*

CHARTWELL PUBLISHERS CANADA
1050 BIRCHMONT ROAD
SCARBOROUGH, ONTARIO M1K 5G4
(416) 752-8900   TELEX 06-96781   FAX (416) 752-3966

March 20, 199x

Ms. Sheila Miller
2569 Notre Dame Avenue
Winnipeg, MB R3H OJ9

Dear Ms. Miller:

SUBJECT: YOUR MARCH 15 BOOK ORDER NO. 2980

The books requested in your Order No. 2980 will be shipped from our
Toronto distribution centre and should reach you by April 1.

The volumes you have ordered are among our best-selling editions and
will certainly generate good sales for you at your spring book fair.

For your interest we are enclosing a list of contemporary issues recently
released. If you place an order from this list or from our general catalogue,
you will be eligible for special terms that we are offering for a limited time.
For each $10 worth of books ordered at full list price, we will issue a $4
credit toward the purchase of additional books—as long as all the books
are ordered at the same time.

We are genuinely pleased, Ms. Miller, to be able to help supply the books
for your fair. Please take advantage of our special terms and place your
next order soon.

Sincerely,

Charles Bailey

Charles Bailey
Marketing Division

CB:wuh
Enclosure

*The writer respond-
ing to customer
claims seeks to
rectify the wrong,
regain customer
confidence, and
promote future
business.*

Large organizations have customer service departments that handle most
claims. Smaller organizations respond individually to customer claims.

An individual who writes letters responding to claims has three goals:

- To rectify the wrong, if one exists
- To regain the confidence of the customer
- To promote future business

When a claim is received, you must first gather information to determine what happened and how you will respond. Some organizations automatically comply with customer claims—even when the claim may be
unjustified—merely to maintain good public relations.

Once you have gathered information, you must decide whether to
grant the claim. If you respond positively, your letter will represent good

news to the reader. Use the direct strategy in revealing the good news. If your response is negative, arrange the message indirectly (Chapter 8). Here's a writing plan that responds favorably to a claim.

WRITING PLAN FOR GRANTING A CLAIM

Transparency 7.6

- *Subject line (optional)*—identifies the previous correspondence.
- *Opening*—grants the request or announces the adjustment immediately, and includes resale or sales promotion if appropriate.
- *Body*—provides details about how you are complying with the request, tries to regain the customer's confidence, and includes resale or sales promotion if appropriate.
- *Closing*—ends positively with a forward-looking thought, expresses confidence in future business relations, and avoids apologizing or referring to unpleasantness.

STREAMLINING REFERENCE IN THE SUBJECT LINE

A subject line streamlines the reference to the reader's correspondence. Although it is optional, a subject line enables you to reserve the first sentence for announcing the most important information. Here are examples of subject lines that effectively identify previous correspondence:

A subject line enables you to save the first sentence for the main idea.

SUBJECT: YOUR JUNE 3 INQUIRY ABOUT INVOICE 3569

SUBJECT: REQUEST FOR EXTENSION OF WEAREVER TIRE WARRANTY

SUBJECT: YOUR DECEMBER 7 LETTER ABOUT YOUR SNO-FLAKE ICE CRUSHER

REVEALING GOOD NEWS IN THE OPENING

Since you have decided to comply with the reader's claim, reveal the good news immediately:

A second shipment of toner cartridges for your printers has been sent by UPS and should reach you by April 25.

Readers want to learn the good news immediately.

We agree with you that the warranty on your Arizona Instruments programmable calculator Model AI 25C should be extended for six months.

You may take your Sno-Flake ice crusher to Ben's Appliances at 310 First Street, Myrtle Beach, where it will be repaired at no cost to you.

The enclosed check for $325 demonstrates our desire to satisfy our customers and earn their confidence.

In announcing that you will grant a claim, do so without a grudging tone—even if you have reservations about whether the claim is legitimate. Once you decide to comply with the customer's request, do so happily. Avoid half-hearted or reluctant responses like the following:

Although the Sno-Flake ice crusher works well when it is used properly, we have decided to allow you to take yours to Ben's Appliances for repair at our expense.

Don't begin your letter with an apology such as *We are sorry that you are having trouble with your Sno-Flake ice crusher.* This negative approach reminds the reader of the problem and may rekindle the heated emotions or unhappy feelings experienced when the claim was written. Also, such an opening is indirect. It doesn't tell the reader the good news first.

EXPLAINING COMPLIANCE IN THE BODY

Most businesses comply with claims because they want to promote customer goodwill.

In responding to claims, most organizations sincerely want to correct a wrong. They want to do more than just make the customer happy. They want to stand behind their products and services; they want to do what's right.

In the body of the letter, then, explain how you are complying with the claim. In all but the most routine claims, you should also seek to regain the confidence of the customer. You might reasonably expect that a customer who has experienced difficulty with a product, with delivery, with billing, or with service has lost faith in your organization. Rebuilding that faith is important for future business. How to rebuild lost confidence depends on the situation and the claim. If procedures need to be revised, explain what changes will be made. If a product has defective parts, tell how the product is being improved. If service is faulty, describe genuine efforts to improve it. Sincere and logical explanations do much to reduce hard feelings.

Sometimes the problem is not with the product but with the way it's being used. In other instances customers misunderstand warranties or inadvertently cause delivery and billing mix-ups by supplying incorrect information. Again, rational and sincere explanations will do much to regain the confidence of unhappy customers.

Because negative words suggest blame and fault, avoid them in letters that attempt to build customer goodwill.

In your explanation avoid using negative words that convey the wrong impression. Words like *trouble, regret, misunderstanding, fault, defective, error, inconvenience,* and *unfortunately* carry connotations of blame and wrongdoing. Try to use as few negative words as possible. Keep your message positive and upbeat.

In regaining the confidence of the reader, it may be appropriate to include resale information. If a customer is unhappy with a product, explain its features and applications in an effort to resell it. Depending on the situation, new product information could also be promoted.

SHOWING CONFIDENCE IN THE CLOSING

End your letter by looking ahead positively, not apologizing.

End positively by expressing confidence that the problem has been resolved and that continued business relations will result. Don't apologize excessively or call the customer's attention to unpleasantness associated with the claim. You might mention the product in a favorable light, suggest a new product, express your appreciation for the customer's business, or anticipate future business. It's often appropriate to refer to the desire to be of service and to satisfy customers. Do the following closings achieve the objectives suggested here?

> Your Sno-Flake ice crusher will help you remain cool and refreshed this summer. For your additional summer enjoyment, consider our Smokey Joe tabletop gas grill shown in the enclosed summer catalog. We genuinely value your business and look forward to your future orders.

> We hope that this refund check convinces you of our sincere desire to satisfy our customers. Our goal is to earn your confidence and continue to justify that confidence with quality products and matchless service.

You were most helpful in telling us about this situation and giving us an opportunity to correct it. We sincerely appreciate your cooperation.

In all your future dealings with us, you will find us striving our hardest to merit your confidence by serving you with efficiency and sincere concern.

EFFECTIVE AND INEFFECTIVE RESPONSES TO CLAIMS

Transparencies 7.7 and 7.8

The letter shown in Figure 7.6 is a response to an angry letter from Bud Stubbs of Sound, Inc., who did not receive a shipment of electronic equipment from Electronic Warehouse. Mr. Stubbs wants his shipment sent immediately. When Glenda Emerson of Electronic Warehouse investigated, she found that the order was sent to the address shown on Sound, Inc., stationery. The claim letter Ms. Emerson just received was written on Sound, Inc., stationery with a different address. Mr. Stubbs seems to be unaware of the discrepancy.

A confused address causes a shipping mix-up that necessitates a claim.

This response gets off to a bad start by failing to address Mr. Stubbs personally. Then, instead of telling Mr. Stubbs when he might expect this shipment, the opening sentence contains an apology. This serves only to remind him of the unpleasant emotions he felt when he wrote his original letter.

The tone of the letter does not promote goodwill. In a subtle way it blames Sound, Inc., for the shipping problem as it grudgingly agrees to send the second shipment. The closing apologizes again—and insincerely at that—while at the same time sharply reminding Mr. Stubbs of the address difficulty.

The claim from Mr. Stubbs does represent a problem to Electronic Warehouse. Ms. Emerson must decide if a second shipment is justified. If so, who should pay the shipping and restocking fee? In this instance Ms. Emerson decides to promote goodwill by sending a second shipment and

Ineffective Writing

FIGURE 7.6   Poor Response Claim Letter

Gentlemen:

We deeply regret the inconvenience you suffered in relation to your recent order for speakers, VCRs, headphones, and other electronic equipment.

Starts negatively with effusive apology.

Our investigators looked into this problem and determined that the shipment in question was indeed shipped immediately after we received the order. According to the shipper's records, it was delivered to the warehouse address given on your stationery: 3590 University Avenue, St. Paul, Minnesota 55114. No one at that address would accept delivery, so the shipment was returned to us. I see from your current stationery that your company has a new address. With the proper address, we probably could have delivered this shipment.

Blames customer for problem situation.

Although we feel that it is entirely appropriate to charge you shipping and restocking fees, as is our standard practice on returned goods, in this instance we will waive those fees.

Adopts grudging and reluctant tone.

Once again, please accept our apologies for the delay in filling this order. We hope this second shipment finally catches up with you at your current address.

Fails to promote future business.

Sincerely,

FIGURE 7.7   **Effective Claim Response Letter—Modified Block Style**

*E**W** ELECTRONIC WAREHOUSE*
930 Abbott Park Place
Providence, RI 02903-5309

February 21, 199x

Mr. Bud Stubbs
Sound, Inc.
2293 Second Avenue
St. Paul, MN 55120

Dear Mr. Stubbs:

SUBJECT: YOUR FEBRUARY 18 LETTER REGARDING YOUR JANUARY 20
    PURCHASE ORDER

Announces good news immediately.

You should receive by February 25 a second shipment of the speakers, VCRs, head-phones, and other electronic equipment that you ordered January 20.

Regains confidence of customer by explaining what happened and by suggesting plans for improvement.

The first shipment of this order was delivered January 28 to 3590 University Avenue, St. Paul, Minnesota 55114. When no one at that address would accept the shipment, it was returned to us. Now that I have your letter, I see that the order should have been sent to 2293 Second Avenue, St. Paul, Minnesota 55120. When an order is undeliver-able, we usually try to verify the shipping address by telephoning the customer. Some-how the return of this shipment was not caught by our normally painstaking shipping clerks. You can be sure that I will investigate shipping and return procedures with our clerks immediately to see if we can improve existing methods.

Closes confidently with genuine appeal for customer's respect.

As you know, Mr. Stubbs, our volume business allows us to sell wholesale electronics equipment at the lowest possible prices. However, we do not want to be so large that we lose touch with our customers. Over the years it is our customers' respect that has made us successful, and we hope that the prompt delivery of this shipment will earn yours.

Sincerely,

Glenda Emerson

Glenda Emerson
Distribution Manager

c David Cole
   Shipping Department

---

by having her company absorb the extra costs. Once this decision was made, the good news should be announced immediately and positively.

An effective claim response does not blame the customer nor begrudge compliance with the claim.

Figure 7.7 shows an improved version of the response to Mr. Stubbs. In this letter Ms. Emerson explains what happened to the first shipment. She also graciously accepts blame for the incident, even though the customer is probably equally guilty for not providing the proper shipping address.

Notice in Ms. Emerson's improved letter how effectively she achieves two of the three goals of an adjustment letter. She rectifies the wrong suf-fered by the customer and successfully regains his confidence. She treats

FIGURE 7.8   Simple But Effective Claim Response Letter

Dear Mrs. Eustice:

We are indeed intrigued by your CompuCap 2-X computer mystery and authorize you to send your 2-X to our Diagnostic Department for inspection.

Announces good news in first sentence.

Normally, we try to have our computers repaired locally to minimize transportation costs and to reduce stress to internal parts. However, your mystery case may require our special attention. We are enclosing a return authorization slip with instructions on how to pack your computer for shipping.

Explains company procedures and explains how company is complying with request.

Most 2-X users find that they can't get along without their computers for even a day. We will do our best to have your 2-X on its way back to you within four working days of its receipt here in Sunnyvale. We hope that this speedy service indicates to your our sincere interest in satisfying our customers.

Ends confidently and promises quick return of computer.

Sincerely,

the third goal—promoting future business—tactfully in the closing, without the use of resale or sales promotion.

Some claims involve minimal loss of customer confidence. In the letter shown in Figure 7.8, Mrs. Eustice (see her request letter shown in Figure 6.5) is happy with her computer but asks a favor of the company. She wants the company to solve her computer's mystery malfunction. In responding to her request, the company could merely have sent Mrs. Eustice instructions for packing and shipping the computer. Instead, it took this opportunity to maintain and promote customer goodwill with a friendly letter explaining the company's service policy. Notice that the letter avoids mentioning negatives, such as the malfunctioning computer. In the closing, rather than dwelling on the loss of her computer while it's being repaired, the letter emphasizes the customer's happiness with her computer by referring to her dependence on it. The letter ends with a forward-looking promise of the computer's speedy return.

In this chapter you learned to write letters that respond favorably to information requests, orders, and claims. These messages employ the deductive strategy; that is, they begin directly with the primary idea. In the next chapter you will learn to use the inductive strategy in conveying negative news.

APPLICATION AND PRACTICE—7

Discussion
1. Why is it advisable to use a subject line in responding to requests?
2. Since brevity is valued in business writing, is it ever advisable to respond with more information than requested? Discuss.
3. Why is it a good business practice to send a personalized acknowledgment of an order?
4. Distinguish between resale and sales promotion.

5. Discuss the policy of granting all customer claims, regardless of merit.

Short Answers

6. What is the most important position in a letter?
   The first sentence

7. Name two ways to open a letter that responds to multiple questions.
   1. Answer the most important question first.
   2. Start with a summary statement.

8. Name three instances when it is particularly appropriate to send a personalized order acknowledgment.
   1. New accounts
   2. Large accounts
   3. Customers who haven't placed orders recently

9. What do customers want to know first about their orders?
   They want to know when and how their orders will be shipped.

10. Give an example of resale.
    The tires you have just purchased are the finest we make.

11. List five situations when claim letters might be written by customers.
    1. Goods were not delivered.
    2. A product failed.
    3. Shipment was late.
    4. Service was poor.
    5. Billing was fouled up.

12. What are three goals that the writer strives to achieve in responding to customer claims?
    1. To right the wrong, if one exists
    2. To regain the confidence of the customer
    3. To promote future business

13. Name at least five negative words that carry impressions of blame and wrongdoing.
    Trouble, regret, misunderstanding, fault, defective, error, inconvenience, unfortunately

14. What should be included in the subject line of a response to a claim?
    Identification of the previous correspondence

15. What's wrong with a salutation like *Dear Sirs?*
    It is dated, impersonal, and possibly offensive.

⊃ *Instructor: Writing Improvement Exercises are available on diskette.*

Transparency Master 7.1

Writing Improvement Exercises

Subject Lines.   Write effective subject lines for the following messages that appeared in this chapter.

16. Information response letter addressed to Mr. Meyers, page 129.
    SUBJECT: TWO MISSING NEC COMPUTER MONITORS

17. Simple but effective response addressed to Mrs. Eustice, page 137.
    SUBJECT: SHIPMENT OF YOUR COMPUCAP 2-X COMPUTER

Letter Openers.   Place a check mark to indicate whether the following letter openers are direct or indirect. Be prepared to explain your choices.

		DIRECT	INDIRECT
18.	Thank you for your letter of December 2 in which you inquired if we have No. 19 bolts in stock.		√
19.	We have an ample supply of No. 19 bolts in stock.	√	
20.	This will acknowledge receipt of your letter of December 2.		√
21.	Yes, the Princess Cruise Club is planning a 15-day Mediterranean cruise beginning October 20.	√	
22.	I am pleased to have the opportunity to respond to your kind letter of July 9.		√
23.	Your letter of July 9 has been referred to me because Mr. Halvorson is away from the office.		√
24.	We sincerely appreciate your recent order for plywood wallboard panels.		√
25.	The plywood wallboard panels that you requested were shipped today by Coastal Express and should reach you by August 12.	√	

Opening Paragraph

26. Revise the following opening paragraph of an information response.

> Thank you for letter of March 3 inquiring about the RefreshAire electronic air cleaner. I am pleased to have this opportunity to provide you with information. You asked how the RefreshAire works and specifically if it would remove pollen from the air. Yes, the RefreshAire removes pollen from the air—and smoke and dust as well. It then recirculates clean air. We think it makes offices, conference rooms, and cafeterias cleaner and more healthful for everyone.
>
> *Yes, the RefreshAire removes not only pollen from the air but also smoke and dust. It then recirculates clean air, making offices, conference rooms, and cafeterias cleaner and healthier for everyone.*

Closing Paragraph

27. The following concluding paragraph to a claim letter response suffers from faults in strategy, tone, and emphasis. Revise and improve.

> According to your instructions, we are sending a replacement shipment of air conditioners by InterMountain Express. It should reach you by June 5. Once again, please accept our sincere apologies for the inconvenience and lost sales you have suffered as a result of this unfortunate incident.
>
> *Your replacement shipment of air conditioners was sent by InterMountain Express and should reach you by June 5. We sincerely hope that this shipment convinces you of our earnest desire to satisfy our customers. We look forward to serving you with quality products and prompt service in the future.*

Transparency Master 7.3

⊃ *Instructor: See p. 47–49 in the Instructor's Manual for solutions to 7-1, 7-2, and 7-3.*

CASE 7-1 ....

FAVORABLE RESPONSE TO CLAIM

You are Peter Mosgrove, manager of WoodDoors, Inc., a firm that manufactures quality precut and custom-built doors and frames. You have received a letter dated March 21 from Geraldine Johnson, 38221 Evergreen Road, Lansing, MI 48909. Ms. Johnson is an interior designer, and she complains that the oak French doors she ordered for a client recently were made to the wrong dimensions.

Although they were the wrong size, she kept the doors and had them installed because her clients were without outside doors. However, her carpenter charged an extra $286.50 to install them. She claims that you should reimburse her for this amount, since your company was responsible for the error. You check her order and find that she is right. Instead of measuring a total of 11 feet 8⅛ inches, the doors were made to measure 11 feet 4⅛ inches. At the time her doors were being constructed, you had two new craftsmen in the factory, and they may have misread or mismeasured her order. Normally, your Quality Control Department carefully monitors custom jobs. You don't know how this error was missed. You resolve, however, to review personally the plant's custom product procedures.

Ms. Johnson is a successful interior designer and has provided WoodDoors with a number of orders. You value her business and decide to send her a check for the amount of her claim. You want to remind her that WoodDoors has earned a reputation as the manufacturer of the finest wood doors and frames on the market. Your doors feature prime woods, and the craftsmanship is meticulous. The design of your doors has won awards, and the engineering is ingenious. You have a new line of greenhouse windows that are available in three sizes. Include a brochure describing these windows.

Before you write your letter, answer the following questions.

1. What is the good news that should be revealed in the first sentence of this letter?
   You are granting the claim and sending a check for the amount requested.

2. What item requires resale? How can you do that?
   The oak French doors should be resold. They feature prime woods, meticulous craftsmanship, award-winning design, and ingenious engineering.

3. What can you say to regain the faith of this customer?
   Explain how the error probably occurred and what measures are being taken to prevent its reoccurrence.

4. Should you include sales promotional items in this letter? How and where?
   Yes. Mention your new line of greenhouse windows in the body or in the closing.

5. Should you apologize for the inconvenience your error caused?
   No.

6. How can you close this letter?
   Show confidence in your product and look forward to future business. You may wish to include sales promotional material here.

Review the writing plan for granting a claim. Use this letter for class discussion or write a response to Ms. Johnson on a separate sheet. Use block style.

CASE 7-2

....

RESPONSE TO INFORMATION REQUEST

Analyze the following poorly written message from an insurance company to one of its policyholders, Mrs. Helen Hindlin, executive vice president, Satellite Cable of Minnesota, 3980 East Fourth Street, St. Paul, MN 55101. List its major faults. Outline a writing plan for a response to an information request. Then, on a separate sheet, rewrite the message rectifying the faults. Use block style.

⊃ *Instructor: Case 7-2 is available on diskette.*

Dear Helen:

SUBJECT: ACCIDENT LOSSES

Per your request by telephone on July 11, I have been thinking about your need for ways to make a reduction in your company's losses due to employee accidents. In response to your request, as I promised, I came up with some recommendations for things that I have found from our experience to be helpful in reducing company losses resulting from employee accidents.

One of the things you must do is ask your managers to complete an accident report whenever an accident occurs. It is also important that all employees be instructed in safe practices and safety requirements in their departments. In addition, we have found that a manager or supervisor must follow up any reported accident with an investigation. This investigation is necessary so that you can take corrective action in preventing a reoccurrence of the same kind of accident. Another recommendation regards the work site. Someone should inspect to be sure that employees are following safe procedures. Are they wearing required protective clothing? Are they using safety equipment as required? Most important, of course, is that all employees be first instructed in the safe practices and safety requirements of their departments.

We have found, Helen, that no loss-prevention program will be successful if the supervisors and management of the organization do not give their 100 percent cooperation. If you think that your managers and supervisors might have trouble implementing the suggestions made above, a seminar in loss prevention might be arranged for you. If I may be of further assistance, please do not hesitate to call upon me.

Ineffective writing

Transparency Master 7.4

1. List at least five faults.
    1. *Starts indirectly with explanation of why the letter is being written.*
    2. *Uses outdated expressions* (per your request) *and wordiness throughout.*
    3. *Provides information in illogical, poorly organized manner.*
    4. *Overemphasizes "I."*
    5. *Uses negative instead of positive presentation in last paragraph* (no loss-prevention program . . .).
    6. *Closes with an impersonal, overused ending.*

2. Outline a writing plan for a response to an information request.

    Subject line: *Identifies previous correspondence.*
    Opening: *Delivers the most important information first.*
    Body: *Arranges information in a logical sequence, explains and clarifies, provides additional information, and builds goodwill.*
    Closing: *Ends pleasantly.*

CASE 7-3  ....

ORDER RESPONSE

*Transparency
Master 7.5*

Analyze the following poorly written message to Sam Stinson, McPherson Hardware, 4821 Shafter Avenue, Oakland, CA 94609. List its major faults. Outline a writing plan for an order response. Then, on a separate sheet, rewrite the message rectifying its faults. Use block style.

Ineffective Writing

Gentlemen:

We have your kind order under date of November 25. Permit me to say that most of the order will be shipped soon.

Only the Brown & Drecker heavy-duty contour sanders will be delayed. We've had quite a run on these sanders, and we just can't keep them in stock. Therefore, they will be sent separately from Buffalo, New York, and will probably arrive sometime around December 15. All the other items (the lightweight drill sets, saber saw blade assortments, and steel router tables) are being sent today by Rocky Mountain Express and will, in all probability, reach you by December 5.

We also have some new items that your hardware store might like. One item is especially interesting. It's a rotary/orbital-action sander that does the job with less fatigue. Attached please find a brochure describing some of our newer items.

If we can be of further service, do not hesitate to call upon us.

Sincerely,

1. List at least five faults.
    1. Uses dated, wordy expressions in the opening.
    2. Presents negative news about the shipping delay before the good news.
    3. Fails to capitalize on the popularity of the item ordered.
    4. Fails to resell the items ordered.
    5. Lacks emphasis on reader benefits.
    6. Promotes new items poorly.
    7. Concludes with a cliché.

2. Outline a writing plan for an order response.

    Subject line: *Identifies previous correspondence.*
    Opening: *Grants the request or announces the adjustment immediately; includes resale information, if appropriate.*
    Body: *Provides details regarding compliance with request, attempts to regain the reader's confidence, and includes resale or promotion.*
    Closing: *Ends positively with a forward-looking thought and expresses confidence in future business; avoids apology or reference to unpleasantness.*

CASE 7-4

RESPONSE TO REQUEST FOR INFORMATION

A friend in a distant city is considering moving to your area for more education and training in your field. This individual wants to know about your program of study. Write a letter describing a program in your field (or any field you wish to describe). What courses must be taken? Toward what degree, certificate, or employment position does this program lead? Why did you choose it? Would you recommend this program to your friend? How long does it take? Add any information you feel would be helpful.

CASE 7-5

FAVORABLE RESPONSE TO CLAIM

Assume that you are a manager in the business in which you now work (or one about which you have some knowledge). Imagine that a customer, colleague, or employee has made a legitimate claim against your organization. Write a letter granting the claim. Make the letter as realistic and factual as possible.

Additional Problems

1. As Rochelle Cornell, owner of Oregon High, producer of freeze-dried backpacking foods, answer the inquiry of Marc Vannault (described in Chapter 6, page 119, Additional Problem No. 1). You are eager to have Mr. Vannault sample your new all-natural line of products containing no preservatives, sugar, or additives. You want him to know that you started this company two years ago after you found yourself making custom meals for discerning backpackers who rejected typical camping fare. Some of your menu items are excellent for individuals on restricted diets. Some dinners are cholesterol-, fat-, and salt-free, but he'll have to look at your list to see for himself. You will send him your complete list of dinner items and the suggested retail prices. You will also send him a sample "Saturday Night on the Trail," a four-course meal that comes with fruit candies and elegant appetizers. All your food products are made from choice ingredients in sanitary kitchens that you personally supervise. They are flash frozen in a new vacuum process that you patented. Although your dried foods are meant to last for years, you don't recommend that they be kept beyond 18 months because they may deteriorate. This could happen if a package were punctured or if the products became overheated. Your products are currently available at Pacific Camper, 2035 Redondo Avenue, Long Beach, CA 90804. Large orders may be placed directly with you. You offer a 5 percent discount on direct orders. Write a response to Marc Vannault, 3175 Fujita Street, Torrance, CA 90505.

2. Play the role of Clifford Bianchi, director, Employee Development Division, Pratt and Whitney (described in Chapter 6, page 119, Additional Problem No. 2). You are eager to respond to the request of

Edith Sterling, assistant vice president, Bank of Virginia, 7943 Main Street, Alexandria, VA 22308. Send her a copy of an article you wrote for *Personnel Today* describing the employee suggestion program you implemented at Pratt and Whitney. In answer to her specific questions, you encourage employees to participate by publicizing the suggestion plan. You post notices on bulletin boards in all departments, you insert announcements into pay envelopes, and you place articles describing employees who have won awards for their suggestions in the company newsletter and local newspapers. As your article states, suggestions are first screened by department managers. The best ones are then sent to an evaluation committee. You base your awards on the savings that result for the company. Employees receive a percentage of the actual savings. Your largest award was made to an engineer who suggested a way to discard fewer parts in jet engine inspections, saving Pratt and Whitney $9.7 million! You have found that an individual response to every suggestion is excellent for employee morale. You cover such problems as legal considerations and employee protests in your article. You have one important piece of advice for Ms. Sterling. She should enlist the support of top management immediately before working on the details of a program. You think that your results-oriented suggestion program has forged a stronger partnership between employees and management. Write a response to Ms. Sterling.

3. Respond to the order placed by Greg Fontecilla, manager, Datatronics, Inc., 2003 Maple Street, Litchfield, CT 06759 (described in Chapter 6, page 120, Additional Problem No. 3). Yes, all of the prices listed in your old catalog have increased. That's the bad news. The good news is that you have in stock nearly everything he ordered. The only item not immediately available is the desktop organizer, Item No. 23-K. That has to be shipped from the manufacturer in Pittsburgh, Pennsylvania. You've been having trouble with that supplier lately, perhaps because of heavy demand. However, you think that the organizer will be shipped no later than three weeks from the current date. You're pleased to have Datatronics' order. They might be interested in your new line of office supply products at discount prices. Send him a new catalog and call his attention to the low, low price on continuous-form computer paper. It's just $39.95 for a box containing 2,700 sheets of 9½- by 11-inch, 20-pound printout paper. All the items he ordered, except the organizer, are on their way by UPS and should arrive in three days.

4. As the customer relations manager at Toys-R-Us, you are responding to a letter from Susan Lee (described in Chapter 6, page 120, Additional Problem No. 4). You think that the toy she has described is the "Wild Mantis," a battery-operated, four-wheel-drive toy racing car (your store No. 825990-2). It is remote controlled and climbs over most obstacles. Wild Mantis has operating headlights, forward/reverse gears, and controlled steering. It requires four "C" batteries, and it costs $24.97. It weighs 6 pounds and will cost $5.37 to ship to Maui, but it should arrive within her three-week deadline. The California sales tax is 6½ percent. Tell her that you are sending Wild Mantis and that you have charged the total amount (figure it out) to her Visa card. Write this order response to Susan Lee, 845 Wainee Street, Lahaina, Maui, HI 96761.

5. Assume that you are Mike Murphy, sales manager, Idaho Wood Products. It is your job to reply to customer claims, and today you must respond to Sandra Fenwick, president, Fenwick Consulting Services, 2248 26th Avenue West, Seattle, WA 98199 (described in Chapter 6, page 120, Additional Problem No. 5). You are disappointed that she is returning the executive desk (Invoice No. 3499), but your policy is to comply with customer wishes. If she doesn't want to keep the desk, you will certainly return the purchase price plus shipping charges. On occasion, desks are damaged in shipping, and this may explain the marred finish and the sticking drawers. You want her to give Idaho Wood Products another chance. After all, your office furniture and other wood products are made from the finest hand-selected woods by master artisans. Since she is apparently furnishing her office, send her another catalog and invite her to look at the traditional conference desk on page 10-E. This is available with a matching credenza, file cabinets, and accessories. She might be interested in your furniture-leasing plan, which can produce substantial savings. You promise that you will personally examine any furniture she may order in the future. Write her a letter granting her claim.

6. Assume the role of Marilyn Thatcher, customer service representative, Ever-Cool Manufacturing Company. You are responding to the claim of Paul Friedman, purchase manager, Datatronics, Inc., 2569 Missouri Street, Mesa, AZ 85016 (described in Chapter 6, page 121, Additional Problem No. 6). Tell Mr. Friedman that the Ever-Cool air conditioner can be taken to A–Z Appliance Repairs, 2320 Cactus Avenue, Phoenix, AZ 84290, for warrantied repair. Rarely do these heavy-duty room air conditioners need service. You are happy to honor the warranty. If Datatronics would like faster service, Ever-Cool has an agreement with Victory Mobile Service. For a nominal fee ($80), Victory will come to his office and, if possible, make the repair on the spot. This is sometimes more convenient than removing a heavy, mounted room air conditioner. He can make an appointment with Victory by calling (800) 574-8900. Write to Datatronics.

GRAMMAR/MECHANICS CHECKUP—7

COMMAS 2

Review the Grammar/Mechanics Handbook Sections 2.05–2.09. Then study each of the following statements and insert necessary commas. In the space provided write the number of commas that you add; write *0* if no commas are needed. Also record the number of the G/M principle(s) illustrated. When you finish, compare your responses with those shown below. If your answers differ, study carefully the principles shown in parentheses.

Example: When businesses encounter financial problems, they often reduce their administrative staffs.   *1*   **2.06a**

1. As stated in the warranty, this printer is guaranteed for one year.   *1*   **(2.06a)**
2. Today's profits come from products currently on the market, and tomorrow's profits come from products currently on the drawing boards.   *1*   **(2.05)**

_0_ _(2.05)_   3. Companies introduce new products in one part of the country and then watch how the product sells in that area.

_2_ _(2.06c)_   4. One large automobile manufacturer, which must remain nameless, recognizes that buyer perception is behind the success of any new product.

_1_ _(2.08)_   5. The imaginative, promising agency opened its offices April 22 in Cambridge.

_0_ _(2.06c)_   6. The sales associate who earns the highest number of recognition points this year will be honored with a bonus vacation trip.

_2_ _(2.09)_   7. Darren Wilson, our sales manager in the Redwood City area, will make a promotion presentation at the June meeting.

_1_ _(2.05)_   8. Our new product has many attributes that should make it appealing to buyers, but it also has one significant drawback.

_1_ _(2.06a)_   9. Although they have different technical characteristics and vary considerably in price and quality, two or more of a firm's products may be perceived by shoppers as almost the same.

_1_ _(2.07)_   10. To motivate prospective buyers, we are offering a cash rebate of $2.

Review of Commas 1 and 2

_2_ _(2.06a, 2.04a)_   11. When you receive the application, please fill it out and return it before Monday, January 3.

_2_ _(2.03, 2.08)_   12. On the other hand, we are very interested in hiring hard-working, conscientious individuals.

_1_ _(2.06c)_   13. In March we expect to open a new branch in Concord, which is an area of considerable growth.

_3_ _(2.06a, 2.04a)_   14. As we discussed on the telephone, the ceremony is scheduled for Thursday, June 9, at 3 p.m.

_1_ _(2.05)_   15. Dr. Adams teaches the morning classes, and Mrs. Wildey is responsible for evening sections.

---

1. (1) warranty, (*2.06a*) 3. 0 5. (1) imaginative, (*2.08*) 7. (2) Wilson, area, (*2.09*)
9. (1) quality, (*2.06a*) 11. (2) application, Monday, (*2.06a, 2.04a*) 13. (1) Concord, (*2.06c*)
15. (1) classes, (*2.05*)

GRAMMAR/MECHANICS CHALLENGE—7

Transparency 7.9

DOCUMENT FOR REVISION

The following letter has faults in grammar, punctuation, spelling, number form, and negative words. Use standard proofreading marks (see Appendix B) to correct the errors. When you finish, your instructor can show you the revised version of this letter.

Poor Letter

May 3, 199x

Mr. Ragu Raghaven

Medical Supplies, Inc.

P.O. Box 489

Missouri City, TX 77489

Dear Mr. Raghavan:

You will be recieving shortly the rubbermaid service and utility carts you ordered along with 5 recycling stack bins. Unfortunately, the heavy duty can crusher is not available but it will be sent from the factory in Albany New York and should reach you by May 31st.

You may place any future orders, by using our toll free telephone number (1-800-577-9241), or our toll free fax number (1-800-577-2657). If you need help with any items ask for one of the following sales representatives, Bill Small, Susan Freed, or Rick Woo. When the items you order are in our currant catalog it will be shipped the same day you place you're order. For products to be custom imprinted please provide a typed or printed copy with your order.

Remember we are the only catalog sales company that guarantees your full satisfaction. If you are not pleased we'll arrange for a prompt refund, credit or replacement. We'll also refund or credit all shipping costs associated with the returned items. We want your business!

Yours truly,

IV

Conveying Negative, Persuasive, and Special Messages

8

LETTERS AND MEMOS THAT CARRY NEGATIVE NEWS

IN THIS CHAPTER YOU WILL LEARN TO DO THE FOLLOWING:

- Identify the need for indirectness in delivering bad news.
- Recognize six components in an effective indirect strategy.
- Apply skillful writing techniques in refusing requests.
- Retain goodwill while refusing claims.
- Demonstrate tact in refusing credit requests.

Instructor: See p. 51 for author's suggested lesson plan for Chapter 8.

As you have learned, the first step in writing a business letter or memo is analyzing your message and the effect you expect to have on the reader. If you think the message will antagonize, disappoint, upset, hurt, or anger the recipient, an indirect strategy may be more effective than the direct method you have been using up to now. Examples of letters that deliver disappointing news are those that deny requests, refuse claims, reveal price increases, decline invitations, announce shipping delays, turn down job applicants, discontinue services, or deny credit. In this chapter you'll learn how to apply the indirect method to bad-news messages.

If your message delivers bad news, use the indirect method.

ANALYZING THE MESSAGE

Recipients of good news like to learn the news quickly. That's why the direct strategy is most effective. Directness, however, is not usually effective for bad news. Blurting out bad news at the beginning of a letter may upset the reader. He or she is in a poor frame of mind to receive the remainder of the letter. Or, worse yet, the bad news may cause the reader to stop reading altogether. Reasons for the refusal and explanations that follow may never be seen. The principal goal of the indirect strategy is this:

The indirect method allows the writer to explain before announcing the bad news.

we want the reader to read our reasons and explanations *before* we reveal the bad news.

The indirect strategy, which we will discuss shortly, is *generally* better for negative news—but not *always.* Some readers may prefer frankness and directness. If you know the reader well, the direct strategy may be appropriate even for negative messages. For example, assume that Dave Nelson, a good customer with whom you are friendly, must be told that his company's order can't be filled immediately. You know that Dave is a no-nonsense, up-front fellow who values candor. For him the direct strategy may be appropriate. Further, if you have been unsuccessful in getting your message across by writing one or more messages using the indirect strategy, you may decide that bluntness is needed. The direct approach, for example, might be appropriate in responding to Sally Kelly. She has been told twice, in memos using an indirect strategy, that she does not qualify for a promotion because she lacks college training in her field. She applied for the promotion a third time and still had not enrolled in the necessary courses. This time her superior wrote a direct memo that spelled out the denial immediately and then explained the reasons for the denial.

Typically, though, we try to soften the blow of bad news by delaying it until after we have explained reasons justifying it. Delaying the bad news is just one part of an overall strategy that has proved effective in delivering messages with negative news. The indirect strategy includes six elements, which we will consider now.

INDIRECT STRATEGY
- Buffer
- Transition
- Explanation
- Bad news
- Alternative(s)
- Goodwill closing

Transparency 8.1

APPLYING THE INDIRECT STRATEGY

Before applying the indirect strategy, analyze the reasons underlying the bad news.

The indirect strategy gives you a general outline for presenting negative news. Before implementing it, however, you need to analyze each step and study illustrations that show how these steps are used in writing letters and memos. After you have examined the steps, you'll learn how to put them together in writing letters for common business situations that involve delivering negative news. By developing skill in using this strategy in the most common situations, you should be able to adapt it to similar business problems.

We'll discuss the indirect strategy in the order shown, but the thinking process actually follows a slightly different order. Skillful writers first decide whether their message will likely elicit a positive or negative reaction from the reader. If a request must be denied or a claim refused, they analyze their reasons for refusing. If they don't have good reasons, they can't write convincing letters. Thus, the explanation shapes the rest of the letter and determines the content and tone. Although the letter begins with a buffer, the thinking process begins with the reasons for delivering the bad news.

DEVELOPING A GOOD BUFFER

Transparency 8.2

A buffer is a device that reduces shock. In denying a request or delivering other bad news, we can reduce the shock a reader may suffer by opening with a buffer paragraph. This opening should put the reader in a receptive frame of mind. Our objective, remember, is to induce the recipient to read the entire letter. We want the reader to understand our reasons and explanations before we disclose the bad news.

An effective buffer generally possesses three characteristics: (1) it is *neutral,* (2) it is *upbeat,* and (3) it is *relevant.* A buffer is neutral when it does not signal the bad news that is to follow nor falsely suggest that good news will be forthcoming. A buffer is upbeat if it emphasizes something positive for the reader. The positive element could be resale material that relates to a product, a compliment or praise for the reader, or a statement that builds goodwill. A buffer is relevant if it refers to the situation at hand. A buffer statement that describes the unusually good weather may be neutral and upbeat, but it has no relation to the bad news.

An effective buffer is neutral, upbeat, and relevant.

Here are a number of buffer statements for negative letters. The first is the opening statement for a letter delivering the news that a candidate did not receive a job for which he was interviewed. The buffer refers to the interview positively but does not suggest that the candidate will be hired:

> I enjoyed talking with you last week about your background and the excellent business administration program at Louisiana Tech.

A letter denying a request for credit for merchandise that a customer wishes to return employs a resale buffer:

> Your selection of an Ambassador top-grain pigskin leather attaché case is a smart one, Mrs. Silva, because these cases combine fashionable styling with fine workmanship and peerless leathers.

Try not to forecast bad news nor falsely imply good news.

A letter refusing an invitation to speak at an awards banquet begins with a compliment to the reader:

> You have done a splendid job of organizing the program for the October 5 awards banquet of Sigma Alpha.

A letter denying an adjustment to a customer's account opens with a warm statement regarding the customer's past payment record:

> We genuinely appreciate the prompt payments you have always made in response to our monthly billings.

BUILDING A SMOOTH TRANSITION

After the opening buffer statement, use a transition that guides the reader to the explanation that follows. Avoid red-flag words like *but, unfortunately,* and *however* because they are dead giveaways that bad news is to come.

Reference to a key word or idea builds a transition between the buffer and the following explanation.

Experienced writers try to plant a key word or idea in the buffer or transition that leads the reader naturally to the reasons for the refusal. In this next example a business must refuse a request for campaign contributions for a city council candidate. Notice how the key words *candidate* and *contribution* form a link between the buffer and the explanation for refusing the request:

> Your efforts to build a campaign chest for city council candidate Jackie Ohlson are commendable. This candidate deserves the support of civic-minded businesses and individuals who are able to make *contributions.*

Buffer

Transition

Explanation

Your *candidate,* if elected, will help administer funds to municipal departments and offices. As you may know, a significant portion of our business involves providing supplies for city offices. City council members who have accepted campaign contributions from vendors supplying city

Bad news

accounts may be accused of conflict of interest. Rather than place your candidate in this awkward position, our attorney advises us to avoid mak-

Alternative

ing financial contributions to the campaigns of city council candidates. Although we are unable to provide financial support, many of our employees will be contributing their time and efforts to work personally for the election of your candidate.

Goodwill closing

We hope that the participation of our staff will contribute to a successful campaign for Jackie Ohlson.

PRESENTING THE EXPLANATION BEFORE THE BAD NEWS

The success of a negative letter depends on how well the explanation is presented.

In the preceding example, key words in the buffer and transition lead the reader smoothly to the explanation. As you know, the explanation is the most important part of a negative letter. Without sound reasons for denying a request or refusing a claim, the letter will fail, no matter how cleverly it is written. The explanation is, after all, the principal reason for using the indirect method. We want to be able to explain before refusing.

In the explanation, as in the transition, don't let red-flag words *(but, however, unfortunately)* signal the refusal. Your explanation should show that you have analyzed the situation carefully. Tell clearly why a refusal is necessary: an item is no longer under warranty or was never warrantied in the first place, or a cash refund cannot be granted for an item that cannot be resold, or a product failed because it was misused. In some instances, such as the denial of credit or the refusal to allow damaged goods to be returned, the explanation can emphasize reader benefits. The reader, along with other customers, benefits from lower prices if a business is able to avoid unnecessary credit costs and unfair returns.

Strive to project an unemotional, objective, and helpful tone. Don't lecture or patronize *(If you will read the operating instruction carefully . . .),* avoid sounding presumptuous *(I'm sure the salesperson who demonstrated this unit explained that . . .),* and don't hide behind company policy *(Our company policy prevents us from granting your request).* Explain specifically why the company policy is necessary. If you have more than one reason for refusing, begin with the strongest reason. Present the bad news, and then continue with additional reasons for refusing.

Source: Duffy. Reprinted with permission of Universal Press Syndicate.

BREAKING THE BAD NEWS

In Chapter 4 you learned stylistic techniques for deemphasizing ideas. Now we will expand on those techniques and apply them as you learn to break bad news.

You can soften the blow of bad news by using some of these seven techniques.

Transparency 8.3

- *Avoid the spotlight.* Don't put the bad news in a conspicuous position. The most emphatic positions in a letter are the first and last sentences. Other conspicuous spots are the beginnings and ends of sentences and paragraphs. The reader's attention is drawn to these positions and lingers there. Strategically, then, these are not good places for announcing bad news. To give the least emphasis to an idea, place it in the middle of a sentence or in the middle of a paragraph partway through your letter.

- *Use a long sentence.* Short sentences emphasize content. Since you want to deemphasize bad news, avoid short, simple sentences *(We cannot ship your goods)*. Longer sentences diffuse the bad news and also give you a chance to explain the bad news or offer alternatives.

- *Put the bad news in a subordinate clause.* Grammatical attention in a sentence is always focused on the independent clause. To deemphasize an idea, then, put it in a less conspicuous spot, like a subordinate clause *(Although your credit application cannot be approved at this time, we welcome your cash business)*. The bad news is subordinated in the dependent clause *(Although your credit application)* where the reader is less likely to dwell on it.

Be selective in applying these techniques whenever you break bad news.

Transparency 8.4

- *Use the passive voice.* The active voice, recommended for most business writing, is direct and identifies the subject of a sentence *(I cannot allow you to examine our personnel files)*. To be less direct and to avoid drawing unnecessary attention to yourself as writer, use the passive voice *(Examination of our personnel files cannot be permitted because . . .)*. The passive voice focuses attention on actions rather than personalities; it helps you be impersonal and tactful.

- *Be clear but not overly graphic.* Bad news is best received when it is clear but not painfully vivid. For example, the following refusal is unnecessarily harsh because it provides too many details:

Bad news should be clear but not overly emphasized.

> We cannot pay for your freelance services in cash, as you request. Such payment is clearly illegal and violates federal law. All freelance services that we authorize must be supported by check payments to individuals whose social security numbers are included in the record of the payment.

This refusal would be more tactful if it were less direct and less graphic:

> Federal law requires that payments to freelancers be made by check and be supported by social security numbers.

- *Imply the refusal.* In certain instances a refusal does not have to be stated directly. In the preceding example the tactful revision does not actually say *We cannot pay you in cash*. Instead, the refusal is implied. Recall the letter refusing campaign funds:

> Rather than place your candidate in this awkward position, our attorney advises us to avoid making financial contributions to the campaigns of city council candidates.

Instead of hammering home the bad news *(Therefore, we cannot contribute to this campaign),* the author spared the feelings of the reader by implying the refusal.

Here's another example of an implied refusal. Instead of refusing an invitation to speak at a campus job fair, a business executive writes:

> Although my appointment schedule is completely booked during the week of your employment fair, I wish you success with this beneficial event.

Implied refusals are effective only if they are not so subtle that the reader misses the point.

Implying a refusal is not quite as devastating as an explicit denial. Such subtleness saves the feelings of both the writer and the reader. Be very careful, however, in using this technique. It is imperative that the reader understand the refusal. Don't be so vague that additional correspondence is required to clarify the refusal.

- *Offer an alternative.* If appropriate, suggest some recourse to the reader. You might offer a compromise, a substitute, or an alternative offer:

> For security reasons visitors are never allowed inside Building J. It is possible, however, to tour our assembly facility in the fall during our Open House.

> My schedule prevents me from speaking to your group, but I have asked my colleague, Dr. George R. Duffy, to consider addressing your conference.

CLOSING WITH GOODWILL

Provide a courteous, pleasant, and forward-looking closing that doesn't refer directly to the bad news.

After explaining the bad news clearly and tactfully, shift to an idea that renews good feelings between the writer and the reader. In the letter refusing to pay a freelancer in cash, the closing regains her confidence:

> We hope that we may continue to use your services as a freelancer in the future.

If an alternative is presented, make it easy to accept:

> Dr. Duffy is an excellent speaker, and I'm sure your group would enjoy his presentation. I am including Dr. Duffy's address so that you may write him directly.

When writing to customers, encourage continued business relations. Resale or sales promotional material may be appropriate:

> I am enclosing a sample of a new imported fragrance and a coupon to save you $15 on your initial purchase. We look forward to serving you soon.

For the most effective closings, avoid these traps:

- *Don't refer to the bad news.* Focus on positive, friendly remarks. Don't needlessly revive the reader's emotions regarding the bad news.
- *Don't apologize.* You have valid reasons for refusing, and you've explained these reasons clearly. An apology at the end of your message undermines your explanation.

Irony is the use of words to express something other than, and especially opposite to, the literal meaning.

- *Don't conclude with clichés.* Remarks such as *If we may be of further service* or *Thank you for understanding our position* sound particularly insincere and ironic in messages delivering negative news.
- *Don't invite further correspondence.* Expressions such as *If you have any further questions* or *If you would like to discuss this further* suggest that the matter is still open for discussion. Don't encourage a pen-pal relationship. Your decision is fair and final.

REFUSING REQUESTS

When you must refuse a request and you feel that the refusal is likely to antagonize, upset, hurt, or anger the reader, use an indirect approach, such as the following writing plan illustrates.

WRITING PLAN FOR REFUSING A REQUEST OR CLAIM

Transparency 8.5

- *Buffer*—identifies previous correspondence incidentally or in a subject line and begins with neutral statement on which both the reader and the writer can agree.
- *Transition*—plants key idea or word that leads naturally to the explanation.
- *Explanation*—presents valid reasons for refusal, avoids red-flag words that forecast bad news, and includes resale or sales promotion material if appropriate.
- *Bad news*—softens the blow by deemphasizing the refusal.
- *Alternative*—suggests a compromise, alternative, or substitute if possible.
- *Closing*—renews good feelings with a positive statement, avoids referring to the bad news, and doesn't apologize.

EXPERT AND FAULTY LETTERS THAT REFUSE REQUESTS

Transparency 8.6

The request refusal letter shown in Figure 8.1 begins well enough. The opening sentence is neutral, although it contains unnecessary information that could be implied. But the letter deteriorates quickly with a blunt refusal of a magazine writer's request for information about employee salaries. It creates a harsh tone with such negative words as *sorry, must refuse, violate,* and *liable.* Since the refusal precedes the explanation, the reader probably will not be in a receptive frame of mind to accept the reasons for refusing. Notice, too, that the bad news is emphasized by its placement in a short sentence at the beginning of a paragraph. It stands out here and hurts the reader by its conspicuousness. The refusal explanation is overly graphic, containing references to possible litigation.

FIGURE 8.1   Blunt Request Refusal

Dear Mrs. Marcus:

I have your letter of October 21 in which you request information about the salaries and commissions of our top young salespeople.

I am sorry to inform you that we cannot reveal data of this kind. I must, therefore, refuse your request. To release this information would violate our private employee contracts. Such disclosure could make us liable for damages, should any employee seek legal recourse. I might say, however, that our salespeople are probably receiving the highest combined salary and commissions of any salespeople in this field.

If it were possible for us to help you with your fascinating research, we would certainly be happy to do so.

Sincerely yours,

Ineffective Writing

States obvious information.

Sounds harsh, blunt and unnecessarily negative.

Switches to insincere tone.

FIGURE 8.2   Skillful Request Refusal—Modified Block Style

**CANON
ELECTRONICS**

115 Fifth Avenue
New York, NY 10011-1010
(212) 593-1098

January 15, 199x

Mrs. Sylvia Marcus
1305 Elmwood Avenue
Buffalo, NY 14222-2240

Dear Mrs. Marcus:

The article you are now researching for *Business Management Weekly*
sounds fascinating, and we are flattered that you wish to include our organization. We do have many outstanding young salespeople, both male and
female, who are commanding top salaries.

Each of our salespeople operates under an individual salary contract.
During salary negotiations several years ago, an agreement was reached
in which both sales staff members and management agreed to keep the
terms of these individual contracts confidential. Although specific salaries
and commission rates cannot be released, we can provide you with a
ranked list of our top salespeople for the past five years. Three of the current top salespeople are under the age of thirty-five.

Enclosed is a fact sheet regarding our top salespeople. We wish you every
success with your article, and we hope to see our organization represented in it.

Cordially,

Lloyd Kenniston

Lloyd Kenniston
Executive Vice President

LK:je
Enclosure: Sales Fact Sheet

Buffer shows genuine interest, and transition sets up explanation.

Explanation gives good reasons for refusing request.

Refusal is softened by substitute.

Closing is pleasant and forward looking.

When you must refuse and you have no alternatives to suggest, the explanation and reasoning must be particularly logical.

Instead of offering constructive alternatives, this letter reveals only tiny
bits of the desired data. Finally, the insincere-sounding closing does not
build goodwill.

Figure 8.2 shows a letter in which the same request is refused more
skillfully. Its opening reflects genuine interest in the request but does not
indicate compliance. The second sentence acts as a transition by introducing the words *salespeople* and *salaries,* repeated in the following paragraph. Reasons for refusing this request are objectively presented in an
explanation that precedes the refusal. Notice that the refusal (*Although
specific salaries and commission rates cannot be released*) is a subordinate
clause in a long sentence in the middle of a paragraph. To further soften
the blow, the letter offers an alternative. The cordial closing refers to the
alternative, avoids mention of the refusal, and looks to the future.

It's always easier to write refusals when alternatives can be offered to
soften the bad news. But often no alternatives are possible. The refusal

FIGURE 8.3   Tactful Memo Refusing Request and Offering No Alternatives

TO: The Staff   July 8, 199x

FROM: Barbara Stordevent, Manager, Document Production **BS**

SUBJECT: DEPARTMENT USE OF LICENSED SOFTWARE

A number of computer users have expressed interest in the licensed word processing program WordWindows, which we recently acquired for the microcomputers in our Document Production Department.

This program, like many licensed programs, requires that each purchased copy be used only on a single machine. The agreement not only forbids that the program be copied for home use but also forbids making copies for additional machines within the office. One can easily understand why a software company must protect its programs from indiscriminate copying. If a business organization purchased one program and then allowed multiple copies to be made for other computers within the company or for employees to take home, the software company would find it impossible to earn enough profit to make the development of any future software program worthwhile.

When we purchased the WordWindows program, we agreed to limit its use to a single machine. Although this program must not be copied, we look forward to using it for many of your documents here in the Document Production Department.

Please drop by to see our new graphics and presentation capabilities.

Opens with relevant but neutral buffer.

Transition picks up key word licensed.

Explanation neither preaches nor patronizes.

Deemphasized refusal diverts attention to reader benefits.

Closes with an off-the-subject but friendly remark.

letter shown in Figure 8.3 involves a delicate situation in which a manager has been asked by her superiors to violate a contract. Several of the attorneys for whom she works have privately asked her to make copies of a licensed software program for them. They apparently want this program for their personal computers. Making copies is forbidden by the terms of the software licensing agreement, and the manager refuses to do this. Rather than saying no to each attorney who asks her, she writes the memo in Figure 8.3 using the indirect strategy.

The opening tactfully avoids suggesting that any attorney has actually asked to copy the software program. These professionals may prefer not to have their private requests made known. A transition takes the reader to the logical reasons against copying. Notice that the tone is objective, neither preaching nor condemning. The refusal is softened by being linked with a positive statement. To divert attention from the refusal, the memo ends with a friendly, off-the-subject remark.

REFUSING CLAIMS

All businesses offering products or services will receive occasional customer claims for adjustments. Claims may also arise from employees. Most of these claims are valid, and the customer or employee receives a positive response. Even unwarranted claims are sometimes granted because businesses genuinely desire to create a good public image and to maintain friendly relations with employees.

Some claims, however, cannot be approved because the customer or employee is mistaken, misinformed, unreasonable, or possibly even dishonest. Letters responding to these claims deliver bad news. The indirect strategy breaks bad news with the least pain. It also allows the writer to explain why the claim must be refused before the reader realizes the bad news and begins resisting.

EFFECTIVE LETTER THAT REFUSES CLAIM

In the letter shown in Figure 8.4, the writer denies a customer's claim for the difference between the price the customer paid for speakers and the price he saw advertised locally (which would have resulted in a cash refund of $151). While Galaxy does match any advertised lower price, the price-matching policy applies *only* to exact models. This claim must be rejected because the advertisement the customer submitted shows a different, older speaker model.

The letter to Robert Bond opens with a buffer that agrees with a statement in the customer's letter. It repeats the key idea of product confidence as a transition to the second paragraph. Next comes an explanation of the price-matching policy. The writer does not assume that the customer is trying to pull a fast one. Nor does she suggest that the customer is a dummy who didn't read or understand the price-matching policy. The safest path is a neutral explanation of the policy along with precise distinctions between the customer's speakers and the older ones. The writer also gets a chance to resell the customer's speakers and demonstrate what a quality product they are. By the end of the third paragraph, it's evident to the reader that his claim is unjustified.

Notice how most of the components in an effective claim refusal are woven together in this letter: buffer, transition, explanation, and pleasant closing. The only missing part is an alternative, which was impossible in this situation.

REFUSING CREDIT

Banks, other financial institutions, and businesses often deny credit by using impersonal form letters. These letters may list a number of possible reasons for the credit rejection, such as insufficient credit references, irregular employment, delinquent credit obligations, insufficient income, inadequate collateral, temporary residence, or inability to verify income.

Form letters announcing credit refusals are efficient for the sender but may displease the receiver.

Form letters are convenient for the writer, but they often antagonize the reader because they are unclear, inappropriate, or insensitive. Even when individuals are poor credit risks (and they probably know this), they may be hurt by tactless and blunt form letters. Form-letter refusals or poorly written letters not only hurt the feelings of the reader but also

FIGURE 8.4 Tactful Claim Refusal—Block Style

Galaxy Sound Sales
829 Morgan Boulevard
Salt Lake City, UT 85033
Phone: 801-677-2401   Fax: 801-677-5532

July 15, 199x

Mr. Robert M. Bond
2410 Russell Street
Pleasant Grove, UT 84060

Dear Mr. Bond:

You're absolutely right, Mr. Bond. We do take pride in selling the finest products at rock-bottom prices. The Boze speakers you purchased last month are premier concert hall speakers. They're the only ones we present in our catalog because they're the best.

We have such confidence in our products and prices that we offer the price-matching policy you mention in your letter of July 6. That policy guarantees a refund of the price difference if you see one of your purchases offered at a lower price for 30 days after your purchase. To qualify for that refund, customers are asked to send us an advertisement or verifiable proof of the product price and model. As our catalog states, this price-matching policy applies only to exact models with USA warranties.

Our Boze AM-5 II speakers sell for $749. You sent us a local advertisement showing a price of $598 for Boze speakers. This advertisement, however, described an earlier version, the Boze AM-4 model. The AM-5 speakers you received have a wider dynamic range and smoother frequency response than the AM-4 model. Naturally, the improved model you purchased costs a little more than the older AM-4 model that the local advertisement describes. Your speakers have a new three-chamber bass module that virtually eliminates harmonic distortion. Finally, your speakers are 20 percent more compact than the AM-4 model.

You bought the finest compact speakers on the market, Mr. Bond. If you haven't installed them yet, you may be interested in ceiling mounts, shown in the enclosed catalog on page 48. We value your business and invite your continued comparison shopping.

Sincerely yours,

Rachael M Rosen

Rachael M. Rosen
Customer Service

Enclosure

Begins with neutral statement on which both reader and writer can agree.

Explains price-matching policy and how reader's purchase is different from lower-priced model.

Without actually saying no, shows why the claim can't be honored.

Renews good feelings by building confidence in wisdom of purchase.

ignore an opportunity to solicit future business. An individual or business that is a poor credit risk today may become a good credit risk and a potential customer in the future.

An effective plan for writing a credit refusal follows the principles of the indirect strategy.

WRITING PLAN FOR A CREDIT REFUSAL

- *Buffer*—expresses appreciation for an order or a credit application, and includes resale information if appropriate.
- *Transition*—moves from buffer to explanation logically and repeats key idea or word if possible.

Credit refusals use five-part strategy to break the bad news.

- *Explanation*—describes submission of application to credit-reporting agency but does not specify reasons for denial; uses objective language.
- *Bad news*—implies refusal or states it respectfully, offers alternatives, and suggests possible extension of credit in the future.
- *Closing*—projects an optimistic look to the future and includes resale or sales promotion material.

CREDIT REFUSALS THAT RETAIN BUSINESS

Credit agencies report applicant's record.

As much as companies want business, they can extend credit only when payment is likely to follow. Credit applications, from individuals or from businesses, are generally approved or disapproved on the basis of the applicant's credit history. This record is supplied by a credit-reporting agency, such as TRW Information Services. After reviewing the applicant's record, a credit manager applies the organization's guidelines and approves or disapproves the loan.

Avoid causing hard feelings or lawsuits. Encourage cash business and prepare for future credit.

If you must deny credit to prospective customers, you have four goals in conveying the refusal:

- Avoiding language that causes hard feelings
- Avoiding information that could cause a lawsuit (such as specific reasons for the denial)
- Retaining customers on a cash basis
- Preparing for possible future credit—without raising false expectations

Credit applicants often will continue to do business with an organization even if they are denied credit. Naturally, you'll want to do everything possible to encourage that patronage. Thus, keep the refusal respectful, sensitive, and upbeat. To avoid possible litigation, some organizations give no explanation of the reasons for the refusal. Instead, they provide the name of the credit-reporting agency and suggest that inquiries be directed to it.

The credit refusal shown in Figure 8.5 strives to retain the business represented by a customer's order. It opens with a buffer that discusses good qualities of the product ordered. This buffer/introduction sets up a transition to the explanation *(We'd like to see this fine product distributed by your full-service dealership)*. Next comes the explanation for the refusal. Actually, not much explaining has to be done. Most companies today do not try to interpret a bad credit report; they simply refer the applicant to the reporting agency.

This letter then suggests an alternative that helps the customer obtain the merchandise desired but on a cash basis. Notice how the writer emphasizes the *you* view and shows reader benefits. The conclusion is pleasant and looks forward to future business.

Retaining the reader's goodwill is the goal in any credit refusal. And tone is the key to keeping that goodwill. Notice in Figure 8.5 how respectful and objective the words sound. It's not easy to say no and remain friends; but it can be done, as this letter illustrates.

ETHICS AND THE INDIRECT STRATEGY

You may worry that the indirect organizational strategy is unethical or manipulative because the writer deliberately delays the main idea. But consider the alternative. Breaking bad news bluntly can cause pain and

FIGURE 8.5   Effective Credit Refusal—Modified Block Style

UNIFAC COMMUNICATION SYSTEMS

3490 Franklin Street • Auburn, NY 13902
(212) 355-8792

February 19, 199x

Mr. Greg Sargema
Federated Sound Suppliers
320 Orchard Park Boulevard
Buffalo, NY 14127-2110

Dear Mr. Sargema:

You've come to the right place for cordless phone systems, Mr. Sargema, and we appreciate your February 14 order. The Nomad 400 model that you have ordered offers outstanding features, including two-way paging, pulse dialing, and intercom capabilities.

Because we'd like to see this fine product distributed by your full-service dealership, we submitted your credit application to TRS Information Services. After reviewing their report, we find that credit cannot be extended at this time. To learn more about your record, you may call a TRS credit counselor at (212) 369-3211. When your firm's financial situation improves, we would sincerely like to serve you on a credit basis.

In the meantime, please consider this plan. Order one dozen of the Nomad 400 units today. By paying for this reduced order with cash, you would receive a 2 percent cash discount. After you have sold these fast-moving units, place another cash order through our toll-free order number. We promise to deliver your items immediately so that your inventory is never depleted. In this way, you can obtain the units you want now, you can enjoy cash discounts, and you can replace your inventory almost instantaneously.

We're proud of our quality products and our competitive prices. If we can do business with you now or in the future, please call us at 1-800-896-3320.

Yours truly,

Margaret Gorman

Margaret Gormann, Manager
Marketing Unit One

MG:fty

Opens confidently with resale and sets up transition.

Explains use of credit service.
States denial objectively.

Uses passive-voice verb for deemphasis. Suggests alternative plan for cash purchase.

Looks forward optimistically to future business.

---

hard feelings. How many times have you heard the comment "I didn't mind the news so much as the *way* I was told."

By delaying bad news, you soften the blow somewhat, as well as ensure that your reasoning will be read while the receiver is still receptive. Your motives are not to deceive the reader or to hide the news. Rather, your goal is to be a compassionate, yet effective communicator.

The key to ethical communication lies in the motives of the sender. Unethical communicators *intend to deceive.* For example, Victoria's Secret, the clothing and lingerie chain, offered free $10 gift certificates. However, when customers tried to cash the certificates, they found that they were required to make a minimum purchase of $50 worth of merchandise.[1] For this misleading, deceptive, and unethical offer, the chain paid a $100,000

Ethical communicators using the indirect strategy do not intend to deceive.

fine. The indirect strategy provides a setting in which to announce bad news; it does not avoid or misrepresent the truth.

ADAPTING THE INDIRECT STRATEGY

Application of the principles of indirectness is often successful in solving personal problems.

In this chapter you learned how to use the indirect strategy for refusing requests, refusing claims, and denying credit. The same general principles of indirectness are appropriate whenever bad news must be delivered. For example, a company announcement reducing health coverage for employees would certainly represent bad news to the employees. The indirect strategy would be best for such an announcement. News that a supplier is out of a needed item or that a certain item is no longer manufactured or that the price of an item has risen—all these messages will be irritating to a customer. The indirect strategy is again most effective.

We have applied this strategy only to written business messages. The strategy is, however, also appropriate in oral communication and in interpersonal relations. If you must tell a friend that you can't fulfill a promise, a good explanation preceding the refusal may help you retain the friendship. If you must tell your brother that you dented the fender of his car, the indirect strategy will help you announce the bad news. Now that you've learned this strategy, you'll be able to adapt it to many situations beyond the letter and memo writing plans illustrated here.

APPLICATION AND PRACTICE—8

Discussion

1. Discuss at least five situations in which the indirect strategy would be appropriate for delivering a negative message.
2. Does the indirect strategy represent an effort to manipulate the reader?
3. Discuss the idea that organization and development of a message delivering negative news begins with the explanation.
4. Analyze the effectiveness of the following opening statements for negative news letters:
   a. Unfortunately, we would like to approve your credit application but we cannot.
   b. I enjoyed talking with you last week when you came in to be interviewed for the position of assistant to the registrar.
   c. The weather recently has certainly been pleasant for this time of the year, hasn't it?
5. Analyze the effectiveness of the following closing statements for negative letters:
   a. Once again, please let me say that we would like to grant your request but we cannot allow outsiders to use our confidential company files even for such worthy research as you describe.
   b. If you have any further questions about this matter, please remember that I am available to serve you.
   c. Although we regret very much any inconvenience our shipping error has caused you, we trust that you will understand our position in this matter.

Short Answers

6. The indirect strategy should be used when you expect what kind of reader reaction?
   When you expect a reader to be antagonized, upset, hurt, or angered

7. List in proper sequence the six elements involved in organizing a negative message according to the indirect strategy.
   1. *Buffer*   4. *Bad news*
   2. *Transition*   5. *Alternatives*
   3. *Explanation*   6. *Goodwill closing*

8. What is a buffer, and when should it be used?
   A buffer reduces shock. It should be used in the opening of a letter to soften the delivery of bad news.

9. What are three characteristics of a good buffer?
   A good buffer is neutral, upbeat, and relevant.

10. How can a writer develop a transition between the opening of a letter and an explanation that follows?
    Plant a key word or idea in the buffer that can be repeated in moving to the explanation.

11. List seven ways to deemphasize bad news. Be prepared to discuss each.
    1. *Avoid the spotlight.*
    2. *Use a long sentence.*
    3. *Put the bad news in a subordinate clause.*
    4. *Use the passive voice.*
    5. *Be clear but not overly graphic.*
    6. *Imply the refusal.*
    7. *Offer an alternative.*

12. List four ways that you should *not* close a negative message.
    1. *Don't refer to the bad news.*
    2. *Don't apologize.*
    3. *Don't conclude with clichés.*
    4. *Don't invite further correspondence.*

13. Name three red-flag words.
    but, however, unfortunately

14. Write *passive* or *active* to indicate the voice of the verbs in the following sentences.
    a. We cannot refund the full purchase price.
       Active
    b. The full purchase price cannot be refunded.
       Passive
    c. The shipment of your order has been delayed.
       Passive
    d. Our delivery service has delayed shipment of your order.
       Active

15. Name four emphatic positions in a letter.
    1. *First sentence*
    2. *Last sentence*
    3. *Beginning of sentence*
    4. *End of sentence*

⊃ *Instructor:*
Writing Improvement Exercises are available on diskette.

Transparency Master 8.1

Writing Improvement Exercises

Subordinate Clauses.   You can soften the effect of bad news by placing it in a subordinate clause that begins with *although, since,* or *because.* The emphasis in a sentence is on the independent clause. Instead of saying *We cannot serve you on a credit basis,* try *Since we cannot serve you on a credit basis, we invite you to take advantage of our cash discounts and sale prices.*

Revise the following refusals so that the bad news appears in a subordinate clause.

16. We no longer manufacture the Model SF-7. However, we now make a substitute, the Model SF-9, which we would like to send you.
    Although we no longer manufacture the Model SF-7, we would like to send you a substitute, the Model SF-9.

17. We hope to have our plant remodeling completed by October. We cannot schedule tours of the bottling plant until after we finish remodeling.
    Although we cannot schedule tours of the bottling plant until after we finish remodeling, we hope to be ready in October.

18. Island Airways cannot accept responsibility for expenses incurred indirectly from flight delays. However, we do recognize that this delay inconvenienced you.
    Although responsibility cannot be assumed for expenses incurred indirectly from flight delays, we do recognize that this delay inconvenienced you.

Passive-Voice Verbs.   Passive-voice verbs may be preferable in breaking bad news because they enable you to emphasize actions rather than personalities. Compare these two refusals:

ACTIVE VOICE: I cannot authorize you to take three weeks of vacation in July.
PASSIVE VOICE: Three weeks of vacation in July cannot be authorized.

Revise the following refusals so that they use passive-voice instead of active-voice verbs.

19. We cannot refund cash for the items you purchased on credit.
    Cash cannot be refunded for credit purchases.

20. I have already filled my schedule on the date you wish me to speak.
    My schedule is already filled for the date you wish me to speak.

21. We do not examine patients until we have verified their insurance coverage.
    Examination of patients cannot be made until their insurance coverage is verified.
    Or, *Patients can be examined after verification of insurance coverage.*

Transparency Master 8.2

Implied Refusals.   Bad news can be deemphasized by implying a refusal instead of stating it directly. Compare these refusals:

DIRECT REFUSAL: We cannot send you a price list nor can we sell our lawn mowers directly to customers. We sell only through dealers, and your dealer is HomeCo, Inc.
IMPLIED REFUSAL: Our lawn mowers are sold only through dealers, and your dealer is HomeCo, Inc.

Revise the following refusals so that they are implied.

22. We cannot open a credit account for you because your application states that you have no regular employment. This allows us to serve you only as a cash customer.

    Because you have no regular employment, we can serve you only as a cash customer.

    Or, Credit accounts may be opened only for individuals with regular employment.

23. I find it impossible to contribute to the fund-raising campaign this year. At present all the funds of my organization are needed to lease new equipment and offices for our new branch in Richmond. I hope to be able to support this fund in the future.

    Although all my present funds are needed to lease new equipment and offices for our new branch in Richmond, I hope to be able to support this campaign in the future.

24. We cannot ship our fresh fruit baskets c.o.d. Your order was not accompanied by payment, so we are not shipping it. We have it ready, though, and will rush it to its destination as soon as you call us with your credit card number.

    We have your fresh fruit basket ready and will ship it as soon as you call us with your credit card number.

CASE 8-1

FAVOR REFUSAL

Transparency Master 8.3

Imagine that you are Ron Levin, manager of Datatech Computers. You have received a letter from Professor Lydia Keuser, at nearby San Jose City College, who wants to bring her class of 30 office automation students to your showroom to see the latest microcomputer hardware and software. You are eager to have 30 potential customers visit your showroom, where you carry a comprehensive line of microcomputers, compatible printers, and state-of-the-art software. But you can't possibly accommodate 30 people at once. Your workstations are arranged for demonstrations to only one or two viewers at a time. You must refuse Professor Keuser's request. However, since you hate to pass up this opportunity, suggest to her that you could bring a computer to her classroom for a demonstration, or she could divide her class into smaller groups for demos at the showroom.

Consider the refusal letter to Professor Keuser. Analyze the following options in relation to the indirect strategy. Circle the letters representing the most appropriate possibilities for the refusal letter.

Instructor: See pp. 52–55 in the Instructor's Manual for solutions to 8-1, 8-2, 8-3, and 8-4.

1. To open this letter appropriately, you might
   a. Point out immediately that your showroom is too small to accommodate her entire class at once.
   b. Express appreciation that Professor Keuser and her office automation class are interested in the microcomputers and software offered by Datatech Computers.
   c. Explain that Datatech Computers carries only professional programs and that your stock does not include computer games, in which some college students may be interested.

    d. Suggest that she divide her class into thirds and let you demonstrate your comprehensive line at three different times.

2. A logical transition for this letter might be for you to
    a. Use sales promotion by describing the outstanding features of your best-selling computer and one of your software programs.
    b. Warn Professor Keuser that 30 students gathered around one screen would create an impossible viewing situation.
    c. Mention that you normally demonstrate your comprehensive line of microcomputers, printers, and software programs to individual customers.
    d. Inquire regarding the level of computer expertise represented by the students in this class.

3. In explaining why you cannot accommodate the class, you might say that
    a. Demonstrating to this large student group would interfere with sales to genuine customers in your showroom.
    b. Customers usually come in singly or in pairs; hence, you are prepared for demonstrations to small groups only.
    c. You never demonstrate to large groups because individuals complain that they can't see what's on the screen or hear what's being said.
    d. You would prefer not to demonstrate to students because many will not understand the complexities of computers; moreover, they are unlikely to make purchases in the near future.

4. Which of the following sentences softens the refusal most effectively?
    a. Although your class cannot be accommodated in our showroom, we might be able to arrange a demonstration in your classroom.
    b. We cannot accommodate your class in our showroom because your class is too large.
    c. Although we might be able to arrange a demonstration in your classroom, we cannot accommodate your class in our showroom.
    d. We sincerely regret that we cannot allow your class to come to Datatech Computers for a demonstration.

Use this problem for discussion. At the option of your instructor, write the entire letter (individually or as a class project) to Professor Lydia Keuser, San Jose City College, 2100 Moorpark Avenue, San Jose, CA 95128-2799. You may wish to incorporate some of the sentences you selected here, but consider this a skeleton. Flesh out your letter with explanations, examples, appropriate connecting thoughts, and a goodwill closing. Use modified block style with indented paragraphs.

CASE 8-2

REQUEST REFUSAL

Analyze the following poorly written message and list some of its major faults. Outline a writing plan for refusing a request. Then, on a separate sheet, rewrite the message, rectifying the faults.

TO: Vicki Samuels, Records Manager   DATE: June 20, 199x
FROM: Karen Klein, President
SUBJECT: CONFERENCE

Ineffective Writing

Please be informed that I have taken under advisement your request to be allowed to attend the conference of the Association of Records Managers and Administrators, Inc., in New York. Unfortunately, this conference is six days long and comes in September, a very critical time for us.

I'm sorry to have to deny your request, because it looks like a worthwhile conference. It would afford an opportunity for records management personnel, like you, to learn more about current procedures and technologies. You've been doing an outstanding job of helping us begin the conversion of our files to microforms.

But to have you gone for a period of six days in September, when, as you know, we complete our budget requests for the following fiscal year is out of the question. We need you at our budget planning meetings, particularly since you have proposed the purchase of computer equipment that will generate micrographs directly. Another reason that you can't go in September, in spite of the fact that I would like to see you go, is that Cathy Watson, in your department, has requested the months of August through October for her maternity leave. Your absence, together with hers, would put us in a real bind.

For these reasons, I cannot allow you to leave in September. However, if there is a suitable conference at some other time in the year when your absence would be less critical, I would be happy to let you go. I'm sorry about this matter, Vicki. This is certainly little thanks for the excellent progress you are making in the massive task of converting our filing system.

1. List at least five faults.
   1. *Subject line is too brief to be helpful.*
   2. *The first sentence and much of the message are wordy.*
   3. *Tone is uneven—sometimes formal, sometimes casual.*
   4. *Refusal comes before the explanation.*
   5. *Organization is jumbled; transitions are missing.*
   6. *Language is unnecessarily negative.*
   7. *The bad news is emphasized by its repetition, negative wording, and placement.*
   8. *The closing contains an apology, which weakens the reasons for refusal.*

2. Outline a writing plan for a request refusal.
   See page 157.

Transparency Master 8.5

Ineffective Writing

CASE 8-3

CREDIT REFUSAL

Analyze the following poorly written credit refusal and list its major faults. Outline a writing plan for refusing credit. Then, on a separate sheet, rewrite the message rectifying its faults. Address the letter to Mr. Eric H. Davis, 876 Avenue H, Winter Haven, FL 33880. Use modified block style with indented paragraphs.

Dear Mr. Davis:

Thank you very much for your April 23 order for computer paper, copy paper, and other supplies. We are delighted by your interest in our quality products and our company. Unfortunately, we cannot fill your order because of your current poor credit rating.

As is our company policy, we submitted your credit application to Eastern Information Services, a credit-reporting agency. Its report made it absolutely clear to us that extending credit to your dealership was not a good idea at this time. Our credit rules prohibit us from extending credit to anyone who does not pass a EIS investigation. We hope you will understand our desire to avoid any credit losses. Although your dealership seems to be growing, we deem it unwise to offer credit to you at this point in time. If you want to talk with EIS directly, its number is (882) 466-3902.

Meanwhile, we invite you to let us fill your order on a cash basis. Presently we have in stock all the items that you requested. We can't send them, though, unless you have cash. If you would like these items rushed to you, call me personally at (212) 468-2220. If I can be of further service, don't hesitate to call upon me.

Sincerely,

1. List at least five faults.
   1. *The opening sentences mislead the reader.*
   2. *Bad news precedes the explanation.*
   3. *Blunt language* (poor credit rating) *offends the reader.*
   4. *Emphasizes writer, not reader, benefits.*
   5. *Goodwill is not promoted.*
   6. *Language is wordy.*
   7. *Closes with an insincere-sounding cliché.*

2. Outline a writing plan for refusing credit.
   See page 160.

CASE 8-4 ....

CLAIM REFUSAL

For class discussion analyze the following poorly written message. Discuss its major faults, and suggest a writing plan for refusing the claim. Then, at the option of your instructor, on a separate sheet rewrite the message, rectifying its faults. Address the letter to Mrs. Lois Sullivan, 422 Paramus Road, Paramus, NJ 97652. Use modified block style with indented paragraphs.

*Transparency
Master 8.6*

Dear Mrs. Sullivan:

We have your letter of May 23 demanding repair or replacement for your newly purchased BeautyTest mattress. You say that you enjoy sleeping on it; but in the morning when you and your husband get up, you claim that the mattress has body impressions that remain all day.

Unfortunately, Mrs. Sullivan, we can neither repair nor replace your mattress because those impressions are perfectly normal. If you will read your warranty carefully, you will find this statement: "Slight body impressions will appear with use and are not indicative of structural failure. The body-conforming coils and comfort cushioning materials are beginning to work for you and impressions are caused by the natural settling of these materials."

When you purchased your mattress, I'm sure your salesperson told you that the BeautyTest mattress has a unique, scientifically designed system of individually pocketed coils that provide separate support for each person occupying the bed. This unusual construction, with those hundreds of independently operating coils, reacts to every body contour, providing luxurious comfort. At the same time, this system provides firm support. It is this unique design that's causing the body impressions that you see when you get up in the morning.

Although we never repair or replace a mattress when it merely shows slight impressions, we will send our representative out to inspect your mattress, if it would make you feel better. Please call for an appointment at (800) 322-9800. Remember, on a BeautyTest mattress you get the best night's rest possible.

Cordially,

Ineffective Writing

1. List at least five faults.
   1. *The opening does not put reader in receptive frame of mind to accept refusal.*
   2. *Negative and red-flag words* (demanding, you claim, unfortunately) *create a harsh tone.*
   3. *Tone is preachy* (if you will read your warranty carefully).
   4. *The language is presumptuous* (I'm sure your salesperson told you).
   5. *Bad news is given before the explanation.*
   6. *No effort is made to promote goodwill.*
   7. *Resale is ineffective.*

2. Outline a writing plan for a message that refuses a claim.
   See page 147.

Additional Problems

1. As the sales manager of Wholesale Copier Exchange, you are faced with a difficult decision. The daughter of one of your best friends

operates Eastland Escrow Services. For the past ten months, as a favor, you have allowed her to lease from you a full-featured Toshiba copier at a low rate of $200 per month. Now she wants to purchase the Toshiba, and she wants you to apply the lease payments against the purchase price. That means that she wants to deduct $2,000 from the basic purchase price of $7,695. Your quoted purchase price is already at rock bottom. You have been able to build business by selling a high volume of units while keeping your margin of profit quite low. Although you do have a limited leasing business, none of your leasing agreements include an option to apply the lease payments toward the purchase of a unit. Other companies may permit such an arrangement, but their purchase prices are probably much higher than yours. Even at $7,695, you will be earning a very slim profit. To allow a $2,000 discount would certainly mean a loss for you; and even for the daughter of a friend, you don't want to absorb a $2,000 loss. Eastland seems to like the performance received from this Toshiba, Model DC-3E. You have slightly cheaper models, but they have fewer features. If Eastland wants to give up the reduction and enlargement capability as well as the automatic paper selection device, you might be able to bring the purchase price down $1,500. Regardless of what Toshiba model Eastland purchases, you guarantee 6-hour emergency service and a 1-million-copy or 8-year warranty. Write a letter to Rachael Ramberg, Eastland Escrow Services, 4801 First Street North, Arlington, VA 22203, retaining her friendship and business but refusing her request.

2. Assume that you are plant operations manager for United Growers Association. You have received a letter from Reverend Donald T. Webster, pastor of the First Church of Christ. Reverend Webster writes at the suggestion of Victor Cortez, whom you know well as the supervisor of your shipping fleet and one of your most valued employees. Mr. Cortez is a deacon at the First Church of Christ and has been instrumental in collecting food and clothing for poor families in Mexico. He has suggested to his pastor that United Growers might allow the church to borrow a small cargo truck over a weekend to pick up articles in the Oxnard and Ventura areas and deliver them to the church's mission in Ensenada, Mexico. You have sympathy with the plight of the poor and would like to encourage this worthwhile endeavor. However, company trucks cannot be loaned to outside organizations or individuals, even for worthy causes. Your liability insurance limits equipment coverage to specific deliveries, routes, and licensed drivers. You cannot allow any company truck to be borrowed officially (or unofficially), even by a trusted company employee for an admirable project. Write a refusal letter that recognizes the worth of this charitable project and acknowledges the high regard you hold for Mr. Cortez. Address the letter to Reverend Webster, First Church of Christ, 269 Anacapa View Drive, Ventura, CA 91076, and send a copy to Victor Cortez in the company mail.

3. As Lentax consumer affairs representative, you must refuse the claim of Gabriella Marconi, a professional photographer who purchased a Lentax macrofocusing teleconverter lens two years ago. Ms. Marconi wants the lens replaced, claiming that it no longer works properly, although it worked well for two years. Your service department has examined the returned teleconverter and determined that either it

was improperly attached to another lens or it was dropped, causing a lack of synchronization with Ms. Marconi's aperture-priority camera. Lentax products are built to the highest-quality standards and should provide years of satisfaction. The Lentax Limited 5-Year Warranty clearly states the following: "Malfunctions resulting from misuse, tampering, unauthorized repairs, modifications, or accident are not covered by this warranty." Refuse the request for replacement. Tell her, however, that since she purchased this lens from an authorized dealer, she may receive a 25 percent discount on repairs. Write to Ms. Gabriella Marconi, 120 Carlisle Street, Hanover, PA 17221.

4. As Richard Green, owner of Greenscapes, Inc., you must refuse the following request. Mr. and Mrs. John Nabor have asked that you replace the landscaping in the home they recently purchased in Kettering. You had landscaped that home nearly a year ago for the former owner, Mrs. Dryden, installing a sod lawn and many shrubs, trees, and flowers. It looked beautiful when you finished, but six months later, Mrs. Dryden sold the property and moved to Dayton. Four months elapsed before the new owners moved in. After four months of neglect and a hot, dry summer, the newly installed landscaping suffered. You guarantee all your work and normally would replace any plants that do not survive. Under these circumstances, however, you do not feel justified in making any refund because your guarantee necessarily presumes proper maintenance on the part of the property owner. Moreover, your guarantee is made only to the individual who contracted with you—not to subsequent owners. You would like to retain the goodwill of the new owners, since this is an affluent neighborhood and you hope to attract additional work here. On the other hand, you can't afford to replace the materials invested in this job. You believe that the lawn could probably be rejuvenated with deep watering and fertilizer. You would be happy to inspect the property and offer suggestions to the Nabors. In reality, you wonder if the Nabors might not have a claim against the former owner or the escrow agency for failing to maintain the property. Clearly, however, the claim is not against you. Write to Mr. and Mrs. John Nabor, 4716 Highgate Drive, Kettering, OH 45429.

5. As manager of The Sports Connection, you must refuse the application of Geri Meyers for an extended membership in your athletic club. This is strictly a business decision. You liked Geri very much when she applied, and she seems genuinely interested in fitness and a healthful lifestyle. However, your "extended membership" plan qualifies the member for all your testing, exercise, aerobics, and recreation programs. This multiservice program is necessarily expensive and requires a solid credit rating. To your disappointment, however, you learn that Geri's credit rating is decidedly negative. Her credit report indicates that she is delinquent in payments to four businesses, including Holiday Health Spa, your principal competitor. You do have other programs, including your "Drop In and Work Out" plan that offers use of available facilities on a cash basis. This plan enables a member to reserve space on the racquetball and handball courts; the member can also sign up for exercise and aerobics classes, space permitting. Since Geri is far in debt, you would feel guilty allowing her to plunge in any more deeply. Refuse her credit application, but encourage her cash business. Suggest that she make an

inquiry to TRS Information Services to learn about her credit report. Write to Geri Meyers, Stratford Apartments No. 4, 15053 Sherman Way, Van Nuys, CA 91405.

6. As manager of Exbrook Restaurant Supply, you are sorry to have to refuse an order because of the poor credit rating of Mary Stephens. She is opening a new gourmet catering business in Fort Lauderdale called "The GodMother." You were delighted with her initial order for $1,430. However, when you checked her credit, you learned that she owes substantial sums for her catering truck and kitchen equipment. In fact, she seems to have no solid financial assets. You cannot allow a credit order. You know that every businessperson has to get started somehow, and you wish you could help her out in this fledgling business. You feel that her international menu (including unusual items like pasta primavera, moussaka, duck lasagna, and chicken fettuccine verde) will be quite successful, especially if she uses your quality ingredients. Suggest that she make an inquiry to Eastern Information Services to learn more about her credit report. Write a sympathetic but firm credit refusal to Mary Stephens, The GodMother, 905 North Gulf Drive, Fort Lauderdale, FL 33334.

GRAMMAR/MECHANICS CHECKUP—8

COMMAS 3

Review the Grammar/Mechanics Handbook Sections 2.10–2.15. Then study each of the following statements and insert necessary commas. In the space provided write the number of commas that you add; write *0* if no commas are needed. Also record the number of the G/M principle(s) illustrated. When you finish, compare your responses with those shown below. If your answers differ, study carefully the principles shown in parentheses.

2   **(2.21)**   **Example:** It was Ms. Jeffreys, not Mr. Simpson, who was assigned the Madison account.

2   **(2.14a)** 1. "The choice of a good name," said President Gordon, "cannot be overestimated."

4   **(2.10)**   2. Lois A. Wagner, Ph.D., and Marilyn S. Smith, M.B.A., were hired as consultants.

1   **(2.14b)** 3. Their August 15 order was shipped on Monday, wasn't it?

0   **(2.15)**   4. Brand names are important in advertising specialty goods such as refrigerators and television sets.

1   **(2.12)**   5. The bigger the investment, the greater the profit.

Review Commas 1, 2, 3

3   (2.06a, 2.01)   6. As you requested, your order for ribbons, file folders, and envelopes will be sent immediately.

2   **(2.03)**   7. We think, however, that you should reexamine your networking system and that you should consider electronic mail.

2   (2.07, 2.06c)   8. Within the next eight-week period, we hope to hire Sue Richards, who is currently working in private industry.

2   (2.01, 2.15)   9. Our convention will attract more participants if it is held in a resort location such as San Diego, Monterey, or Las Vegas.

1   (2.06a, 2.06c) 10. If everyone who applied for the position were interviewed, we would be overwhelmed.

11. Our chief goal is to provide quality products backed by prompt, efficient service.   *1*   *(2.08, 2.15)*

12. In the past ten years, we have employed over 30 well-qualified individuals, many of whom have selected banking as their career.   *2*   *(2.07, 2.09)*

13. Your shipment has been charged to your new account, which we were pleased to open on the basis of your excellent credit.   *1*   *(2.06c, 2.15)*

14. Steven Sims, who spoke to our class last week, is the author of a book entitled *Writing Winning Résumés.*   *2*   *(2.05c, 2.15)*

15. Mrs. Hartung uses market research extensively and keeps a close watch on her own operations, her competition, and the market in order to identify the latest trends.   *2*   *(2.01)*

---

1. (2) name," Gordon, (*2.14a*)   3. (1) Monday, (*2.14b*)   5. (1) investment, (*2.12*)   7. (2) think, however, (*2.03*)   9. (2) Diego, Monterey, (*2.01, 2.15*)   11. (1) prompt, (*2.08, 2.15*) 13. (1) account, (*2.06c, 2.15*) 15. (2) operations, competition, (*2.01*)

GRAMMAR/MECHANICS CHALLENGE—8
••

DOCUMENT FOR REVISION

The following memo has faults in grammar, punctuation, spelling, number form, wordiness, and negative words. Use standard proofreading marks (see Appendix B) to correct the errors. When you finish, your instructor can show you the revised version of this memo.

Transparency 8.8

Poor Memo

TO: Kevin Wang   DATE: May 25, 199x

FROM: Roger Freed

SUBJECT: REQUEST TO ATTEND CONFERENCE IN THE MONTH OF SEPTEMBER

Ineffective Writing

The Management Counsel and me are extremely pleased with the leadership you have provided in setting up live video transmission to our regional offices. As a result of your professinal comittment, Kevin I can understand your desire to attend the conference of the Tellecommunication specialists of America September 23rd to the 28th in atlanta.

Unfortunately, the last two weeks in September has been set aside for budget planing. Just between you and I we've only just scratched the surface of our teleconferencing projects for the next 5 years. As a result of the fact that you are the specialist, and we rely heavily on your expertise, we need you hear for those planning sessions.

If your able to attend a simular conference in the Spring, and if our work loads permit, we'll try to send you then. Your a valueable player, Kevin and I'm greatful your on our MIS team.

••

9

LETTERS AND MEMOS

THAT PERSUADE

⊃ *Instructor: See p. 57 for author's suggested lesson plan for Chapter 9.*

IN THIS CHAPTER YOU WILL LEARN TO DO THE FOLLOWING:

- Use the indirect strategy to persuade.
- Write convincing claim request letters.
- Request favors persuasively.
- Present new ideas in persuasive memos.
- Analyze techniques used in sales letters.
- Compose carefully planned sales letters.

The ability to use persuasion skillfully is a primary factor in personal and business success.

he ability to persuade is a key factor in the success you achieve in your business messages, in your career, and in your interpersonal relations. Persuasive individuals are those who present convincing arguments that influence or win over others. Because their ideas generally prevail, these individuals become decision makers—managers, executives, and entrepreneurs. This chapter will examine the techniques for presenting ideas persuasively.

PERSUASIVE REQUESTS

Use persuasion when you must change attitudes or produce action.

Persuasion is necessary when resistance is anticipated or when ideas require preparation before they can be presented effectively. For example, if Kim Owens purchased a new Ford and the transmission repeatedly required servicing, she might be forced to write to Ford's district office asking that the company install a new transmission in her car. Kim's claim letter should be persuasive; she must convince Ford that replacement, not repair, is needed. Routine claim letters, such as those you wrote in Chapter 6, are straightforward and direct. Persuasive requests, on the other hand, are generally more effective when they are indirect. Reasons and explanations should precede the main idea. To overcome possible resistance, the writer lays a logical foundation before the request is delivered. A writing plan for a persuasive request requires deliberate development.

WRITING PLAN FOR A PERSUASIVE REQUEST

Transparency 9.1

- *Opening*—obtains the reader's attention and interest.
- *Persuasion*—explains logically and concisely the purpose of the request and proves its merit.
- *Closing*—asks for a particular action and shows courtesy and respect.

CLAIM REQUEST

The organization of an effective persuasive claim centers on the closing and the persuasion. First, decide what action you want taken to satisfy the claim. Then, decide how you can prove the worth of your claim. Plan carefully the line of reasoning you will follow in convincing the reader to take the action you request. If the claim is addressed to a business, it is generally effective to appeal to the organization's pride in its products and its services. Refer to its reputation for integrity and your confidence in it. Show why your claim is valid and why the company will be doing the right thing in granting it. Most organizations are sincere in their efforts to produce quality products that gain consumer respect.

The most important parts of a claim letter are the sections describing the desired action and the proof that such action is reasonable.

Anger and emotional threats toward an organization do little to achieve the goal of claim letters. Claims are generally referred to a customer service department. The claims adjuster answering the claim probably bears no responsibility for the design, production, delivery, or servicing of the product. An abusive letter may serve only to offend the claims adjuster, thus making it difficult for the claim to be evaluated rationally.

Transparencies 9.2 and 9.3

The most effective claim captures the attention of the reader immediately in the opening and sets up the persuasion that follows. In the body of the claim, you should present convincing reasons to justify the claim. Try to argue without overusing negative words, without fixing blame for the problem, and without becoming emotional. To create the desired effect, arrange the reasons in a logical, orderly manner with appropriate transitions to guide the reader through the persuasion.

Claim letters should avoid negative and emotional words and should not attempt to attribute blame.

Following the persuasion, spell out clearly the desired action in the closing. Remember, the most successful claims are respectful and courteous.

Transparency 9.4

Observe how the claim letter shown in Figure 9.1 illustrates the preceding suggestions. The opening statements secure the reader's attention and at the same time set up the description of events and persuasive arguments to follow. Notice the absence of rancor and harsh words, although the writer probably experienced anger over these events. Notice, too, that the closing rounds out the letter by referring to the opening statement.

FAVOR REQUEST

Asking for a favor implies that you want someone to do something for nothing—or for very little. Common examples are requests for the donation of time, money, energy, name, resources, talent, skills, or expertise. On occasion, everyone needs to ask a favor. Small favors, such as asking a co-worker to lock up the office for you on Friday, can be straightforward

When you anticipate resistance to a favor request, use persuasive techniques.

FIGURE 9.1   Claim Request—Block Style

AMS
ALBANY MOVING & STORAGE

Local   4950 Pretoria Avenue
National   Albany, Georgia 31705
International   (912) 883-3918

January 23, 199x

G. Bendix, Inc.
3350 Peachtree Center
Atlanta, GA 35891

Ladies and Gentlemen

SUBJECT: BUTONE MODEL 150 HOT-WATER HEATING SYSTEM

Gains attention with favorable comments about the company.

Your Butone hot-water heating system appealed to my company for two reasons. First, it promised high-efficiency heat with a 36 percent savings in our heating oil costs. Second, your firm has been in the heating business for forty years, and such a record must indicate a reputation of concern for your customers.

We think that we were right about your heating system. Now we wonder if we're right about your reputation.

Explains events in orderly, logical fashion.

Last September we purchased a Butone oil-fired Model 150 and had it installed in our eight-room office building by your dealer, Pecan Heating Contractors. For two weeks it heated our offices comfortably. One morning, though, we arrived and found our rooms cold. We called Pecan Heating Contractors, and its technician came out to inspect our system. He reported that the automatic ignition device had failed. He replaced it, and the system worked well for two days. Then, on the third day after this repair, a fire developed in the combustion area of the heating unit, destroying the circulating pump and its motor. Technicians from Pecan Heating returned immediately and replaced the entire heating unit.

We assumed this replacement was covered by the system's 5-year warranty. That's why we were surprised two days ago to receive from Pecan Heating Contractors a bill for $255.92 covering installation of the new unit. In a telephone conversation, James Wilkins, of Pecan Heating, said that the warranty covers only replacement of the unit. The cost of the installation is extra.

Argues convincingly that charge is unjustified.

We feel that this charge is unjustified. The fire that destroyed the unit resulted from either a defective unit or faulty servicing by Pecan Heating Contractors. Since we feel responsibility for neither of these conditions, we believe that we should bear no charges. Our insurance carrier shares this view.

Closes with action request that ties in with opening.

Please pay the attached bill or instruct Pecan Heating Contractors to cancel it. This would indicate to us that we were right both about your product and about your reputation.

Sincerely

Pamela Dougherty

Pamela Dougherty
Office Manager

PD:rpw

---

and direct, since you anticipate little resistance. Larger favors generally require careful planning and an indirect strategy. Consider the appeal to a busy executive to serve on a committee to help handicapped children, or to a florist to donate table arrangements for a charity fund-raiser, or to an eminent author to speak before a local library group. In each instance persuasion is necessary to overcome natural resistance.

The letter shown in Figure 9.2 illustrates a poorly conceived favor request. An organization without funds hopes to entice a well-known

Transparencies 9.5 and 9.6

FIGURE 9.2   Weak Favor Request

> Dear Dr. Wickersham:
>
> Would you be willing to speak to the American Personnel Managers Association's regional conference in Boston March 23?
>
> Although we understand that your research, teaching, and consulting must keep you extremely busy, we hope that your schedule will allow you to be the featured speaker at our conference. We are particularly interested in the article you recently published in the *Harvard Business Review*. A number of our members indicated that your topic, "Cost/Benefit Analysis for Human Resources," is something we should learn more about. Perhaps you could select a topic that would be somewhat more practical and not so theoretical, since most of our members are human resources managers.
>
> We have no funds to pay you, but we would like to invite you and your spouse to be our guests at the banquet following the day's sessions.
>
> We hope that you will be able to speak before our group.
>
>   Sincerely,

Ineffective Writing

Provides easy excuse for reader to refuse.

Point of view is writer-centered instead of reader-centered.

Emphasizes negative statement.

Fails to tell reader how to respond.

authority to speak before its regional conference. Such a request surely requires indirectness and persuasion, but this ineffective letter begins with a direct appeal. The reader is given an opportunity to refuse the request before the writer has a chance to present reasons for accepting. The second paragraph also provides an easy opportunity to refuse the request. Moreover, this letter contains little to convince Dr. Wickersham that she has anything to gain by speaking to this group. Finally, the closing suggests no specific action to help her accept, should she be so inclined.

A favor request is doomed to failure if the writer fails to consider its effect on the reader.

Notice, now, how the letter to Dr. Wickersham in Figure 9.3 applies the indirect strategy to achieve its goal. The opening catches her interest and makes her want to read more regarding the reaction to her article. By showing how Dr. Wickersham's interests are related to the organization's, the writer lays a groundwork of persuasion before presenting the request. The request is then followed by reasoning that shows Dr. Wickersham how she will benefit from accepting this invitation. This successful letter concludes with an action closing.

PERSUASIVE MEMO

Within an organization the indirect strategy is appropriate when persuasion is needed in presenting new ideas to management or to colleagues, in requesting action from employees, and in securing compliance with altered procedures. Whenever resistance is anticipated, a sound foundation of reasoning should precede the main idea so that the idea will not be rejected prematurely.

New ideas can be expected to generate resistance, whether they are moving downward as directives from management, moving upward as suggestions to management, or moving laterally among colleagues. Resistance to change is natural. When asked to perform differently or to try something new, some individuals resist because they are lazy. Others resist because they fear failure. Still others resist because they feel threatened—

FIGURE 9.3   Successful Favor Request Letter—Modified Block Style

American Personnel Managers Association
P.O. Box 5893
Boston, Massachusetts 02148
(617) 543-8922

January 4, 199x

Professor Beverly J. Wickersham
Central Texas College
Killeen, TX 76941

Dear Dr. Wickersham:

Grabs attention of reader by appealing to her interests.

Cost/benefit analysis applied to human resources is a unique concept. Your recent article on that topic in the *Harvard Business Review* ignited a lively discussion at the last meeting of the Boston chapter of the American Personnel Managers Association.

Persuades reader that her expertise is valued.

Many of the managers in our group are experiencing the changes you describe. Functions in the personnel area are now being expanded to include a wide range of salary, welfare, benefit, and training programs. These new programs can be very expensive. Our members are fascinated by your cost/benefit analysis that sets up a formal comparison of the costs to design, develop, and implement a program idea against the costs the idea saves or avoids. We'd like to know more about how this can be done.

Softens negative aspects of request with reader's benefits.

The members of our association have asked me to invite you to be the featured speaker March 23 when we hold our annual East Coast regional conference in Boston. About 150 personnel management specialists will attend the all-day conference at the Park Plaza Hotel. We would like you to speak at 2 p.m. on the topic of "Applying Cost/Benefit Analysis in Human Resources Today." Although we cannot offer you an honorarium, we can offer you an opportunity to help human resources managers apply your theories in solving some of their most perplexing problems. You will also be able to meet managers who might be able to supply you with data for future research into personnel functions. In addition, the conference includes two other sessions and a banquet, to which you and a guest are invited.

Ends confidently with specific action to be taken.

Please call me at (617) 543-8922 to allow me to add your name to the program as the featured speaker before the American Personnel Managers Association March 23 at 2 p.m.

Respectfully yours,

Joan Northern

Joan Northern
Executive Secretary

jjo

the proposed changes may encroach on their status or threaten their security. Some individuals resist new ideas because they are jealous of the individual making the proposal.

Whatever the motivation, resistance to new ideas and altered procedures should be expected. You can prepare for this resistance by anticipating objections, offering counterarguments, and emphasizing benefits. Don't assume that the advantages of a new plan are obvious and therefore may go unmentioned. Use concrete examples and familiar illustrations in presenting arguments.

In the memo shown in Figure 9.4, Miguel Ortiz, supervisor, argues for the purchase of new equipment and software. He expects the director to resist this purchase because the director knows little about computing and because the budget is already overextended. Miguel's memo follows the writing plan for a persuasive request. It begins by describing a costly problem in which Miguel knows the reader is interested. To convince the director of the need for these purchases, Miguel must first explain the background of his request. Instead of using generalities, Miguel cites specific examples of how the new scanner and software would function in their company and how much savings it would produce. Miguel also anticipates the limitations of the purchases and discusses their effect on the

FIGURE 9.4   Successful Persuasive Memo

TO: Marla Franklin, Director, Operations   DATE: April 7, 199x

FROM: Miguel Ortiz, Supervisor, Central Services *M. O.*

SUBJECT: REDUCING OVERTIME AND IMPROVING TURNAROUND TIME

Last month we paid nearly $5,400 in overtime to word processing specialists who were forced to work 50- and 60-hour weeks to keep up with the heavy demand for printed documents. Despite this overtime the average turnaround time for documents submitted to Central Services is now five working days.

Captures attention of reader with a problem that can be solved.

Many of the documents submitted to us are already keyed or are in print and must be rekeyed into our word processing system by our operators. For example, some of the engineers in Systems Design bring us rough-draft proposals they have produced on their computers, but their programs are not compatible with ours. Hence, we are forced to rekey the material.

Explains background and rationale before making proposal.

I estimate that we could eliminate at least 40 percent of our overtime and also reduce turnaround time on documents by two days if our operators had two items: (a) a scanner and (b) conversion software. A scanner is an optical character reader that converts printed images to electronic forms. Conversion software makes different word processing programs compatible.

Although these two items will not solve all our problems, they could offer considerable relief. Scanners can read most printed material accurately, but 100 percent accuracy cannot be guaranteed. Some hard-to-read fonts and dark paper backgrounds reduce scanning accuracy. Software conversion programs, too, are not perfect. Only the most popular word processing programs can be converted to our system. Despite these limitations I believe that the addition of a scanner and conversion software promises three significant benefits:

Anticipates objections and answers them.

1. Savings of at least $2,700 in overtime each month by reducing rekeying of printed documents.

2. Reduction of turnaround time from five days to a maximum of three days.

3. Improved morale of word processing specialists.

Summarizes benefits.

For these reasons, I recommend that we purchase a Quad Turbo Scanner, Model 2000, along with Software Labs "Disk Magic" coversion software. The purchase price of these two items, approximately $5,000, will be recovered within one month, as a result of reduced overtime payments.

Delays mention of price until after convincing arguments are presented.

Enclosed are details of the recommended scanner and conversion software. Please give me authorization to submit a purchase order for these two items by June 1 so that Central Services may improve turnaround time before we are asked to begin work on the fiscal reports in July.

Ends with explicit request and provides end dating.

proposal. In the closing Miguel asks for a specific action and provides support documentation to speed his request. He also includes end dating, which prompts the director to act by a certain date.

SALES LETTERS

Direct-mail selling is a rapidly growing, multibillion-dollar industry. The professionals who specialize in direct-mail marketing have made a science of analyzing a market, developing an appropriate mailing list, studying the product, preparing a comprehensive presentation that appeals to the needs of the target audience, and motivating the reader to act. This carefully orchestrated presentation typically culminates in a sales letter accompanied by a brochure, a sales list, illustrations of the product, testimonials, and so forth.

We are most concerned here with the sales letter: its strategy, organization, and appeals. You'll want to learn the secrets of these messages for many reasons. Although the sales letters of big organizations are usually written by professionals, many smaller companies cannot afford such specialized services. Entrepreneurs and employees of smaller businesses may be called on to write their own sales messages. For example, one enterprising graduate started a secretarial service and immediately had to write a convincing letter offering her services. Another employee went to work for a small company that installs security systems. Because of his recent degree (other employees were unsure of their skills), he was asked to draft a sales letter outlining specific benefits for residential customers.

Recognizing and applying the techniques of sales writing can be helpful even if you never write an actual sales letter.

From a broader perspective nearly every letter we write is a form of sales. We sell our ideas, ourselves, and our organizations. Learning the techniques of sales writing will help you be more effective in any communication that requires persuasion and promotion. Moreover, recognizing the techniques of selling will enable you to respond to such techniques more rationally. You'll be a better-educated consumer of ideas, products, and services if you understand how sales appeals are made.

The following writing plan for a sales letter attempts to overcome anticipated reader resistance by creating a desire for the product and by motivating the reader to act.

Transparency 9.7

WRITING PLAN FOR A SALES LETTER

- *Opening*—captures the attention of the reader.
- *Body*—emphasizes a central selling point, appeals to the needs of the reader, creates a desire for the product, and introduces price strategically.
- *Closing*—stimulates the reader to act.

ANALYZING THE PRODUCT AND THE READER

Both the product and the reader require careful analysis before a successful sales letter can be written.

Before implementing the writing plan, it's wise to study the product and the target audience so that you can emphasize features with reader appeal.

To sell a product effectively, learn as much as possible about its construction, including its design, raw materials, and manufacturing process. Study its performance, including ease of use, efficiency, durability, and applications. Consider warranties, service, price, and special appeals. Be knowledgeable not only about your product but also about the competitor's product so you can emphasize your product's strengths against the competitor's weaknesses.

The most effective sales letters are sent to targeted audiences. Mailing lists for selected groups can be purchased or compiled. For example, the manufacturer of computer supplies would find an appropriate audience for its products in the mailing list of subscribers to a computer magazine. By using a selected mailing list, a sales letter writer is able to make certain assumptions about the readers. Readers may be expected to share certain characteristics, such as interests, abilities, needs, income, and so forth. The sales letter, then, can be adapted to appeal directly to this selected group. In working with a less specific audience, the letter writer can make only general assumptions and must use a shotgun approach, hoping to find some appeal that motivates the reader.

A target audience is one that is preselected for characteristics that make it a good market for a particular product.

CAPTURING THE READER'S ATTENTION

Gaining the attention of the reader is essential in unsolicited or uninvited sales letters. In solicited sales letters, individuals have requested information; thus, attention-getting devices are less important.

Attention-getting devices are especially important in unsolicited sales letters.

Provocative messages or unusual typographical arrangements can be used to attract attention in unsolicited sales letters. These messages may be found within the body of a letter or in place of the inside address.

OFFER: Your free calculator is just the beginning!

PRODUCT FEATURE: Your vacations—this year and in the future—can be more rewarding thanks to an exciting new book from National Geographic.

Transparency 9.8

INSIDE-ADDRESS OPENING: We wonder, Mrs. Crain,
                              If You Would Be Interested
                              In Losing 5 Pounds This Week

STARTLING STATEMENT: Extinction is forever. That's why we need your help in preserving many of the world's endangered species.

STORY: On a beautiful late spring afternoon, twenty-five years ago, two young men graduated from the same college. They were very much alike, these two young men. . . . Recently, these men returned to their college for their 25th reunion. They were still very much alike. . . . But there was a difference. One of the men was manager of a small department of [a manufacturing company]. The other was its president.

Other effective openings include a bargain, a proverb, a solution to a problem, a quote from a famous person, an anecdote, and a question.

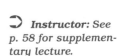 *Instructor: See p. 58 for supplementary lecture.*

APPEALING TO THE READER

Persuasive appeals generally fall into two broad groups: emotional appeals and rational appeals. Emotional appeals are those associated with the senses; they include how we feel, see, taste, smell, and hear. Strategies that arouse anger, fear, pride, love, and satisfaction are emotional. Rational strategies are those associated with reason and intellect; they appeal to the mind. Rational appeals include references to making money, saving money, increasing efficiency, and making the best use of resources.

Emotional appeals relate to the senses; rational appeals relate to reasoning and intellect.

In general, use rational appeals when a product is expensive, long-lasting, or important to health and security. Use emotional appeals when a product is inexpensive, short-lived, or nonessential.

Banks selling checking and savings services frequently use rational appeals. They emphasize saving money in checking fees, earning interest on accounts, receiving free personalized checks, and saving time in opening the account. In contrast, a travel agency selling a student tour to the Mexican Riviera uses an emotional strategy by describing the "sun, fun, rockin' and partying" to be enjoyed. Many successful selling campaigns combine appeals, emphasizing perhaps a rational appeal while also including an emotional appeal in a subordinated position.

EMPHASIZING CENTRAL SELLING POINTS

In sales letters develop one or two central selling points and stress them.

Although a product may have a number of features, concentrate on just one or two of those features. Don't bewilder the reader with too much information. Analyze the reader's needs and tailor your appeal directly to the reader. The letter selling a student tour to the Mexican Riviera emphasized two points:

1. **We see to it that you have a great time.** Let's face it. By the end of the semester, you've earned your vacation. The books and jobs and stress can all be shelved for a while.

2. **We keep our trips cheap.** Mazatlan 1A is again the lowest-priced adventure trip in the entire United States.

The writer analyzed the student audience and elected to concentrate on two appeals: (1) an emotional appeal to the senses (having a good time) and (2) a rational appeal to saving money (paying a low price).

CREATING A DESIRE FOR THE PRODUCT

In convincing readers to purchase a product or service, you may use a number of techniques:

- *Reader benefit.* Discuss product features from the reader's point of view. Show how the reader will benefit from the product:

   You will be able to extend your swimming season by using our new solar pool cover.

- *Concrete language.* Use concrete words instead of general or abstract language:

   Our Mexican tour provides more than just a party. Maybe you've never set eyes on a giant 60-foot saguaro cactus . . . or parasailed 1,000 feet above the Pacific Ocean . . . or watched a majestic golden sunset from your own private island.

- *Objective language.* Avoid language that sounds unreasonable. Overstatements using words like *fantastic, without fail, foolproof, amazing, astounding,* and so forth do not ring true. Overblown language and preposterous claims may cause readers to reject the entire sales message.
- *Product confidence.* Build confidence in your product or service by assuring customer satisfaction. You can do this by offering a free trial, a money-back guarantee, or a free sample, or by providing a guarantee

THE WALL STREET JOURNAL

"It doesn't matter if the salesman convinced you—you just
don't put aluminum siding on a castle, and that's that."

Source: From *The Wall Street Journal.* Reprinted with permission of the Cartoon Features Syndicate, Inc.

warranty. Another way to build confidence is to associate your product with respected references or authorities:

> Our concept of economical group travel has been accepted and sponsored by five city recreation departments. In addition, our program has been featured in *Sunset Magazine,* the *Los Angeles Times,* the *San Francisco Chronicle,* and the *Oakland Tribune.*

- *Testimonials.* The statements of satisfied customers are effective in creating a desire for the product or service:

> A student returning from Mazatlan's cruise last year said, "I've just been to paradise."

INTRODUCING PRICE STRATEGICALLY

If product price is a significant sales feature, use it early in your sales letter. Otherwise, don't mention price until after you have created the reader's desire for the product. Some sales letters include no mention of price; instead, an enclosed order form shows the price. Other techniques for deemphasizing price include the following:

Introduce price early if it is a sales feature; otherwise, delay mentioning it.

- *Show the price in small units.* For instance, instead of stating the total cost of a year's subscription, state the magazine's price in terms of each issue. Or describe insurance premiums in terms of their cost per day.
- *Show how the reader is saving money by purchasing the product.* In selling solar heating units, for example, explain how much the reader will save on heating-fuel bills.
- *Compare your prices with competitors'.* Describe the savings to be realized when your product is purchased.
- *Make your price a bargain.* For instance, point out that the special introductory offer is one-third off the regular price, or the price includes a special discount if the reader acts immediately.

Price can be deemphasized by using one of these five techniques.

- *Associate the price with reader benefits.* Note, for example, that "for as little as $3 a month, you'll enjoy emergency road and towing protection, emergency trip-interruption protection, and nine other benefits."

Notice in Figure 9.5 how price is directly linked to customer benefits. Century Federal Bank opens its promotional letter by telling the reader how much money can be saved on its checking account. This central selling feature is then developed throughout the letter, although the selling points are also mentioned.

FIGURE 9.5   Effective Sales Letter—Modified Block Style

Century Federal Bank

3200 East 30th Avenue, Eugene, OR 97405-3201

Marg Taylor
AVP & Manager
Personal Financial Center

April 3, 199x

Mr. Frank Lawrence
1045 Redwood Drive
Eugene, OR 97431

Dear Mr. Lawrence:

Captures attention with appealing offer.

Why pay $50, $100, or even $150 a year in checking account service charges when Century Federal has the right price for checking—FREE!

Emphasizes central selling point but also introduces other services.

At Century Federal we want your business. That's why we're offering "Totally Free Checking." Compare the cost of your present checking account. We know you'll like the difference. We also have six other personalized checking plans, one of which is certain to be right for you.

Focuses on rational appeals.

In addition to the best price on checking accounts, we provide a variety of investment opportunities and two hassle-free credit-line programs. Once you qualify, you can use your credit line at any time without applying for a new loan each time you need money. With one of our credit-line programs, you can write a check for just about anything, including a vacation, home improvements, major purchases, unexpected medical bills, or investment opportunities.

Suggests specific reader benefits.

If you have not yet heard about Century Federal, you'll find that we have eight convenient locations to serve you.

Makes it easy for reader to open account.

Check out the details of our services described in the enclosed pamphlets. Then check us out by stopping in to open your free checking account at one of our eight convenient locations. You can also open your account by simply filling out the enclosed postage-paid card and returning it to us.

Offers incentive for action before given date.

If you open your Century Federal checking account before June 15, we'll give you 200 free checks and we'll buy back any unused checks you have from your present checking account. Act now to start saving money. We look forward to serving you.

Sincerely yours,

Marg Taylor

Marg Taylor
Accounts Vice President

mt:egh
Enclosures

STIMULATING ACTION

The closing of a sales letter has one very important goal: stimulating the reader to act. A number of techniques help motivate action:

You can encourage the reader to act by applying one or more of these methods.

- *Make the action clear.* Use specific language to tell exactly what is to be done:

    Fill out the enclosed postage-paid card.

    Call this toll-free number.

    Send the enclosed reservation card along with your check.

- *Make the action easy.* Highlight the simple steps the reader needs to take:

    Just use the enclosed pencil to indicate the amount of your gift. Drop the postage-paid card in the mail, and we'll handle the details.

- *Offer an inducement.* Encourage the reader to act while low prices remain in effect. Offer a gift or a rebate for action:

    Now is a great time to join the Chevron Travel Club. By joining now, you'll receive a handsome black and gold-tone electronic calculator and a quartz pen-watch.

- *Limit the offer.* Set a specific date by which the reader must act in order to receive a gift, a rebate, benefits, low prices, or a special offer:

    Act quickly, because I'm authorized to make this special price on solar greenhouses available only until May 1.

- *Make payment easy.* Encourage the reader to send a credit card number or to return a card and be billed later.

Transparencies 9.9 and 9.10

The sales letter shown in Figure 9.6 sounds casual, but it actually required considerable planning on the part of the writer. This letter announces a newsletter of legal tips to help managers avoid conduct that might result in expensive lawsuits. The letter concentrates on a central selling point (the need for current legal information) as it leads up to the action to be taken (returning a reservation form). Notice how the writer uses both emotional and rational appeals. Emotional appeals refer to a fear that managers might accidentally stumble into messy lawsuits. Rational appeals center on the cost of attorneys' fees compared with the low cost of the newsletter. The price of the newsletter subscription is linked with reader benefits, followed by a satisfaction guarantee. In the closing the writer requests action and makes it easy to take. A strategic postscript offers a final incentive: a free gift for prompt action. This letter typifies successful sales letters. It sounds conversational, it offers reader benefits, and it motivates action.

The ability to persuade is a powerful and versatile communication tool. In this chapter you learned to apply the indirect strategy in writing claim letters, making requests, writing sales letters, and overcoming resistance to new ideas. The techniques suggested here will be useful in many other contexts beyond the writing of these business documents. You will find that logical organization of arguments is also extremely effective in expressing ideas orally.

In coming chapters you will learn how to modify and generalize the techniques of direct and indirect strategies in preparing goodwill messages as well as writing short and long reports.

FIGURE 9.6   Successful Sales Letter—Modified Block Style

Legal Services Institute, Inc.
533 Meadowridge Drive
Lynchburg, VA 24503

February 13, 199x

Mr. C. D. Avery, President
Avery Enterprises, Inc.
2043 Powers Ferry
Marietta, GA 30067

Dear Mr. Avery:

Attracts attention with starting statement.

If you had told me a couple of years ago that any time I hired, fired, or appraised an employee I could be facing a million-dollar lawsuit, I'd have said you were crazy.

Just last October, though, I read about an employee who claimed that he had been fired because he had complained that his company had not kept its promises to him. A Wisconsin jury dropped a $12.1 million award in his lap! You're probably as alarmed as I am at the exploding number of lawsuits for hiring discrimination, libel, wrongful termina-tion, sexual harassment, and employee testing. Employees are demanding their rights more than ever, often using the courts to support their claims.

Builds interest with emotional appeals.

As a business owner, you may know about these dangerous litigious topics. But what about all the managers in your company who aren't as knowledgable? How can you train them to avoid stumbling accidentally into expensive lawsuits?

Announces product and creates desire.

The best way to prepare your managers is with our easy-to-read newsletter called the MANAGER'S LEGAL UPDATE. Twice a month, this four-page letter delivers valuable advice to the managers you pick. They will learn to avoid those "red flag" promises, practices, and actions that a hungry lawyer can use to bring legal action against your firm. And with legal fees starting at $200 and $300 an hour, you know how costly it is to defend against any claim. That's where MANAGER'S LEGAL UPDATE can save you thousands of dollars—and at a cost of less than 85 cents a copy.

Associates price with reader benefit.

Makes it easy to respond.

To start your protection immediately, just sign the enclosed reservation form. Fill in the number of copies you want, and return the form in the postage-paid envelope. I'll take care of the rest.

Sincerely,

Winston M. Bacon

Winston M. Bacon, President

WMB:rjt

Motivates action with free gift.

P.S. Respond within ten days and we'll rush you THE EMPLOYER'S LEGAL HAND-BOOK, a special reference book selling for $39.95 in bookstores.

APPLICATION AND PRACTICE—9

Discussion

1. Why is the ability to persuade a significant trait in both business and personal relations?
2. The organization of a successful persuasive claim centers on the reasons and the closing. Why?
3. Should favor requests be written directly or indirectly? Discuss.
4. Why do individuals resist change?

5. Some individuals will never write an actual sales letter. Why is it nevertheless important for them to learn the techniques for doing so?

6. How is a sales letter like a persuasive claim letter? How is it different?

Short Answers

7. In the indirect strategy, what should precede the main idea?
Reasons, explanations, persuasion

8. List at least four examples of favor requests.
Donations of time, money, energy, name, resources, talent, skills, or expertise

9. Name at least eight items a salesperson should know about a product before attempting to sell it.

1. Design	*8. Durability*
2. Raw materials	*9. Reliability*
3. Manufacturing process	*10. Service*
4. Testing	*11. Warranties*
5. Performance applications	*12. Special features*
6. Ease of use	*13. Marketability*
7. Efficiency	*14. Price*

10. The most effective sales letters are sent to what kind of audience?
A targeted or preselected audience

11. What is an unsolicited sales letter? Give an example.
An unsolicited sales letter is one that is not requested. An example is a direct-mail letter selling leather briefcases.

12. What is a solicited sales letter? Give an example.
A solicited sales letter responds to a request for information about a product. An example is a letter answering questions about leasing programs for new cars.

13. List at least five ways to gain a reader's attention in the opening of a sales letter.

1. Typographical arrangements	*7. A bargain*
2. Attractive offer	*8. A proverb*
3. A product feature	*9. Solution to a problem*
4. Inside-address opening	*10. A quote*
5. Startling statement	*11. An anecdote*
6. A story	*12. A question*

14. In selling a product, when are rational appeals most effective?
When the product is expensive, long-lasting, or important to health and security

When are emotional appeals most effective?
When the product is inexpensive, short-lived, or nonessential

15. Name six writing techniques that stimulate desire for a product.
1. Show how the product benefits the reader.
2. Use concrete and objective language.
3. Build product confidence through testimonials.
4. Offer warranties.
5. Give a free trial.
6. Offer a money-back guarantee.

⊃ *Instructor: Writing Improvement Exercises are available on diskette.*

Writing Improvement Exercises

Strategies.   For each of the following situations, check the appropriate writing strategy.

	DIRECT STRATEGY	INDIRECT STRATEGY
16. An appeal for a contribution to Children's World, a charity		✓
17. An announcement that henceforth all dental, health, and life insurance benefits for employees will be reduced		✓
18. A request to another company for verification of employment regarding a job applicant	✓	
19. A letter to a painting contractor demanding payment for replacing ceramic floor tiles damaged by sloppy painters		✓
20. A request for information about an oak desk and computer workstation	✓	
21. A letter to a grocery store asking for permission to display posters advertising a school fund-raising car wash		✓
22. A request for a refund of the cost of a computer program that does not perform the functions it was expected to do		✓
23. A request for a refund of the cost of a hair dryer that stopped working after a month's use (the hair dryer carries a one-year warranty)	✓	
24. An invitation to a prominent author to speak before a student rally		✓
25. A memo to employees describing the schedule and selections of a new mobile catering service	✓	

Transparency Master 9.1

CASE 9-1

···

PERSUASIVE REQUEST LETTER

Analyze the following poorly written persuasive claim and list its major faults. Outline an appropriate writing plan for a persuasive claim. After class discussion, your instructor may ask you to rewrite this message, rectifying its faults. Address your letter to International Copy Services, 1506 West Thomas Road, Phoenix, AZ 85013. Assume that you are writing on your company's letterhead. Use block style.

Ineffective Writing

Gentlemen:

Our Regal compact system copier SP-270F has caused us nothing but trouble since it was installed. It was purchased in September, and repairs have been needed no less than five times since September. This means that we have been without our copier at times when we desperately needed it. Therefore, we want you to replace this copier that won't work and bring us a new unit—or you can refund the amount that it cost when it was purchased.

Just after it was installed, the automatic document feeder jammed. Your technician, after our telephone call, came out to promptly fix it. But we still lost almost a day of copier use. It wasn't long before another repair was needed. In October the document feeder jammed again, and our copies were looking light in appearance. On October 12 your technician made a replacement of parts in the document assembly; the toner apparatus was also cleaned by him. This worked fine for five days. Next the collator jammed. We tried different paper, as recommended by your technician, but it still doesn't work well. In just four months of ownership, that copier has required five repair calls. That means that we have been without a copier a lot of the time. And we are very angry about the time and energy required to have it serviced.

We selected the Regal SP-270F copier because it promised automatic document feeding, that two-sided copies could be made at once and it had automatic collation and fast speed.

Attached please find a copy of our service record with this SP-270F copier. We believed your advertisement that said that Regal made "tough copiers for tough customers." Now I'm getting tough. Call me at 469-2900 immediately because I want action by February 1.

Angrily,

Instructor: See pp. 60–61 in the Instructor's Manual for solutions to 9-1 and 9-2.

1. List at least five faults.
    1. *Fails to use indirect strategy*
    2. *Opens negatively with complaint*
    3. *Places the main idea (replacement or refund) in the first paragraph.*
    4. *Confuses reader with disorganized, incoherent description of events*
    5. *Wastes reader's time with wordy constructions* (attached please find) *and redundancies* (light in appearance, fast speed)
    6. *Makes unclear references with vague pronouns* (it, that, this)

2. Outline a writing plan for a persuasive request.
    See page 177.

CASE 9-2
··

PERSUASIVE REQUEST MEMO

Imagine that you are Dan McMasters, president of Jelly Belly, Inc. The sales of your company's jelly beans have skyrocketed since Kevin King, star of a popular TV show, featured Jelly Bellies on his show. The big problem now is that you can't keep track of your inventories. You need to know how long your jelly beans have been on the shelves of your retailers so that you can replace the candy with fresh inventories when needed. Initially, you kept track of inventories by hand; then you moved to keypunched cards. However, sales are now so great that you can no longer keep adequate records. Your company cannot expand until you solve these inventory control and distribution problems. You believe that a computer-controlled system could be the answer.

Instructor: Case 9-2 is available on diskette.

Transparency Master 9.2

However, Jane Braverton, manager of your Marketing Division, considers herself a people-oriented person, not a machine-oriented person. She's not keen on computers. Jane has been with the company since its inception. She's an excellent manager, and you want to keep her. You must convince her that automating inventory and distribution is essential if the business is to compete today and to grow in the future.

You want her to meet with you and Herman Goltz to begin the process of selecting and implementing a computer hardware and software package to help solve your problems. Since her division is greatly affected, you must have her cooperation. You will give her release time to learn about computer systems. You will work with her, and you will also hire consultants to help. You expect her department to run more efficiently after the system is installed. The overall workload for Jane and her staff should decrease.

Write a memo to Jane discussing your concerns. To get you started, answer these questions.

1. What is the main idea in this message?
   Your company must automate inventory control and distribution functions.

2. What action do you want Jane to take?
   You want her to meet with you to begin planning for automating inventory control and distribution.

3. What strategy should your memo follow?
   Indirect strategy with the main idea delayed until after explanations

4. What are some benefits that Jane will experience as a result of automating her division?
   Her division's work will be accomplished more easily and efficiently. The company's profits will increase, thus improving her future earnings.

5. What objections do you expect Jane to have to your proposal?
   She doesn't have the time or the necessary ability to select or implement a computer system.

6. What counterarguments can you offer to offset her anticipated objections?
   You can give her release time to study computer systems. You can assure her that you will work with her and that you will hire consultants to help her.

CASE 9-3 ....

PERSONAL PERSUASIVE REQUEST

In your own work or organization experience, identify a situation where persuasion is necessary. Should a procedure be altered to improve performance? Would a new or different piece of equipment help you perform your work more efficiently? Do you want to work other hours or perform other tasks? Do you deserve a promotion?

Once you have identified a situation requiring persuasion, write a memo to your boss or organization head. Use actual names and facts. Employ the concepts and techniques in this chapter to help you convince your boss that your idea should prevail. Include concrete examples, anticipate objections, emphasize reader benefits, and end with a specific action to be taken.

CASE 9-4

SALES LETTER ANALYSIS

Select a one-page sales letter that you or a friend has received. (If you are unable to find one, your instructor may be able to help.) Read the letter carefully. Then answer the following questions.

Transparency 9.11

1. At what audience is the letter aimed?
2. Is the appeal emotional or rational? Is the appeal effective? Explain.
3. What techniques capture the reader's attention?
4. Is the opening effective? Explain.
5. Is a central selling point emphasized? Explain.
6. Does the letter emphasize reader benefits? Explain.
7. Is concrete language used?
8. How is confidence in the product or service developed?
9. How is price introduced?
10. What action is to be taken, and how is the reader motivated to take that action?

After class discussion your instructor may ask you to write an improved version of this letter. Implement suggestions from this chapter.

CASE 9-5

PERSONAL SALES LETTER

Identify a situation in your own job or a previous job in which a sales letter is needed. Using suggestions from this chapter, write an appropriate sales letter. Promote a product or service. Use actual names, information, and examples. Make your sales letter as realistic as possible.

Additional Problems

1. Assume you are office manager for First Federal Savings. You have noticed lately that employees are selling things in the office—one person is a cosmetics representative, another shows catalogs of shoes, and one is a part-time Tupperware distributor. You have observed that employees can get very involved in these transactions—on First Fed's time. What policy should the office adopt toward such salesmanship? Should you allow this selling? If so, when? Write a persuasive memo to the staff describing your position.

Remember that you need their cooperation; you don't want to sound like a dictator.

2. Prepare a form letter (see page 209) that you will send to several local or national companies. Address it to the personnel director (by name, if possible). Persuade that individual to send you one or more sample copies of résumés that are typical in this field. Encourage the personnel director to mask any confidential information. Explain that you are interested in the format and content of the résumés since you will be applying for employment shortly. Mail the letters. Share with the class any responses you receive.

3. You are the business manager for Rudolpho's, a producer of gourmet ice cream. Rudolpho's has 12 ice cream parlors in the San Francisco area and a reputation for excellent ice cream. Your firm was approached by an independent ice cream vendor who wanted to use Rudolpho's name and recipes for ice cream to be distributed through grocery stores and drugstores. As business manager you worked with a law firm, Lancomb, Pereigni, and Associates, to draw up contracts regarding the use of Rudolpho's name and quality standards for the product. When you received the bill from Louis Lancomb, you couldn't believe it. The bill itemized 38 hours of attorney preparation, at $300 per hour, and 55 hours of paralegal assistance, at $75 per hour. The bill also showed $415 for telephone calls, which might be accurate because Mr. Lancomb had to converse with Rudolpho's owners, who were living in Manila at the time. Write a persuasive letter to Mr. Lancomb. You doubt that an experienced attorney would require 38 hours to draw up the contracts in question. Perhaps some error was made in calculating the total hours. Moreover, you have checked with other businesses and found that excellent legal advice can be obtained for $150 per hour. Rudolpho's would like to continue using the services of Lancomb, Pereigni, and Associates for future legal business. Such future business is unlikely if an adjustment is not made on this bill. Write a persuasive request to Louis Lancomb, Attorney at Law, Lancomb, Pereigni, and Associates, 2690 Mission Street, San Francisco, CA 94103.

4. The following memo was actually sent (the names have been changed) to cashiers in a retail store persuading them to promote the store's own credit card. Write an improved version of this poor memo.

Ineffective Writing

TO: All Cashiers
FROM: Robert M. Johnson, Manager

Don't forget. *Every* Visa and MasterCharge card user that comes through your checkstand is wasting money! It is your duty (as well as your job responsibility) to explain this to them and to convince them to convert to our Premier Card.

Red pens are to be used to circle Visa and Master Charge fees and this is going to be monitored by the supervisory staff, as well as by security for they check every receipt that leaves the building. Those that fail to circle will be reported to me and to the supervisory staff and corrective action will be taken. If you need a red pen, ask a supervisor. When you close down to go home, leave the red pen in your drawer for the next cashier. We need to boost our Premier sales higher in order to meet company standards, and you are a vital part in helping us attain this.

I need all of you to sign at the bottom stating you have read and understand the policy. Thank you.

5. Your school has no internship program in your field. You realize that work experience is invaluable both to acquaint you with the field and to help you find employment. You write to Marvin Clarkson, personnel manager of The Selby Company, asking him to hire you as an intern. Although you're taking a full load of courses, you feel you could work 12 to 15 hours per week for one semester. You would have to arrange the internship hours around your existing class schedule. Describe your desire to function in a specific capacity, but express your willingness to serve wherever the company can accommodate you. Of course, you expect no remuneration, but you will be receiving up to three units of credit if Selby can take you for one semester. Write a persuasive letter to Marvin Clarkson, Personnel Manager, The Selby Company, 1901 San Antonio Avenue, Houston, TX 77027.

6. As employee relations manager of Blue Cross of California, one of your tasks is to promote Project H.E.L.P. (Higher Education Learning Program), an on-the-job learning opportunity. Project H.E.L.P. is a combined effort of major corporations and the Los Angeles Unified School District. You must find 12 employees who will volunteer as instructors for 50 or more students. The students will spend four hours a week at the Blue Cross Encino facility earning an average of five units of credit a semester. This semester the students will be serving in Medical Review Claims, Word Processing, Corporate Media Services, Library, and Administrative Support departments. Your task is to write a memo to the employees in these departments to encourage them to volunteer. They will be expected to supervise and instruct the students. Employees will receive two hours of release time per week to work with the students. The program has been very successful thus far. School officials, students, and employees alike express satisfaction with the experience and the outcomes. Write a persuasive memo with convincing appeals that will bring you 12 volunteers to work with Project H.E.L.P.

7. You are corresponding secretary of Alpha Psi Omega, your campus business honorary organization. For your installation banquet you have been instructed to invite Donald T. Brannock, personnel director, RWR Corporation, to speak. RWR is a large computer manufacturer in your city, and some graduates from your school are hired by RWR each year. Alpha Psi Omega members are interested in the changes that technology is creating in employment at RWR. They're also eager for advice on the kinds of entry-level jobs at RWR and the skills required for these positions. You know Mr. Brannock is busy, so you want to think of some way to make this invitation appealing. Because RWR encourages its executives to participate in community affairs, you might appeal to his organization's excellent record of civic involvement. By the way, you would also include Mrs. Brannock in this invitation. Provide details of the event. Write a favor request to Donald T. Brannock, Director, Personnel Services, RWR Corporation, 2931 Crosby Street, Stamford, CT 06926.

GRAMMAR/MECHANICS CHECKUP—9

SEMICOLONS AND COLONS

Review Sections 2.16–2.19 in the Grammar/Mechanics Handbook. Then study each of the following statements. Insert any necessary punctuation. Use the delete sign (⌐/) to omit unnecessary punctuation. In the space provided indicate the number of changes you made and record the number of the G/M principle(s) illustrated. (When you replace one punctuation mark with another, count it as one change.) If you make no changes, write *0*. This exercise concentrates on semicolon and colon use, but you will also be responsible for correct comma use. When you finish, compare your responses with those shown below. If your responses differ, study carefully the specific principles shown in parentheses.

_2_ _(2.16a)_	**Example:**	The job of Mr. Wellworth is to make sure that his company has enough cash to meet its obligations**;** moreover**,** he is responsible for locating credit when needed.

_3_ _(2.03, 2.16b)_ 1. Short-term financing refers to a period of under one year; long-term financing, on the other handy, refers to a period of ten years or more.

_2_ _(2.16a)_ 2. Cash resulting from product sales does not come in until December; therefore, our cash flow becomes critical in October and November.

_3_ _(2.01, 2.17a)_ 3. We must negotiate short-term financing during the following months: September, October, and November.

_1_ _(2.17b)_ 4. Some of the large American corporations that offer huge amounts of trade credit are, Ford Motor Company, General Electric Company, Gulf Oil Company, and USX Corp.

_1_ _(2.06a, 2.16b)_ 5. Although some firms rarely, if ever, need to borrow short-term money, many businesses find that they require significant credit to pay for current production and sales costs.

_3_ _(2.03, 2.16a)_ 6. A supermarket probably requires no short-term credit; a greeting card manufacturer, however, typically would need considerable short-term credit.

_3_ _(2.01, 2.17a)_ 7. We offer three basic types of credit: open-book accounts, promissory notes, and trade acceptances.

_9_ _(2.16d, 2.17)_ 8. Speakers at the conference on credit include the following business people: Sheridan Black, financial manager, Lytton Industries; Miriam Minkoff, comptroller, Citibank; and Mark Kendall, legal counsel, Security Federal Bank.

_1_ _(2.05)_ 9. The prime interest rate is set by one or more of the nation's largest banks, and this rate goes up or down as the cost of money to the bank itself fluctuates.

_5_ _(2.16e)_ 10. Most banks are in business to lend money to commercial customers; for example, retailers, service companies, manufacturers, and construction firms.

_2_ _(2.06c, 2.16c)_ 11. Avionics, Inc., which is a small electronics firm with a solid credit rating, recently applied for a loan; but First Federal refused the loan application because the bank was short on cash.

_2_ _(2.06a, 2.17b)_ 12. When Avionics, Inc., was refused by First Federal, its financial managers submitted applications to: Fidelity Trust, Farmers Mutual, and Mountain Federal.

13. The cost of financing capital investments at the present time is very high; therefore, Avionics' managers may elect to postpone certain expansion projects.   <u>2</u>   *(2.16)*

14. If interest rates reach as high as 18 percent, the cost of borrowing becomes prohibitive; and many businesses are forced to reconsider or abandon projects that require financing.   <u>2</u>   *(2.06a, 2.16c)*

15. Several investors decided to pool their resources; then they could find attractive investments.   <u>1</u>   *(2.16b)*

---

1. (3) year; financing, hand, (*2.03, 2.16b*)   3. (3) months: September, October, (*2.10, 2.17a*)
5. (1) money, (*2.06a, 2.16b*)   7. (3) credit: accounts, notes, (*2.01, 2.17a*)   9. (1) banks,
(*2.05*)   11. (3) rating, loan; (*2.06c, 2.16c*)   13. (2) high; therefore, (*2.16*)
15. (1) resources; (*2.16b*)

GRAMMAR/MECHANICS CHALLENGE—9

DOCUMENT FOR REVISION

Transparency 9.12

The following letter has faults in grammar, punctuation, spelling, number form, wordiness, and repetition. Use standard proofreading marks (see Appendix B) to correct the errors. When you finish, your instructor can show you the revised version of this letter.

Ineffective Writing

Poor Letter

October, 199x

Ms. Christie Young

637 Elkhart Street

Aurora, CA 80011

Dear Ms. Young:

Enclosed are copies of this years Sportour ski brochure. This year, in addition to our charter program (which include all our charter trips to the rockies and Europe and canada we are introducing a new program in conjunction with western airlines.

The combination of these 2 programs, offer our customers the most complete ski package we have every created. Value, flexability and variety are all amalgamated in this years program.

Due to the fact that many dates and destinations are all ready begining to fillup please select your trip and complete and fill out the reservation form included in the brochure. Send your deposit of two hundred dollars and forward to the Sportours Main Office as soon as possible.

We invite you to ski with us this comming season, and look forward to serving you, as a special incentive we're taking fifty dollars off the complete package price against the first 25 people who send in there reservations.

Sincerely,

. . . .

10

SPECIAL MESSAGES

IN THIS CHAPTER YOU WILL LEARN TO DO THE FOLLOWING:

- Recognize opportunities for writing goodwill messages.
- Appreciate how special messages can build goodwill.
- Write letters of appreciation, congratulations, and sympathy.
- Write letters of recommendation and introduction.

Instructor: See p.199 for author's suggested lesson plan for Chapter 10.

This chapter presents a diverse group of special messages that require you to adapt the strategies and writing techniques you have learned in previous chapters. Some of the messages convey personal goodwill, and others carry business information of a special nature. None of them has a specific writing plan. You will find, as you progress in your development of the craft of writing, that you are less dependent on writing plans to guide you. Although you will not be provided with detailed writing plans here, we will point out similarities between situations and make suggestions regarding appropriate strategies. This chapter will be helpful not only for its opportunities to adapt strategies but also for the models provided.

GOODWILL LETTERS

Goodwill letters carry good wishes, warm feelings, and sincere thoughts to friends, customers, and employees. These are letters that do not *have* to be written—and often are not written for a number of reasons. Because these letters are not urgent and because words do not come readily to mind, it's easy for writers to procrastinate. Writers may feel an urge to express thanks or congratulations or sympathy, but they put it off until the moment passes. Then it's too late. Yet, there's hardly an individual who doesn't appreciate receiving sincere thanks or words of congratulations. It

Transparency 10.1

199

is human nature to desire social approval: we want to be accepted, remembered, consoled, appreciated, and valued. Although busy or unsure business writers may avoid writing goodwill letters, these messages are worth the effort because they gratify both sender and receiver and because they fulfill important human needs.

Letters that convey social approval satisfy deep human needs for both the sender and the receiver.

Greeting cards and commercial thank-you notes provide ready-made words, but these messages fail to express personal thoughts. When you receive a card, what do you read first—the printed words of the card maker or the penned-in remarks of the sender? The personal sentiments of the sender are always more expressive and more meaningful to the reader than is the printed message.

Transparency 10.2

Goodwill messages are most effective when they are immediate, spontaneous, sincere, and personal. They should follow a direct strategy:

- Identify the situation.
- Include specific details and personal thoughts.
- Close with a forward-looking thought or a concluding remark.

LETTERS OF APPRECIATION

Extend thanks and show appreciation when someone has done you a favor or whenever an action merits praise. Letters of appreciation may be written

Awards and special letters provide recognition, thus developing the goodwill of employees, customers, and others.

to customers for their business, to hosts and hostesses for their hospitality, to colleagues for jobs well done, and to individuals for kindnesses performed. (See Figures 10.1, 10.2, and 10.3.)

FIGURE 10.1   Appreciation for a Customer's Business

Holidays are excellent opportunities for goodwill greetings.

Dear Mrs. Panko:

Staffing your organization with temporary office workers for the past six years has been our pleasure, and we are grateful for your business.

As we begin the new year, I want you to know, Mrs. Panko, that you may continue to count on us for temporaries who are as productive as your permanent personnel. As a regular user of our services, you know how cost-effective it is to keep a lean staff, calling on us to help you fill in with temporaries during peak periods and for special projects.

Thank you for allowing us to send you our qualified temporaries. We appreciate the confidence you have shown in our agency for these past six years, and we look forward to at least six more years of mutually profitable dealings.

Sincerely,

FIGURE 10.2   Letter of Appreciation for Favor

Dear Ms. Blankenship:

Your excellent guided tour of the Communications Services Center at Atlantic Labs was the highlight of the semester for our class.

Your lucid description of the Center's operations and equipment enabled our business communication class to better understand some of the technical applications in this field. We very much appreciated, Ms. Blankenship, learning how authors originate letters and reports using your Dextran central dictation system. Equally interesting was the flow of these documents through the entire production process. Your careful preparation for our group and your painstaking organization of the tour schedule allowed our class to see numerous operations in a short time. Many students commented on your enthusiastic and knowledgeable presentation.

Our trip to Atlantic was entertaining and instructive. We enjoyed the modern interior design, the "urban Eden" of indoor plants and trees, the colorful artwork and furniture, and the lovely employee lounges. Most important, though, we appreciated your tour because it helped bridge the gap between classroom information and real-world applications in the field of communications.

Sincerely,

pc* Mrs. Carmen Sevelas
          Manager, Communication Services

This thank-you letter goes to the employee but a photocopy goes to her supervisor.

Give the reader the spotlight by concentrating on his or her accomplishments.

FIGURE 10.3   Letter of Appreciation for Hospitality

Dear Professor and Mrs. Shelton:

Thanks for inviting me and the other members of our business club to your home for dinner last Saturday.

The warm reception you gave us made the evening very special. Your gracious hospitality, the delicious dinner served in a lovely setting, and the lively discussion following dinner all served to create an enjoyable evening that I will long remember.

We appreciate the opportunity you provided for us students to become better acquainted with each other and with you.

Sincerely,

Thank-you letters generally refer to the fine food, warm hospitality, and good company provided.

LETTERS OF CONGRATULATIONS

Letters of congratulations deliver recognition for special events, such as a promotion, appointment, award, graduation, or significant honor, and also mark personal events, such as an engagement, marriage, anniversary, or birth. These messages contain warmth, approval, and praise. Avoid mechanical phrases like *Congratulations on your promotion. You certainly deserve it.* Try to include personal references and specific details that make your thoughts different from the bland and generalized expressions in greeting cards. Often brief and conversational, congratulatory letters may be handwritten or keyboarded. If a news clipping announced the good news, it's a nice touch to attach the article to your congratulatory letter.

Personalized references and details about the individual distinguish good congratulatory messages from commercial cards.

*pc means "photocopy" and replaces the carbon copy notation (cc).

Successful administrators build cordial employee relations by writing personal letters of appreciation and congratulations (see Figure 10.4).

FIGURE 10.4   Letter Congratulating Employee on Promotion

Dear Pam:

Your promotion to the position of supervisor of Reprographics, Pam, is wonderful news! It seems only yesterday that you were an inexperienced part-time assistant who came to my office with excellent skills, bubbling enthusiasm, and a desire to succeed.

We missed you when you left our department, but we take great pride in your accomplishments and wish you every success in your new position.

Sincerely,

LETTERS OF SYMPATHY

A letter of sympathy should console the reader, point out virtues in the loved one, and express willingness to help.

Grief is easier to bear when we know others care. Whatever the misfortune, show your concern with sympathetic words. Depending on the situation, express the loss that you feel, console the reader, and extend your willingness to help in any way possible. You'll want to recognize virtues in the loved one and assure the reader that he or she is not alone in this unhappy moment. If you need ideas regarding what to say in a message of sympathy, examine the model here. Inspiration can also be gleaned from the thoughts expressed in commercially prepared cards. Study the cards, adapt some of the ideas, and then write your own individual message.

Figure 10.5 shows a letter written by a manager to a division secretary who lost her husband.

FIGURE 10.5   Letter of Sympathy

Dear Jane,

We were deeply saddened to learn of your loss. Although words are seldom adequate to express sympathy, I want you to know that I count myself among your many friends who share your grief and understand the profound loss that you are experiencing.

Henry's kind nature, his patience, and his devotion to you were apparent to all. He will be missed. If there is any way that we may ease your sorrow, you know that we are here.

Sincerely,

SPECIAL INFORMATION LETTERS

Another group of special letters employing the direct strategy includes messages that introduce individuals and that ask for or offer recommendations.

FIGURE 10.6   Letter of Introduction

Dear Fred:

Miss Natalie Kienzler, the daughter of one of my closest friends, will soon be moving to Hartford. Natalie just graduated from Lane Community College in Eugene, Oregon, and she seeks employment in a law firm.

As an attorney in Hartford, Fred, you may have some suggestions for her when she arrives and begins her job search. I've given her your telephone number and encouraged her to call you.

You have my sincere appreciation for any assistance you can extend to Natalie.

Cordially,

LETTERS OF INTRODUCTION

On occasion, a letter of introduction, such as the one in Figure 10.6, is helpful to expedite social or business activities or to reduce red tape, especially when an individual is far from home. Such letters establish a person's character or status and are supported by the writer's character or status. They may be written for friends, employees, or business acquaintances. In a letter of introduction, (1) identify your relationship, (2) explain why you are writing, (3) request help, and (4) express appreciation.

A letter of introduction should identify the writer's relationship with the subject, explain the reason for writing, ask for assistance, and convey thanks.

LETTERS REQUESTING RECOMMENDATIONS

When you apply for employment, for admission to special programs, or for acceptance to some social organizations, you may need to request letters of recommendations.

Naturally, before you list anyone as a reference, you will ask for permission. This is not only courteous but also prudent. By offering the opportunity to accept or refuse, you can find individuals who will write favorable recommendations.

Always ask permission before listing someone as a reference.

Figure 10.7 shows a letter asking for permission to list an instructor as a reference. Notice that the writer uses a persuasive strategy, with explanations and kind words preceding the request. The writer also makes it easy for the receiver to agree to the request by including an addressed postcard.

If an instructor or someone else agrees to write a recommendation, you can assist that person by supplying a résumé, data sheet, or fact sheet. If you know the position for which you are applying, furnish specifics about what the job requires and what you would like the recommender to cover. Your recommender wants to help you succeed. Give that person details about the job requirements and your qualifications. For example, if the job description states "must have strong interpersonal skills and excellent written and oral communication skills," tell your recommenders of these specifications. Also provide concrete examples explaining how you feel that you meet the specifications so that your recommenders can write a targeted recommendation.

Help your recommender by supplying data about the job and about you.

FIGURE 10.7   **Letter Requesting Permission for Recommendation**

Opens with compli-
ment and
explanation.

Dear Professor Earle:

Your course in retail merchandising was my introduction to the field, and your instruction provided an excellent background in this career area. Because you know this field well and because you also know my work as a student, may I use your name as a reference when I apply for employment?

Provides informa-
tion to help reader
to comply with
request.

As I will complete my course work at Heald Business College in June, I will be looking for employment shortly. Being able to list your name as a reference would assist my efforts greatly. Enclosed is a fact sheet listing information that may be helpful to you when you write about me.

Expresses apprecia-
tion and supplies
postcard for quick
reply.

I am grateful to you both for the excellent foundation you provided in merchandising and for any help you can provide in my job search. Please indicate your willingness to serve as a reference by mailing the enclosed postage-paid card.

Sincerely,

LETTERS OF RECOMMENDATION

Transparencies
10.3–10.5

A letter of recommendation evaluates an individual. Recommendations may be written to nominate people for awards and for membership in organizations. Most often, however, they are written by employers to appraise the performance of current or past employees. As you progress in your career into supervisory and management roles, you can expect to write such recommendations.

You'll be expected to
write recommenda-
tions as you pro-
gress in your career.

In today's litigious times, letters of recommendation can represent a real danger zone. The accompanying box describes some of the problems and provides specific guidelines that every business writer should follow.

If you decide to write a letter of recommendation for a job applicant, ask the candidate to supply you with personal and professional data. Request a data sheet or a résumé, and ask what information the applicant wants emphasized.

Recommendations often have three parts: opening, body, and conclusion. In the opening of an employment recommendation, you should give the name of the candidate and the position sought, if it is known. State that your remarks are confidential, and suggest that you are writing at the request of the applicant. Describe your relationship with the candidate, as shown here:

The opening of a
recommendation
names the candi-
date, states that the
message is confi-
dential, and
describes your
relationship.

Ms. Cindy Rosales, whom your organization is considering for the position of media trainer, requested that I submit confidential information on her behalf. Ms. Rosales worked under my supervision for the past two years in our Video Training Center.

Letters that recommend individuals for awards may open with more supportive statements, such as *I'm very pleased to nominate Robert Walsh for the Employee-of-the-Month award. For the past sixteen months, Mr. Walsh served as staff accountant in my division. During that time he distinguished himself by . . .*

DANGER ZONE: LETTERS OF RECOMMENDATION

Many companies today, fearing lawsuits, prohibit their managers from recommending ex-employees. Instead, when these companies are asked about former employees, they provide only the essentials, such as date of employment and position held. Employers are gun-shy because former employees have sued—and won—charging defamation of character. Letters of recommendation carrying negative statements can damage reputations, thus preventing former employees from gaining employment.

Yet, companies that no longer allow recommendations to be written for former employees face still another legal problem. Because silence can lead to bad hiring decisions, former employers can be sued for withholding pertinent information (if, for example, a past employer did not reveal information about a child molester who applied for work with a school).

Despite all the news about employment lawsuits, research suggests that the fear of litigation over recommendations is exaggerated. In fact, the number of defamation suits that went to trial between 1965 and 1990 actually declined, and the average monetary award decreased.[1]

Most businesspeople today are still writing recommendations because they recognize the value of such messages in conveying personnel data. Yet, they are cautious in writing them. Observing the following guidelines can help you stay out of trouble:

- *Write only in response to requests.* Don't volunteer information, particularly if it's negative.
- *State that your remarks are confidential.* While such a statement does not prevent legal review, it does suggest the intentions of the writer.
- *Provide only job-related information.* Avoid commenting on behavior or activities away from the job.
- *Avoid vague or ambiguous statements.* Keep in mind that imprecise, poorly explained remarks *(she left the job suddenly)* may be made innocently but could be interpreted quite differently.
- *Supply specific evidence for any negatives.* Support any damaging information with verifiable facts.
- *Stick to the truth.* Avoid making any doubtful statements. Truth is always a valid defense against libel or slander.

The body of an employment recommendation letter should describe the applicant's job performance and potential. Employers are particularly interested in such traits as communication, organizational, and people-skills, ability to work both with a team and independently, honesty, dependability, ambition, loyalty, and initiative. In describing these traits, though, be sure to back them up with evidence. One of the biggest weaknesses in letters of recommendation is that writers tend to make global, nonspecific statements *(He was careful and accurate* versus *He completed eight financial statements monthly with about 99 percent accuracy).* Employers prefer definite, task-related descriptions:

The body describes the applicant's job performance and characteristics.

Try to provide specifics rather than generalities.

> As a training development specialist, Ms. Rosales demonstrated superior organizational and interpersonal skills. She started as a Specialist I, writing scripts for interactive video modules. After six months she was promoted to

team leader. In that role she supervised five employees who wrote, produced, evaluated, revised, and installed 14 computer/videodisc training courses over a period of eighteen months.

Be especially careful to support any negative comments with verification (not *He was slower than other customer service reps* but *He answered 25 calls an hour, while most service reps average 40 calls an hour*). In reporting deficiencies be sure to *describe* behavior *(Her last two reports were late and had to be rewritten by her supervisor)* rather than *evaluate* it *(She is unreliable and her work is careless)*.

Provide an overall evaluation in the conclusion.

In the final paragraph of a letter of recommendation, you should offer an overall evaluation. Indicate how you would rank this person in relation to others in similar positions. Many managers add a statement indicating whether they would rehire the applicant, given the chance. If you are strongly supportive, summarize the candidate's best qualities. In the closing you might also offer to answer questions by telephone. Such a statement, though, could suggest that the candidate has weak skills and that you will make damaging statements orally but not in print. Here's how our sample letter might close:

> Ms. Rosales is one of the most productive employees I have supervised. I would rank her in the top 10 percent of all the media specialists with whom I have worked. Were she to return to Bridgeport, we would be pleased to rehire her. If you need additional information, call me at (517) 443-9902.

General letters of recommendation, written when the candidate has no specific position in mind, often begin with the salutation TO PROSPECTIVE EMPLOYERS. More specific recommendations, to support applications to known positions, address an individual. When the addressee's name is unknown, consider using the simplified letter format, shown in Figure 10.8, which avoids a salutation.

Figure 10.8 illustrates a complete letter of recommendation for employment. After naming the applicant and the position sought, the letter describes the applicant's present duties. Instead of merely naming positive qualities *(personable, superior people skills, works well with a team, and creative)*, the writer demonstrates these attributes with specific examples and details.

The following list summarizes suggestions for writing effective letters of recommendation for employment. Notice how many of these topics were covered in the letter of recommendation in Figure 10.8.

- Identify the reason for writing.
- Suggest the confidentiality of the recommendation.
- Establish your relationship with the applicant.
- Identify the length of employment and job duties, if relevant.
- Describe the applicant's professional and personal qualities.
- Describe the applicant's relations with others.
- Include specific details and examples that illustrate the applicant's personality and performance.
- Compare the applicant with others in his or her field.
- Offer an overall rating of the applicant.
- Summarize the significant attributes of the applicant.
- Draw a conclusion regarding the recommendation.

Even recommendations that are not about employment cover many of the preceding points. The letter in Figure 10.9 recommends an employee for an award. It does not, however, mention confidentiality. In this

**FIGURE 10.8   Letter of Recommendation for Employment—
Simplified Style**

St. Elizabeth's Hospital
4230 North Clark Street
Chicago, Illinois 60640

January 9, 199x

Director, Human Resources
MedicPlan Health Services
5440 Memorial Highway
Tampa, FL 33634

RECOMMENDATION OF GREGORY M. MAY

At the request of Gregory M. May, I submit this confidential information in support of his application for the position of assistant director of your Human Resources Department. Mr. May served under my supervision as assistant director of Guest Relations at St. Elizabeth's Hospital for the past four years.

Mr. May was in charge of many customer service programs for our 550-bed hospital. A large part of his job involved monitoring and improving patient satisfaction. Because of his personable nature and superior people skills, he got along well with fellow employees, patients, and physicians. His personnel record includes a number of "Gotcha" citations, given to employees caught in the act of performing exemplary service.

Mr. May works well with a team, as evidenced by his participation on the steering committee to develop our "Service First Every Day" program. His most significant contributions to our hospital, though, came as a result of his own creativity and initiative. He developed and implemented a patient hotline to hear complaints and resolve problems immediately. This enormously successful telephone service helped us improve our patient satisfaction rating from 7.2 last year to 8.4 this year. That's the highest rating in our history, and Mr. May deserves a great deal of the credit.

We're sorry to lose Mr. May, but we recognize his desire to advance his career. I am confident that his resourcefulness, intelligence, and enthusiasm will make him successful in your organization. I recommend him without reservation.

Suzanne M. Lindsey

SUZANNE M. LINDSEY, SUPERVISOR, GUEST RELATIONS

SML:egi

Identifies applicant, cites confidentiality, and tells relationship of writer.

Supports general qualities with specific details.

Describes and interprets accomplishments.

Summarizes main points and offers evaluation.

instance the writer did not consider her comments to be private; she would not object if her letter were shown to others or published.

FORM AND GUIDE LETTERS

Form letters are prewritten, printed messages used to deliver repetitious and routine information. To save the expense of composing, transcribing, and printing individual letters, many organizations prepare standardized form letters for recurring situations. Form letters contain blanks for such variables as names and addresses, dates, balances, and other specific

Form letters contain blanks to be filled in.

FIGURE 10.9   Recommendation for Award

TO: Awards Selection Commitee   DATE: April 12, 199x

FROM: Cinda Skelton, Manager *C·S.*
             Information Services

SUBJECT: RECOMMENDATION OF KELLY MCKINLEY

It is with great pleasure that I recommend Kelly McKinley for the Employee of the Year award.

Kelly has been employed by First National Bank in the Word Processing Division for nearly five years. For the past three years, I have been able to observe her performance carefully when she worked first as an Administrative Secretary I and later as an Administrative Assistant II in my division.

Kelly's excellent language skills and keyboarding ability enable her to turn out documents rapidly and accurately. Because of her superior skills in transcribing dictated material, she is in great demand. Kelly also demonstrates genuine interest in and aptitude for the many kinds of equipment she has been required to operate. She is so knowledgeable that I asked her to serve on the selection commitee when a new word processing system was reviewed recently. While serving on this committee, Kelly suggested a new method for coding and distributing work to our secretaries. Using Kelly's plan, the secretaries now enjoy greater variety in their work tasks and the supervisor can track the distributed tasks more efficiently.

In addition to her keyboarding, transcribing, and problem-solving skills, Kelly interacts well with her superiors and with her fellow workers. Her sunny disposition, flexible attitude, and cheerful outlook make her a very pleasant person with whom to work.

I rank Kelly among the top 2 percent of all the employees I've ever supervised. Her skills are outstanding; her work, excellent; and her attitude, exemplary. Few employees have ever deserved to be named Employee of the Year more than Kelly McKinley.

Identifies reason for writing.

Establishes relationship with applicant.

Describes candidate's skills and professional accomplishments with specific details.

Describes personal attributes.

Compares candidate with others in her field and offers an overall rating.

---

data. Form letters are efficient for sales messages, personnel policy announcements, procedural explanations for customers and suppliers, order acknowledgments, and other repetitive information.

Guide letters use prewritten sentences and paragraphs but, unlike form letters, are individually printed. Although somewhat more personalized, guide letters serve the same functions as form letters. Insurance companies, for example, send thousands of guide letters to policyholders to answer routine questions regarding their coverage. Rather than compose individual responses, company representatives select appropriate paragraphs from a book of ready-made answers and instruct a transcriptionist to use these paragraphs in preparing a letter on word processing equipment.

Form and guide letters unquestionably save time and money. Well-written, repetitive messages used appropriately are expedient and accepted by readers. Poorly written or misused letters, on the other hand, are doubly offensive. Readers' feelings are hurt because they are treated

Guide letters are individually typed, but they are composed of prewritten sentences and paragraphs.

When used properly, form and guide letters are efficient and cost-effective.

mechanically, and they are also confused because a letter did not apply to them or did not answer their questions.

Word processing software makes the preparation and processing of form and guide letters simple. If you decide to use this means of delivering messages, follow these guidelines:

- Be certain that your form and guide letters are appropriate to the situation for which they will be used.
- Compose your letters so that they are responsive and yet require insertion of a minimum number of variables.
- Test your form and guide letters over a long period to see if they are effective.
- Revise your letters based on reader reactions.

The guide letter in Figure 10.10 shows how repetitive messages can be tailored to individual circumstances by inserting variable data in the places provided. Word processing software merges a shell document with variable data to produce personalized letters quickly and economically.

FIGURE 10.10   Repetitive Letter with Variables

(Name) _____

(Address) _____

_____

Dear _____ :

We appreciate your interest in our English/American study program offered to Japanese students. The enclosed pamphlet describes the program in detail and shows pictures of students who have participated in the past.

In brief, our organization, Connections International, supplies transportation, tours, and cultural/social programs for Japanese students coming to America to study the English language and American culture.

Our next group is scheduled to arrive _____, and the tentative cost is _____ per student per week. This payment covers transportation, travel, and entertainment as outlined in the enclosed pamphlet. An advance payment of _____ at least three weeks in advance of departure is required. This payment is necessary in order to set the program in operation, retain proper vehicles, and make necessary hotel and lodging reservations. This deposit will be deducted from the total payment for the group.

Thank you very much for considering the cultural immersion programs of Connections International. We look forward to providing warm and rewarding experiences for your students.

Sincerely,

APPLICATION AND PRACTICE—10

Discussion

1. Why do we frequently put off writing goodwill letters?
2. Why write a letter of sympathy or congratulations when a greeting card will accomplish the same end?
3. Under what circumstances would a letter of introduction be appropriate?
4. Why should an applicant ask permission before listing an individual's name as a reference?
5. As a means of screening candidates, are letters of recommendation a valid source of information?

Short Answers

6. In goodwill messages the writer typically covers what three areas?
   1. *Identifies the situation*
   2. *Includes specific details and personal thoughts*
   3. *Closes with a forward-looking thought or concluding remark*

7. Name three instances when letters of appreciation are appropriate.
   1. *To customers in appreciation of their business*
   2. *To hosts and hostesses in appreciation of their hospitality*
   3. *To individuals for kindnesses performed*

8. Why should a copy of a letter of appreciation be sent to an employee's supervisor?
   Words of praise regarding an employee's work should be shared with the supervisor so that the employee receives just credit and reward.

9. What four kinds of information or topics can you include in a letter of sympathy?
   1. *Express the loss you feel.*
   2. *Console the reader.*
   3. *Recognize virtues in the loved one.*
   4. *Extend your willingness to help.*

10. Name three instances when letters of recommendation, other than for employment, might be written.
    1. *To nominate individuals for awards*
    2. *To support applications for memberships*
    3. *To admit individuals to special programs*

11. What six guidelines can help you stay out of dangerous territory in writing employment letters of recommendation?
    1. *Write only in response to requests.*
    2. *State that your remarks are confidential.*
    3. *Provide only job-related information.*
    4. *Avoid vague or ambiguous statements.*
    5. *Supply specific evidence for any negatives.*
    6. *Stick to the truth.*

12. List ten suggestions regarding information to be included in a letter of recommendation.

 1. *Identify the reason for writing.*
 2. *Suggest the confidentiality of the recommendation.*
 3. *Establish the relationship with the applicant.*
 4. *Describe the applicant's professional and personal qualities.*
 5. *Describe the applicant's relations with others.*
 6. *Include specific details and examples that illustrate the applicant's personality and performance.*
 7. *Compare the applicant with others in his or her field.*
 8. *Offer an overall rating of the applicant.*
 9. *Summarize the significant attributes of the applicant.*
 10. *Draw a conclusion regarding the recommendation.*

13. How can the writer of a letter of recommendation avoid generalities?

Include specific examples illustrating a candidate's personal and professional attributes. Instead of saying Tim is innovative, provide an example of Tim's method of indexing customer orders.

14. Most goodwill letters would follow which strategy, direct or indirect?

Direct

15. How are form letters different from guide letters?

Form letters are prewritten, printed messages used to deliver repetitious and routine information. Guide letters use prewritten sentences and paragraphs but are individually printed.

CASE 10-1

EMPLOYMENT RECOMMENDATION

Assume that you are Ross Neil, manager of Builder's City. Alan B. Khory, one of your favorite department managers, has now completed his college education and will be leaving the store. Mr. Khory asks you to write a recommendation for him to enter a management trainee program for a large retailer. You know that he is a quiet, unassertive individual; but he has been an excellent hardware manager for you these past three years.

You ask Mr. Khory to refresh your memory about his performance at Builder's City. He reminds you that he started as a clerk and became department manager at the Winnetka store within six months, while at the same time working toward a college degree. His department has five employees. Within his department he tried to streamline operations. He reduced crowded displays so that the store wasn't so cluttered. He tried to increase inventory turnarounds so that fewer duplicate items were stored in the retail display area. He solved some problems that increased sales and, of course, increased profits. When the new computerized inventory system was introduced, he was very interested in it; his department was operational long before some others.

You feel that Mr. Khory has been one of your most enterprising and responsible department managers. You hate to lose him, but you can understand his desire to achieve his long-term goal in administrative management. In your letter you want to show that he has those traits

Instructor: See pp. 64-65 in the Instructor's Manual for solutions to 10-1 and 10-2.

Instructor: Case 10-1 is available on diskette.

Transparency Master 10.1

that are necessary to be a good manager. Your opinion is that he will be an excellent management trainee. Instead of saying that Mr. Khory is able to solve problems and possesses initiative, you want to show how he demonstrates these qualities. You also want to present a fair picture. You feel that you should mention that Mr. Khory is quiet, though he gets along well both with customers and with those employees that he supervises. He was, after all, responsible for training all new employees hired for the hardware department. He was also responsible for planning a work schedule that kept the employees happy and provided adequate sales coverage.

Before you begin writing this letter of recommendation, outline a plan. The information presented here is unorganized and poorly expressed. Improve it. Add any realistic data necessary to create a good letter. Conclude your letter with a statement regarding the potential success of Mr. Khory. Use block style. Address your letter to Ms. Jane Bennett, Personnel Director, Federated Stores, Inc., 3900 East Carson Street, Long Beach, CA 90808.

Transparency Master 10.2

C A S E 10 - 2

LETTER OF APPRECIATION

You are genuinely appreciative of the care shown by Eleanore Chu, R.N., for your bedridden mother over the past two years. You decide to send her a box of chocolates and the following note:

> Dear Eleanore:
>
> Thanks for everything you have done for Mother. We really appreciate your visits over the past two years. You helped us through some very difficult times. Thanks again for your help.
>
> Most sincerely,

Then you reconsider. You decide to write a longer letter that expresses your gratitude and also lets her employer know what an outstanding employee she is. Here are some facts you should include in your letter. Nurse Chu not only took care of your mother's medical needs but also taught you how to care for your mother. She was enthusiastic and always had lots of cheerful conversation; everyone felt better when she visited. She made suggestions and even gave you demonstrations of professional techniques for easing your mother's discomfort. The entire family appreciated Ms. Chu's compassion and concern for your mother. She visited for two years. During that time your mother's condition improved, and now it has stabilized. You feel that she is an extraordinary nurse and an excellent representative of her employer, HomeCare, Inc.

Write the letter to Eleanore Chu, R.N., HomeCare, Inc., 2105 East Henrietta Road, Rochester, NY 14620. Use a modified block style. Add any necessary information. Be sure that her employer, Dr. Chandler H. Alexander, President, HomeCare, Inc., is informed of your praise.

CASE 10-3

LETTER OF SYMPATHY

Assume that the spouse of a colleague or friend has died. Write a letter of sympathy. Include enough detail to make your letter significantly different from greeting card messages.

CASE 10-4

LETTER OF APPRECIATION

Write a letter of appreciation to your boss (supervisor, manager, vice president, president, or chief executive officer) and his or her spouse. Assume that you and other members of your immediate staff were entertained at an elegant dinner during the winter holiday season. Include specific details that make your letter personal, sincere, and concrete.

CASE 10-5

REQUEST FOR RECOMMENDATION

Write to an instructor or a previous employer asking for permission to use that individual as a reference.

CASE 10-6

LETTER OF RECOMMENDATION

You are about to leave your present job. When you ask your boss for a letter of recommendation, to your surprise he tells you to write it yourself and then have him sign it. [Actually, this is not an unusual practice today. Many businesspeople find that employees are very perceptive and accurate when they evaluate themselves.] Use specifics from a current or previous job. If you have not worked, interview a fellow student. Assume that you are the student's instructor; write a letter of recommendation for the student.

Additional Problems

1. As corresponding secretary of Alpha Psi Omega, campus business honorary organization, write to Donald T. Brannock, thanking him for the informative and entertaining talk he presented at the installation banquet (see Chapter 9, page 196, Additional Problem No. 7). Provide details. Send to the RWR employee newsletter a copy of your letter and a photograph of Mr. Brannock delivering his speech before your group.

2. Dirk Sondberg, a part-time worker in your department for the past three years, has just completed the requirements for a B.S. in accounting. Although he will probably be leaving, you are very happy for him. Write a letter of congratulations.

3. The mother of one of your coworkers died after a lengthy illness. Death was inevitable, but your friend was devastated. Write a letter of condolence.

4. One of your instructors has been nominated for a teaching award. Selected students have been asked to write letters in support of the nomination. Write a letter recommending an instructor of your choice to Professor Thomas Watkins, Teaching Award Committee, School of Business.

5. As office manager of the law firm of Ernst, Katz, and Ernst, you have been asked to write a letter describing the service of Wendy White, who is moving to another city with her husband. Wendy has been a fine legal secretary, and you are happy to accommodate her. Since she has not asked you to address the letter to a specific individual, write an undirected letter of recommendation.

6. After finishing the course of instruction at your school, you have taken a job in your field. One of your instructors was especially helpful to you when you were a student. This instructor also wrote an effective letter that was instrumental in helping you obtain your job. Write a letter thanking your instructor.

7. Write a form or guide letter to selected students at your college. These students have filled out applications to graduate, but a computer search of their records indicates that they are missing some requirement. Leave a blank space to fill in the missing requirement(s). Tell these students that a mistake may have been made; perhaps their records have an error or are not up to date. Regardless, the students must come in for a conference with a records officer. Since time is limited, the conferences have already been scheduled. Leave a blank space for the date of the conference to be filled in for each student.

GRAMMAR/MECHANICS CHECKUP—10

POSSESSIVES

Review Sections 2.20–2.22 in the Grammar/Mechanics Handbook. Then study each of the following statements. Underscore any inappropriate form. Write a correction in the space provided and record the number of the G/M principle(s) illustrated. If a sentence is correct, write *C*. When you finish, compare your responses with those provided below. If your answers differ, study carefully the principles shown in parentheses.

years'   (2.20b)   **Example:** In just two <u>years</u> time, the accountants and managers devised an entirely new system.

Mr. Wilson's (2.20a;
         2.21)   1. Two supervisors said that <u>Mr. Wilsons</u> work was excellent.

year's   (2.20a)   2. In less than a <u>years</u> time, the offices of both attorneys were moved.

weeks'   (2.20b)   3. None of the employees in our Electronics Department had taken more than two <u>weeks</u> vacation.

4. All the secretaries agreed that Ms. <u>Lanhams</u> suggestions were practicable.

Lanham's   *(2.21)*

5. After you obtain your <u>boss</u> approval, send the application to Personnel.

boss's   *(2.20b)*

6. We tried to sit at our favorite <u>waitress</u> station, but all her tables were filled.

waitress's   *(2.20b)*

7. Despite <u>Harold</u> grumbling, his wife selected two bonds and three stocks for her investments.

Harold's   *(2.22)*

8. The apartment owner requires two <u>months</u> rent in advance from all applicants.

months'   *(2.20b)*

9. Four <u>companies</u> buildings were damaged in the fire.

companies'   *(2.20b)*

10. In one <u>months</u> time we hope to be able to complete all the address files.

month's   *(2.20a)*

11. Only one <u>ladies</u> car had its engine running.

lady's   *(2.20a)*

12. One <u>secretaries</u> desk will have to be moved to make way for the computer.

secretary's   *(2.20a)*

13. Several <u>sellers</u> permits were issued for two years.

sellers'   *(2.20b)*

14. <u>Marks</u> salary was somewhat higher than <u>David</u>.

Mark's David's   *(2.20a)*

15. <u>Lisas</u> job in accounts receivable ends in two months.

Lisa's   *(2.20a)*

---

1. Mr. Wilson's (*2.20a, 2.21*)   3. weeks' (*2.20b*)   5. boss's (*2.20b*)   7. Harold's (*2.22*)
9. companies' (*2.20b*)   11. lady's (*2.20a*)   13. sellers' (*2.20b*)   15. Lisa's (*2.20a*)

GRAMMAR/MECHANICS CHALLENGE—10

DOCUMENT FOR REVISION

The following letter has faults in grammar, punctuation, spelling, number form, wordiness, and word use. Use standard proofreading marks (see Appendix B) to correct the errors. When you finish, your instructor can show you the revised version of this letter.

Transparency 10.6

Ineffective Writing

Poor Letter

October 4, 199x

Ms. Roxanne Waters

Human Resources Department

Travelers Investment Corporation

Briedgeport, CT 08606

Dear Ms. Waters:

This is to inform you that Mr. Darrell Dix who you are considering for a systems' programmer position, ask me to submit confidential information, on his behalf.

I had responsibility for supervision of Mr. Dix for the passed two years, when he worked as a part time computer technician in our computer users center. In assisting our employees who use computers solve their computing problems; his computer expertise and creativity were demonstrated.

Mr. Dix excepted direction easily, but could also work independent when necessary. For example when I ask him to bring about the organization of our software storage; he did a good job with no supervision whatsoever.

Of all the technicians we have employed Mr. Dix ranks among the top 1/3. Its a pleasure to reccomend him; and I feel certain that he will be successful as a systems programer.

Sincerly,

· ·

V

REPORTING DATA

11

INFORMAL REPORTS

IN THIS CHAPTER YOU WILL LEARN TO DO THE FOLLOWING:

- Gather data from four primary sources to write informal business reports.
- Organize report data deductively or inductively.
- Present data objectively to gain credibility.
- Write information and recommendation reports.
- Write justification and progress reports.
- Write proposals and minutes of meetings.
- Write summaries and to-file reports.

⊃ *Instructor: If you would like to assign a long report (but not necessarily a formal report), see the author's sugges- tion on p. 2. For author's suggested lesson plan for Chapter 11, see p. 67.*

Informal reports are relatively short (under ten pages) and are usually written in memo or letter format.

Like letters and memos, reports play a significant role in delivering information within and among organizations. You can learn to write good reports by examining basic techniques and by analyzing appropriate models. In this chapter we'll concentrate on infor- mal reports. These reports tend to be short (usually under ten pages), use memo or letter format, and are personal in tone.

EIGHT KINDS OF INFORMAL REPORTS

In this chapter we'll consider eight categories of informal reports fre- quently written in business. In many instances the boundaries of the cat- egories overlap; distinctions are not always clear-cut. Individual situations, goals, and needs may make one report take on some charac- teristics of a report in another category. Still, these general categories help beginning writers get started. They are presented here in a brief overview. Later in the chapter they will be illustrated and discussed in more detail.

Transparency 11.1

- *Information reports.* Reports that collect and organize information are informative or investigative. They may record routine activities, such as daily, weekly, and monthly reports of sales or profits. They may investigate options, performance, or equipment. Although they provide information, they do not analyze that information.

- *Recommendation reports.* Recommendation reports are similar to informative reports in that they present information. However, they offer analysis in addition to data. They attempt to solve problems by evaluating options and offering recommendations. These reports are solicited; that is, the writer has been asked to investigate and report.

- *Justification reports.* Like recommendation reports, justification reports attempt to solve problems. However, they are unsolicited; that is, the writer generates the report on his or her own. He or she observes a problem, analyzes alternatives, and describes a potential solution.

- *Progress reports.* Progress reports monitor the headway of unusual or nonroutine activities. For example, progress reports would keep management informed about a committee's preparations for a trade fair 14 months from now. Such reports usually answer three questions: (1) Is the project on schedule? (2) Are corrective measures needed? (3) What activities are next?

Reports that provide data are informational; reports that draw conclusions and make recommendations are analytical.

- *Proposals.* A proposal is an offer to perform a service, sell a product, investigate a subject, or solve a problem. Proposals attempt to convince an audience that the writer is the best person to perform the task. For example, Coca-Cola seeks help in appealing to a younger market. It solicits proposals from market research companies, who then submit bids detailing their qualifications and their plans for solving the problem.

- *Minutes of meetings.* A record of the proceedings of a meeting is called "the minutes." This record is generally kept by a secretary. Minutes may be kept for groups that convene regularly, such as the monthly meeting of a club, or for groups that meet irregularly, such as committees.

- *Summaries.* A summary condenses the primary ideas, conclusions, and recommendations of a longer report or publication. Employees may be asked to write summaries of technical reports. Students may be asked to write summaries of periodical articles or books to sharpen their writing skills.

- *To-file reports.* Reports prepared to document an idea or action are called "to-file" reports. These useful reports provide a written record of conversations, directives, and decisions. In today's often litigious business world, such reports are becoming increasingly important.

REPORT FORMATS

How should a report look? The following four formats are frequently used:

Transparency 11.2

Informal reports may appear in four formats: in memo, letter, or report form, or on prepared forms.

- *Letter format*—appropriate for informal reports prepared by one organization for another. These reports are much like letters except that they are more carefully organized, using headings and lists where appropriate.

- *Memo format*—appropriate for informal reports written for circulation within an organization. They follow the conventions of memos that you learned in Chapter 5—with the addition of headings.

- *Report format*—used for longer and somewhat more formal reports. Printed on plain paper (instead of letterhead or memo forms), these reports begin with a title followed by carefully displayed headings and subheadings. (See an illustration of report format in Figure 11.8, formal minutes of a meeting.)

- *Prepared forms*—useful in reporting routine activities, such as police arrest reports or merchandise inventories. Standardized headings on these forms save time for the writer; forms also make similar information easy to locate.

Today's reports and other business documents are far more sophisticated than typewritten documents of the past. If you've worked with a computer and a laser printer, you know how easy it is to make your documents look as if they were professionally printed. In fact, reports are no longer *typed;* today, they are *designed.* You must learn to use type sizes, fonts, margins, and a host of word processing capabilities to fashion attractive documents. The accompanying box, "Ten Tips for Designing Better Documents," offers suggestions to make sure you avoid common traps.

GUIDELINES FOR WRITING INFORMAL REPORTS

DEFINING THE PROJECT

Begin the process of report writing by defining your project. This definition should include a statement of purpose. Ask yourself: Am I writing this report to inform, to analyze, to solve a problem, or to persuade? The answer to this question should be a clear, accurate statement identifying your purpose. In informal reports the statement of purpose may be only one sentence; that sentence usually becomes part of the introduction. Notice how the following introductory statement describes the purpose of the report:

Transparency 11.3

Begin a report by formulating a statement of purpose: Why are you writing this report?

> This report presents data regarding in-service training activities coordinated and supervised by the Human Resources Department between the first of the year and the present.

After writing a statement of purpose, analyze who will read your report. If your report is intended for your immediate supervisors and they are supportive of your project, you need not include extensive details, historical development, definition of terms, or persuasion. Other readers, however, may require background data and persuasive strategies.

The expected audience for your report influences your writing style, your research method, your vocabulary, your areas of emphasis, and your communication strategy. Remember, too, that your audience may consist of more than one set of readers. Reports are often distributed to secondary readers who may need more details than the primary reader.

GATHERING DATA

A good report is based on solid, accurate, verifiable facts. Typical sources for such facts include (1) company records, (2) observation, (3) surveys, questionnaires, and inventories, (4) interviews, and (5) research.

Company Records   Many business-related reports begin with analysis of company records and files. From these records you can observe past per-

---

TEN TIPS FOR DESIGNING BETTER DOCUMENTS

Desktop publishing packages, high-level word processing programs, and laser printers now make it possible for you to turn out professional-looking documents. The temptation, though, is to overdo it by incorporating too many features in one document. Here are ten tips for applying good sense and good design principles in "publishing" your documents:

- *Analyze your audience.* Sales brochures and promotional letters can be flashy—with color print, oversized type, and fancy borders—to attract attention. But such effects are out of place for most conservative business documents. Also consider whether your readers will be reading painstakingly or merely browsing. Lists and headings help those readers who are in a hurry.
- *Choose an appropriate type size.* For most business memos, letters, and reports, the body text should be 10 or 11 points tall (a point is $\frac{1}{72}$ of an inch). Larger type looks amateurish, and smaller type is hard to read.
- *Use a consistent type font.* Although your software may provide a variety of fonts, stay with a single family of type within one document—at least until you become more expert. The most popular fonts are Times Roman and Helvetica. For emphasis and contrast, you may vary the font size and weight with **bold,** *italic,* ***bold italic,*** and other selections.
- *Generally, don't justify right margins.* Textbooks, novels, newspapers, magazines, and other long works are usually set with justified (even) right margins. However, for shorter works ragged-right margins are recommended because such margins add white space and help readers locate the beginnings of new lines. Slower readers find ragged-right copy more legible.
- *Separate paragraphs and sentences appropriately.* The first line of a paragraph should be indented or preceded by a blank line. To separate sen-

---

The facts for reports are often obtained from company records, observation, surveys, interviews, and research.

formance and methods used to solve previous problems. You can collect pertinent facts that will help determine a course of action.

Observation   Another logical source of data for many problems lies in personal observation and experience. For example, if you were writing a report on the need for additional computer equipment, you might observe how much the current equipment is being used and for what purpose.

Surveys, Questionnaires, and Inventories   Data from groups of people can be collected most efficiently and economically by using surveys, questionnaires, and inventories. For example, if you were part of a committee investigating the success of a campus recycling program, you might begin by using a questionnaire to survey students and faculty.

Interviews   Talking with individuals directly concerned with the problem produces excellent first-hand information. Interviews also allow for one-on-one communication, thus giving you an opportunity to explain your questions and ideas in eliciting the most accurate information.

tences, typists have traditionally left two spaces. This spacing is still acceptable for most business documents. If you are preparing a newsletter or brochure, however, you may wish to adopt printer's standards, leaving one space after end punctuation.

- *Design readable headlines.* Presenting headlines and headings in all caps is generally discouraged because solid blocks of capital letters interfere with recognition of word patterns. To further improve readability, select a sans serif typeface (one without cross strokes or embellishment), such as Helvetica.

- *Strive for an attractive page layout.* In designing title pages or visual aids, provide for a balance between print and white space. Also consider placing the focal point (something that draws the reader's eye) at the optical center of a page—about three lines above the actual center. Moreover, remember that the average reader scans a page from left to right and top to bottom in a Z pattern. Plan your visuals accordingly.

- *Use graphics and clip art with restraint.* Images created with spreadsheet or graphics programs can be imported into documents. Original drawings, photographs, and clip art can also be scanned into documents. Use such images, however, only when they are well drawn, relevant, purposeful, and appropriately sized.

- *Avoid amateurish results.* Many beginning writers, eager to display every graphic device a program offers, produce busy, cluttered documents. Too many typefaces, ruled lines, oversized headlines, and images will overwhelm readers. Strive for simple, clean, and forceful effects.

- *Develop expertise.* Learn to use the desktop publishing features of your current word processing software, or investigate one of the special programs, such as Ventura, PageMaker, Harvard Graphics, Powerpoint, or CorelDraw. Although the learning curve for many of these programs is steep, such effort is well spent if you will be producing newsletters, brochures, announcements, visual aids, and promotional literature.

Research Brochures and company literature can provide significant data. In addition, the library and electronic databases can provide an unlimited source of current and historical information. For short, informal reports the most usable data will probably be found in periodicals. The *Business Periodicals Index* is the best source for business magazines and short publications. Chapter 12 contains more detailed suggestions about library research.

Many reports begin with secondary research in libraries or company records.

DETERMINING ORGANIZATION

⊃ *Instructor: See p. 68 for supplementary lecture, "Six Methods for Organizing Data."*

Like correspondence, reports may be organized inductively (indirectly) or deductively (directly). Placement of the main idea (recommendations or conclusions) is delayed in the inductive approach. Figures 11.1 and 11.2 show the same material for a report organized two different ways.

In Figures 11.1 and 11.2 you see only the skeleton of facts representing a complex problem. However, you can see the effects of organization. The inductive approach brings the reader through the entire process of analyzing a problem. It mirrors our method of thinking: problem, facts, analysis, recommendation. As you learned earlier, this strategy is successful when persuasion is necessary. It's also useful when the reader lacks knowledge and must be informed. However, busy executives or readers already familiar with the problem may want to get to the point more quickly.

The difference between inductive and deductive strategy is the placement of conclusions and recommendations.

The deductive approach is more direct; recommendations and conclusions are presented first so that readers have a frame of reference for reading the following discussion and analysis. Business reports are commonly organized deductively. Analyze your audience and purpose to determine the best overall strategy.

BEING OBJECTIVE

Reports are more believable if the author is impartial, separates fact from opinion, uses moderate language, and cites sources.

Reports are convincing only when the facts are believable and the writer is credible. You can build credibility in a number of ways:

- *Present both sides of an issue.* Even if you favor one possibility, discuss both sides and show through logical reasoning why your position is superior. Remain impartial, letting the facts prove your point.

- *Separate fact from opinion.* Suppose a supervisor wrote, *Our department works harder and gets less credit than any other department in the company.* This opinion is difficult to prove, and it damages the credibility of the writer. A more convincing statement might be, *Our productivity has increased 6 percent over the past year, and I'm proud of the extra effort my employees are making.* After you've made a claim or presented an important statement in a report, ask yourself, Is this a verifiable fact? If the answer is no, rephrase your statement to make it sound more reasonable.

- *Be sensitive and moderate in your choice of language.* Don't exaggerate. Instead of saying *most people think . . . ,* it might be more accurate to say *some people think . . .* Obviously, avoid using labels and slanted expressions. Calling someone a *bozo,* an *egghead,* or an *elitist* demonstrates bias. If readers suspect that a writer is prejudiced, they may discount the entire argument.

- *Cite sources.* Tell your readers where the information came from. For example, *In a telephone interview with Thomas Boswell, director of transportation, October 15, he said . . .* Or *The Wall Street Journal (August 10, p. 40) reports that . . .* By referring to respected sources, you lend authority and credibility to your statements. Your words become more believable, and your argument more convincing.

USING EFFECTIVE HEADINGS

Transparency 11.4

Good headings are helpful to both the report reader and the writer. For the reader they serve as an outline of the text, highlighting major ideas and

FIGURE 11.1   Inductive Organization

Inadequate student parking on campus during prime class times.	*Problem*
10,000 permits sold for 3,000 parking spaces; some parking lots unusable in bad weather; large numbers of visitors without permits fill parking spaces; no land for new lots.	*Facts*
Carpool? Try shuttles from distant parking lots? Enforce current regulations more strictly? Charge premium for parking in prime locations or during prime times? Build double-deck parking structures? Restrict visitors?	*Discussion*
Short-term: begin shuttle program. Long-term: solicit funds for improving current lots and building new multistory structures.	*Recommendations*

FIGURE 11.2   Deductive Organization

Inadequate student parking on campus during prime class times.	
Short-term: begin shuttle program. Long-term: solicit funds for improving current lots and building new multistory structures.	*Problem* *Recommendations*
10,000 permits sold for 3,000 parking spaces; some lots unusable in bad weather; large numbers of visitors without permits fill spaces; no land for new lots.	*Facts*
Carpool? Try shuttles from distant parking lots? Enforce current regulations more strictly? Charge premium for parking in prime locations or during prime times? Build double-deck parking structures? Restrict visitors?	*Discussion*

categories. They also act as guides for locating facts and in pointing the way through the text. Moreover, headings provide resting points for the mind and for the eye, breaking up large chunks of text into manageable and inviting segments. For the writer headings force organization of the data into meaningful blocks.

Functional heads (like *Problem, Summary,* and *Recommendations*) help the writer outline a report. But talking heads (like *Students Perplexed by Shortage of Parking* or *Short-Term Parking Solutions*) provide more information to the reader. Many of the examples in this chapter use functional heads for the purpose of instruction. It's sometimes possible to make headings both functional and descriptive, such as *Recommendations: Shuttle and New Structures*. Whether your heads are talking or functional, keep them brief and clear.

Functional headings show the outline of a report; talking heads provide more information.

Most informal reports are simple, requiring only one level of heading. Longer, more formal reports demand subdividing the topic into levels of headings (see page 284, Chapter 12).

Here are general tips on displaying headings effectively:

- *Strive for parallel construction.* Use balanced expressions such as *Visible Costs* and *Invisible Costs* rather than *Visible Costs* and *Costs That Don't Show.*
- *Don't enclose headings in quotation marks.*
- *Don't use headings as antecedents for pronouns like* this, that, these, *and* those. For example, if the heading reads *Laser Printers,* don't begin the next sentence with *These are often used with desktop publishing software.*

INFORMATION REPORTS

Information reports usually contain three parts: introduction, findings, and summary.

Information reports provide information without drawing conclusions or making recommendations. Some information reports are highly standardized, such as police reports, hospital admittance reports, monthly sales reports, or government regulatory reports. Essentially, these are fill-in reports using prepared forms for recurring data. Other information reports are more personalized, as illustrated in Figure 11.3. They often include these sections:

• *Introduction.* This part may also be called *Background.* In this section do the following: (1) explain why you are writing, (2) describe what methods and sources were used to gather information and why they are credible, (3) provide any special background information that may be

FIGURE 11.3   Information Report—Letter Format

J A G E R   S E R V I C E S ,   I N C .
3920 Santa Monica Boulevard
Los Angeles, California 90066-0120
(213) 478-3201

August 4, 199x

Ms. Karen Butts, Promotions Manager
Universal Records, Inc.
5890 Hollywood Boulevard
Hollywood, CA 90382

Dear Ms. Butts:

SUBJECT: AVAILABILITY OF NAMES FOR NEW RECORDING SERIES

Here is the report you requested regarding the availability of names for use in a new recording series within the Universal Records label.

Introduction

The following information is based on trademark searches of the U.S. Patent and Trademark Office, the Copyright Office, several other sources of patent data within the music industry, and the services of our attorneys. My staff conducted a full search of the five names you submitted. Of this group we find that two names are possible for your use.

Discussion of Findings

1. Gold Label. Our research disclosed one recording company using the "Gold Label" name, and this causes us some concern. However, our outside counsel advises us that the name "Gold Label" is available for Universal's use in light of the trademark registrations for "Gold Note" currently owned by your affiliated companies.

2. The Master Series. Several registrations containing the word "Master" appear in the Patent and Trademark Office. Since many registrations exist, no one can assert exclusive rights to that word. Therefore, Universal's use of the name "The Master Series" is not precluded.

Identifies report and authorization.

Discusses research methods.

Enumerates research findings.

necessary, (4) give the purpose of the report, if known, and (5) offer a preview of your findings.

- *Findings.* This section may also be called *Observations, Facts, Results,* or *Discussion.* Important points to consider in this section are organization and display. Since information reports generally do not include conclusions or recommendations, inductive or deductive organization may be less appropriate. Instead, consider one of these methods of organization: (1) chronological, (2) alphabetical, (3) topical, or (4) most to least important.

To display the findings effectively, number the paragraphs, underline or boldface the key words, or indent the paragraphs. Be sure that words used as headings are parallel in structure. If the findings require elaboration, either include this discussion with each segment of the findings or place it in a separate section entitled *Discussion.*

FIGURE 11.3   continued

Ms. Karen Butts   Page 2   August 4, 199x

3. Heavenly Voices. Our search of copyright records disclosed that approximately seven songs were recorded in 1993 on the "Heavenly Voices" record label, with an address in Sausalito, California. Repeated attempts to reach this business have been unsuccessful.

4. Celestial Sounds. A record label using this name produced 12 titles in 1991. Apparently the recording company is now defunct, but the trademark registration, No. 1,909,233, persists.

5. Cherubim. This name has at least one currently operating outstanding trademark, Trademark Registration No. 2,109,900 for "Cherubim Music."

Summary

Of the five names discussed here, the first two appear to be open to you: "Gold Label" and "The Master Series." The names "Heavenly Voices" and "Celestial Sounds" require additional research. Since "Cherubim" is trademarked, it is unavailable for your consideration.

Should you have any other names you would like us to check, please call me at 478-3201. It's always a pleasure to serve you.

Sincerely,

Robert Jager
President

RJ:era

Summarizes significant findings.

- *Summary.* This section is optional. If it is included, use it to summarize your findings objectively and impartially.

The information report shown in Figure 11.3 supplies information from an investigator about names available for a new recording series. The writer, an information specialist and consultant, used functional headings (*Introduction, Discussion of Findings,* and *Summary*). These headings immediately announce the report's organization, but they give no hint of what the sections actually reveal.

Notice how easy this information report is to read. Short paragraphs, ample use of headings, white space, concise writing, and an enumerated list all contribute to improved readability.

FIGURE 11.4   Recommendation Report—Memo Format

DataCom, Inc.

Internal Memorandum

TO:	Thomas A. Varner, Director Personnel Services	DATE: June 3, 199x

FROM: Judy Gray, Manager   *Judy*
        Information Services

SUBJECT: DEVELOPING PROCEDURES FOR USING TEMPORARY EMPLOYEES

Includes signature here rather than at end.

At your request I am submitting this report detailing my recommendations for improving the use of temporary employees in all departments within DataCom. My recommendations are based on my own experience with hundreds of temporary employees in my department and on my interviews with other department managers.

Announces report and establishes sources of data.

Background

DataCom has increased its number of service accounts from 58 to 97 over the past three years. During that same period the number of permanent employees has increased only 12 percent. Because we have not been able to find qualified individuals to hire as full-time employees, we have been forced to rely on temporary employees more heavily than ever before. During the past year DataCom has required the services of 189 temporary employees, an increase of 76 over the previous year.

Presents facts that suggest significance of problem.

Joe Hernandez in Personnel reports that he does not expect the employment picture to improve in the future. He feels that DataCom will probably continue to hire large numbers of temporary employees for at least the next two years.

Problem

Temporary employees are hired by department managers who have little experience in acquiring temps, planning their work, or supervising them. As a result, the productivity of the temps is not always as great as it could be. Moreover, we sometimes hire expensive, highly skilled individuals for routine tasks. These workers are bored with their assigned tasks and dissatisfied with their experience at DataCom; hence they refuse to return.

Provides details that justify need for change.

RECOMMENDATION REPORTS

Recommendation reports present information and analysis intended to solve a problem. They are usually written in response to requests by superiors. The writer is expected to analyze data, draw conclusions, and make recommendations. The report may be arranged inductively or deductively, depending on the problem, audience, and purpose. To arrange a report deductively, place the conclusions and recommendations near the beginning. For inductive arrangement, place them toward the end.

The recommendation report shown in Figure 11.4 presents information about procedures for hiring and using temporary employees. Orga-

Unlike information reports, recommendation reports include conclusions and recommendations.

FIGURE 11.4   **continued**

Thomas A. Varner   Page 2   June 3, 199x

Conclusions

   DataCom could improve the productivity, effectiveness, and morale of its temporary employees by instituting changes in three areas: (1) establishing standardized procedures to be followed by all departments requesting temps, (2) introducing techniques for department managers to follow when temps first arrive, and (3) providing suggestions for adequate supervision after temps are on the job.

Recommendations

   System for Requesting Temps. I recommend that Personnel prepare a form that supervisors complete when they need temporary employees. The form will require department managers to indicate precisely what skills are required for the tasks to be completed. We should not request a secretary for a task that a typist could perform. Requests for temps should then be channeled through one office, such as Personnel.

   Procedures for Introducing Temps to Workforce. When temps are hired, department managers can improve their productivity by following these suggestions:

   1. Lay out and organize the work to be completed.

   2. Simplify the tasks as much as possible.

   3. Ensure that supplies and operating equipment are available.

   4. Provide ample directions.

   5. Encourage the temp to ask questions clarifying tasks.

   Follow-up Supervision. Probably the most important suggestion involves supervision. As soon as a temp starts on the job, assign a nearby supervisor. Spot-check the temp an hour after work is begun and at intervals throughout the entire task. Don't wait until a task is completed to discover a misunderstood direction.

Limitations

   The success of these recommendations is limited by two factors. First, the Personnel Division must agree to assume the task of regulating the hiring of all temporary employees. Second, department managers must be supportive of the new procedures. To secure their cooperation, an in-service training workshop should be provided to instruct managers in working with temps.

Draws conclusions from preceding facts.

Itemizes specific actions to solve problem.

Gains credibility by acknowledging limitations of recommendations.

nized inductively, this report begins with a description of the background and problem. Conclusions and recommendations follow. Because the writer thought the reader would require persuasion, she arranged the report to follow logical thought processes.

In addition to illustrating inductive organization, the recommendation report in Figure 11.4 shows the memo format. This report was internal; therefore, it used company memo stationery.

The headings in this report include *Background, Problem, Conclusions, Recommendations,* and *Limitations.* Other possible section headings for a recommendation report follow:

Introduction	Analysis of Facts
Background	Options
Problem	Rejected Alternatives
Method of Collecting Data	Limitations
Findings	Conclusions
Presentation of Facts	Recommendations

FIGURE 11.5   **Justification Report—Memo Format**

M E M O R A N D U M

TO: Orene Harder, Vice President   DATE: June 11, 199x
          Operations Division

FROM: Jack Harris, Office Manager *J. H.*
              Accounting Department

SUBJECT: INSTALLATION OF FLAT, UNDERCARPET WIRING TO UPDATE
                CURRENT ELECTRICAL, DATA PROCESSING, AND
                COMMUNICATION WIRING SYSTEM

Presents main idea (proposal) immediately.

Proposal

Because the Accounting Department of Hershey Chocolate Company needs a flexible, economical wiring system that can accommodate our ever-changing electrical, communication, and data processing needs, I propose that we install a flat, undercarpet wiring system.

Describes problem, emphasizing current deficiencies.

Present System

At present our department has an outdated system of floor ducts and power poles and a network of surface wiring that is overwhelmed by the demands we are now placing on it. The operation of 27 pieces of electrical equipment and 34 telephones requires extensive electrical circuits and cabling. In addition, our overhead lighting, consisting of fluorescent fixtures in a suspended egg-crate structure, has resulted in excessive wiring above the drop ceiling.

We have outgrown our present wiring system, and future growth is contingent on the availability of power. Since Hershey's goal is to have a computer terminal at every workstation, we must find a better way to serve our power needs than through conventional methods.

JUSTIFICATION REPORTS

Justification reports include information, analysis, and recommendations. Unlike recommendation reports, however, they are *unsolicited*—that is, the idea for a justification report starts with the writer instead of with a superior. The writer may wish to purchase equipment, change a procedure, or revise existing policy. Typically, the desired change will be obvious to the reader. Therefore, persuasion should not be a primary factor. Start directly with the proposal or problem. Follow this with some or all of the following topics: Present System, Proposed System, Advantages, Cost and Savings, Methods or Procedures, Conclusion, and Discussion. Figure 11.5 shows a justification report within Hershey Chocolate Company.

Justification reports are unsolicited; that is, the idea originates with the writer.

FIGURE 11.5   continued

Vice President Harder   Page 2   June 11, 199x

Advantages of Proposed System

Power, telephone, and data cables are now available in a flat form only .043 inches thick. This flat, flexible cable can be installed underneath existing carpeting, thus preventing costly and disruptive renovation necessary for installing additional round cables. Because flat cables can be moved easily, an undercarpet system would provide great flexibility. Whenever we move a computer or add a printer or a fax machine, we can easily make necessary changes in the wiring.

Undercarpet wiring would allow us to eliminate all power poles. These poles break up the office landscaping and create distracting shadows about which employees complain.

Installation of an undercarpet wiring system in the Accounting Department would enable Hershey to evaluate the system's effectiveness before considering it for other areas, such as sales, customer services, and field warehousing.

Cost and Savings

The AMP Products Corporation of Harrisburg estimates that undercarpet wiring for the Accounting Department would cost about $29,000. If we were to use conventional methods to install round wiring, we would have to renovate our entire department, costing over $200,000. Undercarpet wiring, then, saves Hershey over $170,000. Equally important, however, is the savings in terms of productivity and employee satisfaction, which would deteriorate if renovation were required.

Shows how new system would solve problems.

Relates costs to savings and benefits.

PROGRESS REPORTS

*Progress reports
generally answer
three questions:
(1) Is the project on
schedule? (2) Are
corrective measures
needed? (3) What
activities are next?*

Progress reports describe the headway of unusual or nonroutine projects. Most progress reports include these four parts: (1) the purpose and nature of the project, (2) a complete summary of the work already completed, (3) a thorough description of work currently in progress, including personnel, methods, obstacles, and attempts to remedy obstacles, and (4) a forecast of future activities in relation to the scheduled completion date, including recommendations and requests. In Figure 11.6 Gail Desler explains the construction of a realty company branch office. She begins with a statement summarizing the construction progress in relation to the

FIGURE 11.6   Progress Report

M E M O R A N D U M

TO: Jeanne Dostourian, President   DATE: April 20, 199x

FROM: Gail Desler   *y. p.*
          Development Officer

SUBJECT: CONSTRUCTION PROGRESS OF MALIBU BRANCH OFFICE

Summary

*Introduces report;
heading ("Sum-
mary") could be
omitted.*

Construction of Dostourian Realty's Malibu branch office has entered Phase 3. Although we are one week behind the contractor's original schedule, the building should be ready for occupancy August 15.

Past Progress

*Describes completed
work concisely.*

Phase 1 involved development of the architect's plans; this process was completed February 5. Phase 2 involved submission of the plans for county building department approval. The plans were then given to four contractors for estimates. The lowest bidder was Holst Brothers Contractors. This firm began construction on March 25.

Present Status

*Itemizes current
activities.*

Phase 3 includes initial construction procedures. The following steps have been completed as of April 20:

1. Demolition of existing building at 27590 Pacific Coast Highway.

2. Excavation of foundation footings for the building and for the surrounding wall.

3. Installation of steel reinforcing rods in building pad and wall.

4. Pouring of concrete foundation.

The contractor indicated that he was one week behind schedule for the following reasons. The building inspectors required additional steel reinforcement not shown on the architect's blueprints. Further, excavation of the footings required more time than the contractor anticipated because the 18-inch footings were all below grade.

Future Schedule

*Projects future
activities.*

Despite some time lost in Phase 3, we are substantially on target for the completion of this office building by August 1. Phase 4 includes framing, drywalling, and plumbing.

expected completion date. She then updates the reader with a brief recap of past progress. She emphasizes the present status of construction and concludes by describing the next steps to be taken.

PROPOSALS

A proposal is an offer or a bid to sell a product, provide a service, explore a topic, or solve a problem. As such, it must persuade or sell the reader on a plan of attack for solving the problem or performing the service. Typically, informal proposals include the following parts.

Introduction.   Most proposals begin by briefly explaining the reasons for the proposal and by highlighting the writer's qualifications. To make an introduction more persuasive, try to provide a "hook" to capture the interest of the reader. One proposal expert suggests these possible hooks.

- Hint at extraordinary results with details to be revealed shortly.
- Promise low costs or speedy results.
- Mention a remarkable resource (well-known authority, new computer program, well-trained staff) available exclusively to you.
- Specify a key issue or benefit that you feel is the heart of the proposal.

Background, problem, purpose.   The background section identifies the problem and discusses the goals or purposes of the project. In an unsolicited proposal, your goal is to convince the reader that a problem exists. Thus, you must present the problem in detail, discussing such factors as monetary losses, failure to comply with government regulations, or loss of customers. In a solicited proposal your aim is to persuade the reader that you understand the problem completely. Many proposals respond to requests for proposals (RFPs). RFPs are prepared by organizations that know exactly what they want. In their RFP these companies specify their exact requirements. Smart proposal writers often repeat the language of the RFP to show their familiarity with the specifications.

Shorter proposals, such as that shown in Figure 11.7, may combine the introduction and background sections. Notice that in the proposal from Computer Assistance, Inc., the introduction includes a description of the needs of Lowe & Associates Accountancy. This explanation assures the reader that the writer understands the problem and is prepared to solve it.

Proposal, plan, schedule.   In the proposal section itself, you should discuss your plan for solving the problem. In some proposals this is tricky because you want to disclose enough of your plan to secure the contract without giving away so much information that your services are unneeded. Without specifics, though, your proposal has little chance, so you must decide how much to reveal. Tell what you propose to do and how it will benefit the reader. Remember, too, that a proposal is a sales presentation. Sell your methods, product, and "deliverables"—items that will be left with the client. In this section some writers specify how the project will be managed and how its progress will be audited. Most writers also include a schedule of activities. Notice in Figure 11.7 that the proposal itemizes three phases of the project for installing software and training employees in its use.

FIGURE 11.7   Proposal—Letter Style

Computer Assistance, Inc.
2390 Marshall Avenue
Arlington, West Virginia 23403

May 15, 199x

Ms. Nedra K. Lowe, CPA
Lowe & Associates Accountancy
5492 Lavalette Boulevard
Huntington, West Virginia 25705

Dear Ms. Lowe:

Explains the purpose of the report.

As you requested, we have prepared a proposal for assisting Lowe & Associates Accountancy in computerizing its accounting data.

Introduction

Reviews client's specifications and provides brief history of company.

We understand that Lowe & Associates wishes to install hardware and software that will enable it to operate each of its four regional offices with separate, single-user computers and software. Each regional office needs to automate its general ledger and accounts payable functions. The Huntington office wishes to combine the information generated by the regional offices on a monthly basis for reporting purposes.

Our organization was formed in 1985 to assist businesses like yours select and implement PC-based accounting systems. Since then we have successfully installed a multitude of systems, serving customers from accounting firms to restaurants to wholesale distributors. To learn more about our satisfied customers, please see the attached brochure.

Proposal

Spells out exactly what will be done.

We propose that you allow us to demonstrate two software packages appropriate for your firm: MAS90 and ACCPAC Plus. Both of these software packages provide custom financial statements, and they support departmentalization and company consolidation. We will highlight the features of each program so that you can choose the one you prefer. We will install the program you select and provide training on-site or in our training room. If you engage us, we would divide the project into three phases:

1. System Design and Setup. The tasks to be performed in this phase include the following:

    • Determine the computer and peripheral equipment to be used in each office

    • Establish the procedure for transporting data to home office (by modem or mail)

Staffing

Promotes qualifications of staff.

Beverly Husak, our talented software consultant trained at Huntington University, will demonstrate the two packages. Hardware hookup and installation of software will be done by our veteran technician, William Andrews, who has installed dozens of systems over the past five years. Training and follow-up support will be provided by Ms. Husak.

Staffing.   The staffing section of a proposal describes the credentials and expertise of the project participants. It may also identify the size and qualifications of the support staff, along with other resources such as computer facilities and special programs for analyzing statistics. In longer proposals, résumés of key people may be provided. The staffing or personnel section is a good place to endorse and promote your staff, as illustrated in Figure 11.7.

Budget or cost.   A central item in most proposals is the budget, a list of proposed project costs. You need to prepare this section carefully because it represents a contract; you can't raise the price later—even if your costs

FIGURE 11.7   continued

Ms. Nedra K. Lowe   Page 2   May 15, 199x

Schedule

    We expect to complete a substantial portion of the project within four to five weeks after starting. Implementation follow-up will occur in the weeks immediately after the initial phase. Technical and accounting support is available as needed following installation. We will require a meeting with the management staff involved in this project to clarify the specific installation and training requirements as described in this proposal prior to beginning the actual installation.

Cost

    Our fees are based on the number of hours spent on the job by our staff multiplied by their respective billing rates. Our current rates are as follows:

Technicians	$ 60/hr
Software consultant	80/hr
President	250/hr

    See Attachment 1 for a detailed listing of the projected costs for consulting, software, installation, and training.

Authorization

    If this information correctly anticipates your needs and meets your expectations, please sign the enclosed duplicate copy and return it to us. In addition, include a retainer for the amount of the software plus $5,000 as authorization for us to begin the project. The figures in this proposal remain in effect until June 30. We look forward to working with you.

Sincerely,

Linda Wilkinson
President

LW:psf

Enclosures

Includes detailed daily, weekly, or monthly schedule.

Discusses fees; because proposals are legally binding, all facts and figures must be accurate.

Requests approval and sets deadline.

---

increase. You can—and should—protect yourself with a deadline for acceptance. In the cost section, some writers itemize hours and fees; others present a total sum only. In the proposal from Computer Assistance, hourly costs are presented, although they are described more fully on an attached sheet.

Authorization.   Informal proposals often close with a request for approval or authorization. In addition, the closing might remind the reader of key benefits and motivate action. It should also include a deadline date beyond which the offer is invalid.

FORMAL MINUTES

Minutes provide a summary of the proceedings of meetings. Formal, traditional minutes, illustrated in Figure 11.8, are written for large groups and legislative bodies. The following items are usually included in the sequence shown:

- Name of group, date, time, place, name of meeting
- Names of people present; names of absentees, if appropriate
- Disposition of previous minutes
- Old business, new business, announcements, reports
- Motions, vote, action taken
- Name and signature of individual recording minutes

FIGURE 11.8 **Minutes of Meeting, Traditional—Report Format**

Identifies name, date, time, and place of meeting.

Shows attendees and absentees.

Describes disposition of previous minutes and old business.

Summarizes new business and announcements.

Records discussion, motions, votes, and action taken.

Shows name and signature of person recording minutes.

PSA Professional Secretaries Association

1995 International Convention
Planning Committee Meeting
October 23, 1995, 10 a.m.
Conference Room A, Century Towers

Present: Marilyn Andrews, Melody Franklin, June Gonzales, Brenda Miller, Margaret
Zappa, Martha Zebulski

Absent: Amy Costello

The meeting was called to order by Chair Margaret Zappa at 10:05 a.m. Minutes from the June 22 meeting were read and approved.

Old Business

Brenda Miller and Martha Zebulski reviewed the information distributed at the last meeting about hotels being considered for the Houston conference. Brenda said that the Hilton Regency has ample conference rooms and remodeled interiors. Martha reported that the Embassy Suites Houston also has excellent banquet facilities, adequate meeting facilities, and rooms at $82 per night. Melody Franklin moved that we hold the PSA International Convention at the Embassy Suites Houston. Brenda Miller seconded the motion. The motion passed 5-1.

New Business

The chair announced three possible themes for the convention, all of which focused on technology and the changing role of the secretary. June Gonzales suggested the following possible title: "The New, The Tried and True, and The Unusual." Martha Zebulski suggested a communication theme. Several other possibilities were discussed. The chair appointed a subcommitee of June and Martha to bring to the next committee meeting two or three concrete theme ideas.

Reports

Brenda Miller reported on convention exhibits and her desire to involve more companies and products. Discussion followed regarding how this might be accompanied. Brenda Miller moved that the PSA office staff develop a list of possible exhibitors. Marilyn Andrews seconded the motion. It passed 6-0.

The meeting was adjourned at 11:45 by Margaret Zappa.

Respectfully submitted,

Melody Franklin

Melody Franklin, Secretary

INFORMAL MINUTES

The minutes of business meetings and small organizations may be recorded informally, as illustrated in Figure 11.9. These minutes are usually shorter and easier to read than formal minutes. Informal minutes place less emplasis on the conventions of reporting and do not attempt to record the exact wording of individual statements. Instead, informal minutes concentrate on the following:

- Summaries of important discussions
- Decisions reached
- Items on which action must be taken, including people responsible and due dates

FIGURE 11.9   Minutes of Meeting, Informal—Report Format

San Jacinto Homeowners' Association

Board of Directors Meeting
April 12, 199x

MINUTES

Directors Present: J. Weinstein, A. McGraw, J. Carson, C. Stefanko, A. Pettus
Directors Absent: P. Hook

Summary of Topics Discussed

1. Report from Architectural Review Committee. Copy attached.

2. Landscaping of center divider on Paseo Canyon. Three options considered: hiring private landscape designer, seeking volunteers from community, assigning association handyman to complete work.

3. Collection of outstanding assessments. Discussion of delinquent accounts and possible actions.

4. Use of beach club by film companies. Pros: considerable income. Cons: damage to furnishings, loss of facility to homeowners.

5. Nomination of directors to replace those with two-year appointments.

Decisions Reached

1. Hire private landscaper to renovate and plant center divider on Paseo Canyon.

2. Attach liens to homes of members with delinquent assessments.

3. Submit to general membership vote the question of renting the beach club to film companies.

Action Items

Item	Responsibility	Due Date
1. Landscaping bid	J. Carson	May 1
2. Attorney for liens	P. Hook	April 20
3. Creation of nominating committee	A. Pettus	May 1

Smaller, less formal organizations may use streamlined, more efficient minutes.

SUMMARIES

A summary condenses the primary ideas, conclusions, and recommendations of a longer publication.

A summary compresses essential information from a longer publication. Employees are sometimes asked to write summaries that condense technical reports, periodical articles, or books so that their staffs or superiors may grasp the main ideas quickly (see Figure 11.10). Students are often asked to write summaries of articles, chapters, or books to sharpen their writing skills and to confirm their knowledge of reading assignments. A summary includes primary ideas, conclusions, and recommendations. It usually omits examples, illustrations, and references. Organized for readability, a summary often includes headings and enumerations. It may include the reactions of the reader.

FIGURE 11.10   Summary of Article—Memo Format

MEMO TO: Professor Valerie Evans   DATE: November 18, 199x

FROM: Edwin Hwang *E. H.*

SUBJECT: ANALYSIS OF COMPUTER MAINTENANCE ARTICLE

Introduces report.

In response to your request, here is an analysis of "Taking the Sting Out of Computer Repair," which appeared in the July 1994 issue of Office Administration and Automation.

Major Points

The author, Michael B. Chamberlain, discusses four alternatives available to computer users seeking service. Each has advantages and disadvantages.

1. Factory service. The user sends the equipment back to the factory for repairs. Expert service is provided, but generally the time required is impossibly long.

2. Customer self-service. Large companies may maintain in-house repair departments, but their technicians find it difficult to keep abreast of changing hardware and software.

Summarizes primary ideas and conclusions.

3. Third-party service. Independent computer maintenance organizations offer convenience, but they can't always handle multivendor systems.

The author favors the third option and provides many tips on how to work with third-party maintenance companies. Before choosing such an organization, he warns, make sure that it has experts who can work with your particular computer configuration.

Strengths and Weaknesses

Omits examples, illustrations, and references.

The strength of this article lies in the discussion on how to choose a service organization. The author also provides helpful preventive maintenance tips.

This article had two weaknesses. First, the author failed to support his choice of third-party maintenance companies effectively. Second, the article is poorly organized. It was difficult to read because it was not developed around major ideas. Better headings would have helped readers recognize significant data.

TO-FILE REPORTS

To-file reports document oral decisions, directives, and discussions. They create a concise, permanent record that may be important for future reference. Because individuals may forget, alter, or retract oral commitments, a written record should often be established. However, to-file reports should not be made for minor events.

To-file reports provide a record of conversations for future reference.

To-file reports typically include the names and titles of involved individuals, along with a summary of the decision. A copy of the report is sent to involved individuals so that corrections or amendments may be made before the report is filed. Figure 11.11 shows a to-file report in memo format.

The eight types of reports discussed and illustrated in this chapter are representative of commonly seen reports in business transactions. All of the examples in this chapter are considered relatively informal. Longer, more formal reports are necessary for major investigations and research. These reports, along with suggestions for research methods, are presented in Chapter 12.

FIGURE 11.11   To-File Report—Memo Format

DataCom, Inc.

Internal Memo

TO: Wayne McEachern   DATE: February 4, 199x
             Chief Counsel

FROM: Jean Taylor *JT*
             Business Manager

SUBJECT: DISPOSITION OF UNORDERED MERCHANDISE

This confirms our telephone conversation today in which you advised me regarding the disposition of unordered merchandise sent to my office by vendors. It is my understanding that I am under no obligation to return this merchandise since its delivery was unauthorized. I further understand that after reasonable time has elapsed, we may use this merchandise or dispose of it as we see fit.

Please let me hear from you by February 10 if this record of our conversation is inaccurate.

Provides record of conversation.

Repeats major ideas.

Requests correction if necessary.

APPLICATION AND PRACTICE—11

Discussion

1. How do business reports differ from business letters?
2. Of the reports presented in this chapter, discuss those that require inductive development versus those that require deductive development.

3. How are the reports that you write for your courses similar to those presented here? How are they different?

4. Compare and contrast traditional and informal minutes of meetings. Why would some organizations require traditional minutes?

5. Compare and contrast justification reports and proposals.

Short Answers

6. List eight kinds of short reports. Be prepared to describe each.

1. Information	*5. Proposals*
2. Recommendation	*6. Minutes of meetings*
3. Justification	*7. Summaries*
4. Progress	*8. To-file*

7. List four formats suitable for reports. Be prepared to discuss each.

1. Memo	*3. Letter*
2. Report	*4. Prepared forms*

8. From the lists that you made above, select a report category and appropriate format for each of the following situations.

   a. Your supervisor asks you to read a long technical report and tell him or her the important points.
   Summary, memo format

   b. You want to tell management about an idea you have for improving a procedure that you think will increase productivity.
   Justification report, memo format

   c. You just completed a telephone conversation with a union representative detailing your rights in a disagreement you had with your supervisor.
   To-file report, memo format

   d. You are asked to record the proceedings of a meeting of your school's student association.
   Minutes, report format

   e. You want to describe how the products of your company, Pacific Tile, can be used by Del Webb Company in its new housing project.
   Proposal, letter format

   f. As Engineering Department office manager, you have been asked to describe your highly regarded computer system for another department.
   Information report, memo or report format

   g. As a police officer, you are writing a report of an arrest.
   Information report, prepared form

   h. You write a report describing how 5 acres of empty beachfront could be developed into luxury condominiums.
   Proposal, letter or report format

9. What is the primary distinction between a recommendation report and a justification report?
   Recommendation reports are usually solicited; justification reports are not.

10. Name five or more sources of information for reports.
    1. *Company records*
    2. *Observation*
    3. *Surveys, questionnaires, inventories*
    4. *Interviews*
    5. *Research*

11. If you were about to write the following reports, where would you gather information? Be prepared to discuss the specifics of each choice.
    a. You are a student representative on a curriculum committee. You are asked to study the course requirements in your major and make recommendations.
       Observation, interviews, surveys, library research

    b. As department manager, you must write job descriptions for several new positions you wish to establish in your department.
       Company records, observation, possibly surveys and interviews

    c. You are proposing to management the replacement of a copier in your department.
       Company records, observation, research (library and other)

    d. You must document the progress of a 12-month campaign to alter the image of Levi-Strauss jeans.
       Company records, observation, surveys, interviews

12. What three questions do progress reports typically address?
    1. *Is the project on schedule?*
    2. *Are corrective measures needed?*
    3. *What activities are next?*

13. What one factor distinguishes reports developed inductively from those developed deductively?
    Placement of conclusions and recommendations

14. List six items that the writer of a proposal should include.
    1. *Introduction (problem)*
    2. *Proposed solution*
    3. *Staffing*
    4. *Schedule*
    5. *Cost*
    6. *Authorization*

15. What is the purpose of a to-file report?
    Documenting oral decisions, directives, and discussions

16. Information reports that are not organized inductively or deductively may be arranged by what four methods?
    1. *Chronologically*
    2. *Alphabetically*
    3. *Topically*
    4. *Most important to least important*

17. Why are informal minutes usually easier to read than traditional minutes?
    They condense discussions, use headings, include tables, omit standard conventions, and omit who said what.

18. An article summary that your employer asks you to write should include what items?
    A summary of primary points and conclusions as well as optional recommendations.

19. Proposals offer to do what?
   Sell a product, provide a service, explore a topic, solve a problem.

20. In formal minutes how are motions treated?
   The wording, the action taken, and the vote are recorded.

CASE 11-1

⊃ *Instructor: Case 11-1 is available on diskette.*

Transparency Masters 11.1 and 11.2

INFORMATION REPORT

Your instructor wants to learn about your employment. Select a position you now hold or one that you have held in the past. (If you have not been employed, select an organization to which you belong.) Write an information report describing your employment. As an introduction describe the company and its products or services, its ownership, and its location. As the main part of the report, describe your position, including its tasks and the skills required to perform these tasks. Summarize by describing the experience you gained. Your report should be 1½ to 2 pages, single-spaced, and should follow memo format.

CASE 11-2

⊃ *Instructor: See pp. 69–70 for supplementary handouts for Case 11-2.*

INFORMATION REPORT

Gather information about a position for which you might be interested in applying. Learn about the nature of the job. Discover whether certification, licenses, or experience is required. Describe the working conditions in this field. Collect information regarding typical entry-level salaries and potential for advancement.

If your instructor wishes to make this an extended report, collect information about two companies where you might apply. Investigate each company's history, products and/or services, size, earnings, reputation, and number of employees. Describe the functions of an employee working in the position you have investigated. To do this, interview one or more individuals who are working in that position. Devote several sections of your report to the specific tasks, functions, duties, and opinions of these individuals. You can make this into a recommendation report by drawing conclusions and making recommendations. One conclusion that you could draw relates to success in this career area. Who might be successful in this field?

CASE 11-3

RECOMMENDATION REPORT

An employer for whom you worked last year regarded you highly. Although you are no longer employed there, this individual called to ask your candid opinion on how to retain employees. He is concerned about the high rate of turnover. What advice can you offer? How do similar businesses recruit and retain their employees? Using actual experiences, write a letter report responding to this request.

CASE 11 - 4

JUSTIFICATION REPORT

You have been serving as a student member of a college curriculum advisement committee. Examine the course requirements for a degree or certificate in your major. Are the requirements realistic and practical? What improvements can you suggest? Interview other students and faculty members for their suggestions. Write to the dean of your college proposing your suggestions.

CASE 11 - 5

JUSTIFICATION REPORT

In your work or your training, identify equipment that needs to be purchased or replaced (computer, printer, VCR, copier, camera, etc.). Write a justification report comparing two or more brands.

CASE 11 - 6

PROGRESS REPORT

You made an agreement with your parents (or spouse, relative, or significant friend) that you would submit a progress report at this time describing headway toward your educational goal (employment, certificate, degree). Write that report in memo format.

CASE 11 - 7

PROPOSAL

You want to start your own business (fast food franchise, secretarial service, pet-grooming service, photocopy store, etc.) and you need financial backing. Write a convincing proposal to your parents, rich uncle, or philanthropist friend that will get you the capital you need. Do research to learn how much investment is required.

CASE 11 - 8

MINUTES

Attend an open meeting of an organization at your school or elsewhere. Record the proceedings in formal or informal minutes.

CASE 11-9

SUMMARY

Your boss, Russell M. Silver, is worried about computer viruses (or a topic your instructor approves). He asks you to find a good article (at least 1,000 words long) in a magazine that suggests ways to avoid the problem in his company. Look in *Datamation, Personal Computing, Byte,* or some other magazine to find an appropriate article. Write a one- or two-page summary for him.

CASE 11-10

TO-FILE REPORT

You just saw your office manager in the hall, and she told you that you could take a three-week vacation in August. You know she has a bad memory, and you don't want her to forget or renege on her promise. Write her a to-file report.

CASE 11-11

LONGER REPORT

Identify a problem in a business or organization with which you are familiar, such as sloppy workmanship, indifferent service, poor attendance at organization meetings, uninspired cafeteria food, antique office equipment, arrogant management, lack of communication, underappreciated employees, wasteful procedures, and so forth. Describe the problem in detail. Assume you are to report to management (or to the leadership of an organization) about the nature and scope of the problem. Decide which kind of report to prepare (information, recommendation, justification), and choose the format. How would you gather data to lend authority to your conclusions and recommendations? Determine the exact topic and report length after consultation with your instructor.

GRAMMAR/MECHANICS CHECKUP—11

OTHER PUNCTUATION

Although this checkup concentrates on Sections 2.23–2.29 in the Grammar/Mechanics Handbook, you may also refer to other punctuation principles. Insert any necessary punctuation. In the space provided, indicate the number of changes you make and record the number of the G/M principle(s) illustrated. Count each mark separately; for example, a set of parentheses counts as 2. If you make no changes, write *0*. When you finish, compare your responses with those shown below. If your responses differ, study carefully the specific principles shown in parentheses.

Example: (De-emphasize.) The consumption of Mexican food products is highest in certain states (California, Arizona, New Mexico, and Texas), but this food trend is spreading to other parts of the country.

2   *(2.27)*

1. (Emphasize.) The convention planning committee has invited three managers —Jim Lowey, Frank Beyer, and Carolyn Wong —to make presentations.

2   *(2.26a, 2.27)*

2. Would you please, Miss Sanchez, use your computer to recalculate these totals?

3   *(2.02, 2.23a)*

3. (Deemphasize.) A second set of demographic variables (see Figure 13 on page 432) includes nationality, religion, and race.

2   *(2.27)*

4. Because the word "recommendation" is frequently misspelled, we are adding it to our company style book.

3   *(2.06a, 2.28c)*

5. Recruiting, hiring, and training—these are three important functions of a personnel officer.

1   *(2.26c)*

6. The office manager said, "Who placed an order for 15 dozen ribbon cartridges?"

2   *(2.28f)*

7. Have any of the research assistants been able to locate the article entitled "How Tax Reform Will Affect You"?

3   *(2.28e, 2.28f)*

8. (Emphasize.) The biggest oil-producing states —Texas, California, and Alaska —are experiencing severe budget deficits.

2   *(2.26a)*

9. Have you sent invitations to Mr. Ronald E. Harris, Miss Michelle Hale, and Ms. Sylvia Mason?

4   *(2.23b, 2.24)*

10. Dr. Y. W. Yellin wrote the chapter entitled "Trading on the Options Market" that appeared in a book called Securities Markets.

3   *(2.28e)*

11. James said, "I'll be right over"; however, he has not appeared yet.

2   *(2.16, 2.28f)*

12. In business the word liability may be defined as "any legal obligation requiring payment in the future."

3   *(2.28d)*

13. Because the work was scheduled to be completed June 10, we found it necessary to hire temporary workers to work June 8 and 9.

1   *(2.06)*

14. Did any c.o.d. shipments arrive today?

4   *(2.23b, 2.24)*

15. Hooray! I have finished this checkup, haven't I?

3   *(2.24, 2.25)*

---

1. (2) managers— Wong— *(2.26a, 2.27)*   3. (2) *(2.27)*
5. (1) training— *(2.26c)*   7. (3) "How You"? *(2.28e, 2.28f)*
9. (4) Mr. E. Ms. Mason? *(2.23b, 2.24)*   11. (2) over"; however, *(2.16, 2.28f)*
13. (1) June 10, *(2.06)*   15. (3) Hooray! checkup, I? *(2.24, 2.25)*

GRAMMAR/MECHANICS CHALLENGE—11

DOCUMENT FOR REVISION

The following progress report has faults in grammar, punctuation, spelling, number form, wordiness, and word use. Use standard proofreading marks (see Appendix B) to correct the errors. When you finish, your instructor can show you the revised version of this report.

Transparency Master 11.5

Poor Report

Ineffective Writing

TO: Jon Peterson   DATE: January 6, 199x

          Executive Producer

FROM: Tiffany Taylor-Payton

          Location Manager

SUBJECT: SITE FOR "REDWOOD BAY" TELEFILM

This memo describes the progress of my exploration for an appropriate rustic home, villa or ranch to be used in connection with the wine country sequences in the telefilm "Redwood Bay".

<u>Work Completed:</u> To prepare for this assignment several sites in the Russian River area were visited. Possible locations include turn of the century estates, victorian mansions and rustic farmhouses. One acceptional cite is the country meadow inn a 97 year old farmhouse nestled amoung vine yards with a breath taking view of vallies, redwoods, and distant mountains.

<u>Work to Be Completed:</u> In the next 5 days I'll search the sonoma county countryside including winerys at Korbel, Field Stone, and Napa. Many old winerys contain charming structures that may present exactly the degree of atmosphere and mystery we seek, these winerys have the added advantage of easy acess.

My final report in regards to the 3 most promising locations are nearly completed. You will in all probability be able to visit these cites January 21st.

· ·

12

FORMAL REPORTS

IN THIS CHAPTER YOU WILL LEARN TO DO THE FOLLOWING:

- Write a meaningful statement of purpose for a formal report.
- Collect data from both primary and secondary sources.
- Research topics from books, periodicals, and computer databases.
- Recognize three methods for documenting data sources.
- Distinguish among five organizational strategies.
- Outline topics and use appropriate heading format.
- Illustrate data, using tables, charts, and graphs.
- Sequence 13 parts of a formal report.

Instructor: If you would like to assign a long report (but not necessarily a formal report), see the author's suggestion on p. 2. For author's suggested lesson plan for Chapter 12, see p. 75.

Formal reports, whether they offer only information or whether they also analyze that information and make recommendations, typically have three characteristics: formal tone, traditional structure, and length. Although formal reports in business are infrequently seen, they serve a very important function. They provide management with vital data for decision making. In this chapter we will consider the entire process of writing a formal report: preparing to write; collecting, documenting, organizing, and illustrating data; and presenting the final report.[1]

The primary differences between formal and informal reports are tone, structure, and length.

PREPARING TO WRITE

Like informal reports, formal reports begin with a definition of the project. Probably the most difficult part of this definition is limiting the scope of the report. Every project has limitations. Decide at the outset what constraints influence the range of your project and how you will achieve your purpose. How much time do you have for completing your report? How much space will you be allowed for reporting on your topic? How accessible are the data you need? How thorough should your research be? For

The planning of every report begins with a statement of purpose explaining the goal, significance, and limitations of the project.

Transparency 12.1

example, if you are writing about low morale among swing-shift employees, how many of your 475 employees should you interview? Should you limit your research to company-related morale factors, or should you consider external factors over which the company has no control? In investigating variable-rate mortgages, should you focus on a particular group, such as first-time homeowners in a specific area, or should you consider all mortgage holders? The first step in writing a report, then, is determining the precise boundaries of the topic.

Once you have defined the project and limited its scope, write a statement of purpose. The statement of purpose should describe the goal, significance, and limitations of the report. Notice how the following statement pinpoints the research and report:

> The purpose of this report is to explore employment possibilities for entry-level paralegal workers in the city of San Francisco. It will consider typical salaries, skills required, opportunities, and working conditions. This research is significant because of the increasing number of job openings in the paralegal field. This report will not consider legal secretarial employment, which represents a different employment focus.

COLLECTING DATA

Transparency 12.2

Effective reports, whether formal or informal, are founded on accurate data. Data collected for a report may be grouped into two categories, primary and secondary. Primary information is obtained from first-hand observation and experience. Secondary information comes from reading what others have observed or experienced.

PRIMARY SOURCES

Because they generally seek to solve current problems, formal business reports rely heavily on primary source material. Five logical sources of primary information for a report are (1) company records, (2) observation, (3) interviews, (4) surveys, and (5) experiments.

Primary data are facts that have not already been collected and recorded by someone else.

Company Records   Information for reports regarding company operations often originates in company records. Accounting and marketing reports would necessarily include data on previous performance taken from existing records.

Observation   In business reports personal observation often provides essential data. For example, if Sam Erwin, a marketing manager, were writing a report recommending changes in sales territories, he would probably begin by carefully observing the current territories and analyzing sales coverage. If Samantha Jones, a student, were reporting on employment possibilities, she might begin by observing classified ads in a local newspaper.

Interviews   Collecting information by talking with individuals gives the researcher immediate feedback and provides a chance for explanation of questions if necessary. If the information collected is to be used scientifically or systematically, the interviewer should follow an interview schedule—that is, the same questions, stated identically, should be addressed to all interviewees.

Surveys If many questions need to be asked of a large group of individuals and if costs must be kept down, then surveys may be used to collect data. Good surveys, however, cannot be conducted casually. Questions should be carefully written and tested on sample groups before actually being administered. Thought should be given to how the results will be tabulated and interpreted.

Experiments Although experimentation is more common to the physical and social sciences, decision makers in business may also use this technique to gather information. In promoting a new product, for example, a business might experiment with an ad in two different newspapers and compare the results.

SECONDARY SOURCES

The most important information in formal business reports usually comes from first-hand, primary sources. Yet, the research process for every business report should begin with secondary sources. Secondary data usually come from library resources, both manual and electronic. Beginning with a search of secondary sources provides an overview of the project. Often, something has already been written about your topic. Reviewing secondary sources can save time and effort and prevent you from "reinventing the wheel."

Many formal business reports require library research to provide background data.

For a business report you'll probably consult one or more of the following major sources of secondary information: (1) library catalogs, (2) periodicals and newspapers, (3) encyclopedias, dictionaries, and handbooks, and (4) electronic databases.

Library Catalog Libraries in the past indexed all their books on 3- by 5-inch cards alphabetized by author and/or by subject. Many libraries today, however, have computerized their card catalogs. Some systems are fully automated, showing the user not only whether the library has a book but also whether it is currently available. When you start to use a computer terminal to search for data, don't hesitate to request help from clerks or librarians. In using the library catalog system, remember that books provide excellent historical, in-depth data on a subject. For many business problems, however, books are inadequate because the material is outdated. Periodicals are more timely.

Periodicals and Newspapers Magazines, pamphlets, and journals are called *periodicals* because of their recurrent publication. Journals, by the way, are compilations of scholarly articles. Journals and other periodicals generally provide the most up-to-date information on a topic. To locate articles in general-interest magazines (such as *Time, Newsweek, The New Yorker,* and *U.S. News & World Report*), consult *The Readers' Guide to Periodical Literature.* To locate articles in business, industrial, and trade magazines and journals (such as *Business Week, Management Review, Barron's,* and *Forbes*), consult the *Business Periodicals Index.*

Newspapers from around the country and the world also supply current information, as well as being fascinating to read. Locating articles on a topic, however, is difficult unless you limit yourself to the newspapers that index their articles. Some indexes to consider are *Barron's Index, Index of the Christian Science Monitor, Los Angeles Times Index, National Observer Index, New York Times Index,* and *The Street Journal Index.* Most of these indexes are also available in print or electronically through the *National Newspaper Index.*

Encyclopedias, Dictionaries, and Handbooks The reference section of a library contains special collections of helpful material. General encyclopedias include *Encyclopedia Americana, The Concise Columbia Encyclopedia,* and *Encyclopaedia Britannica.* Specialized encyclopedias include *Encyclopedia of American Economic History, Encyclopedia of Business Information Sources, Exporter's Encyclopedia,* and *Accountant's Encyclopedia.* The reference section may also house excellent dictionaries that function as encyclopedias, such as Prentice-Hall's *Encyclopedic Dictionary of Business.* Handbooks provide current data in specialized fields. For employment information consult the *Occupational Outlook Handbook* (published by the U.S. Department of Labor). Other handbooks include *Handbook of Auditing Methods, Handbook of Business Administration, Management Handbook,* and *Handbook for Office Professionals* (published by South-Western and coordinated with this textbook).

Databases Databases are collections of information usually accessed by computer. Vast amounts of data are now stored in computerized databases, making them huge electronic libraries. You can use them to conduct literature searches, check references, confirm statistics, quote experts, locate specific publications, and, in some instances, read entire documents. Because the computer can find items faster than even the most skilled researcher, these databases are rapidly becoming the principal source of secondary data today. In addition to speed, electronic databases provide access to stores of information that rival the holdings of the largest university and public libraries. Moreover, bibliographic data are constantly updated. Thus, database references are more current than printed indexes, which may lag as much as a year behind the publications they cite.

Databases can be grouped into three broad categories:

- *In-house databases*—consist of information related to the operations of a particular organization. Employees are able to access style manuals showing, for example, preferred spellings, document formats, and language usage. In-house systems also include user manuals for equipment, company policies and procedures, engineering drawings, and letters, memos, and specialized reports.
- *Statistical databases*—hold huge stores of numerical data, such as census information, employment figures, stock and bond values, and indexes, like the Consumer Price Index. The U.S. government supplies much of the statistics in databases.
- *Bibliographic databases*—contain listings of books, magazine articles, newspaper stories, and other publications. They may show a title, a summary, or the full text of an article. Most commonly used by researchers, these databases are rented to users who are charged for

every minute of search time. Two popular databases for business users are BRS (Bibliographic Retrieval Services) and DIALOG Information Services. For information about service and rates, call 1-800-555-1212 to obtain their toll-free numbers.

DOCUMENTING DATA

To give formal reports credibility and authority, researchers generally rely on a certain amount of secondary data obtained in print or electronically.

RESEARCH

To search for secondary data, consider the following tips:

- *Become acquainted with your library's resources, both print and electronic.* It pays to discuss your project with the reference librarian. By the way, several years ago a *Wall Street Journal* poll revealed that librarians are among the friendliest, most approachable people in the working world.
- *Before you begin working with listings of periodicals, find out what magazines your library has on-shelf.* It's most disappointing to find fascinating titles for articles in magazines that your library doesn't carry.
- *Don't allow yourself to become a victim of information overload.* You can't read everything that's been written about your subject. Look up only *relevant* and *current* references. Be selective.
- *Be resourceful and persevering when searching for data.* For example, if you're looking for information about speaking skills for businesspeople, you might look under such descriptors as *speech, communication, language, public relations,* and *conversation.* Don't forget to ask your librarian for help with key words.
- *Take excellent notes.* Place each reference on a separate card or sheet of paper. Record the author's name, title of the article or book, and complete publication information, in addition to your notes regarding the content of the references.
- *Limit the quotations in your report.* Good writers use direct quotes only to (1) emphasize opinions because of the author's status as an expert, (2) duplicate the exact wording before criticizing, or (3) repeat identical phrasing because of its precision, clarity, or aptness.

CITING REFERENCES

If you use data from secondary sources, the data must be acknowledged; that is, you must indicate where the data originated. Even if you paraphrase (put the information in your own words), the ideas must be documented. In Appendix C you will find three methods of documentation: (1) the footnote method, (2) the endnote method, and (3) the parenthetic or MLA method.

To document a formal report with secondary sources, you must take good notes, include source notes in the report, and list all references in a bibliography.

BIBLIOGRAPHY

A bibliography is an alphabetic list of all books, articles, and other sources of data cited or consulted in preparing a formal report. This list is useful to readers and a necessary component in a long, formal report. Instructions for preparing a bibliography are also given in Appendix C.

ORGANIZING DATA

Transparency 12.3

The overall presentation of a topic may be inductive or deductive, while parts of the report are chronological (such as the background) or topical (such as discussion of findings).

The readability of a report is greatly enhanced by skillful organization of the facts presented. You have already studied numerous strategies or plans of organization for shorter documents. Here is a brief overview of possible plans for the organization of formal reports:

- *Deductive.* As you recall from earlier instruction, the deductive strategy presents main ideas first. In formal reports that would mean beginning with proposals, recommendations, or findings. For example, if you were studying five possible locations for a proposed shopping center, you would begin with the recommendation of the best site and follow with discussion of other sites. Use this strategy when the reader is supportive and knowledgeable.

- *Inductive.* Inductive reasoning presents facts and discussion first, followed by conclusions and recommendations. Since formal reports generally seek to educate the reader, this order of presentation is often most effective. Following this sequence, a study of possible locations for a shopping center would begin with data regarding all proposed sites followed by analysis of the information and conclusions drawn from that analysis.

- *Chronological.* Information sequenced along a time frame is arranged chronologically. This plan is effective for presenting historical data or for describing a procedure. A description of the development of a multinational company, for example, would be chronological. A report explaining how to obtain federal funding for a project might be organized chronologically. Often topics are arranged in a past-to-present or present-to-past sequence.

- *Geographical or spatial.* Information arranged geographically or spatially is organized by physical location. For instance, a report analyzing a company's national sales might be divided into sections representing different geographical areas such as the East, South, Midwest, West, and Northwest.

- *Topical or functional.* Some subjects lend themselves to arrangement by topic or function. A report analyzing changes in the management hierarchy of an organization might be arranged in this manner. First, the report would consider the duties of the CEO followed by the function of the general manager, business manager, marketing manager, and so forth.

In organizing a formal report, you may find that you combine some of the preceding plans. However it's done, you must break your topic into major divisions, usually three to six. These major divisions then can be partitioned into smaller subdivisions. To identify these divisions, you may use functional heads (such as *Introduction, Findings, Discussion, Conclusions, Recommendations*) or talking heads that explain the contents of the text. You may wish to review the suggestions for writing effective headings that appeared in Chapter 11, page 224.

OUTLINING

Most writers agree that the best way to organize a report is by recording its divisions in an outline. Although this outline is not part of the final report, it is a valuable tool of the writer. It shows at a glance the overall organization of the report. Figure 12.1 shows an abbreviated outline of a report about forms of business ownership. Rarely is a real outline so perfectly balanced; some sections are usually longer than others. Remember, though, not to put a single topic under a major component. If you have only one subpoint, integrate it with the main item above it or reorganize. Use details, illustrations, and evidence to support subpoints.

Transparency 12.4

The format of your report headings is closely related to your outline. Figure 12.2 discusses and illustrates levels of headings.

ILLUSTRATING DATA

Tables, charts, graphs, illustrations, and other visual aids can play an important role in clarifying, summarizing, and emphasizing information. Numerical data become meaningful, complex ideas are simplified, and visual interest is provided by the appropriate use of graphics. Here are general tips for making the most effective use of visual aids:

The tips presented here for generating and implementing graphics in formal reports are useful in other presentations as well.

- Clearly identify the contents of the visual aid with meaningful titles and headings.
- Refer the reader to the visual aid by discussing it in the text and mentioning its location and figure number.
- Locate the table close to its reference in the text.
- Strive for vertical placement of visual aids. Readers are disoriented by horizontal pages in reports.
- Give credit to the source if appropriate.

FIGURE 12.1   Outline Format

FORMS OF BUSINESS OWNERSHIP

I. Sole proprietorship (*first main topic*)
  A. Advantages of sole proprietorship (*first subdivision of Topic I*)
    1. Minimal capital requirements (*first subdivision of Topic A*)
    2. Control by owner (*second subdivision of Topic A*)
  B. Disadvantages of sole proprietorship (*second subdivision of Topic I*)
    1. Unlimited liability (*first subdivision of Topic B*)
    2. Limited management talent (*second subdivision of Topic B*)
II. Partnership (*second main topic*)
  A. Advantages of partnership (*first subdivision of Topic II*)
    1. Access of capital (*first subdivision of Topic A*)
    2. Management talent (*second subdivision of Topic A*)
    3. Ease of formation (*third subdivision of Topic A*)
  B. Disadvantages of partnership (*second subdivision of Topic II*)
    1. Unlimited liability (*first subdivision of Topic B*)
    2. Personality conflicts (*second subdivision of Topic B*)

FIGURE 12.2   **Levels of Headings in Reports**

Center main heading in all-capital letters.

Center first-level subheadings and capitalize initial letters of main words.

Start second-level subheadings at left margin and capitalize initial letters of main words.

Indent third-level subheadings as part of paragraph and capitalize first letter.

REPORT, CHAPTER, AND PART TITLES

The title of a report, chapter heading or major part (such as CONTENTS or NOTES) should be centered in all caps. If the title requires more than one line, arrange it in an inverted triangle with the longest lines at the top. Begin the text a triple space (two blank lines) below the title, as shown here.

First-level Subheading

Headings indicating the first level of division are centered and underlined. Capitalize the first letter of each main word. Whether a report is single-spaced or double-spaced, most typists triple-space (leaving two blank lines) before and double-space (leaving one blank line) after a first-level subheading.

Every level of heading should be followed by some text. For example, we could not jump from "First-level Subheading," shown above, to "Second-level Subheading," shown below, without some discussion between.

Good writers strive to develop coherency and fluency by ending most sections with a lead-in that introduces the next section. The lead-in consists of a sentence or two announcing the next topic.

Second-level Subheading

Headings that divide topics introduced by first-level subheadings are underlined and begin at the left margin. Use a triple space above and a double space below a second-level subheading. If a report has only one level of heading, use either a first- or second-level subheading style.

Always be sure to divide topics into two or more subheadings. If you have only one subheading, eliminate it and absorb the discussion under the previous major heading. Try to make all headings within a level grammatically equal. For example, all second-level headings might use verb forms *(Preparing, Organizing,* and *Composing)* or noun forms *(Preparation, Organization,* and *Composition).*

Third-level subheading. Because it is part of the paragraph that follows, a third-level subheading is also called a "paragraph subheading." Capitalize only the first word and proper nouns in the subheading. Underline the subheading and end it with a period. Do not underline the period. Begin typing the paragraph text immediately following the period, as shown here. Double-space before a paragraph subheading.

TABLES

Probably the most frequently used visual aid in reports is the table. A table presents quantitative information in a systematic order of columns and rows. Be sure to identify columns and rows clearly. In Figure 12.3 *Years of Schooling Required* represents the row heading; *Current Jobs* and *New Jobs* represent column headings.

CHARTS AND GRAPHS

A chart or graph clarifies data by showing the relationship between one variable and another.

FIGURE 12.3   Table

TABLE 1

**SCHOOLING REQUIRED FOR CURRENT
AND FUTURE EMPLOYMENT**

YEARS OF SCHOOLING REQUIRED	CURRENT JOBS	JOBS IN YEAR 2000
8 years or less	6%	4%
1 to 3 years of high school	12%	10%
4 years of high school	40%	34%
1 to 3 years of college	20%	22%
4 years of college or more	22%	30%

Source: Bureau of Labor Statistics, Hudson Institute.

Pie Charts   Pie, or circle, charts help readers visualize a whole and the proportions of its components, as shown in Figure 12.4. Pie charts are particularly useful in showing percentages. In preparing pie charts, begin dividing the pie at the 12 o'clock position. It's helpful to include both a description and the actual percent of the total with each segment. To avoid visual clutter, group a number of small components into one segment. All segments should total 100 percent. Labels are easiest to read when typed horizontally outside the segments.

Line Charts   Line charts are useful in showing changes in quantitative data over time. Like many visual aids, line charts cannot show precise data; instead, they give an impression of a trend or movement. Notice in Figure 12.5 that the time variable (years) is shown horizontally and the quantitative variable (pounds of production) is shown vertically.

FIGURE 12.4   Pie Chart

New Entrants to U.S. Labor Force by Year 2000
Distributed by Sex and Citizenship

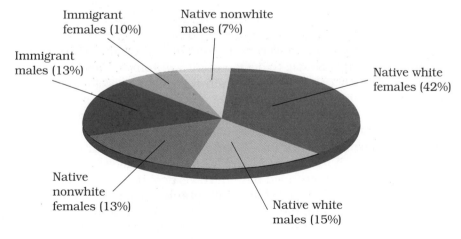

Source: U.S. Bureau of Labor Statistics

FIGURE 12.5   **Line Chart**

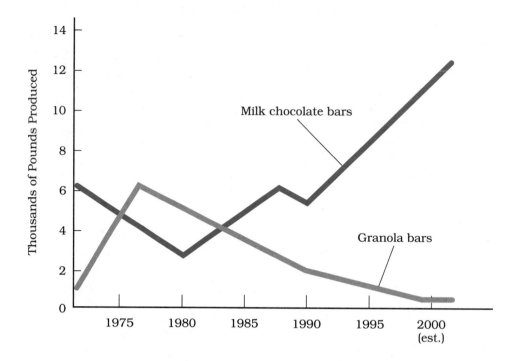

TRENDS IN CANDY BAR PRODUCTION

Bar Charts   A bar chart uses horizontal bars or vertical columns to compare information. Figure 12.6 shows fast-growing occupations projected to the year 2000. Could this information have been meaningfully expressed in a pie chart?

Organization Chart   An organizational chart shows management structure and lines of authority. The chart in Figure 12.7 defines the hierarchy of authority from the board of directors to individual managers.

USING YOUR COMPUTER TO PRODUCE CHARTS

Designing effective bar charts, pie charts, figures, and other graphics is easy with today's software. Spreadsheet programs—such as Lotus 1-2-3, Excel, and QuattroPro—and presentation graphics programs—such as Harvard Graphics, Microsoft PowerPoint, and Lotus Freelance Graphics— allow even nontechnical people to design quality graphics. These graphics can be printed directly on paper for written reports or used for transparency masters and slides for oral presentations. The benefits of preparing visual aids on a computer are near-professional quality, shorter preparation time, and substantial savings in costs.

    To prepare a computer graphic, begin by assembling your data, usually in table form (such as that in Figure 12.3). Next, choose what type of chart you want: pie chart, grouped bar chart, vertical bar chart, horizontal bar chart, organization chart, or some other graphic. To make a pie chart, key in the data or select the data from an existing file. Add a title for the chart, as well as any necessary labels. For a bar or line chart, indicate the horizontal and vertical axes (reference lines or beginning points). Most programs will automatically generate legends for figures.

FIGURE 12.6   Bar Chart

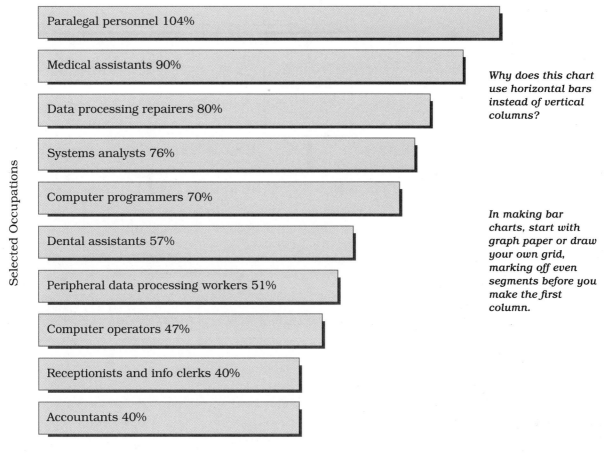

Percent of Growth

Selected Occupations

- Paralegal personnel 104%
- Medical assistants 90%
- Data processing repairers 80%
- Systems analysts 76%
- Computer programmers 70%
- Dental assistants 57%
- Peripheral data processing workers 51%
- Computer operators 47%
- Receptionists and info clerks 40%
- Accountants 40%

Why does this chart use horizontal bars instead of vertical columns?

In making bar charts, start with graph paper or draw your own grid, marking off even segments before you make the first column.

Fast-Growing Occupations, 1990–2000
Source: Bureau of Labor Statistics

The finished chart can be printed on paper or imported into your word processing document to be printed with your finished report.

PRESENTING THE FINAL REPORT

Long reports generally are organized into three major divisions and a number of subdivisions. The order and contents of three divisions in a formal report are outlined here.

PREFATORY PARTS (PARTS PRECEDING THE BODY)
Title fly*
Title page
Letter of authorization*
Letter or memo of transmittal
Table of contents
Abstract, synopsis, epitome, or executive summary

Transparency 12.5

Long, formal reports contain three major sections: prefatory parts, body, and supplementary parts.

*Not illustrated in our model formal report.

FIGURE 12.7   **Organization Chart**

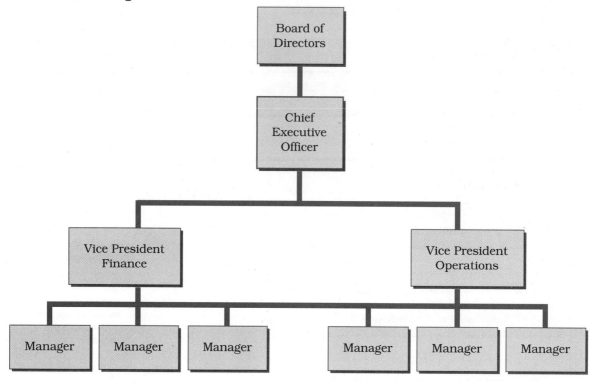

BODY
Introduction or background
Discussion of findings
Summary, conclusions, recommendations

SUPPLEMENTARY PARTS
Endnotes or works cited
Bibliography
Appendix*

Now let's look more carefully at the individual parts of a long, formal report. Refer to Figure 12.8 on page 261 for illustration of most of these parts.

- *Title fly.* A single page with the title begins a formal report. In less formal reports, the title fly is omitted. Compose the title of your report carefully so that it shows immediately what the report covers and what it does not cover.
- *Title page.* In addition to the title, the title page shows the author, the individual or organization who authorized the report, the recipient of the report, and the date.
- *Letter of authorization.* If a letter or memo authorized the report, it may be included in the prefatory material. This optional part is omitted from the model in Figure 12.8.

*Not illustrated in our model formal report.

- *Letter of transmittal.* This is the first impression the reader receives of the report; as such, it should be given serious consideration. Use the direct strategy and include some or all of the suggestions here:

  1. Deliver the report ("Here is the report you authorized").
  2. Present an overview of the report.
  3. Suggest how to read or interpret it.
  4. Describe limitations, if they exist.
  5. Acknowledge those who assisted you.
  6. Suggest follow-up studies, if appropriate.
  7. Express appreciation for the assignment.
  8. Offer to discuss the report personally.

- *Table of contents.* Identify the name and location of every part of the report except the title fly, title page, and table of contents itself. Use spaced periods (leaders) to join the part with its page number.
- *Abstract, synopsis, epitome, or executive summary.* A summary condensing the entire report may carry any of these names. This time-saving device summarizes the purpose, findings, and conclusions.
- *Introduction or background.* After the prefatory parts, begin the body of the report with an introduction that includes any or all of the following items:

  1. Explanation of how the report originated and why it was authorized
  2. Description of the problem that prompted the report and the specific research questions to be answered
  3. Purpose of the report
  4. Scope (boundaries) and limitations or restrictions of the research
  5. Sources and methods of collecting data
  6. Summary of findings, if the report is written deductively
  7. Preview of the major sections of the report to follow, thus providing coherence and transition for the reader

- *Discussion of findings.* This is the main section of the report and contains numerous headings and subheadings. It is unnecessary to use the title *Discussion of Findings;* many business report writers prefer to begin immediately with the major headings into which the body of the report is divided. As with short reports, you may organize the body deductively, inductively, chronologically, geographically, or topically. Present your findings objectively, avoiding the use of first-person pronouns (*I, we*). Include tables, charts, and graphs if necessary to illustrate findings. Analytic and scientific reports may include another section entitled *Implications of Findings,* in which the findings are analyzed and related to the problem. Less formal reports contain the author's analysis of the research findings within the *Discussion* section.
- *Summary, conclusions, recommendations.* If the report has been largely informational, it ends with a summary of the data presented. If the report analyzes research findings, then it ends with conclusions drawn from the analyses. An analytic report frequently poses research questions. The conclusion to such a report reviews the major findings and answers the research questions.

If a report seeks to determine a course of action, it may end with conclusions and recommendations. The recommendations regarding a course of action may be placed in a separate section or incorporated with the conclusions.

- *Footnotes, endnotes, or works cited.* See Appendix C for details on how to document sources. In the footnote method the source notes appear at the foot of each page. In the endnote method they are displayed immediately after the text on a page called *Notes.* In the parenthetic or MLA method of documentation, the notes are listed on a page called *Works Cited* or *Works Consulted.*

- *Bibliography.* Most formal reports will include a bibliography that lists all sources consulted in the report research—whether they were actually cited in notes or not. See Appendix C regarding the bibliography.

- *Appendix.* The appendix contains any supplementary information needed to clarify the report. Charts and graphs illustrating significant data are generally part of the report proper. However, extra information that might be included in an appendix are such items as a sample questionnaire, a questionnaire cover letter, correspondence relating to the report, maps, other reports, and optional tables.

FIGURE 12.8 Model Formal Report

Title Page

Transparency Masters 12.5–12.14

ECONOMIC IMPACT OF ROXBURY INDUSTRIAL PARK
ON THE CITY OF BOSTON

Prepared for
The Boston City Council
Boston, Massachusetts

Prepared by
Diana Del Rio
Senior Research Consultant
Monroe, Del Rio Research Consultants

January 10, 199x

Includes report title in all caps with longer line above shorter line.

Highlights name of report recipient.

Identifies report writer.

Omits page number.

The title page is usually arranged in four evenly balanced areas. If the report is to be bound on the left, move the left margin and center point $\frac{1}{4}$ inch to the right. Notice that no page number appears on the title page, although it is counted as page i. If you use scalable fonts and a laser printer to enhance your report, be careful to avoid anything unprofessional—such as too many type fonts, oversized print, and inappropriate graphics.

Letter of Transmittal

MONROE, DEL RIO INDUSTRIAL CONSULTANTS
588 Park Avenue
Boston, Massachusetts 02116

January 12, 199x

City Council
City of Boston
Boston, MA 02290

Ladies and Gentlemen:

Announces report and identifies authorization.

The attached report, requested by the Boston City Council in a letter to Goldman-Lyon & Associates dated May 20, describes the economic impact of Roxbury Industrial Park on the city of Boston. We believe you will find the results of this study useful in evaluating future development of industrial parks within the city limits.

Gives broad overview of report purposes.

This study was designed to examine economic impact in three areas:

(1) Current and projected tax and other revenues accruing to the city from Roxbury Industrial Park

(2) Current and projected employment generated by the park

(3) Indirect effects on local employment, income, and economic growth

Describes primary and secondary research.

Primary research consisted of interviews with 15 Roxbury Industrial Park tenants and managers, in addition to a 1994 survey of over 5,000 RIP employees. Secondary research sources included the Annual Budget of the City of Boston, county and state tax records, government publications, professional periodicals, and relevant books. Results of this research, discussed more fully in this report, indicate that Roxbury Industrial Park exerts a significant beneficial influence on the Boston metropolitan economy.

Offers to discuss report; expresses appreciation.

I would be pleased to discuss this report and its conclusions with you at your request. My firm and I thank you for your confidence in selecting our company to prepare this comprehensive report.

Sincerely,

Diana Del Rio

Diana Del Rio
Senior Research Consultant

DDR:mef
Attachment

A letter or memo of transmittal announces the report topic and explains who authorized it. It briefly describes the project and previews the conclusions, if the reader is supportive. Such messages generally close by expressing appreciation for the assignment, suggesting follow-up actions, acknowledging the help of others, or offering to answer questions. The margins for the transmittal should be the same as for the report, about $1\frac{1}{4}$ inches on all sides.

Table of Contents and List of Figures

TABLE OF CONTENTS

LIST OF FIGURES

Uses leaders to guide eye from heading to page number.

Indents secondary headings to show levels of outline.

Includes tables and figures in one list for simplified numbering.

Because the table of contents and the list of figures for this report are small, they are combined on one page. Notice that the titles of major report parts are in all caps, while other headings are a combination of upper- and lowercase letters. The style duplicates those within the report. Advanced word processing capabilities enable you to generate a contents page automatically, including leaders and accurate page numbering—no matter how many times you revise.

Abstract

Opens directly with major research findings.

Identifies data sources.

Summarizes organi- zation of report.

Condenses recommendations.

ABSTRACT

The city of Boston can benefit from the development of industrial parks like the Rox- bury Industrial Park. Both direct and indirect economic benefits result, as shown by this in-depth study conducted by Monroe, Del Rio Industrial Consultants. The study was authorized by the Boston City Council when Goldman-Lyon & Associates sought the City Council's approval for the proposed construction of a G-L industrial park. The City Coun- cil requested evidence demonstrating that an existing development could actually benefit the city.

Our conclusion that the city of Boston benefits from industrial parks is based on data supplied by a survey of 5,000 Roxbury Industrial Park employees, personal interviews with managers and tenants of RIP, city and state documents, and professional literature.

Analysis of the data revealed benefits in three areas:

(1) Revenues. The city of Boston earned nearly $1 million in tax and other revenues from the Roxbury Industrial Park in 1988. By 1995 this income is expected to reach $1.7 million (in constant 1988 dollars).

(2) Employment. In 1988 RIP businesses employed a total of 7,035 workers, who earned an average wage of $24,920. By 1995 RIP businesses are expected to employ directly nearly 15,000 employees who will earn salaries totaling over $450 million.

(3) Indirect benefits. Because of the multiplier effect, by 1995 Roxbury Industrial Park will directly and indirectly generate a total of 38,362 jobs in the Boston metropolitan area.

On the basis of these findings, it is recommended that development of additional industrial parks be encouraged to stimulate local economic growth.

An abstract or executive summary highlights report findings, conclu- sions, and recommendations. Its length depends on the report it sum- marizes. A 100-page report might require a 10-page abstract. Shorter reports may contain 1-page abstracts, as shown here. Unlike letters of transmittal (which may contain personal pronouns and references to the writer), abstracts are formal and impersonal. They use the same margins as the body of the report.

Page 1

ECONOMIC IMPACT OF ROXBURY INDUSTRIAL PARK

PROBLEM

This study was designed to analyze the direct and indirect economic impact of Roxbury Industrial Park on the city of Boston. Specifically, the study seeks answers to these questions:

(1) What current tax and other revenues result directly from this park? What tax and other revenues may be expected in the future?

(2) How many and what kind of jobs are directly attributable to the park? What is the employment picture for the future?

(3) What indirect effects has Roxbury Industrial Park had on local employment, incomes, and economic growth?

BACKGROUND

The development firm of Goldman-Lyon & Associates commissioned this study of Roxbury Industrial Park at the request of the Boston City Council. Before authorizing the development of a proposed Goldman-Lyon industrial park, the City Council requested a study examining the economic effects of an existing park. Members of the City Council wanted to determine to what extent industrial parks benefit the local community, and they chose Roxbury Industrial Park as an example.

For those who are unfamiliar with it, Roxbury Industrial Park is a 400-acre industrial park located in the city of Boston about 4 miles from the center of the city. Most of the area lies within a specially designated area known as Redevelopment Project No. 2, which is under the jurisdiction of the Boston Redevelopment Agency. Planning for the park began in 1980; construction started in 1982.

Lists three problem questions.

Describes authorization for report and background of study.

The first page of a formal report contains the title printed 2 inches from the top edge. Titles for major parts of a report (such as *Problem, Background, Findings,* and *Conclusions*) are centered in all caps. First-level headings (such as *Employment* on page 267) are underscored and printed with upper- and lowercase letters. Second-level headings (such as *Distribution* on page 267) begin at the side. See Figure 12.2 for illustration of heading formats.

Page 2

The park now contains 14 building complexes with over 1.25 million square feet of completed building space. The majority of the buildings are used for office, research and development, marketing and distribution, or manufacturing uses. Approximately 50 acres of the original area are yet to be developed.

Provides specifics for data sources.

Data for this report came from a 1994 survey of over 5,000 Roxbury Industrial Park employees, interviews with 15 RIP tenants and managers, the Annual Budget of the City of Boston, county and state tax records, current books, and articles from professional journals. Projections for future revenues resulted from analysis of past trends and "Estimates of Revenues for Debt Service Coverage, Redevelopment Project Area 2."

DISCUSSION OF FINDINGS

Previews organization of report.

The results of this research indicate that major direct and indirect benefits have accrued to the city of Boston and surrounding metropolitan areas as a result of the development of Roxbury Industrial Park. the research findings presented here fall into three categories: (a) revenues, (b) employment, and (c) indirect effects.

Revenues

Roxbury Industrial Park contributes a variety of tax and other revenues to the city of Boston. Figure 1 summarizes revenues.

Positions figure close to textual reference.

Figure 1

REVENUES RECEIVED BY THE CITY OF BOSTON
FROM ROXBURY INDUSTRIAL PARK

Current Revenues and Projections to 1999

	1994	1999
Sales and use taxes	$604,140	$1,035,390
Revenues from licenses	126,265	216,396
Franchise taxes	75,518	129,424
State gas tax receipts	53,768	92,134
Licenses and permits	48,331	82,831
Other revenues	64,039	111,987
Total	$972,061	$1,668,162

Source: State Board of Equalization *Bulletin*. Boston: State Printing Office, 1994, 103.

2

Notice that this formal report is single-spaced. Many businesses prefer this space-saving format. However, some organizations prefer double-spacing, especially for preliminary drafts. Page numbers may be centered 1 inch from the bottom of the page or placed 1 inch from the upper right corner at the margin. Strive to leave a minimum of 1 inch for top, bottom, and side margins.

Page 3

Sales and Use Revenues

As shown in Figure 1, the city's largest source of revenues from RIP is the sales and use tax. Revenues from this source totaled $604,140 in 1994, according to figures provided by the Massachusetts State Board of Equalization.[1] Sales and use taxes accounted for more than half of the park's total contribution to the city of $972,062.

Other Revenues

Other major sources of city revenues from RIP in 1994 include alcohol licenses, motor vehicle in lieu fees, and trailer coach licenses ($126,265), franchise taxes ($75,518), and state gas tax receipts ($53,768).

Projections

Total city revenues from RIP will nearly double by 1999. producing an income of $1.7 million. This projection is based on an annual growth rate in sales of 8 percent in constant 1990 dollars.

Employment

One of the most important factors to consider in the overall effect of an industrial park is employment. In Roxbury Industrial Park the distribution, number, and wages of people employed will change considerably in the next five years.

Distribution

A total of 7,035 employees currently work in various industry groups at Roxbury Industrial Park, as shown in Figure 2. The largest number of workers (58 percent) is employed in manufacturing and assembly operations. In the next largest category, the computer and electronics industry employs 24 percent of the workers. Some overlap between the manufacturing and computer categories probably exists because electronics assembly could be included in either group. Employees also work in publishing (9 percent), warehousing and storage (5 percent), and other industries (4 percent).

Although the distribution of employees at Roxbury Industrial Park shows a wide range of employment categories, it must be noted that other industrial parks would likely generate an entirely different range of job categories.

3

Continues interpreting figures in table.

Sets stage for next topics to be discussed.

Only the most important research findings are interpreted and discussed for readers. The depth of discussion depends on the intended length of the report, the goal of the writer, and the expectations of the reader. Because the writer wants this report to be formal in tone, she avoids *I* and *we* in all discussions.

Page 4

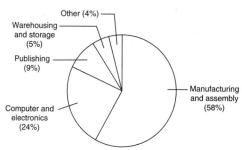

Figure 2

EMPLOYMENT DISTRIBUTION OF INDUSTRY GROUPS

Other (4%)
Warehousing
and storage
(5%)
Publishing
(9%)
Computer and
electronics
(24%)
Manufacturing
and assembly
(58%)

Source: 1994 survey of RIP employees.

Wages

In 1994 employees at RIP earned a total of $181.5 million in wages, as shown in Figure 3. The average employee in that year earned $24,920. The highest average wages were paid to employees in white-collar fields, such as computer and electronics ($32,800) and publishing ($26,300). Average wages for workers in blue-collar fields ranged from $23,400 in manufacturing and assembly to $20,200 in warehousing and storage.

Figure 3

8AVERAGE ANNUAL WAGES BY INDUSTRIAL GROUPS

Roxbury Industrial Park, 1994

Industry Group	Employees	Annual Wages	Total
Manufacturing and assembly	4,073	$23,400	$95,308,200
Computer and electronics	1,657	32,800	55,349,600
Publishing	672	26,300	17,673,600
Warehousing and storage	370	20,200	7,474,000
Other	263	21,900	5,759,700
Total	7,035	$24,920	$181,565,100

Source: 1994 Survey of RIP employees.

4

If you use figures or tables, be sure to introduce them in the text (for example, *as shown in Figure 3*). Although it's not always possible, try to place them close to the spot where they are first mentioned. To save space, you can print the title of a figure at its side. Because this report contains few tables and figures, the writer named them all "Figures" and numbered them consecutively.

Projections

By 1999 Roxbury Industrial Park is expected to more than double its number of employees, bringing the total to over 15,000 workers. The total payroll in 1995 will also more than double, producing over $450 million (using constant 1988 dollars) in salaries to RIP employees. These projections are based on an 8 percent growth rate,[2] along with anticipated increased employment as the park reaches its capacity.

Future development in the park will influence employment and payrolls. One RIP project manager stated in an interview that much of the remaining 50 acres is planned for medium-rise office buildings, garden offices, and other structures for commercial, professional, and personal services.[3] Average wages for employees are expected to increase because of an anticipated shift to higher-paying white-collar jobs. Industrial parks often follow a similar pattern of evolution.[4] Like many industrial parks, RIP evolved from a warehousing center to a manufacturing complex at a time when

Clarifies informa-tion and tells what it means in relation to original research questions.

CONCLUSIONS AND RECOMMENDATIONS

Analysis of tax revenues, employment data, personal interviews, and professional literature leads to the following conclusions and recommendations about the economic impact of Roxbury Industrial Park on the city of Boston:

1. Sales tax and other revenues produced nearly $1 million in income to the city of Boston in 1994. By 1999 sales tax and other revenues are expected to produce $1.7 million in city income.

2. RIP currently employs 7,035 employees, the majority of whom are working in manufacturing and assembly. The average employee in 1994 earned $24,920.

3. By 1999 RIP is expected to employ more than 15,000 workers producing a total payroll of over $450 million.

4. Employment trends indicate that by 1999 more RIP employees will be engaged in higher-paying white-collar positions.

On the basis of these findings, we recommend that the City Council of Boston authorize the development of additional industrial parks to stimulate local economic growth.

5

Summarizes conclusions and recommendations.

After discussing and interpreting the research findings, the writer articulates what she considers the most important conclusions and recommendations. Longer, more complex reports may have separate sections for conclusions and resulting recommendations. In this report they are combined. Notice that it is unnecessary to start a new page for the conclusions.

Notes and Bibliography

**Documents refer-
ences in order of
appearance in text.**

NOTES

1. Massachusetts State Board of Equalization, *Bulletin* (Boston: State Printing Office, 1993) 26.

2. Arthur M. Miller, "Estimates of Revenues for Debt Service Coverage, Redevelopment Project Area No. 2," *Miller and Schroeder Municipals* (New York: Rincon Press, 1993) 78-79.

3. Ivan M. Novack, personal interview, 30 September 1994.

4. Deborah Law and Wayne Barry, *Industrial Development in a Healthy Economy* (New York: Dryden Press, 1991) 320.

5. Law and Barry, 81.

BIBLIOGRAPHY

**Lists all sources
alphabetically in
hanging indented
form.**

City of Boston. *Annual Budget*. Boston, Massachusetts: Municipal Printing Office, 1989.

Cohen, Allen P. "Industrial Parks Invade Suburbia." *The New York Times*, 10 December 1990, Sec. IV, 1, cols. 4-5.

Law, Deborah, and Wayne Barry. "Commercial Developments in Our Future" *Business Week*, 14 June 1992, 91.

Massachusetts State Board of Equalization. *Bulletin*. Boston: State Printing Office, 1990.

**A bibliography may
be omitted if few
sources are cited.**

Miller, Arthur M. "Estimates of Revenues for Debt Service Coverage, Redevelopment Project Area No. 2," *Miller and Schroeder Municipals*. New York: Rincon Press, 1987.

Novack, Ivan M. Personal interview. 30 September 1994.

Suffolk County Auditor-Controller. *Prospectus for Tax Allocated Bonds*. Boston, Massachusetts: County Printing Office, 1989.

All references cited within the text are listed in the Notes. For more information about documentation styles, see Appendix C. Notes entries are arranged as they appear in the text, while bibliography entries are alphabetical. Some writers include all works they investigated in the bibliography. Most word processing software programs today automatically update footnotes within the text and print a complete list for you, thus making documentation almost painless.

APPLICATION AND PRACTICE—12

Discussion

1. If formal reports are seldom written in business, why study them?
2. How is the process of writing a formal report similar to that of writing an informal report?
3. How could a report be organized inductively and topically at the same time?
4. Should every long, formal report have graphic aids? Explain.
5. Distinguish between primary and secondary data. Which are more likely to be useful in a business report?

Short Answers

6. Name five plans for organizing data in a formal report. Be prepared to explain each.
   1. *Deductive*
   2. *Inductive*
   3. *Chronological*
   4. *Geographical or spatial*
   5. *Topical or functional*

7. What is the first step in writing a formal report?
   Defining the project, including limiting its scope

8. If you were writing a formal report on computerizing your company's accounting functions, what primary sources of data would you seek? Be prepared to explain.
   Company records, observation, interviews, possibly surveys and experiments

9. List four sources of secondary information, and be prepared to discuss how each might be useful in writing a formal report on computerizing your company's accounting functions.
   1. *Guide to periodicals (probably most useful)*
   2. *Encyclopedia, dictionary, handbook*
   3. *Card catalog*
   4. *Newspapers*
   5. *Computer databases*

10. List four levels of headings, and explain how they are different.
    1. *First-level headings include main topics. They are typed in all caps and centered.*
    2. *Second-level headings subdivide main topics. They are underscored and centered. Only major words are capitalized.*
    3. *Third-level headings subdivide second-level topics. They are typed at the left margin and underscored. Major words are capitalized.*
    4. *Fourth-level headings subdivide third-level topics. Also called "paragraph headings," they are indented like a paragraph and underscored. Only the first word and proper nouns are capitalized.*

11. Pie charts are most helpful in showing what?
    Parts of a whole (percentages)

12. Line graphs are most effective in showing what?
    Changes in quantitative data over time

13. If you've never used a library or an electronic database, where should you probably begin?
Consult the reference librarian and printed materials describing the use of your library and its electronic search techniques.

14. List the parts of a formal report. Be prepared to discuss each.

Title fly	*Introduction or background*
Title page	*Discussion of findings*
Letter of authorization	*Summary, conclusions,*
Letter of transmittal	* recommendations*
Table of contents	*Footnotes, endnotes, or works cited*
Abstract, synopsis, epitome, or execu-	*Bibliography*
* tive summary*	*Appendix*

15. Should business reports be single- or double-spaced?
Follow the style of the organization authorizing the report.

⊃ **Instructor:** *Writing Improvement Exercises are available on diskette.*

Transparency Master 12.1

Writing Improvement Exercises

Outlining

16. Construct an outline using the following data gathered initially to write a report. Include a title. Assume that you would collect more data later. After you complete the outline, indicate what level of heading each line of the outline would require.

> The operation of a business would be very risky without some form of property insurance. Most fire insurance policies protect against loss to buildings and their contents. Wooden buildings, of course, would cost more than brick buildings to insure. The contents of buildings are valued separately. Insurance experts believe that nearly one-third of all business-related fires may be caused by arson. Another form of property insurance is marine insurance. Ocean marine insurance is the oldest form of insurance in the country. It protects the ship and its cargo. Inland marine insurance, strangely enough, protects against damage to property being transported in three areas: goods transported by ship, truck, or train—that is, goods being moved by any of these three means may be covered with inland marine insurance.
>
> Nearly 30 million automobile accidents occur each year in the United States. Automobile insurance is a form of property insurance. It covers many areas, including bodily injury, medical payment coverage (to protect policyholders, their family members, and any passengers in the car), and uninsured motorist coverage. Auto insurance also includes property damage. This pays the cost of damage to other people's property (such as buildings and cars). Collision insurance is different. It pays for damage to the policyholder's car. You can have full coverage or deductible ($100 to $500).

⊃ **Instructor:** *See solution on page 78.*

Organizing. Assume that you are a research consultant with Search, Inc. Your firm has been asked to find a sales and distribution site in the Denver area for Farrell Electrical Components, 3450 Overland Avenue, Los Angeles, CA 90034. Farrell seeks suitable office space, including a reception area (where three office employees could work), one private office, and a conference/display area. Farrell also wants 3,000 square feet of heated warehouse space. It should be equipped with a sprinkler system and have 18-foot ceilings. If sales are successful, Farrell may need an additional

2,000 square feet of warehouse space in the future. Farrell needs to locate near Stapleton International Airport; moreover, it must be close to trucking terminals and main thoroughfares in an area zoned for light industry. It also seeks an impressive-looking building with a modern executive image. Farrell wants to lease for at least two years with possible renewal. It needs to make a decision within three weeks. If no space is available, it will delay until next year.

You have been assigned the task of researching this assignment and then writing a report that includes a recommendation for Farrell based on your findings.

17. Who is the audience for this long report? Should you include extensive background data explaining why the report is being written? Explain.

Transparency Master 12.2

The audience is the management of Farrell Electrical Components. Because the audience is familiar with the project, it is unnecessary to present extensive background data.

18. Would you rely on primary or secondary research? How would you gather data for this report?
You would probably rely on primary research. Observe newspaper ads to identify agencies that lease commercial properties. Interview leasing agents by telephone and in person. Examine industrial parks and other available facilities.

19. What constraints will limit your research?
Three-week time limit; only one person to do the research; limited funds available

20. What visual aids would enhance this report?
Map showing area under consideration; table comparing rates for proposed sites; table comparing options of proposed sites; picture of recommended site

21. On a separate sheet write a statement of purpose that could become part of the introduction to your report. Include Farrell's requirements.

Instructor: See solution on p. 78.

22. You have narrowed the choices to five locations near Stapleton International Airport. On a separate sheet make a table from the following rough notes. Include a title and subtitle, as well as appropriate columnar headings

Instructor: See solution on p. 79.

(1) The site at 3348 Quebec Street has 1,800 square feet of office space and 3,500 square feet of warehouse space with an option for additional space. Cost: $2,200 per month with a 1-year minimum lease.

(2) A space in the Aurora Industrial Park offers only 1,000 square feet of office space but it has 6,000 square feet of warehouse space. Cost: $2,750 per month with a 3-year lease preferred.

(3) A warehouse at 2280 Monaco Street Parkway has 3,000 square feet of warehouse space with an option to expand. It rents for $1,950 per month with 1,200 square feet for offices. Minimum 1-year lease.

(4) 30 Colfax Center offers 1,000 square feet of office space and 3,500 square feet of warehouse space but cannot guarantee additional warehouse space in the future. Cost: $3,000 per month, with a 2-year lease.

(5) A building at 3340 Montview Avenue will lease for only $1,500 per month. It has a total of 3,800 square feet, of which 800 square feet is office space. The rest is warehousing, 2-year lease. Additional warehouse space is available.

23. Compose a lead-in sentence that introduces the preceding table in your report.
    The following table compares five locations in the Stapleton International Airport area that may satisfy your requirements.

24. What strategy would you follow in organizing this report? Why?
    Arrange the report deductively if you wish to present your conclusions and recommendations first. Arrange the report inductively if you decide to discuss your findings first and then draw conclusions from the findings. (Inductive organization seems most logical to the author.) Within the findings section you will probably arrange the information topically or from most important to least important.

Activities

25. **Visual aids** From *U.S. News & World Report, USA Today, Business Week,* a textbook, or some other publication, locate one example of a table, a pie chart, a line chart, a bar chart, and an organization chart. Bring copies of these visual aids to class. How effectively could the data have been expressed in words, without the graphics? Is the appropriate graphic form used? How is the graphic introduced in the text? Your instructor may wish you to submit a memo discussing visual aids.

26. **Library** Assume that you have been asked to recommend a library to fellow students who have little library experience. Visit your school or public library. Observe its resources, method of operation, shelf lists, electronic capabilities, and personnel. Write a one-page memo report describing your findings.

27. **Bibliography** Select a topic that interests you. Prepare a bibliography of at least five current magazine articles, three books, and five other references that contain relevant information regarding the topic. Your instructor may ask you to divide your bibliography into sections: *Books, Periodicals, Other Resources.* You may also be asked to annotate your bibliography, that is, to compose a brief description of each reference, such as this:

    > Rash, Wayne, Jr. "Dawn of the Dead Disk." *Byte,* July 1993, 137–140. This article discusses the need for timely, complete backups of data stored on hard disks so that when a hard disk crashes, a business may continue with the least interruption.

28. **Computer databases** Compose a list of computer information sources available through a library in your area. What are the charges for receiving data? What is the procedure for using the services? Write a memo describing your findings. Include one or more visual aids to illustrate your data.

CASE 12-1

↪ *Instructor: For additional formal report topics, see pp. 76–77.*

FORMAL REPORT: READABILITY OF INSURANCE POLICIES

The 21st Century Insurance Company is concerned about the readability of its policies. State legislators are beginning to investigate com-

FIGURE 12.9   21st Century Insurance Company Policyholder Survey

RESPONSE TO STATEMENT "I AM ABLE TO READ AND UNDERSTAND THE LANGUAGE AND PROVISIONS OF MY POLICY."

AGE GROUP	STRONGLY AGREE	AGREE	UNDECIDED	DISAGREE	STRONGLY DISAGREE
18–34	2%	9%	34%	41%	14%
35–49	2	17	38	33	10
50–64	1	11	22	35	31
65+	1	2	17	47	33

plaints of policyholders who say they can't understand their insurance policies. One judge lambasted insurers, saying, "The language in these policies is bureaucratic gobbledygook, jargon, double-talk, a form of officialese, federalese, and insurancese that does not qualify as English. The burden upon organizations is to write policies in a manner designed to communicate rather than to obfuscate." Taking the initiative in improving its policies, 21st Century hires you as a consultant to study its standard policy and make recommendations.

Examine a life, fire, or health insurance policy that you or a friend or relative holds. Select one that is fairly complex. Study the policy for jargon, confusing language, long sentences, and unclear antecedents. Evaluate its format, print size, paper and print quality, amount of white space, and use of headings. Does it have an index or glossary? Are difficult terms defined? How easy is it to find specifics, should a policyholder want to check something?

In addition to the data you collect from your own examination of the policy, 21st Century gives you the data shown in Figure 12.9 from a recent policyholder survey. Prepare a report for Heather Garcia, vice president, 21st Century Insurance Company, discussing your analysis, conclusions, and recommendations for improving its basic policy.

CASE 12-2

FORMAL REPORT: FAST-FOOD CHECKUP

Select a fast-food franchise in your area. Assume that the national franchising headquarters has received complaints about the service, quality, and cleanliness of the unit.

You have been sent to inspect and to report on what you see. Visit on two or more occasions. Make notes on how many customers were served, how quickly they received their food, and how courteously they were treated. Observe the number of employees and supervisors working. Note the cleanliness of observable parts of the restaurant. Inspect the restroom as well as the exterior and surrounding grounds. Sample the food. Your boss is a stickler for details; he has no use for general statements like *The restroom was not clean.* Be specific. Draw conclusions. Are the complaints justified? If improvements are necessary, make recommendations. Address your report to Lawrence C. Kelsey, President.

C A S E 12-3

FORMAL REPORT: A PRIVATE PROBLEM

In a business, organization, or field you know, think about a problem or issue that needs investigation. Assume that a president, owner, supervisor, or executive asks you to examine the problem or issue and analyze its causes and ramifications. Consider ways to solve the problem or define the issue. Draw conclusions based on your analysis. Make specific recommendations for implementing changes necessary to achieve the solution. Be sure to narrow the problem sufficiently so that it can be broken into three to five segments or factors.

C A S E 12-4

COLLABORATIVE FORMAL REPORT: INTERCULTURAL COMMUNICATION

American businesses are expanding into foreign markets with manufacturing plants, sales offices, and branch offices abroad. Unfortunately, most Americans have little knowledge of or experience with people from other cultures. To prepare for participation in the global marketplace, collect information for a report focused on a Pacific Rim, Latin American, or European country where English is not spoken. Before selecting the country, though, consult your campus international program for volunteers who are willing to be interviewed. Your instructor may make advance arrangements seeking international student volunteers.

In teams of three to five, collect information about your target country from the library and other sources. Then invite an international student representing your target country to be interviewed by your group. In your primary and secondary research, investigate the topics listed in Figure 12.10. Confirm what you learn in your secondary research by talking with your interviewee. When you complete your research, write a report for the CEO of your company (make up a name and company). Assume that your company plans to explain its operations abroad. Your report should advise the company's executives of social customs, family life, attitudes, religions, education, and values in the target country. Remember that your company's interests are business-oriented; don't dwell on tourist information. Write your report individually or in teams.

FIGURE 12.10　Intercultural Interview Topics and Questions[2]

SOCIAL CUSTOMS

1. How do people react to strangers? Friendly? Hostile? Reserved?

2. How do people greet each other?

3. What are the appropriate manners when you enter a room? Bow? Nod? Shake hands with everyone?

4. How are names used for introductions? Is it appropriate to inquire about one's occupation or family?

5. What are the attitudes toward touching?

6. How does one express appreciation for an invitation to another's home? Bring a gift? Send flowers? Write a thank-you note? Are any gifts taboo?

7. Are there any customs related to how or where one sits?

8. Are any facial expressions or gestures considered rude?

9. How close do people stand when talking?

10. What is the attitude toward punctuality in social situations? In business situations?

11. What are acceptable eye contact patterns?

12. What gestures indicate agreement? Disagreement?

FAMILY LIFE

1. What is the basic unit of social organization? Basic family? Extended family?

2. Do women work outside of the home? In what occupations?

HOUSING, CLOTHING, AND FOOD

1. Are there differences in the kind of housing used by different social groups? Differences in location? Differences in furnishings?

2. What occasions require special clothing?

3. Are some types of clothing considered taboo?

4. What is appropriate business attire for men? For women?

5. How many times a day do people eat?

6. What types of places, food, and drink are appropriate for business entertainment? Where is the seat of honor at a table?

CLASS STRUCTURE

1. Into what classes is society organized?

2. Do racial, religious, or economic factors determine social status?

3. Are there any minority groups? What is their social standing?

POLITICAL PATTERNS

1. Are there any immediate threats to the political survival of the country?

2. How is political power manifested?

3. What channels are used for expression of popular opinion?

4. What information media are important?

5. Is it appropriate to talk politics in social situations?

RELIGION AND FOLK BELIEFS

1. To which religious groups do people belong? Is one predominant?

2. Do religious beliefs influence daily activities?

3. Which places have sacred value? Which objects? Which events?

4. How do religious holidays affect business activities?

ECONOMIC INSTITUTIONS

1. What are the country's principal products?

2. Are workers organized in unions?

3. How are businesses owned? By family units? By large public corporations? By the government?

4. What is the standard work schedule?

5. Is it appropriate to do business by telephone?

6. Is participatory management used?

7. Are there any customs related to exchanging business cards?

8. How is status shown in an organization? Private office? Secretary? Furniture?

9. Are businesspersons expected to socialize before conducting business?

VALUE SYSTEMS

1. Is competitiveness or cooperation more prized?

2. Is thrift or enjoyment of the moment more valued?

3. Is politeness more important than factual honesty?

4. What are the attitudes toward education?

5. Do women own or manage businesses? If so, how are they treated?

6. What are your people's perceptions of Americans? Do Americans offend you? What has been hardest for you to adjust to in America? How could Americans make this adjustment easier for you?

CASE 12-5

FORMAL REPORT: CONSUMER PRODUCT INVESTIGATION

Study a consumer product that you might consider buying. Are you (or your family) interested in purchasing a VCR, camera, microwave, car, van, camcorder, or some other product? Your investigation should include primary data collected from interviews with users, owners, salespersons, service technicians, and so forth. You'll also find rich resources in sales brochures and pamphlets. Conduct secondary research by studying (and citing) magazine articles in such publications as *Consumer Reports*. Be sure to narrow your topic by setting boundaries on your search. For example, are you interested in an economy van with good mileage that will be driven 50 miles daily? Are you in the market for an economical auto-focus camera?

In the introduction discuss why you selected this product and for whom it is intended (for example, a VCR for a middle-class family who would use it primarily for watching rented videocassettes and for time-shift recording of television programs). Perhaps provide some background data about the product gleaned from your reading. In the findings section you might discuss such topics as price, warranty, specific features, and service reputation. Draw conclusions from your data, and make a recommendation. Address the report to your instructor. Your instructor may ask you to work in pairs on this project.

CASE 12-6

FORMAL REPORT: COMMUNICATION SKILLS ON THE JOB

Collect information regarding communication skills used by individuals in a particular career field (accounting, management, marketing, office administration, paralegal, and so forth). Interview three or more individuals in a specific occupation in that field. Determine how much and what kind of writing they do. Do they make oral presentations? How much time do they spend in telephone communication? What recommendations do they have for training for this position? What conclusions can you draw from your research? What recommendations would you make for individuals entering this field? Your instructor may wish you to include a section requiring library research into the perception of businesspeople over the past ten years regarding the communication skills of employees.

GRAMMAR/MECHANICS CHECKUP—12

CAPITALIZATION

Review Sections 3.01–3.16 in the Grammar/Mechanics Handbook. Then study each of the following statements. Circle any lowercase letter that should be capitalized. Draw a slash (/) through any capital letter that you wish to change to lowercase. Indicate in the space provided the number of changes you made in each sentence and record the number of the G/M principle(s) illustrated.* If you made no changes, write *0*. When you finish, compare your responses with those shown below. If your responses differ, study carefully the principle in parentheses.

Example: After consulting our /attorneys for /egal advice, Vice president Mills signed the /ontract.   **4   (3.01, 3.06a)**

1. All american passengers from Flight 402 must pass through Customs inspection at Gate 17 upon arrival at Baltimore international airport.   **5 (3.01, 3.02, 3.07)**
2. Personal tax rates for japanese citizens are low by international standards; rates for japanese corporations are high, according to Iwao Nakatani, an Economics Professor at Osaka university.   **6 (3.01, 3.02, 3.04, 3.06d)**
3. In the end, Business passes on most of the burden to the Consumer: What looks like a tax on Business is really a tax on Consumption.   **4   (3.01, 3.13)**
4. Lisa enrolled in courses in History, Sociology, Spanish, and Computer Science.   **4   (3.05)**
5. Did you see the *Forbes* article entitled "Careers in horticulture are nothing to sneeze at"?   **5   (3.12)**
6. Although I recommend the Minex Diskettes sold under the brand-name Maxidisk, you may purchase any Diskettes you choose.   **2   (3.11)**
7. According to a Federal Government report, any regulation of State and County banking must receive local approval.   **4   (3.10)**
8. The vice president of the united states said, "this country continues to encourage Foreign investments."   **6 (3.01, 3.06c, 3.13)**
9. The Comptroller of Ramjet International reported to the President and the Board of Directors that the internal revenue service was beginning an investigation of their Company.   **6 (3.01, 3.04, 3.06e)**
10. My Mother, who lives near St. Petersburg, reports that protection from the Sun's rays is particularly important in the South.   **2   (3.03, 3.06g, 3.08, 3.14)**
11. Our Managing Editor met with Leslie Hawkins, Manager of the Advertising Sales Department, to plan an Ad Campaign for our special issue.   **5   (3.01, 3.06d, 3.06e, 3.09)**
12. In the fall, Editor in Chief Porter plans an article detailing the astounding performance of the austrian, West german, and italian currencies.   **3   (3.02, 3.06a, 3.16)**
13. To reach Belle Isle park, which is located on an Island in the Detroit river, tourists pass over the Douglas MacArthur bridge.   **4   (3.01, 3.03)**
14. On page 6 of the catalog you will see that the computer science department is offering a number of courses in programming.   **3 (3.05, 3.07, 3.09)**
15. Please consult figure 3.2 in chapter 5 for U.S. census bureau figures regarding non-english-speaking residents.   **5 (3.02, 3.04, 3.07)**

---

1. (5) American, customs inspection, International Airport (*3.01, 3.02, 3.07*)   3. (4) business, consumer, business, consumption (*3.01, 3.13*)   5. (5) Horticulture, Are, Nothing, Sneeze, At (*3.12*)   7. (4) federal government, state, county (*3.10*)   9. (6) comptroller, president, Internal Revenue Service, company (*3.01, 3.04, 3.06e*)   11. (5) managing editor, manager, ad campaign (*3.01, 3.06d, 3.06e, 3.09*)   13. (4) Park, island, River, Bridge (*3.01, 3.03*)   15. (5) Figure, Chapter, Census Bureau, English (*3.02, 3.04, 3.07*)

Note: G/M principles are listed in ascending order.

GRAMMAR/MECHANICS CHALLENGE—12

DOCUMENT FOR REVISION

Transparency 12.6

The following report abstract has faults in grammar, punctuation, spelling, number form, wordiness, and word use. Use standard proofreading marks (see Appendix B) to correct the errors. When you finish, your instructor can show you the revised version of this abstract.

Ineffective Writing

Poor Document

ABSTRACT

On the date of November 10th Dennis W. Wilbur, Director, Human Resources development authorized a study to ascertain whether or not affirmative action guidelines for women was being met at Globex Enterprises.

A research program was developed to make inquiry into each divisions hiring practices. Data in regard to the employment of 23,102 past and present employees was searched by the program to make a determination of the date of employment, division, and sex. Census Bureau data were also examined in way of comparison.

The following findings in regard to the aforementioned study, resulted;

• San Francisco is 5% above the figure for compliance for the 5 year period

• Dallas is 7% below the compliance figure for the 5 year period

On the basis of these findings the EEO Compliance Committee (1) reccomend the developement of an intensive recruiting program to search for and bring qualified females into the Dallas division and (2) the developement of a training program to train females for drafting and design positions in Dallas. The Dallas Division should hire 2 females for every 1 male until such time as 16 extra females are hired. This will bring Dallas in compliance.

EXPANDING

COMMUNICATION

SKILLS

13

COMMUNICATION FOR

EMPLOYMENT

Instructor: See p. 81 for author's suggested lesson plan for Chapter 13.

IN THIS CHAPTER YOU WILL LEARN TO DO THE FOLLOWING:

- Evaluate your assets, career paths, and the job market in preparation for employment.
- Compare and contrast chronological, functional, and combination résumés.
- Organize, format, and produce a persuasive résumé.
- Write a persuasive letter of appreciation to accompany your résumé.
- Write effective employment follow-up letters and other messages.
- Evaluate successful job interview strategies.
- Answer job interview questions skillfully.

Transparencies 13.1–13.3

Whether you are applying for your first permanent position, competing for promotion, or changing careers, you'll be more successful if you understand employment strategies and how to promote yourself. This chapter provides expert current advice in preparing for employment, searching the job market, and writing a persuasive résumé and letter of application. You'll also learn effective interviewing techniques.

PREPARING FOR EMPLOYMENT

You can start the employment process by (1) identifying your interests, (2) evaluating your qualifications, and (3) searching the job market.[1]

IDENTIFYING YOUR INTERESTS

The employment process begins with introspection. This means looking inside yourself to analyze what you like and dislike so that you can make good employment choices. Career counselors charge large sums for

Finding the perfect job demands examining your interests, your qualifications, and the job market.

283

helping individuals learn about themselves. You can do the same kind of self-examination—without spending a dime. For guidance in choosing a field that eventually proves to be satisfying, answer the following questions. If you have already chosen a field, think carefully about how your answers relate to that choice.

- Do I enjoy working with people, data, or things?
- How important is it to be my own boss?
- How important are salary, benefits, and job stability?
- How important are working environment, colleagues, and job stimulation?
- Would I rather work for a large or small company?
- Must I work in a specific city, geographical area, or climate?
- Am I looking for security, travel opportunities, money, power, or prestige?
- What do I consider to be the perfect job, boss, and co-workers?

EVALUATING YOUR QUALIFICATIONS

Answering specific questions about your interests and qualifications helps you choose a career.

In addition to your interests, you must take a hard look at your qualifications. Employers want to know what assets you have to offer them. Your responses to the following questions will target your thinking as well as prepare a foundation for your résumé. Remember, though, that employers seek more than empty assurances; they will want proof of your qualifications.

- What skills have I acquired in school, on the job, or through other activities? How can I demonstrate these skills?
- Do I work well with people? What evidence can I offer from extracurricular activities, clubs, and jobs?
- Am I a leader, self-starter, or manager? What examples can I suggest?
- Do I learn quickly? Am I creative? How can I demonstrate these characteristics?
- Do I communicate well in speech and in writing? How can I verify these talents?
- Do I speak, write, or understand another language?

CHOOSING A CAREER PATH

Career information can be obtained at campus career centers and libraries, in classified ads, through interviews, and from professional organizations.

As a result of job trends and personal choices, the average American changes *careers* at least three times and changes *jobs* at least seven times in a lifetime. Some of you probably have not yet settled on your first career choice; others are returning to college to retrain for a new career. You'll make the best career decisions when you can match your interests and qualifications with the requirements of and rewards from specific careers. But where can you get specific career data? Consider the following possibilities:

- *Visit your campus career or counseling center.* Most have literature, inventories, and software programs that allow you to investigate such fields as accounting, finance, office administration, hotel management, and so forth.
- *Use your library.* Several publications are especially helpful. Consult the latest editions of the *Dictionary of Occupational Titles, Occupational Outlook Handbook,* and *The Jobs Rated Almanac* for information about career duties, qualifications, salaries, and employment trends.

- *Take a summer job, internship, or part-time position in your field.* Trying out a career by actually working in it or in an allied area is the best way to learn about that career. Many companies offer internships and temporary jobs to begin training college students and to develop relationships with them. These relationships sometimes blossom into permanent positions. If your college has no internship program for you, call companies yourself to see if they have such programs.
- *Interview someone in your chosen field.* People are usually flattered when asked to describe their careers. Inquire about needed skills, required courses, financial and other rewards, benefits, working conditions, future trends, and entry requirements.
- *Monitor the classified ads.* Early in your college career, begin scanning wants ads in your career area. Check job availability, qualifications sought, duties, and salary range. Don't wait until you're about to graduate to see how the job market looks.
- *Join professional organizations in your field.* Frequently, these organizations offer student membership status and reduced rates. You'll have an inside track on issues, career news, and possibly jobs.

SEARCHING THE JOB MARKET

Finding the perfect job, even when the economy is flourishing, requires an early start and a determined effort. Moreover, anyone seeking a job today must recognize the value of experience. A serious job seeker must also mount an aggressive job-search campaign, including some or all of the following steps:

A job-search campaign might include checking classified ads and announcements in professional publications, contacting companies, and developing a network of contacts.

- *Check classified ads in local and national newspapers.* Be aware, though, that classified ads represent only about one third of all jobs available. Nearly two thirds, representing the "hidden" job market, are unadvertised.
- *Learn to network.* To locate jobs in the "hidden" market, tell everyone you know that you are looking for a job. Ask questions like "Do you know anyone who might have an opening for a person with my skills?" If they don't, ask, "Do you know anyone else who might know of someone who would?" If not, "Do you know someone who knows lots of people?" Develop contacts; talk with these contacts. Ask the most promising contacts how a person with your background and skills might get started in the field.
- *Contact companies in which you're interested, even if you know of no current opening.* Write an unsolicited letter and include your résumé. Follow up with a telephone call.
- *Sign up for campus interviews with visiting company representatives.* Campus recruiters may open your eyes to exciting jobs and locations.
- *Ask for advice from your professors.* They often have contacts and ideas for expanding your job search.

THE PERSUASIVE RÉSUMÉ

After learning about the employment market and developing job leads, your next step is writing a persuasive résumé. Such a résumé does more than merely list your qualifications. It packages your assets into a con-

Source: Cathy, © Universal Press Syndicate. Reprinted with permission.

A persuasive résumé sells you and your assets; its goal is winning you an interview.

vincing advertisement that sells you for a specific job. The goal of a persuasive résumé is winning an interview. Even if you are not in the job market at this moment, preparing a résumé now has advantages. Having a current résumé makes you look well organized and professional should an unexpected employment opportunity arise. Moreover, preparing a résumé early helps you recognize weak qualifications and might give you two or three years in which to bolster your credentials.

CHOOSING A RÉSUMÉ STYLE

Chronological résumés focus on employment history; functional résumés focus on skills.

Your qualifications and career goal will help you choose from among three résumé styles: chronological, functional, and combination.

Chronological   Most popular with recruiters is the chronological résumé, shown in Figure 13.1. It lists work history job by job, starting with the most recent position. Recruiters favor the chronological style because such résumés quickly reveal a candidate's work stability and promotion record. One recruiter said, "I'm looking for applicable experience; chronological résumés are the easiest to assess."[2] The chronological style works well for candidates who have experience in their fields of employment and for those who show steady career growth.

Transparency 13.4

Functional   The functional résumé shown in Figure 13.2 focuses attention on a candidate's skills rather than on past employment. Like a chronological résumé the functional résumé begins with the candidate's name, address, telephone number, job objective, and education. Instead of listing jobs, though, the functional résumé groups skills and accomplishments in special categories, such as *Supervisory and Management Skills* or *Retailing and Marketing Experience.* This résumé style highlights accomplishments and can deemphasize a negative employment history. People who have changed jobs frequently or who have gaps in their employment records may prefer the functional résumé. Recent graduates with little employment experience may also find the functional résumé useful. Perhaps outweighing its advantages, however, is the fact that some recruiters immediately assume that a functional résumé is hiding something.

Transparency 13.5

Transparency 13.6

Combination   The combination résumé style, shown in Figure 13.3, draws on the best features of the chronological and functional résumés. It emphasizes a candidate's capabilities while also including a complete job history. For recent graduates the combination résumé is a good choice

FIGURE 13.1   Chronological Résumé

ROBERTA SANCHEZ
2350 Batavia Avenue
Downers Grove, IL 60135
(708) 445-2101

OBJECTIVE

Position with financial services organization installing accounting software and providing user support, where computer experience and proven communication and interpersonal skills can be used to improve operations.

Includes detailed objective in response to advertisement.

EXPERIENCE

Accounting software consultant, Financial Specialists, Elmhurst, Illinois
June 1994 to present
- Design and install accounting systems for businesses like 21st Century Real Estate, Illini Insurance, Aurora Lumber Company, and others.
- Provide ongoing technical support and consultation for regular clients.
- Help write proposals, such as recent one that won $250,000 contract.

Uses present-tense verbs for current job.

Office manager (part-time), Post Premiums, Naperville, Illinois
June 1993 to May 1994
- Conceived and implemented improved order processing and filing system.
- Managed computerized accounting system; trained new employees to use it.
- Helped install local area network.

Chronological format arranges jobs and education by dates.

Bookkeeper (part-time), Sunset Avionics, Downers Grove, Illinois
August 1992 to May 1993
- Kept books for small airplane rental and repair service.
- Performed all bookkeeping functions including quarterly internal audit.

EDUCATION

College of DuPage, Glen Ellyn, Illinois
Associate of Arts degree in business administration, June 1994
GPA in major 3.6/4.0

Computer Associates training seminars, summer and fall 1994
Certificates of completion
Seminars in consulting ethics, marketing, and ACCPAC accounting software

SPECIAL SKILLS

- Proficient in WordPerfect, PageMaker, Lotus 1-2-3, and Excel.
- Skilled in ACCPAC Plus, MAS90, and Solomon IV accounting software.
- Trained in technical writing, including proposals and documentation.
- Experienced in office administration and management.
- Competent at speaking and writing Spanish.

White space around headings creates open look.

HONORS AND ACTIVITIES

Dean's list, 3 semesters
Member, Beta Alpha Gamma (business student honorary)
Member, Academic Affairs Advisory Committee, College of DuPage, 1992-94

because it enables them to profile what they can do for a prospective employer. If the writer has a specific job in mind, the items can be targeted to that job description.

ARRANGING THE PARTS

Although résumés have standard parts, their arrangement and content must be strategically planned. The most persuasive résumés emphasize skills and achievements aimed at a particular job or company. They show a candidate's most important qualifications first, and they deemphasize any weaknesses. In arranging the parts, try to create as few headings as possible; more than six generally gives a cluttered look.

Résumés targeted to specific positions have the best chance of being read.

FIGURE 13.2   **Functional Résumé**

ROB L. McLAIN
5 Pinecroft Drive
Downingtown, PA 19335
(215) 945-3301

Uses general objective for all-purpose résumé.	OBJECTIVE	Position in sales or marketing with opportunity for advancement and travel.
	SALES/ MARKETING SKILLS	• Demonstrated lawn-care equipment in central and western Pennsylvania. • Achieved product sales amounting to 120 percent of forecast in competitive field. • Personally generated over $25,000 in telephone subscriptions as part of President's Task Force for the Penn Foundation. • Conducted telephone survey of selected businesses in two counties to determine potential users of farm equipment and to promote company services. • Successfully served 40 or more retail customers daily as clerk in electrical appliance department of national home hardware store.
Emphasizes relevant skill for sales/ marketing position.	COMMUNICATION SKILLS	• Conducted survey, analyzed results, and wrote 20-page report regarding the need for developing a recycling program at Penn State. • Presented talks before selected campus classes and organizations encouraging students to participate in recycling program. • Spoke for award-winning delegation defending U.S. policies before mock U.N. meeting. • Announced sports news for WGNF, college radio station.
Employs action verbs to describe skills.	ORGANIZATIONAL/ MANAGEMENT SKILLS	• Helped conceptualize, organize, and conduct highly successful campus campaign to register student voters. • Scheduled events and arranged weekend student retreat for Newman Club. • Trained and supervised two counter employees at Pizza Bob's. • Organized my courses, extracurricular activites, and part-time employment to graduate in seven semesters. Earned 3.4 grade-point average (A = 4.0).
	EDUCATION	Pennsylvania State University, State College, PA. B.S., 1995 Major: Business Administration with sales and marketing emphasis GPA in major: 3.6 (A = 4.0) Community College of Alleghany County, Monroeville, PA Courses in General Studies and Business Administration
Uses periods at ends of lines only after complete sentences.	EMPLOYMENT	1994–1995, Pizza Bob's, State College, Pennsylvania Summer 1993, Bellefonte Manufacturers Representatives, Pittsburgh Summer 1992, Home Depot, Inc., Pittsburgh
	INTERESTS	Basketball, soccer, mountain biking, skiing

Most résumé writers study models and adapt a style they like. A word of warning, though: you'll probably be disappointed in your result if you use a typewriter, computer, or printer with standard, draft spacing. You really need proportional spacing or scalable fonts to fit more words, spaces, and lines on a page.

No two résumés are ever exactly alike, but you'll probably want to consider the following parts.

Main Heading Your résumé should always begin with your name, address, and telephone number. If possible, include a number where messages may be left for you. Prospective employers tend to call the next applicant when no one answers. Avoid showing both permanent and temporary

FIGURE 13.3   Combination Résumé

VICKI SUE CARLSON
Route 1, Box 210
Dodgeville, Wisconsin 53533

Residence: (608) 935-3196   Messages: (608) 935-4399

SKILLS AND CAPABILITIES	-Type 70 wpm on computer or electronic typewriter. -Take symbol shorthand at 90 wpm with accurate transcription. -Skilled in the production of legal documents and correspondence. -Competent in producing mailable copy from machine transcription. -Experienced in personal computer use, including the following software: WordPerfect 5.1, WordPerfect for Windows, Lotus 1-2-3, and dBASE III+. -Ability to perform office tasks and interact effectively using excellent written and oral communication skills.
EXPERIENCE	Word Processing Operator 1, Limited-term employee University of Wisconsin-Madison, May 1994 to August 1994 -Transcribed confidential letters, memos, reports, and other documents from machine dictation using WordPerfect 5.1. -Proofread documents for other operators, marking grammar and content errors. Student assistant Southwest Wisconsin Technical College, Fennimore, WI 53809, June 1993 to August 1993 -Typed memos and input financial aid data on terminal to mainframe; printed and verified monthly report totals for $70,000 budget. -Helped financial aid applicants understand and complete five-page form. -Screened incoming telephone calls for supervisor and three counselors. Part-time cook and cashier Souprrr Subs, Fennimore, WI 53809, May 1992 to May 1993 -Prepared menu items, accepted customer payments, and balanced cash drawer.
EDUCATION	Southwest Wisconsin Technical College, Fennimore, WI 53809 Major: Office assistant and word processing specialist programs AA degree expected May 1995. GPA in major: 3.6 (4.0 = A)
ACTIVITIES AND AWARDS	-Received the Fennimore Times award from Southwest Wisconsin Technical College Foundation for academic excellence and contribution to campus life. -Elected secretary of Business Professionals of America Club. Represented SWTC chapter at state and national competitions.

REFERENCES

Ms. Shirley A. Yost	Professor Lois Wagner	Mr. James W. Loy
College of Letters & Science	SW Wisconsin Technical College	SW Wisconsin Technical College
University of Wisconsin	Highway 18 East	Highway 18 East
Madison, WI 53489	Fennimore, WI 53809	Fennimore, WI 53809
(413) 390-4491	(608) 822-8931	(608) 822-8749

Omits job objective to keep all options open.

Focuses on skills and aptitudes that employers seek.

Arranges employment by job title for easy reading.

Combines activities and awards to fill out section.

Includes references because local employers expect them (most résumés omit them).

---

addresses; some specialists say that dual addresses immediately identify about-to-graduate college students. Keep the main heading as uncluttered and simple as possible. And don't include the word *résumé;* it's like putting the word *letter* above correspondence.

Career Objective   Opinion is divided on the effect of including a career objective on a résumé. Recruiters think such statements indicate that a candidate has made a commitment to a career. Moreover, career objectives make the recruiter's life easier by quickly classifying the résumé. But such declarations can also disqualify a candidate if the stated objective doesn't match a company's job description. One expert warned that putting a job

Generally, include a specific career objective for targeted jobs only.

objective on a résumé has "killed more opportunities for candidates . . . than typos."[3]

You have three choices regarding career objectives. One option is to include a career objective when applying for a specific, targeted position. For example, the following responds to an advertised position: *Objective: To work in the health care industry as a human resources trainee with exposure to recruiting, training, and benefit administration.* A second choice—one that makes sense if you are preparing an all-purpose résumé—is to omit the career objective. A third possibility involves using a general statement, such as *Objective: Challenging position in urban planning* or *Job Goal: Position in sales/marketing.* Some consultants warn against using the words *entry-level* in your objective, because such words emphasize lack of experience.

Many aggressive job applicants today prepare individual targeted résumés for each company or position sought. Thanks to word processing, the task is easy.

Educational achievements should precede employment history on a résumé only when they are more noteworthy.

Education   The next component is your education—if it is more noteworthy than your work experience. In this section you should include the names and locations of schools, dates of attendance, major fields of study, and degrees received. Your grade-point average and/or class ranking are important to prospective employers. One way to enhance your GPA is to calculate it in your major courses only (for example, *3.6/4.0 in major*). A list of completed courses makes dull reading; refer to courses only if you can relate them to the position sought. When relevant, include certificates earned, seminars attended, and workshops completed. Because employers are interested in your degree of self-sufficiency, you might wish to indicate the percentage of your education for which you paid. If your education is incomplete, include such statements as *B.S. degree expected 6/96* or *80 units completed in 120-unit program.* Entitle this section *Education, Academic Preparation,* or *Professional Training.*

Work Experience   If your work experience is significant and relevant to the position sought, this information should appear before education. List your most recent employment first and work backwards, including only those jobs that you think will help you win the targeted position. A job application form may demand a full employment history, but your résumé may be selective. (Be aware, though, that time gaps in your employment history will probably be questioned in the interview.) For each position show the following:

- Employer's name, city, and state
- Dates of employment, including month and year
- Most important job title
- Significant duties, activities, accomplishments, and promotions

The work experience section of a résumé should list specifics and quantify achievements.

Describe your employment achievements concisely but concretely. Avoid generalities like *Worked with customers.* Be more specific, with statements such as *Served 40 or more retail customers a day, Successfully resolved problems about custom stationery orders,* or *Acted as intermediary among customers, printers, and suppliers.* If possible, quantify your accomplishments, such as *Conducted study of equipment needs of 100 small businesses in Phoenix, Personally generated orders for sales of $90,000 annually, Keyboarded all the production models for a 250-page* *employee procedures manual*, or *Assisted editor in layout, design, and news writing for 12 issues of division newsletter.*

In addition to technical skills, employers seek individuals with communication, management, and interpersonal capabilities. This means you'll want to select work experiences and achievements that illustrate your initiative, dependability, responsibility, resourcefulness, and leadership. Employers also want people who can work together in teams. Thus, include statements like *Collaborated with interdepartmental task force in developing 10-page handbook for temporary workers* and *Headed student government team that conducted most successful voter registration in campus history.*

Statements describing your work experience can be made forceful and persuasive by using action verbs, such as those listed in Figure 13.4 and demonstrated in Figure 13.5.

Capabilities and Skills   Recruiters want to know specifically what you can do for their companies. Therefore, list your special skills, such as *Proficient in preparing correspondence and reports using WordPerfect 5.1.* Include your ability to use computer programs, office equipment, foreign languages, or sign language. Describe proficiencies you have acquired through training and experience, such as *Trained in computer accounting, including general ledger, accounts receivable, accounts payable, and payroll.* Use expressions like *competent in, skilled in, proficient with, experienced in* and *ability to*—for example, *Competent in typing, editing, and/or proofreading reports, tables, letters, memos, manuscripts, and business forms.*

> *Emphasize the skills and aptitudes that recommend you for a specific position.*

You'll also want to highlight exceptional aptitudes, such as working well under stress and learning computer programs quickly. If possible, provide details and evidence that back up your assertions—for example, *Mastered the Barrister computer program in 25 hours with little instruction.* Search for examples of your writing, speaking, management, organizational, and interpersonal skills—particularly those talents that are relevant to your targeted job.

For recent graduates this section can be used to give recruiters evidence of your potential. Instead of *Capabilities*, the section might be called *Skills and Abilities.*

Awards, Honors, and Activities   If you have three or more awards or honors, highlight them by listing them under a separate heading. If not, put them with activities. Include awards, scholarships (financial and other), fellowships, honors, recognition, commendations, and certificates. Be sure to identify items clearly. Your reader may be unfamiliar, for example, with Greek organizations, honoraries, and awards; tell what they mean. Instead of saying *Recipient of Star award*, give more details: *Recipient of Star award given by Red River College to outstanding graduates who combine academic excellence and extracurricular activities.*

> *Awards, honors, and activities are appropriate for résumés; most personal data are not.*

It's also appropriate to include school, community, and professional activities. Employers are interested in evidence that you are a well-rounded person. This section provides an opportunity to demonstrate leadership and interpersonal skills. Strive to use action statements. For example, instead of saying *Treasurer of business club*, explain more fully: *Collected dues, kept financial records, and paid bills while serving as treasurer of 35-member business management club.*

FIGURE 13.4   Action Verbs for Persuasive Résumés*

MANAGEMENT SKILLS	COMMUNICATION SKILLS	RESEARCH SKILLS	TECHNICAL SKILLS	TEACHING SKILLS
administered	addressed	clarified	assembled	adapted
analyzed	arbitrated	collected	built	advised
consolidated	arranged	critiqued	calculated	clarified
coordinated	collaborated	diagnosed	computed	coached
delegated	convinced	evaluated	designed	communicated
developed	developed	examined	devised	coordinated
directed	drafted	extracted	engineered	developed
evaluated	edited	identified	executed	enabled
improved	explained	inspected	fabricated	encouraged
increased	formulated	interpreted	maintained	evaluated
organized	interpreted	interviewed	operated	explained
oversaw	negotiated	investigated	overhauled	facilitated
planned	persuaded	organized	programmed	guided
prioritized	promoted	summarized	remodeled	informed
recommended	publicized	surveyed	repaired	instructed
scheduled	recruited	systematized	solved	persuaded
strengthened	translated		upgraded	set goals
supervised	wrote			trained

*The underlined words are especially good for pointing out accomplishments.

Personal Data   The trend in résumés today is to omit personal data, such as birth date, marital status, height, weight, and religious affiliation. Such information doesn't relate to genuine occupational qualifications, and recruiters are legally barred from asking for such information. Some job seekers do, however, include hobbies or interests (such as skiing or photography) that might grab the recruiter's attention or serve as conversation starters. Naturally, you wouldn't mention dangerous pastimes (such as bungee jumping or sports car racing) or time-consuming interests. But you should indicate your willingness to travel or to relocate, since many companies will be interested.

Experts don't agree on including references on a résumé.

References   Listing references on a résumé is favored by some recruiters and opposed by others. Such a list takes up valuable space. Moreover, it is not normally instrumental in securing an interview—few companies check references before the interview. Instead, they prefer that a candidate bring to the interview a list of individuals willing to discuss her or his qualifications. If you do list them, use parallel form. For example, if you show a title for one person *(Professor, Dr., Mrs.),* show titles for all. Include complete addresses with zip codes and telephone numbers with area codes.

Whether or not you include references on your résumé, you should have their names available when you begin your job search. Ask three to five instructors or previous employers whether they will be willing to answer inquiries regarding your qualifications for employment. Be sure, however, to provide them with an opportunity to refuse. No reference is better than a negative one. Do not include personal or character references, such as friends or neighbors, because recruiters rarely consult them. Companies are more interested in the opinions of objective individuals.

FIGURE 13.4   continued

FINANCIAL SKILLS	CREATIVE SKILLS	HELPING SKILLS	CLERICAL OR DETAIL SKILLS	MORE VERBS FOR ACCOMPLISHMENTS
administered	acted	assessed	approved	achieved
allocated	conceptualized	assisted	catalogued	expanded
analyzed	created	clarified	classified	improved
appraised	customized	coached	collected	pioneered
audited	designed	counseled	compiled	reduced (losses)
balanced	developed	demonstrated	generated	resolved (problems)
budgeted	directed	diagnosed	inspected	restored
calculated	established	educated	monitored	spearheaded
computed	founded	expedited	operated	transformed
developed	illustrated	facilitated	organized	
forecasted	initiated	familiarized	prepared	
managed	instituted	guided	processed	
marketed	introduced	motivated	purchased	
planned	invented	referred	recorded	
projected	originated	represented	screened	
researched	performed		specified	
	planned		systematized	
	revitalized		tabulated	

Source: Adapted from Yana Parker, *The Damn Good Résumé Guide* (Berkeley, CA; Ten Speed Press, 1989).

One final note: personnel officers see little reason for including the statement *References furnished upon request.* "It's like saying the sun comes up every morning," remarked one human resources professional.[4]

APPLYING THE FINAL TOUCHES

Because your résumé is probably the most important message you will ever write, you'll revise it many times. With so much information in concentrated form and with so much riding on its outcome, your résumé demands careful polishing, proofreading, and critiquing.

In addition to being well written, a résumé must be carefully formatted and meticulously proofread.

As you revise, be certain to verify all the facts, particularly those involving your previous employment and education. Don't be caught in a mistake, or worse, distortion of previous jobs and dates of employment. These items likely will be checked. And the consequences of puffing up a résumé with deception or flat-out lies are simply not worth the risk.

Transparencies 13.8–13.12

As you continue revising, look for other ways to improve your résumé. For example, consider consolidating headings. By condensing your

Transparency 13.7

FIGURE 13.5   Using Action Verbs to Strengthen Your Résumé

Identified weaknesses in internship program and **researched** five alternate programs.

Reduced delivery delays by an average of three days per order.

Streamlined filing system, thus reducing 400-item backlog to 0.

Organized holiday awards program for 1200 attendees and 140 awardees.

Created a 12-point checklist for managers to use when requesting temporary workers.

Designed five posters announcing new employee suggestion program.

Calculated shipping charges for overseas deliveries and **recommended** most economical rates.

Managed 24-station computer network linking data and employees in three departments.

Distributed and **explained** voter registration forms to over 500 prospective student voters.

information into as few headings as possible, you'll produce a clean, professional-looking document. Study other résumés for valuable formatting ideas. Ask yourself what graphics highlighting techniques you can use to improve readability: capitalization, underlining, indenting, and bulleting. Experiment with headings and styles to achieve a pleasing, easy-to-read message. Moreover, look for ways to eliminate wordiness. For example, instead of *Supervised two employees who worked at the counter,* try *Supervised two counter employees.* Review Chapters 2 and 3 for more tips.

Above all, make your résumé look professional. Avoid anything humorous or "cute," such as a help-wanted poster with your name or picture inside. Eliminate the personal pronoun *I.* The abbreviated, objective style of a résumé precludes the use of personal pronouns. Use white, off-white, or buff-colored heavy bond paper (24-pound).

After revising, proofread, proofread, and proofread again: for spelling and mechanics, for content, and for format. Then, have a knowledgeable friend or relative proofread it again. This is one document that must be perfect.

Studying the model résumés in Figures 13.1–13.3 and Figures 13.6–13.8 should give you many ideas for your own résumé. Notice that the models illustrate the qualifications of job seekers with little experience as well as some with more experience. Remember, you'll get the best results if you use a computer and a good printer.

Finally, be sure to write your résumé yourself because no one knows you as well as you. Don't delegate the task to a résumé-writing service. Such services tend to produce eye-catching, elaborate documents with lofty language, fancy borders, and fuzzy thinking. Here's an example: "Seeking a position that will utilize academic achievements and hands-on experience while providing for career-development opportunities."[5] Save your money and buy a good interview suit instead.

THE PERSUASIVE LETTER OF APPLICATION

Letters of application introduce résumés, relate writer strengths to reader benefits, and seek an interview.

Transparencies 13.13–13.15

To accompany your résumé, you'll need a persuasive letter of application (also called a *cover letter*). The letter of application has three purposes: (1) introducing the résumé, (2) highlighting your strengths in terms of benefits to the reader, and (3) gaining an interview. In many ways your letter of application is a sales letter; it sells your talents and tries to beat the competition. It will, accordingly, include many of the techniques you learned for sales presentations (Chapter 9).

Personnel professionals disagree on how long to make the letter of application. Many prefer short letters with no more than four paragraphs; instead of concentrating on the letter, these readers focus on the résumé. Others desire longer letters that supply more information, thus giving them a better opportunity to evaluate a candidate's qualifications. The latter personnel professionals argue that hiring and training new employees is expensive and time-consuming; therefore, they welcome extra data to guide them in making the best choice the first time. Follow your judgment whether to write a brief or a lengthier letter of application. If you feel, for example, that you need space to explain in more detail what you can do for a prospective employer, do so.

FIGURE 13.6 **Chronological Résumé**

Tran M. Nguyen
923 Pleasant Dale Place
Westlake Village, California 91362
(818) 857-3301

OBJECTIVE: **Word Processing/Secretarial/Administrative/General Office**

EDUCATION: Moorpark College, Moorpark, California, AA degree expected 6/95
Specialization in Office Automation.

EXPERIENCE:
- U.S. Superior Court, Los Angeles, California, 1/95 to 6/95

  Administrative intern
  File memos, find and copy cases from law books, type letters and memos, maintain office supplies, enter cases on computer. Successfully perform all duties in an atmosphere where accuracy and ability to follow detailed instructions are essential. Cleared three-month backlog in five weeks.

- Sav-On Drugs, Agoura, California, 7/92 to 8/94

  Part-time pharmacy clerk
  Accepted and processed prescriptions on computer. Cheerfully answered approximately 40 telephone calls daily. Enjoyed serving up to 50 customers in Pharmacy Department daily.

- Office Technology Department, Moorpark College, Moorpark, California, 9/93 to 6/94

  Student secretary, work-study program
  Selected by department chair to serve as her personal secretary. Created, revised, and retrieved letters, memos, files, and reports using WordPerfect 5.1. Organized departmental computer files so that hundreds of files could be located logically and efficiently.

- Ross Department Stores, Reseda, California, 6/91 to 7/92

  Floor sales associate
  Developed interpersonal and sales skills by assisting customers in sales selections. Worked as part of a successful team that surpassed its national sales goal. Became second assistant manager after six months.

STRENGTHS:
- Keyboard 60 wpm accurately
- Competent in machine transcription, editing, and proofreading
- Computer skills include WordPerfect 5.1, Lotus 1-2-3, and spreadsheets
- Comfortable in either Mac or DOS computer environments
- Ability to work effectively with people, to budget time, and to perform well under stress

Expands opportunities with broad objective.

Uses bullets, boldface, and white space to achieve emphasis and readability.

Emphasizes skills necessary for targeted job.

Regardless of its length, a letter of application should have three primary parts: (1) an opening that gains attention, (2) a body that builds interest and reduces resistance, and (3) a closing that motivates action.

GAINING ATTENTION IN THE OPENING

The first step in gaining the interest of your reader is addressing that individual by name. Rather than sending your letter to the "Personnel Manager" or "Human Resources Department," make an effort to identify the name of the appropriate individual. Make it a rule to call the organization for the correct spelling and the complete address. This personal touch distinguishes your letter and demonstrates your serious interest.

The opener in a letter of application gains attention by addressing the receiver by name.

FIGURE 13.7   Combination Résumé

Uses italics, bold and scalable font features.

Highlights skills named in advertisement.

KEITH M. DAVIES

4938 Mountain View Avenue
Sunnyvale, CA 94255
(415) 479-1982
Messages: (415) 412-5540

Objective: Position as Staff Accountant with progressive Bay Area firm, where my technical, computer, and communication skills will be useful in managing accounts and acquiring new clientele.

SKILLS AND CAPABILITIES
Accounting
- Ability to journalize entries accurately in general and specialized journals.
- Proficient in posting to general ledger, preparing trial balance, and detecting discrepancies.
- Trained in preparing and analyzing balance sheet and other financial statements.

Computer
- Experienced in using Lotus 1-2-3, dBASE III+, and WordPerfect for Windows.
- Comfortable in personal computer (MS-DOS), mainframe, or network environments.
- Ability to learn new computer programs and applications quickly, with little instruction.

Communication and Interpersonal
- Enjoy working with details and completing assignments accurately and on time.
- Demonstrate sound writing and speaking skills acquired and polished in business letter writing, report writing, and speech classes.
- Interact well with people as evidenced in my successful sales, volunteer, and internship work.

Combines skills and experience for most forceful appeal.

EXPERIENCE
Tax Preparer, Volunteer Income Tax Assistance program (VITA)
Sponsored by the Internal Revenue Service and California State University, San Jose. Prepared state and federal tax returns for individuals with incomes under $25,000. Conducted interviews with over 50 individuals to elicit data regarding taxes. Determined legitimate tax deductions and recorded them accurately. (Tax seasons, 1993 to present)

Uses paragraph style to save space.

Accounting Intern, Software, Inc., Accounting Department, Santa Clara, CA
Assisted in analyzing data for weekly accounts payable aging report. Prepared daily cash activity report for sums up to $10,000. Calculated depreciation on 12 capital asset accounts with a total valuation of over $900,000. Researched and wrote report analyzing one division's budget of $150,000. (Spring 1995)

Salesperson, Kmart, Santa Clara, CA
Helped customers select gardening and landscaping supplies. Assisted in ordering merchandise, stocking the department, and resolving customer problems. (Summers 1993, 1994)

Includes activities and awards with education because of limited space.

EDUCATION
California State University, San Jose. B.S. degree expected 6/95
Major: Business Administration
Specialization: Accounting Theory and Practice. GPA: 3.2 (A = 4.0)
Participated as member of Accounting Club for two years.
San Jose Community College. A.A. degree 6/92
Major: Business Administration and Accounting. GPA: 3.4 (A = 4.0)
Received Award of Merit for volunteer work as orientation guide and peer tutor.

How you open your letter of application depends largely on whether the application is solicited or unsolicited. If an employment position has been announced and applicants are being solicited, you can use a direct approach. If you do not know whether a position is open and you are prospecting for a job, use an indirect approach. Whether direct or indirect, the opening should attract the attention of the reader. Strive for openings that are more imaginative than *Please consider this letter an application for the position of . . .* or *I would like to apply for . . .*

Openings for Solicited Jobs   Here are some of the best techniques to open a letter of application for a job that has been announced:

FIGURE 13.8   **Chronological Résumé**

RACHEL M. CHOWDHRY
P.O. Box 3310
Garland, TX 75350   (817) 490-3310

OBJECTIVE: SENIOR FINANCIAL MANAGEMENT

PROFESSIONAL HISTORY AND ACHIEVEMENTS

11/91 to 5/95 CONTROLLER
    United Plastics, Inc., Dallas, TX (extruder of polyethylene film for plastic aprons and
    gloves)
- Directed all facets of accounting and cash management for 160-employee, $3 billion business.
- Supervised inventory and production data processing operations and tax compliance.
- Talked owner into reducing sales prices, resulting in doubling first quarter 1995 sales.
- Created cost accounting by product and pricing based on gross margin.
- Increased line of credit with 12 major suppliers.

11/89 to 10/91 CONTROLLER
    Burgess Inc., Freeport, IL (major manufacturer of flashlight and lantern batteries)
- Managed all accounting, cash, payroll, credit, and collection operations for 175-employee business.
- Implemented a new system for cost accounting, inventory control, and accounts payable, resulting in a $100,000 annual savings in computer operations.
- Reduced staff from 10 persons to 5 with no loss in productivity.
- Successfully reduced inventory levels from $1.1 million to $600,000.
- Helped develop new cash management system that significantly increased cash flow.

8/87 to 8/89 TREASURER/CONTROLLER
    The Builders of Winter, Winter, WI (manufacturer of modular housing)
- Supervised accounts receivable/payable, cash management, payroll, and insurance.
- Directed monthly and year-end closings, banking relations, and product costing.
- Refinanced company with long-term loan, ensuring continued operational stability.
- Successfully lowered company's insurance premiums by 7 percent.

4/83 to 6/87 SUPERVISOR OF GENERAL ACCOUNTING
    Levin National Batteries, St. Paul, MN (local manufacturer of flashlight batteries)
- Completed monthly and year-end closing of ledgers for $2 million business.
- Audited freight bills, acted as interdepartmental liaison, prepared financial reports.

ADDITIONAL INFORMATION

    Education: B.S.B.A. degree, University of Minnesota, major in Accounting, 1982

    Certification: CPA Review, Academy of Accountancy, Minneapolis, Minnesota

    Personal: Will travel and/or relocate.

Emphasizes steady employment history by listing dates FIRST.

Uses action verbs, thus avoiding the deadly "was responsible for" listing of achievements.

De-emphasizes education because work history is more important for mature candidates.

- *Refer to the name of an employee in the company.* Remember that employers always hope to hire known quantities rather than complete strangers:

> Mitchell Sims, a member of your Customer Service Department, recently informed me that DataTech is seeking an experienced customer service representative. The attached summary of my qualifications demonstrates my preparation for this position.

> At the suggestion of Ms. Jennifer Larson of your Human Resources Department, I submit my qualifications for the position of personnel assistant.

Openers for solicited jobs refer to the source of the information, the job title, and qualifications for the position.

- *Refer to the source of your information precisely.* If you are answering an advertisement, include the exact position advertised and the name and date of the publication. For large organizations it's also wise to mention the section of the newspaper where the ad appeared:

> Your advertisement in Section C-3 of the June 1 *Daily News* for a junior accountant greatly appeals to me. With my accounting training and computer experience, I believe I could serve DataTech well.

> The September 10 issue of the *Washington Post* reports that you are seeking a mature, organized, and reliable administrative assistant with excellent communication skills.

> Susan Butler, placement director at Sierra University, told me that Data-Tech has an opening for a technical writer with knowledge of desktop publishing techniques.

- *Refer to the job title and describe how your qualifications fit the requirements.* Personnel directors are looking for a match between an applicant's credentials and the job needs:

> Will an honors graduate with a degree in recreation and two years of part-time experience organizing social activities for a convalescent hospital qualify for your position of activity director?

> Because of my specialized training in computerized accounting at Nicholls State University, I feel confident that I have the qualifications you described in your advertisement for a cost accountant trainee.

Openers for unsolicited jobs show interest in and knowledge of the company, as well as spotlighting reader benefits.

Openings for Unsolicited Jobs. If you are unsure whether a position actually exists, you may wish to use a more persuasive opening. Since your goal is to convince this person to read on, try one of the following techniques:

- *Demonstrate interest in and knowledge of the reader's business.* Show the personnel director that you have done your research and that this organization is more than a mere name to you.

> Since Signa HealthNet, Inc., is organizing a new information management team for its recently established group insurance division, could you use the services of a well-trained business administration graduate who seeks to become a data processing professional?

- *Show how your special talents and background will benefit the company.* Personnel directors need to be convinced that you can do something for them:

> Could your rapidly expanding publications division use the services of an editorial assistant who offers exceptional language skills, an honors degree from Iowa State University, and two years' experience in producing a campus literary publication?

In applying for an advertised job, Carolyn Crockett wrote the solicited letter of application shown in Figure 13.9. Notice that her opening identifies the position and the newspaper completely so that the reader knows exactly what advertisement Carolyn means. More challenging are unsolicited letters of application, such as Rob McLain's shown in Figure 13.10. Because he hopes to discover or create a job, his opening must grab the reader's attention immediately. To do that, he capitalizes on company information appearing in the newspaper. Notice, too, that Rob purposely

FIGURE 13.9   Solicited Letter of Application

1770 Hawthorne Place
Boulder, CO 80304
May 23, 199x

Mr. William A. Caldwell
Director, Human Resources
Del Rio Enterprises
Denver, CO 82511

Dear Mr. Caldwell:

Since I have focused my education and training on sales and marketing, your advertisement for an assistant product manager, appearing May 22 in Section C of the Denver Post, immediately caught my attention.

Your ad states that the job includes "assisting in the coordination of a wide range of marketing programs as well as analyzing sales results and tracking marketing budgets." A recent internship at Ventana Corporation introduced me to similar tasks. I assisted the marketing manager in analyzing the promotion, budget, and overall sales success of two products Ventana was evaluating. My ten-page report examined the nature of the current market, the products' life cycles, and their sales/profit return. In addition to this research, I helped formulate a product merchandising plan and answered consumers' questions at a local trade show. This brief but challenging introduction to product management convinced me that I could be successful and happy in a marketing career.

Intensive coursework in marketing and management, as well as proficiency in computer spreadsheets and databases, has given me the kind of marketing and computing training that Del Rio demands in a product manager. Moreover, I have had some retail sales experience and have been active in campus organizations. I'm confident that my academic preparation, my marketing experience, and my ability to work well with others qualify me for this position.

After you have examined the enclosed résumé for details of my qualifications, I would be happy to answer questions. Please call me to arrange an interview at your convenience so that we may discuss how my marketing, computing, and interpersonal skills could contribute to Del Rio Enterprises.

Sincerely,

Carolyn A. Crockett

Carolyn A. Crockett

Enclosure

kept his cover letter short and to the point because he anticipated that a busy executive would be unwilling to read a long, detailed letter.

Rob's unsolicited letter, Figure 13.10, "prospects" for a job. Some job candidates feel that such letters may be even more productive than efforts to secure advertised jobs, since "prospecting" candidates face less competition.

BUILDING INTEREST IN THE BODY

Once you have captured the attention of the reader, you can use the body of the letter to build interest and reduce resistance. Keep in mind that your

FIGURE 13.10   Unsolicited Letter of Application

5 Pinecroft Drive
Downingtown, PA 19335
May 29, 199x

Mr. Arthur P. Minsberg
Vice President, Operations
Sports World, Inc.
4907 Allegheny Boulevard
Pittsburgh, PA 16103

Dear Mr. Minsberg:

Shows knowledge of company and resourcefulness.

Today's Pittsburgh Examiner reports that your organization plans to expand its operations to include national distribution of sporting goods, and it occurs to me that you will be needing highly motivated, self-starting sales representatives and marketing managers. I have these significant qualifications to offer:

Focuses on three most important qualities.

- Four years of formal training in business administration, including specialized courses in sales management, retailing, marketing promotion, and consumer behavior.

- Practical experience in demonstrating and selling consumer products, as well as successful experience in telemarketing.

- A strong interest in most areas of sports and good communication skills (which helped me become a sportscaster at Penn State radio station WGNF).

Takes initiative for follow-up.

I would like to talk with you about how I can put these qualifications, and others summarized in the enclosed résumé, to work for Sports World as it develops its national sales force. I'll call during the week of June 5 to discuss your company's expansion plans and the opportunity for an interview.

Sincerely yours,

Rob L. McLain

Rob L. McLain

Enclosure

The body of a letter of application should build interest, reduce resistance, and discuss relevant personal traits.

résumé emphasizes what you have *done;* your application letter stresses what you *can do* for the employer.

Your first goal is to relate your remarks to a specific position. If you are responding to an advertisement, you'll want to explain how your preparation and experience fill the stated requirements. If you are prospecting for a job, you may not know the exact requirements. Your employment research and knowledge of your field, however, should give you a reasonably good idea of what is expected for this position.

It's also important to emphasize reader benefits. In other words, you should describe your strong points in relation to the needs of the employer. In one employment survey many personnel professionals expressed the same view: "I want you to tell me what you can do for my organization. This is much more important to me than telling me what courses you took in college or what 'duties' you performed on your previous jobs."[6] Instead of *I have completed courses in business communication, report writing, and technical writing,* try this:

> Courses in business communication, report writing, and technical writing have helped me develop the research and writing skills required of your technical writers.

Choose your strongest qualifications and show how they fit the targeted job. And remember, students with little experience are better off spotlighting their education and its practical applications, as these candidates did:

Spotlighting reader benefits means matching personal strengths to employer needs.

> Because you seek an architect's apprentice with proven ability, I submit a drawing of mine that won second place in the Sinclair College drafting contest last year.

> Successfully transcribing over 100 letters and memos in my college transcription class gave me experience in converting the spoken word into the written word, an exacting communication skill demanded of your administrative assistants.

In the body of your letter, you'll also want to discuss relevant personal traits. Employers are looking for candidates who, among other things, are team players, take responsibility, show initiative, and learn easily. Notice how the following paragraph uses action verbs to paint a picture of a promising candidate:

> In addition to developing technical and academic skills at Mid-State University, I have gained interpersonal, leadership, and organizational skills. As vice president of the business students' organization, Gamma Alpha, I helped organize and supervise two successful fund-raising events. These activities involved conceptualizing the tasks, motivating others to help, scheduling work sessions, and coordinating the efforts of 35 diverse students in reaching our goal. I enjoyed my success with these activities and look forward to applying such experience in your management trainee program.

Finally, in this section or the next, you should refer the reader to your résumé. Do so directly or as part of another statement, as shown here:

> Please refer to the attached résumé for additional information regarding my education, experience, and references.

> As you will notice from my résumé, I will graduate in June with a bachelor's degree in business administration.

Motivating Action in the Closing

After presenting your case, you should conclude with a spur to action. This is where you ask for an interview. If you live in a distant city, you may request an employment application or an opportunity to be interviewed by the organization's nearest representative. However, never ask for the job. To do so would be presumptuous and naive. In requesting an interview, suggest reader benefits or review your strongest points. Sound sincere and appreciative. Remember to make it easy for the reader to agree by supplying your telephone number and best times to call you. And keep in mind that some personnel directors prefer that you take the initiative to call them. Here are possible endings:

The closing of a letter of application should include a request for an interview.

I hope this brief description of my qualifications and the additional information on my résumé indicate to you my genuine desire to put my skills in accounting to work for you. Please call me at (405) 488-2291 before 10 a.m. or after 3 p.m. to arrange an interview.

To add to your staff an industrious, well-trained word processing specialist with proven communication skills, call me at (350) 492-1433 to arrange an interview. I can meet with you at any time convenient to your schedule.

Next week, after you have examined the attached résumé, I will call you to discuss the possibility of arranging an interview.

FINAL TIPS

A letter of application should look professional and suggest quality.

As you revise your letter of application, notice how many sentences begin with *I*. Although it's impossible to talk about yourself without using *I*, you can reduce "I" domination with this writing technique: Make activities and outcomes, and not yourself, the subjects of sentences. For example, rather than *I took classes in word processing and desktop publishing,* say *Classes in word processing and desktop publishing prepared me to . . .* Instead of *I enjoyed helping customers,* say *Helping customers was a real pleasure.*

Like the résumé your letter of application must look professional and suggest quality. This means using a traditional letter style, such as block or modified block. Also, be sure to print it on the same bond paper as your résumé. And, as with your résumé, proofread it several times yourself; then, have a friend read it for content and mechanics.

FOLLOW-UP LETTERS AND OTHER EMPLOYMENT DOCUMENTS

Although the résumé and letter of application are your major tasks, other important letters and documents are often required during the employment process. You may need to make requests, write follow-up letters, or fill out employment applications. Because each of these tasks reveals something about you and your communication skills, you'll want to put your best foot forward. These documents often subtly influence company officials to extend an interview or offer a job.

APPLICATION REQUEST LETTER

Some organizations consider candidates only when they submit a completed application form. To secure a form, write a routine letter of request. But provide enough information about yourself, as shown in the following example, to assure the reader that you are a serious applicant:

Dear Mr. Adams:

Because you expect a positive response, announce your request directly.

Please send me an application form for work in your Human Resources Department. In June I will be completing my studies in psychology and communications at Northwestern University in Evanston, Illinois. My program included courses in public relations, psychology, and communications.

Supply an end date, if appropriate.

I would appreciate receiving this application by May 15 so that I may complete it before making a visit to your city in June. I'm looking forward to beginning a career in personnel management.

APPLICATION OR RÉSUMÉ FOLLOW-UP LETTER

If your letter or application generates no response within a reasonable time, you may decide to send a short follow-up letter like the one below. Doing so (1) jogs the memory of the personnel officer, (2) demonstrates your serious interest, and (3) allows you to emphasize your qualifications or to add new information. Avoid any accusations that might make the reader defensive.

Dear Mrs. Lopez:

Please know that I am still interested in becoming an administrative assistant with DataTech, Inc.

Open by reminding the reader of your interest.

Since I submitted an application in May, I have completed my schooling and have been employed as a summer replacement for office workers in several downtown offices. This experience has honed my word processing and communication skills. It has also introduced me to a wide range of office procedures.

Review your strengths or add new qualifications.

Please keep my application in your active file and let me know when I may put my formal training, technical skills, and practical experience to work for you.

Close by looking forward positively.

INTERVIEW FOLLOW-UP LETTER

After a job interview you should always send a brief letter of thanks. This courtesy sets you apart from other applicants (most of whom will not bother). Your letter also reminds the interviewer of your visit, as well as suggesting your good manners and genuine enthusiasm for the job.

Follow-up letters are most effective if sent immediately after the interview.[7] In your letter refer to the date of the interview, the exact job title for which you were interviewed, and specific topics discussed. Avoid worn-out phrases, such as *Thank you for taking the time to interview me.* Be careful, too, about overusing *I,* especially to begin sentences. Most important, show that you really want the job and that you are qualified for it. Notice how the following letter conveys enthusiasm and confidence:

Dear Ms. Cogan:

Talking with you Thursday, May 23, about the graphic designer position was both informative and interesting.

Mention the interview date and specific position.

Thanks for describing the position in such detail and for introducing me to Ms. Thomas, the senior designer. Her current project designing the annual report in four colors on a Macintosh sounds fascinating as well as quite challenging.

Show appreciation, good manners, and perseverance.

Now that I've learned in greater detail the specific tasks of your graphic designers, I'm more than ever convinced that my computer and creative skills can make a genuine contribution to your graphic productions. My training in Macintosh design and layout ensures that I could be immediately productive on your staff.

Remind the reader of your interpersonal skills and your enthusiasm for this job.

In addition to my technical skills, you will find me an enthusiastic and hard-working member of any team effort. I'm eager to join the graphics staff at your Santa Barbara headquarters, and I look forward to hearing from you soon.

Highlight a specific skill you have for the job.

REJECTION FOLLOW-UP LETTER

If you didn't get the job and you think it was perfect for you, don't give up. Employment consultant Patricia Windelspecht advises, "You should always respond to a rejection letter. . . . I've had four clients get jobs that way." In a rejection follow-up letter, it's okay to admit you're disappointed. Be sure to add, however, that you're still interested and will contact them again in a month in case a job opens up. Then follow through for a couple of months—but don't overdo it. "There's a fine line between being professional and persistent and being a pest," adds consultant Windelspecht.[8] Here's an example of an effective rejection follow-up letter:

Subordinate your disappointment to your appreciation at being notified promptly.

Emphasize your continuing interest. Express confidence in meeting the job requirements.

Refer to specifics of your interview. Tell how you are improving your skills.

Dear Mr. Crenshaw:

Although I'm disappointed that someone else was selected for your accounting position, I appreciate your promptness and courtesy in notifying me.

Because I firmly believe that I have the technical and interpersonal skills needed to work in your fast-paced environment, I hope you will keep my résumé in your active file. My desire to become a productive member of your Transamerica staff remains strong.

I enjoyed our interview, and I especially appreciate the time you and Mr. Samson spent describing your company's expansion into international markets. To enhance my qualifications, I've enrolled in a course in International Accounting at CSU.

Should you have an opening for which I am qualified, you may reach me at (818) 719-3901. In the meantime, I will call you in a month to discuss employment possibilities.

APPLICATION FORM

Some organizations require job candidates to fill out job application forms instead of submitting résumés. This practice permits them to gather and store standardized data about each applicant. Here are some tips for filling out such forms:

- Carry a card summarizing those vital statistics not included on your résumé. If you are asked to fill out an application form in an employer's office, you will need a handy reference to the following data: social security number, graduation dates, beginning and ending dates of all employment; salary history; full names, titles, and present work addresses of former supervisors; and full names, occupational titles, occupational addresses, and telephone numbers of persons who have agreed to serve as references.
- Look over all the questions before starting. Fill out the form neatly, printing if your handwriting is poor.
- Answer all questions. Write *Not applicable* if appropriate.
- Be prepared for a salary question. Unless you know what comparable employees are earning in the company, the best strategy is to suggest a salary range or to write *Negotiable* or *Open*.
- Ask if you may submit your résumé in addition to the application form.

INTERVIEWING FOR EMPLOYMENT

Transparency 13.16

Job interviews, for most of us, are intimidating; no one enjoys being judged and, possibly, rejected. You can overcome your fear of the interview process by knowing how it works and how to prepare for it.

Trained recruiters generally structure the interview in three separate activities: (1) establishing a cordial relationship, (2) eliciting information about the candidate, and (3) giving information about the job and company. During the interview its participants have opposing goals. The interviewer tries to uncover any negative information that would eliminate a candidate. The candidate, of course, tries to minimize faults and emphasize strengths to avoid being eliminated.

You can become a more skillful player in the interview game if you know what to do before, during, and after the interview.

BEFORE THE INTERVIEW

- *Research the organization.* Never enter an interview cold. Visit the library to search for information about the target company or its field, service, or product. Call the company to request annual reports, catalogs, or brochures. Ask about the organization and possibly the interviewer. Learn something about the company's size, number of employees, competitors, reputation, and strengths and weaknesses.

Prior to an interview, applicants should research the organization and plan answers to potential questions.

- *Learn about the position.* Obtain as much specific information as possible. What are the functions of an individual in this position? What is the typical salary range? What career paths are generally open to this individual? What did the last person in this position do right or wrong?

- *Plan to sell yourself.* Identify three to five of your major selling points regarding skills, training, personal characteristics, and specialized experience. Memorize them; then in the interview be certain to find a place to insert them.

- *Prepare answers to possible questions.* Imagine the kinds of questions you may be asked and work out sample answers. Although you can't anticipate precise questions, you can expect to be asked about your education, skills, experience, and availability. The accompanying box shows ten of the most common questions and suggests responses.

- *Prepare success stories.* Rehearse two or three incidents that you can relate about your accomplishments. These may focus on problems you have solved, promotions you have earned, or recognition or praise you have received.

- *Arrive early.* Get to the interview five or ten minutes early. If you are unfamiliar with the area where the interview is to be held, you might visit it before the scheduled day. Locate the building, parking facilities, and office. Time yourself.

- *Dress appropriately.* Heed the advice of one expert: "Dress and groom like the interviewer is likely to dress—but cleaner."[9] Don't overdo perfume, jewelry, or after-shave lotion. Avoid loud colors; strive for a coordinated, natural appearance. Favorite "power" colors for interviews are gray and dark blue. It's not a bad idea to check your appearance in a restroom before entering the office.

DURING THE INTERVIEW

- *Establish the relationship.* Shake hands firmly. Don't be afraid to offer your hand first. Address the interviewer formally ("Hello, Mrs. Jones"). Allow the interviewer to put you at ease with small talk.

- *Act confident but natural.* Establish and maintain eye contact, but don't get into a staring contest. Sit up straight, facing the interviewer. Don't cross your arms and legs at the same time because of the negative message these actions suggest. Don't manipulate objects, like a pencil or keys, during the interview. Try to remain natural and at ease.

↪ *Instructor: See pp. 83–85 for supplementary lectures on legality of interview questions and other tips.*

TEN FREQUENTLY ASKED INTERVIEW QUESTIONS AND RESPONSE STRATEGIES

- *Why do you want to work for us?* Questions like this illustrate the need for you to research an organization thoroughly before the interview. Do library research, ask friends, and read the company's advertisements and other printed materials to gather data. Describe your desire to work for them not only from your perspective but also from their point of view. What have you to offer them?

- *Why should we hire you?* Here is an opportunity for you to sell your strong points in relation to this specific position. Describe your skills, academic preparation, and relevant experience. If you have little experience, don't apologize—the interviewer has read your résumé. Emphasize strengths as demonstrated in your education, such as initiative and persistence in completing assignments, ability to learn quickly, self-sufficiency, and excellent attendance.

- *What can you tell me about yourself?* Use this chance to promote yourself. Stick to professional or business-related strengths; avoid personal or humorous references. Be ready with at least three success stories illustrating characteristics important to this job. Demonstrate responsibility you have been given; describe how you contributed as a team player.

- *What are your strongest (or weakest) personal qualities?* Stress your strengths, such as "I believe I am conscientious, reliable, tolerant, patient, and thorough." Add examples that illustrate these qualities: "My supervisor said that my research was exceptionally thorough." If pressed for a weakness, give a strength disguised as a weakness: "Perhaps my greatest fault is being too painstaking with details." Or, "I am impatient when tasks are not completed on time." Don't admit weaknesses, not even to sound human. You'll be hired for your strengths, not your weaknesses.

- *What do you expect to be doing ten years from now?* Formulate a realistic plan with respect to your present age and situation. The important thing is to be prepared for this question.

- *Do you prefer working with others or by yourself?* This question can be tricky. Provide a middle-of-the-road answer that not only suggests your interpersonal qualities but also reflects an ability to make independent decisions and work without supervision.

- *Have you ever changed your major field of interest during your education? Why?* Another tricky question. Don't admit weaknesses or failures. In explaining changes, suggest career potential and new aspirations awakened by your expanding education, experience, or maturity.

- *What have been your most rewarding or disappointing work (or school) experiences?* If possible, concentrate on positive experiences such as technical and interpersonal skills you acquired. Avoid dwelling on negative or unhappy topics. Never criticize former employers. If you worked for an ungrateful, penny-pinching slave driver in a dead-end position, say that you learned all you could from that job. Move the conversation to the prospective position and what attracts you to it.

- *Have you established any new goals lately?* Watch out here. If you reveal new goals, you may inadvertently admit deficiencies. Instead of "I've resolved to finally learn how to operate a computer," try "Although I'm familiar with basic computer applications, I'm now reading and studying more about computer applications in . . ."

- *What are your long- and short-term goals?* Suggest realistic goals that you have consciously worked out before the interview. Know what you want to do with your future. To admit to an interviewer that you're not sure what you want to do is a sign of immaturity, weakness, and indecision.

- *Don't criticize.* Avoid making negative comments about previous employers, instructors, or others. Such criticism may be taken to indicate a negative personality. Employers are not eager to hire complainers. Moreover, such criticism may suggest that you would do the same to this organization.

- *Stay focused on your strengths.* If the interviewer asks a question that does not help you promote your strongest qualifications, answer briefly. Alternatively, try to turn your response into a positive selling point, such as this: "I have not had extensive paid training in that area, but I have completed a 50-hour training program that provided hands-on experience using the latest technology and methods. My recent training taught me to be open to new ideas and showed me how I can continue learning on my own. I was commended for being a quick learner."

- *Find out about the job early.* Because your time will be short, try to learn all you can about the target job early in the interview. Ask about its responsibilities and the kinds of people who have done well in the position before. Knowing this information early will enable you to shape your responses to the job requirements.

- *Prepare for salary questions.* Remember that nearly all salaries are negotiable, depending on your qualifications. Knowing the typical salary range for the target position helps. The recruiter can tell you the salary ranges—but you will have to ask. If you've had little experience, you will probably be offered a salary somewhere between the low point and the midpoint in the range. With more experience you can negotiate for a higher figure. A word of caution, though. One personnel manager warns that candidates who emphasize money are suspect because they may leave if offered a few thousand dollars more elsewhere.

- *Be ready for inappropriate questions.* If you are asked a question that you think is illegal, politely ask the interviewer how that question is related to this job. Ask the purpose of the question. Perhaps valid reasons exist that are not obvious.

- *Ask your own questions.* Often, the interviewer concludes an interview with "Do you have any questions about the position?" Inquire about career paths, orientation or training for new employees, or the company's promotion policies. Have a list of relevant questions prepared. If the interview has gone well, ask the recruiter about his or her career in the company.

- *Conclude positively.* Summarize your strongest qualifications, show your enthusiasm for obtaining this position, and thank the interviewer for a constructive interview. Be sure you understand the next step in the employment process.

AFTER THE INTERVIEW
- *Make notes on the interview.* While the events are fresh in your mind, jot down the key points—good and bad.
- *Write a thank-you letter.* Immediately write a letter thanking the interviewer for a pleasant and enlightening discussion. Be sure to spell his or her name correctly.

During an interview, applicants should act confident, focus on their strengths, and sell themselves.

APPLICATION AND PRACTICE—13

Discussion

1. Why is the résumé the most important document you may ever write?
2. What is *introspection*, and how does it relate to the employment process?
3. Discuss six ways to gather information about career paths.
4. Discuss five means of searching the job market.
5. What are the three parts of a letter of application, and what is the goal of each part?

Short Answers

6. How are most jobs likely to be found? Through classified ads? Employment agencies? Networking?
   Networking

7. What is the goal of a résumé?
   Gaining an interview

8. Describe a chronological résumé and discuss its advantages.
   A chronological résumé lists work history job by job. Recruiters like this style because they can judge a candidate's employment stability. This style is best for experienced individuals who show steady career growth.

9. Describe a functional résumé and discuss its advantages.
   A functional résumé highlights skills and achievements aimed at a specific job. It does not review a candidate's job history thoroughly. This résumé style is appropriate for candidates with little experience or negative work histories. It also works well for people changing careers.

10. When does it make sense to include a career objective on your résumé?
    Include a specific career objective on a résumé when applying for a targeted position. You can also include a general objective for an all-purpose, general résumé.

11. In addition to technical skills, what traits and characteristics do employers seek?
    Employers seek communication (speaking and writing), management, and interpersonal skills. Specifically, they are looking for such qualities as initiative, dependability, responsibility, resourcefulness, leadership, teamwork, and economy.

12. What are three purposes of a letter of application?
    A letter of application aims to do the following:
    1. Introduce the résumé.
    2. Highlight strengths in terms of reader's benefits.
    3. Gain an interview.

13. Other than a letter of application, name four kinds of letters you might need to write in the employment process.
    Letters written during the employment process could include an application request, an application or résumé follow-up letter, an interview follow-up (thank-you) letter, and a rejection follow-up letter.

14. On a company job application form, how should you respond to questions about salary?
    Unless you know what comparable employees are earning in this company, the best plan is to suggest a salary range or to write Negotiable *or* Open.

15. List seven specific ways that job applicants can prepare for job interviews.

    1. *Research the organization.*
    2. *Learn about the position.*
    3. *Plan to sell themselves.*
    4. *Prepare answers to possible questions.*
    5. *Prepare success stories.*
    6. *Arrive early.*
    7. *Dress appropriately.*

Writing Improvement Exercise

Application Letter

16. Analyze each section of the following letter of application.

Dear Personnel Manager:

(1)   Please consider this letter as an application for the position of staff accountant that I saw advertised in the *Houston Post* on April 27. Accounting has been my major in college, and although I have had no paid work experience in this field, I believe that I could be an asset to Meyers & Jacoby.

(2)   For four years I have studied accounting, and I am fully trained for full-charge bookkeeping as well as computer accounting. I have taken 36 units of college accounting and courses in electronic data processing. I have also taken other courses that may help me in business, including business communication, human relations, report writing, and economics.

(3)   In addition to my course work, during the tax season I have been a student volunteer for VITA. This is a project to help individuals in the community prepare their income tax returns, and I learned a lot from this experience. I have also received some experience in office work and working with figures when I was employed as an office assistant for Copy Quick, Inc.

(4)   I am a competent and responsible person who gets along pretty well with others. I have been a member of some college and social organizations and have even held elective office.

(5)   I feel that I have a strong foundation in accounting as a result of my course work and my experience. Along with my personal qualities and my desire to succeed, I hope that you will agree that I qualify for the position of staff accountant with Meyers & Jacoby.

                              Sincerely,

Make specific suggestions to the writer of this letter for improving each of the five paragraphs.

Address the personnel manager by name. In Paragraph 1 improve the opening by relating your qualifications to the job requirements. Be positive about your work experience. In Paragraph 2 show how your course work will make you a productive employee for this company. Deemphasize "I"; develop reader benefits. In Paragraph 3 name specific tasks that you performed instead of using generalities. In Paragraph 4 demonstrate how the personal qualities that made you successful in college organizations will also make you successful with this company. In the closing (Paragraph 5), refer to your résumé. Ask for an interview at a time that is convenient to the personnel officer.

Activities

17. Learn about employment in your field. Visit your school or local library. Photocopy a page from the *Dictionary of Occupational Titles* that describes a position for which you could apply in two to five years. Photocopy pages from the *Occupational Outlook Handbook* that describe employment in the area in which you are interested. Save these copies to attach to your letter of application.

18. Clip a job advertisement from the classified section of a local or national newspaper. Select an ad describing the kind of employment you will seek in two to five years. (If you can find no advertisement, write one. Construct an advertisement for a legitimate position that could possibly have appeared in an advertisement.) Save this advertisement to attach to your résumé when you submit it.

19. Using information you have gathered from your research and from other sources, describe the successful candidate for the position in Activity No. 18. What education will this individual have? Experience? Skills? Personal qualities? Physical abilities? Appearance?

20. In preparation for writing your résumé, write two career objectives for yourself. Write one that is broad, encompassing both short- and long-term goals. Write another that is narrow and aimed at a specific job.

21. Prepare for writing your résumé by completing inventory lists:

    * *Education.* List degrees, certificates, and training accomplishments. Include courses, seminars, and skills that are relevant to the job you seek.
    * *Experience.* Begin with your most recent job. For each position list the following information: employer, your job title, dates of employment, and three to five accomplishments. Use active verbs and strive to quantify your achievements. Don't merely list duties.
    * *Awards, honors, activities.* List awards, recognition, honors, or activities that recommend you for the targeted job. Look over the examples in this chapter.
    * *Skills, strengths.* Think about skills, talents, or characteristics you possess that relate to the targeted job. Decide whether to use this category or one of the others shown in the models in this chapter. Write statements that demonstrate traits and skills employers seek.

⊃ *Instructor: Activity 22 is described fully on diskette. It includes tips on preparing a résumé on a computer.*

22. Using the data you have just developed, write your résumé. Use a word processor if possible. Revise until it is perfect. Attach a copy of the advertisement from Activity No. 18.

23. Write a letter of application delivering your résumé. Attach the photocopies from Activity No. 17.

24. Assume that you were interviewed for this position. Write a follow-up letter.

25. Write an unsolicited letter seeking a part-time or summer position with an actual firm in your area.

26. Fill in the sample application blank shown in Figure 13.11. Take the time to find all the necessary information. This filled-in form can then be removed and carried with you to serve as a reference when applying for employment.

27. Practice employment interviewing. Choose a partner in your class. Make a list of five employment questions from those shown in the box on page 306. Prepare answers to those questions. In small groups you and your partner will role-play an actual interview. One acts as inter-

viewer; the other is the candidate. Prior to the interview, the candidate tells the interviewer what job and company he or she is applying to. For the interview the interviewer and candidate should dress appropriately and sit in chairs facing each other. The interviewer greets the candidate and makes him/her comfortable. The candidate gives the interviewer a copy of his/her résumé. The interviewer asks several questions from the candidate's list. The interviewer may also ask follow-up questions if appropriate. When finished, the interviewer ends the meeting graciously. After each interview, reverse roles and repeat.

GRAMMAR/MECHANICS CHECKUP—13

NUMBER STYLE

Review Sections 4.01–4.13 in the Grammar/Mechanics Handbook. Then study each of the following pairs. Assume that these expressions appear in the context of letters, reports, or memos. Write *a* or *b* in the space provided to indicate the preferred number style and record the number of the G/M principle illustrated. When you finish, compare your responses with the following. If your responses differ, study carefully the principles in parentheses.

Example: (a) six investments (b) 6 investments *a* *(4.01a)*

1. (a) sixteen credit cards	(b) 16 credit cards	*b*	*(4.01a)*
2. (a) Fifth Avenue	(b) 5th Avenue	*a*	*(4.05b)*
3. (a) 34 newspapers	(b) thirty-four newspapers	*a*	*(4.01a)*
4. (a) July eighth	(b) July 8	*b*	*(4.03)*
5. (a) twenty dollars	(b) $20	*b*	*(4.02)*
6. (a) on the 15th of June	(b) on the fifteenth of June	*a*	*(4.03)*
7. (a) at 4:00 p.m.	(b) at 4 p.m.	*b*	*(4.04)*
8. (a) 8 sixty-four page books	(b) eight 64-page books	*b*	*(4.07)*
9. (a) over 18 years ago	(b) over eighteen years ago	*b*	*(4.08)*
10. (a) 2,000,000 residents	(b) 2 million residents	*b*	*(4.10)*
11. (a) fifteen cents	(b) 15 cents	*b*	*(4.02)*
12. (a) a thirty-day warranty	(b) a 30-day warranty	*b*	*(4.08)*
13. (a) 2/3 of the books	(b) two-thirds of the books	*b*	*(4.12)*
14. (a) two telephones for 15 employees	(b) 2 telephones for 15 employees	*a*	*(4.06)*
15. (a) 6 of the 130 letters	(b) six of the 130 letters	*a*	*(4.06)*

1. b *(4.01a)*   3. a *(4.01a)*   5. b *(4.02)*   7. b *(4.04)*   9. b *(4.08)*   11. b *(4.02)*
13. b *(4.12)*   15. a *(4.06)*

FIGURE 13.11 **Sample Employment Application**

TO OUR APPLICANTS: Please answer all questions completely. If you need help in completing this application, please request assistance from a member of this office. We will be pleased to serve you.

NAME: Last	First	Middle	TODAY'S DATE

PRESENT ADDRESS: No.   Street   City   State   Zip Code

HOME TELEPHONE: ( )	WORK TELEPHONE: ( )	SOCIAL SECURITY NUMBER:

POSITION APPLIED FOR:	SALARY EXPECTED	DATE OPEN FOR HIRE

WOULD YOU WORK —
☐ Full-time?   ☐ Part-time?

REFERRED BY:

WERE YOU PREVIOUSLY EMPLOYED BY US?   IF "YES", WHEN?
☐ Yes   ☐ No

DO YOU HAVE THE LEGAL RIGHT TO BE EMPLOYED IN THE U.S.?   ☐ Yes   ☐ No

VISA NUMBER (if any)   EXPIRATION DATE:

PERSON TO BE NOTIFIED IN CASE OF ACCIDENT OR EMERGENCY: NAME

ADDRESS: TELEPHONE NUMBER: ( )

HAVE YOU SERVED IN THE ARMED SERVICES?   IF "YES", WHEN?
☐ Yes   ☐ No

HAVE YOU EVER BEEN CONVICTED OF A FELONY?
☐ Yes   ☐ No

ON THE LINES BELOW, PLEASE LIST ANY FRIENDS OR RELATIVES WHO ARE STUDENTS HERE OR ARE WORKING FOR US.
Name   Relationship
1.

2.

EDUCATION

NAME AND LOCATION OF HIGH SCHOOL: DID YOU GRADUATE?   ☐ Yes   ☐ No

Name of College, University, Trade or Vocational School	Location	Major Subjects	Degrees or Certificates

SKILLS/ABILITIES

Please list any skills or abilities you have which you think may be used in your employment here. Any craft, trade, office, clerical, professional or administrative skills or abilities may be included. Also list any skills or abilities you gained doing volunteer work, household duties or while pursuing a hobby.

Skill/Ability	Duration of Training	Length of Experience

TYPING SPEED: Manual   Electric   SHORTHAND SPEED: WORD PROCESSING OR DATA ENTRY?   NAME MACHINES OPERATED:

OTHER OFFICE MACHINES OPERATED:

In filling out an employment application, always read the entire application form before you begin filling in answers. For salary questions, it's wise to respond with "Open" or "Negotiable." Remember that an employment application is a legal document. Errors or lying can result in dismissal if discovered after an applicant is hired.

FIGURE 13.11 **continued**

EMPLOYMENT/EXPERIENCE

Please list all jobs and activities for the past ten years or since attending school as a full-time student. Include part-time employment and self-employment. Include experience gained doing volunteer work or community service work. Begin with the most recent employment and activities first.

NAME OF EMPLOYER	YOUR JOB TITLE
ADDRESS OF EMPLOYER	DESCRIBE WORK YOU PERFORMED
SUPERVISOR'S NAME, JOB TITLE AND TELEPHONE NUMBER	

DATE STARTED	DATE ENDED	DURATION	PAY	REASON FOR LEAVING

NAME OF EMPLOYER	YOUR JOB TITLE
ADDRESS OF EMPLOYER	DESCRIBE WORK YOU PERFORMED
SUPERVISOR'S NAME, JOB TITLE AND TELEPHONE NUMBER	

DATE STARTED	DATE ENDED	DURATION	PAY	REASON FOR LEAVING

NAME OF EMPLOYER	YOUR JOB TITLE
ADDRESS OF EMPLOYER	DESCRIBE WORK YOU PERFORMED
SUPERVISOR'S NAME, JOB TITLE AND TELEPHONE NUMBER	

DATE STARTED	DATE ENDED	DURATION	PAY	REASON FOR LEAVING

NAME OF EMPLOYER	YOUR JOB TITLE
ADDRESS OF EMPLOYER	DESCRIBE WORK YOU PERFORMED
SUPERVISOR'S NAME, JOB TITLE AND TELEPHONE NUMBER	

DATE STARTED	DATE ENDED	DURATION	PAY	REASON FOR LEAVING

REFERENCE CHECKS

MAY WE ASK YOUR PRESENT OR PREVIOUS EMPLOYERS ABOUT YOU? ☐ Yes ☐ No	NOT UNTIL I GIVE NOTICE ON (date):

DRIVER'S LICENSE NUMBER:	CLASS (circle one) I II III	STATE WHERE ISSUED:

SIGNATURE: X	DATE:

By my signature above, I certify that all answers and statements on this application are true and complete to the best of my knowledge. I understand that should an investigation disclose untruthful of misleading answers, my application may be rejected, my name removed from consideration, or my employment terminated.

Pay particular attention to statements like the one following the signature above. Many employers thoroughly check all information shown on an employment application. Make sure it is accurate.

GRAMMAR/MECHANICS CHALLENGE—13

Transparency 13.17

DOCUMENT FOR REVISION

The following résumé (shortened for this exercise) has faults in grammar, punctuation, spelling, number form, verb form, wordiness, and word use. Use standard proofreading marks (see Appendix B) to correct the errors. When you finish, your instructor can show you the revised version of this résumé.

Poor Résumé

Ineffective Writing

MEGAN A. RYAN

2450 1st Street

Miami, Flor., 33133

EDUCATION

Coastal Community College, Miami, Florida. Degree expected in June 1995. Major Word Processing.

EXPERIENCE:

- **Office Assistant.**   Host Systems, Miami. 1994 too pressent Responsible for entering data on Macintosh computer. I had to insure accuracy and completness of data that was to be entered. Another duty was maintaining a clean and well-organized office. I also served as Office Courier.

- **Lechter's Housewares.**   Miami Shores. 2nd Asst. Mgr I managed store in absence of mgr. and asst. mgr. I open and close registers. Ballanced daily reciepts. Ordered some mds. I also had to supervise 2 employes, earning rapid promotion.

- **Clerk typist.**   Caribean Cruises Miami. 1992-93. (part time) Entered guest data on IBM PC. Did personalized followup letters to customer inquirys. Was responsible for phones. I also handled all errands as courier.

STRENGTHS

IBM PC, 10-key, transcription, poofreading.

Can type 50 words/per/minute.

I am a fast learner, and very accurate.

Word-perfect, Lotus 123.

14

LISTENING AND SPEAKING

IN THIS CHAPTER YOU WILL LEARN TO DO THE FOLLOWING:

- Identify barriers to effective listening.
- Suggest techniques for becoming an active and effective listener.
- Analyze the audience, organize the content, and prepare visual aids for an oral presentation.
- Select the best method for delivering an oral report.
- Discuss techniques for reducing stage fright.
- Implement techniques of effective speaking.
- Participate in productive and enjoyable meetings.
- Use the telephone as an efficient business tool.
- Master voice mail techniques and applications.

Instructor: See p. 87 for author's suggested lesson plan for Chapter 14.

Successful people, in both their business and their private lives, require a variety of communication skills. Some estimates suggest that adults spend 45 percent of their communicating time listening, 30 percent speaking, 16 percent reading, and 9 percent writing. Writing skills demand the most attention because they are most difficult to develop and because written documents record the most significant events in our lives. However, you should also develop other communication skills that are often taken for granted, such as listening and speaking. Like writing, listening and speaking are talents that can be improved through awareness, study, and practice.

Adults spend about 45 percent of their communicating time listening and 30 percent speaking.

IMPROVING LISTENING SKILLS

Do you ever pretend to be listening when you're not? Do you know how to look attentive in class when your mind wanders far away? Do you ever "tune out" people when their ideas are boring or complex? Do you find it

Instructor: Begin this chapter with listening quiz on p. 88.

Transparencies 14.1 and 14.2

Most individuals listen at only 25 percent efficiency.

Passive listeners don't get involved; active listeners make a physical and mental effort to hear.

difficult to concentrate on ideas when a speaker's appearance or mannerisms are strange?

Most of us would answer yes to one or more of these questions because we have developed poor listening habits. In fact, some researchers suggest that we listen at only 25 percent efficiency. Such poor listening habits are costly in business. Letters must be rekeyed, shipments reshipped, appointments rescheduled, and directions restated. One large corporation postulated that if each of America's 100 million workers made a simple $10 listening mistake, the total loss would be $1 billion. Some business organizations decided that they could not afford to pay the price of poor listening. These companies instituted programs to improve listening habits among their personnel.

For most of us, listening is a passive, unconscious activity. We don't require our minds to work very hard at receiving sounds, and we don't give much thought to whether we're really listening. Only when a message is urgent do we perk up and try to listen more carefully. Then we become more involved in the communication process. We reduce competing environmental sounds; we concentrate on the speaker's words; we anticipate what's coming; we ask questions. Good listeners are active listeners.

To improve listening skills, we first need to recognize barriers that prevent effective listening. Then we need to focus on specific techniques that are effective in improving listening skills.

BARRIERS TO EFFECTIVE LISTENING

Barriers to listening may be physical, psychological, verbal, or nonverbal.

As we learned in Chapter 1, barriers can interfere with the communication process. Some of the barriers and distractions that prevent good listening are discussed here.

Transparency 14.3

- *Physical barriers.* You cannot listen if you cannot hear what is being said. Physical impediments include hearing disabilities, poor acoustics, and noisy surroundings. It's also difficult to listen if you're ill, tired, uncomfortable, or worried.
- *Psychological barriers.* As noted in Chapter 1, every person brings to the communication process a different set of cultural, ethical, and personal values. Each of us has an idea of what is right and what is important. If other ideas run counter to our preconceived thoughts, we tend to "tune out" the speaker and thus fail to hear. For example, if Carolyn Dee thinks that her work is satisfactory, she might filter out criticism from her supervisor. Such selective listening results in poor communication and is unproductive for both the listener and the speaker.
- *Language problems.* We've already learned that jargon and unfamiliar words can destroy the communication process because such words lack meaning for the receiver. In addition, emotion-laden or "charged" words can adversely affect listening. If the mention of words like *abortion* or *overdose* has an intense emotional impact, a listener may be unable to concentrate on the words that follow.
- *Nonverbal distractions.* Many of us find it difficult to listen if the speaker is different from what we consider normal. Unusual clothing, speech mannerisms, body twitches, or a nonconformist hairstyle can cause sufficient distraction to prevent us from hearing what the speaker has to say.
- *Thought speed.* Because thought speed is over three times as great as speech speed, listener concentration flags. Our minds are able to pro-

cess thoughts much faster than speakers can enunciate them. There-fore, we become bored and our minds wander.

Most Americans speak at about 125 words per minute. The human brain can process information at least three times as fast.

- *Faking attention.* Most of us have learned to look as if we are listening even when we're not. Such behavior was perhaps necessary as part of our socialization. Faked attention, however, seriously threatens effective listening because it encourages the mind to flights of uncontrolled fancy. Those who practice faked attention often find it difficult to concentrate even when they want to.
- *Grandstanding.* Would you rather talk or listen? Naturally, most of us would rather talk. Since our own experiences and thoughts are most important to us, we grab the limelight in conversations. We sometimes fail to listen carefully because we're just waiting politely for the next pause so that we can have our turn to speak.

HOW TO BECOME AN ACTIVE LISTENER

You can reverse the harmful effects of poor listening habits by making a conscious effort to become an active listener. Listening actively means becoming involved. You can't sit back and hear whatever a lazy mind happens to receive. These techniques will help you become an active and effective listener.

- *Stop talking.* The first step to becoming a good listener is to stop talking. Let others explain their views. Learn to concentrate on what the speaker is saying, not on what your next comment will be.

Transparency 14.4

To become a good listener, control your surroundings and your mind-set.

- *Control your surroundings.* Whenever possible, remove competing sounds. Close windows or doors, turn off radios and noisy appliances, and move away from loud people or engines. Choose a quiet time and place for listening.
- *Establish a receptive mind-set.* Expect to learn something by listening. Develop a positive and receptive frame of mind. If the message is complex, consider it mental gymnastics. It's hard work but good exercise for the mind to stretch and expand its limits.

Instructor: See p. 89 for supplementary lecture, "Types of Poor Listeners."

- *Keep an open mind.* We all sift and filter information through our own prejudices and values. For improved listening, discipline yourself to listen objectively. Be fair to the speaker. Hear what is really being said, not what you want to hear.
- *Listen for main points.* Concentration is enhanced and satisfaction is heightened when you look for and recognize the speaker's central themes.
- *Capitalize on lag time.* Make use of the quickness of your mind by reviewing the speaker's points. Anticipate what's coming next. Evaluate evidence the speaker has presented. Don't allow yourself to daydream.
- *Listen between the lines.* Focus on both what is spoken and what is unspoken. Listen for feelings as well as for facts.

Transparency 14.5

- *Judge ideas, not appearances.* Concentrate on the content of the message, not on its delivery. Avoid being distracted by the speaker's appearance, voice, or mannerisms.
- *Hold your fire.* Force yourself to listen to the speaker's entire argument or message before reacting. Such restraint may enable you to understand the speaker's reasons and logic before you jump to unwarranted conclusions.
- *Take selective notes.* For some situations thoughtful note-taking may be necessary to record important facts that must be recalled later. Select only the most important points so that the note-taking process

Listening actively may mean taking notes and providing feedback.

does not interfere with your concentration on the speaker's total message.

- *Provide feedback.* Let the speaker know that you are listening. Nod your head and maintain eye contact. Ask relevant questions at appropriate times. Getting involved improves the communication process for both the speaker and the listener.

IMPROVING SPEAKING SKILLS

Listening and speaking make up a large part of the time you spend communicating. How much time you devote to speaking—and, more particularly, to making speeches and oral presentations—depends on your occupation and on the level you reach in your career. Few businesspeople regularly deliver formal speeches. Instead, most of us communicate orally in informal conversations and small-group discussions.

As you advance in your career, the ability to express your ideas orally takes on greater significance.

Yet, every college-educated individual aspiring to a business career is well advised to develop speaking skills. A computer equipment sales representative pitches products before a group of potential customers. An accountant explains the financial position of an organization to management. A travel agent describes an excursion package to a single client or to a group. An office manager clarifies new office procedures, and a structural engineer explains load bearing to a land developer. Just as the need for writing skills increases as you rise in your profession, so does the need for speaking skills. It is no coincidence that most individuals promoted to executive-level positions are effective writers and speakers.

PREPARING AN ORAL REPORT

Transparency 14.6

Before you make an oral presentation, you should analyze the audience, organize your topic, and plan visual aids, if appropriate.

One of the most common speaking functions for businesspeople is the presentation of ideas in an oral report. Such a presentation is most frequently made informally to a superior or to a small group of colleagues. Only occasionally do businesspeople make formal speeches before large groups.

Planning an oral report is similar in many ways to preparing for a written report. You need to analyze the audience, organize the content, and plan visual aids.

ANALYZING THE AUDIENCE

Knowing about your audience will help you decide how to structure your report. The size of the audience influences the formality of your presentation: a large audience generally requires a more formal and less personalized approach. Other factors, such as age, sex, education, experience, and attitude toward the subject, also affect your presentation. Analyze these factors to determine your strategy, vocabulary, illustrations, and level of detail. Your answers to specific questions will guide you in adapting the topic to your audience:

- How will this topic appeal to this audience?
- What do I want the audience to believe?
- What action do I want the audience to take?
- What aspects of the topic will be most interesting to the audience?

- Which of the following will be most effective in making my point: Statistics? Graphic illustrations? Demonstrations? Case histories? Analogies? Cost figures?

ORGANIZING CONTENT

Begin to organize your oral report by defining its purpose. Is your goal to inform? To persuade? To recommend? In describing your goal, write a statement of purpose. For example, the goal of this report is

> To inform all staff members of the benefits and options in the new health care program.

> To persuade the sales vice president that a consolidation of the Ohio and Michigan territories would reduce costs and increase efficiency.

> To recommend to the Board of Directors the establishment of a members' advisory committee that would encourage input from the rank and file of the organization.

A precise statement of purpose helps you organize the content of your presentation.

After you have a firm statement of purpose, organize your report to reach your goal. Like business letters and written reports, oral reports may follow either a direct or an indirect strategy. It seems most logical, though, to organize the report indirectly. Since listeners are generally unfamiliar with the problem, they typically need some explanation or introductory comment to ease them into the topic.

Whether you use a direct or indirect approach, make an outline to guide the organization of your report. Concentrate on two to four main points only. Follow an outline form such as that shown in Chapter 12 for a long report.

Most presentations should focus on only two to four principal points.

Like long reports, oral presentations often contain three parts: introduction, body, and conclusion. One old-timer explains the organization of speeches as follows: *(1) tell them what you're going to tell them, (2) tell them what you have to say, and then (3) tell them what you've just told them.* Such redundancy may seem deadly, but repetition helps the audience retain information.

The audience for oral reports, unlike readers, cannot control the rate of presentation or reread main points. Therefore, knowledgeable speakers help their listeners recognize the organization and main points in an oral report by emphasizing and reiterating them. Good speakers also keep the audience on track by including helpful transitions, reviews, and previews.

Help the listener follow your presentation by describing its organization (introduction, body, and conclusion).

- *Introduction.* At the beginning of your report, identify yourself (if necessary) and your topic. Describe the goal of your report, its organization, and the main points you will cover. Also in your introduction make an effort to capture the attention of the audience with a question, startling fact, joke, story, quotation, or some other device. Make sure, of course, that your attention-getter is relevant to your topic.
- *Body.* Follow your outline in presenting the two to four main points of your topic. Develop each with adequate, but not excessive, support and detail. Keep your presentation simple and logical—listeners have no pages to leaf back through if they should become confused.

The best devices you can use to ensure comprehension are verbal signposts that tell where you've been and point where you're going. Summarize a segment of your report with a summary statement:

Include verbal signposts so that listeners know where you've been and where you're heading in your presentation.

> We see, then, that the two major problems facing management are raw material and labor costs.

Or combine a review with a preview:

> Now that we've learned how sole proprietorships are different from partnerships, let's turn to corporations.

> I've described two good reasons for consolidating sales territories, but the final reason is most important.

Repeat main ideas as you progress. Indicate new topics or shifts in direction with helpful transitional expressions, such as *first, second, next, then, therefore, moreover, on the other hand, on the contrary,* and *in conclusion.*

Conclude your presentation by emphasizing the information that you want your listeners to remember.

- *Conclusion.* You may end a presentation by reviewing the main themes of the talk, or you may round out the presentation by referring to your opening. Concentrate on the information that achieves your purpose. What do you want your listeners to believe? What action do you want them to take? When you finish, ask if audience members have any questions. If silence ensues, remark that you'll be happy to answer questions individually after the program is completed.

PLANNING VISUAL AIDS

Oral reports are most successful when they show and tell.

Show-and-tell is effective not only for grade-schoolers but also for adults. Some authorities suggest that we learn and remember 85 percent of all our knowledge visually. The oral report that incorporates visual aids is twice as likely to be understood and retained as a report lacking visual supplements. By appealing to the senses of both sight and sound, a message can double its impact.

Visual aids are particularly useful for inexperienced speakers because the audience concentrates on the aids rather than on the speaker and because visual aids can jog the memory of the speaker.

When you incorporate visual aids into an oral report, keep a few points in mind:

- Use visual aids only for major points or for information that requires clarification.
- Keep the visual aids simple.
- Make sure the necessary equipment works properly. Have a backup ready.
- Ensure that everyone can see the visual aid.
- Talk to the audience, not to the visual aid.

In selecting ways to illustrate your oral report, you have a number of options, each with its particular uses, advantages, and disadvantages.

- *Transparencies.* Easy and inexpensive to prepare, transparencies can be used to project a message on a screen in a lighted or unlighted room. They are popular in business and education because the masters can be typed or handwritten on plain paper. The masters are transferred onto transparent film by means of a thermograph or photocopy machine. Transparencies can also be printed with laser printers. The transparency is then placed onto an overhead projector, which projects the image onto a screen.

  Typed transparencies are especially useful because they can be made in advance, and they are easy to read when printed in a large font. They emphasize points for the viewers and can serve to prompt the speaker.
- *Flip charts.* Like a giant pad of paper, a flip chart consists of large sheets attached at the top. You may prepare the sheets in advance or write on them as you speak and flip through the pad. Flip charts are usually less visible than transparencies because they are propped on an

easel on a level with the speaker and because the sheets are smaller than the images projected on a screen. Thus, they are less effective with larger audiences. However, flip charts require no special equipment, and they can be quite colorful if you use felt-tip markers.

- *Slides.* For picturesque, nonverbal messages, slides can be colorful and entertaining. Verbal messages on slides are more difficult to achieve unless you use a graphic-design service or computer presentation software. Slides, of course, require a slide projector and a screen as well as an operator. When you project slides in a darkened room, you lose eye contact with the audience and risk putting the audience to sleep.
- *Handouts.* Speakers often use handouts, such as a sheet of paper or a packet, to supplement the presentation. Handouts may consist of an outline, list of selected main points, illustration, flow chart, table, or any other material that helps clarify the report. Members of the audience appreciate handouts because they have ready-made notes to take with them to remind them of the report. The major disadvantage of handouts is that audience members may read the handouts instead of listening to the speaker. For this reason some speakers distribute handouts only at the end of their presentations.

Experienced speakers distribute handouts when they conclude their presentations.

DELIVERING THE ORAL REPORT

Regardless of its excellent preparation and interesting content, a speech will be boring and fail in its purpose if delivered poorly. Good speakers choose an appropriate delivery method, and they practice techniques to hold the attention of the audience.

Transparency 14.7

DELIVERY METHODS

Your audience will be most favorably impressed if your presentation is forceful but natural. Four delivery methods are available:

- *Memorized delivery.* Inexperienced speakers often feel that they must memorize an entire report to be effective. Actually, unless you're a trained actor, a memorized delivery sounds wooden and unnatural. Also, forgetting your place can be disastrous. Therefore, memorizing an entire oral presentation is not recommended. However, memorizing significant parts—the introduction, the conclusion, or a significant quotation—can be dramatic and impressive.

Memorized oral presentations sound artificial and result in catastrophe if you become confused.

- *Reading delivery.* Reading a report to an audience creates a negative impression. It suggests that you don't know your topic very well, so that the audience loses confidence in your expertise. Reading also prevents you from maintaining eye contact with the audience. If you can't see their reactions, you can't benefit from feedback. Worst of all, reading is simply boring. If you must read your report, practice it enough so that you can look up occasionally as you present familiar sections.

If you read an oral presentation, you may put your audience to sleep.

- *Extemporaneous delivery.* The most effective method for presenting oral reports is the extemporaneous delivery. In this method you plan the report carefully and talk from notes containing key sentences. By practicing with your notes, you can talk to your audience in a conversational manner. Your notes should not consist of entire paragraphs, nor should they be single words. Instead, use complete sentences based on the

Write out complete sentences for the key ideas in your talk.

major ideas in your outline. These key ideas will keep you on track and will jog your memory, but only if you have thoroughly practiced the presentation.

- *Impromptu delivery.* An impromptu, or off-the-cuff, delivery is necessary if you are asked to give a spur-of-the-moment report. For example, you might be asked to report on the progress of a March of Dimes collection drive of which you are chairperson. Many activities in business require impromptu oral reports. Usually, you are very familiar with your topic, but you have little time to prepare your thoughts. Presenting accurate, coherent, persuasive, and well-organized information without adequate preparation is very difficult for even the most professional speaker. If you are asked to give an impromptu report, take a few moments to compose your thoughts and to jot down your main points.

Transparency 14.7

DELIVERY TECHNIQUES

Nearly everyone experiences some degree of stage fright when speaking before a group. Such fears are quite natural. You can learn to control and reduce stage fright, as well as to incorporate techniques of effective speaking in your presentations, by studying suggestions from experts. Successful speakers use these techniques before, during, and after their reports.

BEFORE YOU SPEAK

Here are techniques that experts use before, during, and after delivering oral presentations.

- *Prepare thoroughly.* One of the most effective devices to reduce stage fright is the confidence that you know your topic well. Research your topic diligently and prepare a careful sentence outline. Those who try to "wing it" usually suffer the worst butterflies.
- *Rehearse repeatedly.* Practice your entire presentation, not just the first half. Place your outline sentences on separate cards. You may also wish to include transitional sentences to help you move to the next topic. Use these cards as you practice, and include your visual aids in your rehearsal. Record your rehearsal on tape so that you can hear how you sound.
- *Time yourself.* Try to make your presentation in no more than twenty minutes. Most audiences tend to get restless during longer talks. Set a timer during your rehearsal to measure your speaking time.
- *Request a lectern.* Every beginning speaker needs the security of a high desk or lectern from which to deliver a presentation. It serves as a note holder and a convenient place to rest awkward hands and arms.
- *Check the room.* Make sure that a lectern has been provided. If you are using sound equipment or a projector, make sure they are operational. Check electrical outlets and the position of the viewing screen. Ensure that the seating arrangement is appropriate to your needs.

Deep-breathing exercises can significantly reduce stress.

- *Practice stress reduction.* If you feel tension and fear while you are waiting your turn to speak, use stress reduction techniques. Take very deep breaths. Inhale to a count of ten; hold this breath to a count of ten; exhale to a count of ten. Concentrate on your breathing, not on the audience awaiting you.

DURING YOUR PRESENTATION

- *Begin with a pause.* When you first approach the audience, take a moment to adjust your notes and make yourself comfortable. Establish your control of the situation.
- *Present your first sentence from memory.* By memorizing your opening, you can immediately establish rapport with the audience through eye contact. You'll also sound confident and knowledgeable.

- *Maintain eye contact.* Look at your audience. If the size of the audience frightens you, pick out two individuals on the right and two on the left. Talk directly to these people.
- *Control your voice and vocabulary.* Speak in moderated tones but loudly enough to be heard. Eliminate verbal static, such as "ah," "er," and "uh." Silence is preferable to meaningless fillers when you are thinking of your next idea.
- *Put the brakes on.* Many novice speakers talk too rapidly, displaying their nervousness and making it very difficult for audience members to understand their ideas. Slow down and listen to what you're saying.
- *Move naturally.* Use the lectern to hold your notes so that you are free to move about casually and naturally. Avoid fidgeting with your notes, your clothing, or items in your pockets. Learn to use your body to express a point.
- *Use visual aids effectively.* Discuss and interpret each visual aid for the audience. Move aside as you describe it so that it can be seen fully. Use a pointer if necessary.
- *Avoid digressions.* Stick to your outline and notes. Don't suddenly include clever little anecdotes or digressions that occur to you as you speak. If it's not part of your rehearsed material, leave it out so that you can finish on time. Remember, too, that your audience may not be as enthralled with your topic as you are.

  Avoid digressions that occur to you as you speak.
- *Summarize your main points.* Conclude your presentation by reiterating your main points or by emphasizing what you want the audience to think or do. Once you have announced your conclusion, proceed to it directly. Don't irritate the audience by talking for five or ten more minutes.

AFTER YOUR PRESENTATION

- *Distribute handouts.* If you prepared handouts with data the audience will need to have after the presentation, pass them out when you finish.
- *Encourage questions.* If the situation permits a question-and-answer period, announce it at the beginning of your presentation. Then, when you finish, ask for questions. Set a time limit for questions and answers.
- *Repeat questions.* Although the speaker may hear the question, some people in the audience often do not. Begin each answer with a repetition of the question. This also gives you thinking time.

  Keep control of the question-and-answer period by repeating questions for the entire audience to hear and by involving the entire audience.
- *Answer questions directly.* Avoid becoming defensive or debating the questioner.
- *Keep control.* Don't allow one individual to take over. Keep the entire audience involved.
- *End gracefully.* To signal the end of the session before you take the last question, say something like "We have time for just one more question." After you answer the last question, express appreciation to the audience for the opportunity to talk with them.

EVALUATING PRESENTATIONS

The oral report evaluation form shown in Figure 14.1 should be useful to speakers preparing a presentation. It's also helpful to students who will evaluate oral reports in a classroom situation.

FIGURE 14.1   Oral Report Evaluation Form

⊃ *Instructor: See
p. 92 for report
forms ready to
duplicate for class
use.*

SPEAKER'S NAME_____	

Oral Report Evaluation

Excellent	10 points
Above average	8–9
Average	5–7
Needs improvement	4 or below

                                               Points

1. Were the opening and closing clear and well planned?   _____

2. Did the speaker help you remember two to four main points?   _____

3. Were the speaker's movements and eye contact natural?   _____

4. Was the visual aid handled appropriately?   _____

5. Was the report well organized, coherent, and obviously practiced before presentation?   _____

TOTAL POINTS   _____

On the back add a statement of praise and suggest one pointer for improvement.

DEVELOPING SUCCESSFUL MEETINGS AND CONFERENCES

Transparency 14.8

Whether you like attending them or not, meetings and conferences are a necessary part of business today. These meetings can be more successful—and even enjoyable—if leaders and participants sharpen their listening and speaking skills.

Meetings and conferences consist of three or more individuals who meet for discussion. Meetings are called to gather information, clarify policy, seek consensus, and solve problems. Meetings are different from speeches, where one individual talks *at* an audience. In meetings individuals *exchange* ideas.

Meetings differ from conferences in that they are smaller and less formal. We'll concentrate on meetings in this discussion, although most of the advice holds for conferences as well. Meetings can be occasions for successful exchange of information, or they can be boring time wasters.

WHY MEETINGS FAIL

*Poor meetings are
usually the result of
poor planning or
ineffective
leadership.*

Many failed meetings are the result of poor planning. Perhaps the meeting was unnecessary. Alternatives—such as personal conversation, memos, or telephone calls—might have served the purpose as well.

Poor leadership dooms some meetings. The leader fails to keep the group discussing target items. The discussion digresses or flounders on trivia, and no resolution is reached. Then the group must meet again, and no one enjoys additional meetings.

PLANNING MEETINGS

Successful meetings begin with planning. Decide first on a goal or an objective, and then determine whether a meeting is the best way to achieve the goal. If the goal is to announce a new policy regarding the scheduling of vacations, is a meeting the best way to inform employees? Perhaps a memo would be better.

     If a meeting is necessary, prepare an agenda of items to be discussed. The best agendas list topics, an estimate of time for each item, and an ending time. They may also include the names of individuals who are responsible for presenting topics or for performing some action. Send the agenda (and perhaps the minutes of the previous meeting) at least two days prior to the meeting. Notify only those people directly concerned with the business of this meeting. Plan to serve refreshments if you think the participants need them.

Agendas help prepare participants for meetings.

THE WALL STREET JOURNAL

"Jenkins, is there something I should know?"

Source: From *The Wall Street Journal.* Reprinted with permission of the Cartoon Features Syndicate.

CONDUCTING MEETINGS

Conducting good meetings requires real skill, which not every leader immediately has. Such skill comes with practice and with knowledge of the following pointers. To avoid wasting time and irritating the attendees, always start meetings on time—even if some participants are missing. Delaying sets a poor example. Individuals who came on time resent waiting for latecomers. Moreover, latecomers may fail to be on time for future meetings, knowing that the leader doesn't always start punctually.

The most important part of a meeting is the first 5 to 10 minutes when the leader introduces the topic and sets the tone.

Begin with a 3- to 5-minute introduction that includes the following: (1) goal and length of the meeting, (2) background of the problem, (3) possible solutions and constraints, (4) tentative agenda, and (5) procedures to be followed. At this point ask if participants agree with you thus far.

Then assign one attendee to take minutes. It's impossible for the leader to direct a meeting and record its proceedings at the same time. Open the discussion, and from that point forward, say as little as possible. Adhere to the agenda and the time schedule. Keep the discussion on the topic by tactfully guiding speakers back to the main idea. You might say, "Well, gosh, Jeff, I'm afraid I don't understand exactly how your new motorcycle relates to our vacation policy. Can you explain?" Encourage all individuals to participate. You can do this by occasionally asking for the opinions of the smart but silent participants. Try not to let one or two people monopolize the discussion. When the group seems to have reached a consensus, summarize it in your own words and look to see if everyone agrees. Finally, end the meeting at the agreed time. Announce that a report of the proceedings will be sent to all.

PARTICIPATING IN MEETINGS

Meetings give employees an opportunity to impress their superiors.

As a participant, you can get the most out of a meeting and contribute to its success by coming prepared. Read the agenda and gather any information necessary for your knowledgeable participation. One way to make yourself visible in an organization is to shine at meetings. Know the problem, its causes, possible solutions, alternatives, and how others have dealt with it. Careful preparation and wise participation at meetings often cause management to recognize upwardly mobile employees.

Arrive at the meeting on time. Be ready to speak on an issue, but consider your timing. It may be smart to wait for others to speak first so that you can shape your remarks to best advantage. You can help the leader keep the discussion on target with remarks such as, "Sure, I love a bargain, too, Lisa, but right now I'm very concerned about how to solve this problem. Has anyone considered . . . ?"

Productive, enjoyable meetings result from good planning, skillful leadership, and active participation.

IMPROVING TELEPHONE AND VOICE MAIL TECHNIQUES

Transparency 14.9

Telephones and voice mail should promote goodwill and increase productivity.

The telephone is the most universal—and, some would say, the most important—piece of equipment in offices today. The telephone has spawned an entire new industry—voice mail systems, which are rapidly replacing switchboards and receptionists. These computerized message systems save labor costs and provide sophisticated capabilities and flexibility unavailable in the past. Regardless of their advanced technology, though, telephones and voice mail are valuable business tools *only* when they generate goodwill and increase productivity. Poor communication techniques can easily offset any benefits arising from improved equipment. What good is an extensive voice mail system if callers hang up in frustration after waiting through a long list of menu options without learning what they need? Here are suggestions aimed at helping business communicators make the best use of telephone and voice mail equipment.

Source: Reprinted with special permission of North American Syndicate, Inc.

MAKING PRODUCTIVE TELEPHONE CALLS

Before making a telephone call, decide whether the intended call is really necessary. Could you find the information yourself? If you wait a while, would the problem resolve itself? Perhaps your message could be delivered more efficiently by some other means. One West Coast company found that telephone interruptions consumed about 18 percent of staff members' workdays. Another study found that two-thirds of all calls were less important than the work they interrupted. Alternatives to telephone calls include electronic mail (E-mail) messages, memos, or calls to voice mail systems. If a telephone call must be made, consider the following suggestions to make it fully productive:

Making productive telephone calls means planning an agenda, identifying the purpose, being courteous and cheerful, and avoiding rambling.

- *Plan a mini-agenda.* Have you ever been embarrassed when you had to make a second telephone call because you forgot an important item the first time? Before placing a call, jot down notes regarding all the topics you need to discuss. Following an agenda guarantees not only a complete call but also a quick one. You'll be less likely to wander from the business at hand while rummaging through your mind trying to remember everything.

- *Use a three-point introduction.* When placing a call, immediately (1) name the person you are calling, (2) identify yourself and your affiliation, and (3) give a brief explanation of your reason for calling. For example: "May I speak to Larry Lopez? This is Hillary Dahl of Sebastian Enterprises, and I'm seeking information about a software program called 'Power Presentations.'" This kind of introduction enables the receiving individual to respond immediately without asking further questions.

- *Be cheerful and accurate.* Let your voice show the same kind of animation that you radiate when you greet people in person. In your mind try to envision the individual answering the telephone. A smile can certainly affect the tone of your voice, so smile at that person. Moreover, be accurate about what you say. "Hang on a second; I'll be right back" rarely is true. Better to say, "It may take me two or three minutes to get that information. Would you prefer to hold or have me call you back?"

- *Bring it to a close.* The responsibility for ending a call lies with the caller. This is sometimes difficult to do if the other person rambles on. You may need to use suggestive closing language, such as "I've certainly enjoyed talking with you," "I've learned what I needed to know, and now I can proceed with my work," "Thanks for your help," or "I must go now, but may I call you again in the future if I need . . . ?"

- *Avoid telephone tag.* If you call someone who's not in, ask when it would be best for you to call again. State that you will call at a specific time—and do it. If you ask a person to call you, give a time when you can be reached—and then be sure you are in at that time.
- *Leave complete voice mail messages.* Remember that there's no rush when you leave a voice mail message. Always enunciate clearly. And be sure to provide a complete message, including your name, telephone number, and the time and date of your call. Explain your purpose so that the receiver can be ready with the required information when returning your call.

RECEIVING PRODUCTIVE TELEPHONE CALLS

Receiving productive telephone calls means identifying oneself, being responsive and helpful, and taking accurate messages.

With a little forethought you can make your telephone a productive, efficient work tool. Developing good telephone manners also reflects well on you and on your organization.

- *Identify yourself immediately.* In answering your telephone or someone else's, provide your name, title or affiliation, and, possibly, a greeting. For example, "Larry Lopez, Proteus Software. How may I help you?" Force yourself to speak clearly and slowly. Remember that the caller may be unfamiliar with what you are saying and fail to recognize slurred syllables.
- *Be responsive and helpful.* If you are in a support role, be sympathetic to callers' needs. Instead of "I don't know," try "That's a good question; let me investigate." Instead of "We can't do that," try "That's a tough one; let's see what we can do." Avoid "No" at the beginning of a sentence. It sounds especially abrasive and displeasing because it suggests total rejection.
- *Be cautious when answering calls for others.* Be courteous and helpful, but don't give out confidential information. Better to say, "She's away from her desk" or "He's out of the office" than to report a colleague's exact whereabouts.
- *Take messages carefully.* Few things are as frustrating as receiving a potentially important phone message that is illegible. Repeat the spelling of names and verify telephone numbers. Write messages legibly and record their time and date. Promise to give the messages to intended recipients, but don't guarantee return calls.
- *Explain what you're doing when transferring calls.* Give a reason for transferring, and identify the extension to which you are directing the call in case the caller is disconnected.

MAKING THE BEST USE OF VOICE MAIL

Voice mail eliminates telephone tag, inaccurate message-taking, and time-zone barriers; it also allows communicators to focus on essentials.

Voice mail links a telephone system to a computer that digitizes and stores incoming messages. Some systems also provide functions like automated attendant menus, allowing callers to reach any associated extension by pushing specific buttons on a touch-tone telephone. Interactive systems allow callers to receive verbal information from a computer database. For example, a ski resort in Colorado uses voice mail to answer routine questions that once were routed through an operator: "Welcome to Snow Paradise. For information on accommodations, touch 1; for snow conditions, touch 2; for ski equipment rental, touch 3," and so forth.

Voice mail serves many functions, but the most important is message storage. Because half of all business calls require no discussion or feedback (according to AT&T estimates), the messaging capabilities of voice mail can mean huge savings for businesses. Incoming information is delivered without interrupting potential receivers and without all the niceties that most two-way conversations require. Stripped of superfluous chit-chat, voice mail messages allow communicators to focus on essentials. Voice mail also eliminates telephone tag, inaccurate message-taking, and time-zone barriers. Critics complain, nevertheless, that automated systems seem cold and impersonal and are sometimes confusing and irritating.

In any event, here are some ways that you can make voice mail work more effectively for you:

- *Announce your voice mail.* If you rely principally on a voice mail message system, identify it on your business stationery and cards. Then, when people call, they will be ready to leave a message.
- *Prepare a warm and informative greeting.* Make your mechanical greeting sound warm and inviting, both in tone and content. Identify yourself and your organization so that callers know they have reached the right number. Thank the caller and briefly explain that you are unavailable. Invite the caller to leave a message or, if appropriate, call back. Here's a typical voice mail greeting: "Hi! This is Larry Lopez of Proteus Software, and I appreciate your call. You've reached my voice mailbox because I'm either working with customers or talking on another line at the moment. Please leave your name, number, and reason for calling so that I can be prepared when I return your call." Give callers an idea of when you will be available, such as "I'll be back at 2:30" or "I'll be out of my office until Wednesday, May 20." If you screen your calls as a time-management technique, try this message: "I'm not near my phone right now, but I should be able to return calls after 3:30."
- *Test your message.* Call your number and assess your message. Does it sound inviting? Sincere? Understandable? Are you pleased with your tone? If not, says one consultant, have someone else, perhaps a professional, record a message for you.

Employers today are looking for individuals who have developed good communication skills. Active listeners and confident speakers have a competitive edge in the business world, not only for entry-level positions but especially for higher-lever management positions.

APPLICATION AND PRACTICE—14

Discussion

1. If most of our communicating time is spent listening, speaking, and reading, why is a disproportionate amount of time spent learning writing skills?
2. Discuss seven barriers to effective listening and give an example of each from the business world.
3. Discuss the advantages and disadvantages of taking notes while you are listening. When would note-taking be most effective?
4. Compare and contrast the development of oral and written reports.
5. Why is it necessary to keep the audience informed of the organization of an oral report?
6. Discuss the duties of a leader and the functions of a participant at business meetings and conferences.

Short Answers

7. According to some estimates, adults spent what percentage of their communicating time
   a. listening   *45%*
   b. speaking   *30%*
   c. reading   *16%*
   d. writing   *9%*

8. How fast does the average American speak?
   125 words a minute

9. List 11 ways to improve your listening skills. Be prepared to discuss each.
   1. *Stop talking.*
   2. *Control the surroundings.*
   3. *Establish a receptive mind-set.*
   4. *Keep an open mind.*
   5. *Listen for main points.*
   6. *Capitalize on lag time.*
   7. *Listen between the lines.*
   8. *Judge ideas, not appearances.*
   9. *Hold your fire.*
   10. *Take selective notes.*
   11. *Provide feedback.*

10. Name five characteristics that you should identify about your audience before preparing an oral report.
    1. *Age*
    2. *Sex*
    3. *Education*
    4. *Experience*
    5. *Attitude toward the subject*

11. On how many main points should an oral report concentrate?
    Two to four

12. What is the first step in developing an oral report?
    Write a statement of purpose.

13. List the three parts of an oral report. Be prepared to discuss what goes in each part.
    1. *Introduction*
    2. *Body*
    3. *Conclusion*

14. List four kinds of visual aids for oral reports. Be prepared to discuss each.
    1. *Transparencies*
    2. *Flip charts*
    3. *Slides*
    4. *Handouts*

15. List five techniques that are helpful in overcoming stage fright.
    1. *Prepare thoroughly.*
    2. *Rehearse repeatedly.*
    3. *Practice stress reduction.*
    4. *Use a lectern.*
    5. *Deliver your first sentence from memory.*

16. Notes for an oral report should consist of what?
    Complete sentences for each division in your outline recorded on cards or on separate sheets of paper

17. What is an agenda, and what should it include?
    An agenda is a list of topics to be discussed at a meeting. It should include the topics, estimated time for each, names of individuals making presentations, and ending time of meeting.

18. Who takes the minutes of a meeting, and what are done with them?
    The leader appoints a participant to record the minutes, which are then sent to participants following the meeting.

19. Give an example of an efficient three-point opening to a telephone call. Use your own name and data.
    "This is Mark Macho from Contemporary Videos calling Melissa Mason about the order she placed October 3."

20. What is telephone tag, and how can it be avoided?
    Telephone tag results when one individual calls another and leaves a message. The recipient calls back at a bad time and must leave a message. Telephone tag can be avoided by leaving a message including a time when you can be reached or by asking what time you may call again.

Activities

21. Observe the listening habits in one of your classes for a week. Write a memo report to your instructor describing your observations.

22. Analyze your own listening habits. What are your strengths and weaknesses? Decide on a plan for improving your listening skills. Write a memo to your instructor including your analysis and your improvement plan.

23. You are a student in a business management or other class. Your instructor notices that you have good listening habits. Disturbed by the poor listening skills of some other class members, your instructor asks you to do research and to present a program (for extra credit) to help students improve their listening skills. For this presentation:
    a. Write a specific statement of purpose.
    b. Prepare a complete outline
    c. Write the introduction.
    d. List visual aids that would be appropriate and describe their content.

⊃ *Instructor: Activity 23 is available on diskette.*

24. If you are now employed or have been employed, adapt the assignment in Activity No. 23 to your work. Assume that your supervisor has asked you to present an in-service training workshop that helps employees improve listening skills. Respond to the instructions in Items (a) through (d).

25. Visit your library and select a speech from *Vital Speeches of Our Day*. Write a memo report to your instructor in which you analyze the speech in terms of the following items:
    a. Effectiveness of the introduction, body, and conclusion
    b. Evidence of effective overall organization
    c. Use of verbal signposts to create coherence
    d. Emphasis of two to four main points
    e. Effectiveness of supporting facts (use of examples, statistics, quotations, and so forth)

26. Adapt a newspaper or magazine article to an oral report format. Assume that you are to present this report before your business communication class. Submit the outline, introduction, and conclusion to your instructor, or present the report to your class.

27. Write a memo to your instructor describing the fears or anxieties that you have experienced when presenting a speech. Suggest ways to reduce your fears.

28. Interview two or three individuals in your professional field. How is oral communication important in this profession? Does the need for oral skills change as one advances? What suggestions can this individual make for developing proficient oral communication skills among newcomers to the field? Discuss your findings with your class.

29. If you prepared a business report in Chapter 11, deliver it as an extemporaneous report before your class. Your instructor will determine how much time you have. Use visual aids, if appropriate, and be sure to leave enough time for questions and answers. Class members will evaluate the report using the oral report evaluation form (Figure 14.1).

30. Plan a meeting. Assume that the next meeting of your associated students' organization will discuss preparations for a careers day in the spring. The group will hear reports from committees working on speakers, business recruiters, publicity, reservations of campus space, setup of booths, and any other matters you can think of. As president of your ASO, prepare an agenda for the meeting, Compose your introductory remarks to open the meeting. Your instructor may ask you to submit these two documents or use them in staging an actual meeting in class.

31. Listen for instructions. Your instructor will "talk" or explain the facts from one of the letter or memo assignments in an earlier exercise. The instructor may add extraneous information or omit something vital. Take notes from your instructor's presentation. Ask questions, if necessary. Do not look at a written version of the data. Then write the document prescribed.

32. Practice making and taking telephone calls. Your instructor will divide the class into pairs. Read the scenario and take a moment to rehearse your role silently. Then play the role with your partner. If there is time, repeat the scenarios, changing roles.

PARTNER 1

You are the personnel manager of Datatronics, Inc. Call Elizabeth Franklin, office manager at Computers Plus. Inquire about a job applicant, Chelsea Chavez, who listed Ms. Franklin as a reference. Place the call.

Call Ms. Franklin again the following day to inquire about the same job applicant, Chelsea Chavez. Ms. Franklin answers today, but she talks on and on, describing the applicant in great detail. Tactfully close the conversation.

PARTNER 2

You are the receptionist for Computers Plus. The caller asks for Elizabeth Franklin, who is home sick today. You don't know when she will be able to return. Answer the call appropriately.

You are now Ms. Franklin, office manager. Describe Chelsea Chavez, an imaginary employee. Think of someone with whom you've worked. Include many details, such as her ability to work with others, her appearance, her skills at computing, her schooling, her ambition, and so forth.

PARTNER 1

You are now the receptionist for Tom Wing, of Wing Imports. Answer a call for Mr. Wing, who is working in another office, at ext. 134, where he will accept calls.

You are now Tom Wing, owner of Wing Imports. Call your attorney, Michael Murphy, about a legal problem. Leave a brief, incomplete message.

Call Mr. Murphy again. Leave a message that will prevent telephone tag.

PARTNER 2

You are now an administrative assistant for attorney Michael Murphy. Call Tom Wing to verify a meeting date Mr. Murphy has with Mr. Wing. Use your own name in identifying yourself.

You are now the receptionist for attorney Michael Murphy. Mr. Murphy is skiing in Aspen and will return in two days, but he doesn't want his clients to know where he is. Take a message.

Take a message again.

33. Make a five-minute oral presentation. Select a challenging business-related magazine article of at least 1,000 words. Prepare a well-organized presentation that includes the following: (1) an attention-getting opening plus an introduction to the major ideas, (b) three to four main points that are easy for the audience to identify, and (c) a conclusion that reviews the main points and ends by asking for questions. Avoid self-conscious remarks such as "My report is about . . ." or "The article says . . ." or "I guess that ends it." Use one visual aid. Allow no more than three minutes for questions and answers. Your instructor may ask you to distribute copies of your article to the class one or two days prior to your presentation so that they may ask informed questions. Turn in an outline to your instructor before your presentation.

34. Prepare a five- to ten-minute oral report. Use one of the following topics or a topic that you and your instructor agree on. You are an expert who has been called in to explain some aspect of the topic before a group of interested individuals. Since your time is limited, prepare a concise yet forceful report with effective visual aids.

   a. What is E-mail, and how is it used at your company?
   b. What kinds of employment advertisements are legal, and what kinds are potentially illegal?
   c. Would Japanese management techniques work in this country?
   d. Should smoking be allowed in public places?
   e. How should one dress for an employment interview?
   f. What is the economic outlook for a given product (shoes, women's apparel, domestic cars, TV sets, etc.) this year?
   g. What franchise would offer the best opportunities for investment for an entrepreneur in your area?
   h. What brand and model of computer and printer represent the best buys for home use today?
   i. What is the current employment outlook in three career areas of interest to you?
   j. Why should you be hired for a position that you have applied for?
   k. For its sales personnel, should your company rent automobiles, own them, or pay mileage costs on employee-owned vehicles?
   l. Where should your professional organization hold its next convention?
   m. What local plant or animal is endangered, and how can it be protected?

n. What is the Malcolm Baldridge National Quality award, and how do companies win it?

o. How can your school (or company) improve its image?

p. Why should individuals invest in a company or scheme of your choice?

q. What are some common and uncommon ways in which fax messages are being used today?

GRAMMAR/MECHANICS CHECKUP—14

PUNCTUATION REVIEW

Review Sections 1.17 and 2.01–2.29 in the Grammar/Mechanics Handbook. Study each of the following statements and insert any necessary punctuation. In the space provided, indicate the number of marks that you added and record the number of the G/M principle(s) illustrated. When you finish, compare your responses with those shown below. If your responses differ, study carefully the specific principles shown in parentheses.

_1_   _(2.05)_ **Example:** The District of Columbia has never been much of a financial mecca, but suddenly it has attracted some big names in banking.

_3_   _(1.17e, 2.09)_   1. A Cleveland-based law firm, Sanders & Dempsey, has been promoting D.C. banking.

_4_   _(1.17e, 2.16)_   2. D.C. banking may have fewer restrictions; therefore, many large banks are rushing to apply for full-service and limited-service privileges.

_1_   _(2.17)_   3. By April the following four New York banks had applied to open D.C. branches: Chase Manhattan, Morgan, Chemical, and Bankers Trust.

_2_   _(1.17e, 2.20a)_   4. What the bankers seem to be hoping is that the District's liberal banking laws will permit their limited-service banks to offer financial services forbidden elsewhere.

_3_   _(2.09, 2.20a)_   5. George Hancock, who is now an attorney with Sanders & Dempsey, formerly worked in the Comptroller's office.

_3_   _(2.01, 2.07)_   6. During his time with the agency, Mr. Hancock interpreted local, state, and federal banking laws and regulations.

_3_   _(2.03, 2.12)_   7. He was, as a matter of fact, aware of additional banking opportunities, not just those in the District.

_3_   _(2.6a, 2.14a, 2.28f)_   8. When interviewed recently, he said, "No one really knows how far a bank can go because the law has never been fully utilized."

_3_   _(1.17e, 2.16b)_   9. A limited-service bank can acquire other institutions more easily than a full-service bank; its purchases need no approval by the Federal Reserve.

_3_   _(2.20a, 2.27)_   10. (Emphasize.) Three major banks—Chase, Morgan, and Bankers Trust—now have branches in the nation's capital.

_2_   _(2.06a, 2.16c)_   11. When the bank rush began, local officials became concerned; but they did not act until April.

_4_   _(2.28e)_   12. An article entitled "Banks Rush to Set Up Shop in District" appeared in the Washington Post.

_4 (1.17e, 2.03, 2.08)_   13. The District Council, on the other hand, hopes to establish permanent, far-reaching regulations.

14. Acting on behalf of the Council, Councilwoman Reese said that the District may have to examine banks' applications more carefully.   _2_   *(2.07, 2.20b)*

15. Banks must now meet new requirements; for example, they must offer $50 million in the form of loans to local businesses.   _2_   *(2.16)*

---

1. (3) Cleveland-based firm, Dempsey, (*1.17e, 2.09*)   3. (1) branches: (*2.17*)   5. (3) Hancock, Dempsey, Comptroller's (*2.09, 2.20a*)   7. (3) was, fact, opportunities, (*2.03, 2.12*)   9. (3) limited-service full-service bank; (*1.17e, 2.16b*)   11. (2) began, concerned; (*2.06a, 2.16c*)   13. (4) Council, hand, permanent, far-reaching (*1.17e, 2.03, 2.08*)   15. (2) requirements; example, (*2.16*)

GRAMMAR/MECHANICS CHALLENGE—14

DOCUMENT FOR REVISION

The following short presentation has faults in grammar, punctuation, spelling, wordiness, and word use. Use standard proofreading marks (see Appendix B) to correct the errors. When you finish, your instructor can show you the revised version of this abstract.

Poor Document

Ineffective writing

Visual Aids

Before making a business prsentation consider this wise chinese proverb, 'Tell me, I forget. Show me; I remember. Involve me; I understand.' Owing to the fact that your goals as a speaker are to make listeners understand remember and act on your ideas; include visual aides to get them interested and involved. 3 of the most popular visuals are: overhead transparencys, slides and handouts.

Overhead transparencies. Student and proffesional speakers alike rely in large measure on the overhead projecter for a great many reasons. Most meeting areas are equiped with projectors and screens. Moreover acetate transparencys for the overhead are cheap, they are easily prepared on a computer or copier; and they are simple to use.

Slides. Slides deliver excelent resolution, creates an impression of professionalism, and they can be seen by large groups. Yet, their cost, inflexibility, and fairly difficult preparation off-set there advantages. Moreover, because they must be projected in a darkened room; speakers loose eye contact with the audience. He runs the risk of of the problem of putting the viewers to sleep.

Handouts. You can enhance and compliment your presentations by distributing pictures, outlines, brochures, articals, charts, summarys, or other suppliments. You should, however, hold in abeyance the distribution of handouts until such time as you are finished.

REFERENCE GUIDE TO

DOCUMENT FORMATS

Business documents carry two kinds of messages. Verbal messages are conveyed by the words chosen to express the writer's ideas. Nonverbal messages are conveyed largely by the appearance of a document. If you compare an assortment of letters and memos from various organizations, you will notice immediately that some look more attractive and more professional than others. The nonverbal message of the professional-looking documents suggests that they were sent by people who are careful, informed, intelligent, and successful. Understandably, you're more likely to take seriously documents that use attractive stationery and professional formatting techniques.

Over the years certain practices and conventions have arisen regarding the appearance and formatting of business documents. Although these conventions offer some choices (such as letter and punctuation styles), most business letters follow standardized formats. To ensure that your documents carry favorable nonverbal messages about you and your organization, you'll want to give special attention to the appearance and formatting of your letters, envelopes, memos, and fax cover sheets.

APPEARANCE

To ensure that a message is read and valued, you need to give it a professional appearance. Two important elements in achieving a professional appearance are stationery and placement of the message on the page.

Stationery. Most organizations use high-quality stationery for business documents. This stationery is printed on select paper that meets two qualifications: weight and cotton-fiber content.

Paper is measured by weight and may range from 9 pounds (thin onionskin paper) to 32 pounds (thick card and cover stock). Most office stationery is in the 16- to 24-pound range. Lighter 16-pound paper is generally sufficient for internal documents including memos. Heavier 20- to 24-pound paper is used for printed letterhead stationery.

Paper is also judged by its cotton-fiber content. Cotton fiber makes paper stronger, softer in texture, and less likely to yellow. Good-quality stationery contains 25 percent or more cotton fiber.

Spacing.   In preparing business documents on a typewriter or word processor, follow accepted spacing conventions. These conventions include double-spacing after all end punctuation marks (period, question mark, and exclamation point). Business typists also leave two spaces after a colon, except in the expression of time, as shown here:

Two appointments are available: 2:30 and 4:15.

Professional typographers leave only one space after all punctuation marks, as you will notice in books, magazines, and newspapers. Business writers, however, are not working within such tight space constraints. Leaving two spaces after end punctuation and colons helps readers separate ideas.

Justification.   Many word processing programs automatically justify right margins, a print feature you'll want to avoid for letters and memos. Justification adds extra space between words to make all lines of text end evenly (as here). If you have a printer with proportional spacing, these extra spaces are distributed evenly. But many printers lack this capacity, thus resulting in awkward spacing gaps. Moreover, experts tell us that justified right margins make documents more difficult to read, since the eye cannot easily see where individual lines end. Natural resting points for the eye are removed. And justified business letters look computer-generated and thus less personal. This is why smart communicators use ragged (unjustified) right margins for business letters and memos.

Justified right margins, however, are appropriate for special documents, such as formal reports, brochures, newsletters, and announcements. Writers with laser printers and scalable fonts (which permit a variety of type faces and sizes) include justification as one of many techniques to create print-quality output.

LETTER PARTS

Professional-looking business letters are arranged in a conventional sequence with standard parts. Following is a discussion of how to use these letter parts properly. Figure A.1 illustrates the parts in a block-style letter. (See Chapters 6 and 7 for additional discussion of letters and their parts.)

Letterhead.   Most business organizations use 8½- by 11-inch paper printed with a letterhead displaying their official name, address, and tele-

FIGURE A.1 Block and Modified Block Letter Styles

Block style
Open punctuation

Letterhead

island graphics
893 Dillingham Boulevard Honolulu, HI 96817-8817

Dateline

↓ line 13 or 2 lines below letterhead

September 13, 199x

↓ 2 lines to 10 lines

Inside address

Mr. T. M. Wilson, President
Visual Concept Enterprises
1901 Kaumualii Highway
Lihue, HI 96766

↓ 2 lines

Salutation

Dear Mr. Wilson

↓ 2 lines

Subject line

SUBJECT: BLOCK LETTER STYLE

↓ 2 lines

Body

This letter illustrates block letter style, about which you asked. All typed lines begin at the left margin. The date is usually placed two inches from the top edge of the paper or two lines below the last line of the letterhead, whichever position is lower.

This letter also shows open punctuation. No colon follows the salutation, and no comma follows the complimentary close. Although this punctuation style is efficient, we find that most of our customers prefer to include punctuation after the salutation and the complimentary close.

If a subject line is included, it appears two lines below the salutation. The word *SUBJECT* is optional. Most readers will recognize a statement in this position as the subject without an identifying label. The complimentary close appears two lines below the end of the last paragraph.

↓ 2 lines

Complimentary close

Sincerely

↓ 4 lines

Signature block

Mark H. Wong
Graphics Designer

↓ 2 lines

Modified block style
Mixed punctuation

MHW: pil

In the modified block-style letter shown at the left, the date is centered or aligned with the complimentary close and signature block, which start at the center. Paragraphs may be blocked or indented. Mixed punctuation includes a colon after the salutation and a comma after the complimentary close.

phone and fax numbers. The letterhead may also include a logo and an advertising message such as *Great Western Banking: A new brand of banking.*

Dateline.   On letterhead paper you should place the date two lines below the last line of the letterhead or 2 inches from the top edge of the paper (line 13). On plain paper place the date immediately below your return address. Since the date goes on line 13, start the return address an appropriate number of lines above it. The most common dateline format is as follows: *June 9, 1995.* Don't use *th* (or *rd*) when the date is written this way. For European or military correspondence, use the following dateline format: *9 June 1995.* Notice that no commas are used.

Addressee and Delivery Notations.   Delivery notations such as *FAX TRANSMISSION, OVERNIGHT DELIVERY, CONFIDENTIAL,* or *CERTIFIED MAIL* are typed in all capital letters two line spaces above the inside address.

Inside Address.   Type the inside address—that is, the address of the organization or person receiving the letter—single-spaced, starting at the left margin. The number of lines between the dateline and the inside address depends on the size of the letter body, the type size (point or pitch size), and the length of the typing lines. Generally, two to ten lines are appropriate.

Be careful to duplicate the exact wording and spelling of the recipient's name and address on your documents. Usually, you can copy this information from the letterhead of the correspondence you are answering. If, for example, you are responding to *Jackson & Perkins Company,* don't address your letter to *Jackson and Perkins Corp.*

Always be sure to include a courtesy title such as *Mr., Ms., Mrs., Dr.,* or *Professor* before a person's name in the inside address—for both the letter and the envelope. Although many women in business today favor *Ms.,* you'll want to use whatever title the addressee prefers.

Remember that the inside address is not included for readers (who already know who and where they are). It's there to help writers accurately file a copy of the message.

In general, avoid abbreviations (such as *Ave.* or *Co.*) unless they appear in the printed letterhead of the document being answered.

Attention Line.   An attention line allows you to send your message officially to an organization but to direct it to a specific individual, officer, or department. However, if you know an individual's complete name, it's always better to use it as the first line of the inside address and avoid an attention line. Here are two common formats for attention lines:

MultiMedia Enterprises   MultiMedia Enterprises
931 Calkins Road   Attention: Marketing Director
Rochester, NY 14301   931 Calkins Road
                                Rochester, NY 14301
ATTENTION MARKETING DIRECTOR

Attention lines may be typed in all caps or with upper- and lowercase letters. The colon following *Attention* is optional. Notice that an attention line may be placed two lines below the address block or printed as the second line of the inside address. You'll want to use the latter format if you're composing on a word processor because the address block may be copied to the envelope and the attention line will not interfere with the last-line placement of the zip code. (Mail can be sorted more easily if the zip code appears in the last line of a typed address.)

Whenever possible, use a person's name as the first line of an address instead of putting that name in an attention line. Some writers use an attention line because they fear that letters addressed to individuals at companies may be considered private. They worry that if the addressee is no longer with the company, the letter may be forwarded or not opened. Actually, unless a letter is marked "Personal" or "Confidential," it will very likely be opened as business mail. Figure A.2 shows more examples of attention lines.

Salutation.   For most letter styles place the letter greeting, or salutation, two lines below the last line of the inside address or the attention line (if used). If the letter is addressed to an individual, use that person's courtesy title and last name *(Dear Mr. Lanham)*. Even if you are on a first-name basis *(Dear Leslie)*, be sure to add a colon (not a comma or a semicolon) after the salutation. Do not use an individual's full name in the salutation (not *Dear Mr. Leslie Lanham*) unless you are unsure of gender *(Dear Leslie Lanham)*.

For letters with attention lines or those addressed to organizations, the selection of an appropriate salutation has become more difficult. Formerly, *Gentlemen* was used generically for all organizations. With increasing numbers of women in business management today, however, *Gentlemen* is problematic. Because no universally acceptable salutation has emerged as yet, you'll probably be safest with *Ladies and Gentlemen* or *Gentlemen and Ladies*.

One way to avoid the salutation dilemma is to address a document to a specific person. Another alternative is to use the simplified letter style, which conveniently omits the salutation (and the complimentary close). Figure A.2 discusses and illustrates letter addresses and appropriate salutations.

Subject and Reference Lines.   Although experts suggest placing the subject line two lines below the salutation, many businesses actually place it above the salutation. Use whatever style your organization prefers. Reference lines often show policy or file numbers; they generally appear two lines above the salutation.

Body.   Most business letters and memorandums are single-spaced, with double line spacing between paragraphs. Very short messages may be double-spaced with indented paragraphs.

Complimentary Close.   Typed two lines below the last line of the letter, the complimentary close may be formal *(Very truly yours)* or informal *(Sincerely yours* or *Cordially)*. The simplified letter style omits a complimentary close.

Signature Block.   In most letter styles the writer's typed name and optional identification appear three to four lines below the complimentary close. The combination of name, title, and organization information should

FIGURE A.2   Letter Addressees and Salutations

ADDRESSEE	SALUTATION	EXPLANATION
Individual Mr. Leslie Lanham, CEO Atlantic Associates, Inc. 2320 Park Avenue Boston, MA 02115-2320	Dear Mr. Lanham: Dear Leslie:	For specific individuals use a courtesy title (such as *Mr.* or *Ms.*) and the person's last name. For friends use a first-name greeting. When you are unsure of an addressee's gender, include the full name (*Dear Leslie Lanham*). A helpful alternative is the simplified letter style, which omits a salutation.
Organization Pacific Builders Association Sequoia Building, Suite 303 105 Redwood Boulevard Seattle, WA 98104-1105	Ladies and Gentlemen: Gentlemen: Ladies:	When females are part of management or if you are unsure, use *Ladies and Gentlemen.* If you know a company has only male managers, use *Gentlemen.* For a company with only female managers, use *Ladies.* An alternative that avoids this dilemma is the simplified letter style, which omits a salutation.
Individual Within Organization Michigan Fabricators, Inc. Attention: Ms. Lisa Jonas 3038 North Jennings Flint, MI 48433-3088	Ladies and Gentlemen:	Although an attention line is included here, the message is addressed to the organization—hence the salutation *Ladies and Gentlemen.* However, when you know an individual's name, as in this case, it's better to use that name on the first line of the address without *Attention.* Then the salutation would be *Dear Ms. Jonas.*
Position or Department Within Organization Magnaflex Enterprises, Inc. Attention: Sales Manager 200 Main Street Fort Morgan, CO 80701	Ladies and Gentlemen:	When a letter is addressed to an organization for the attention of an individual in a specific position, the salutation should address the organization. If this salutation sounds awkward, use the simplified letter style and avoid a salutation.
Group of People Customers or individuals from a large database.	Dear Customer: Dear Policyholder:	When you are sending form letters to a large group and cannot use individual salutations, use an appropriate general salutation.

be arranged to achieve a balanced look. The name and title may appear on the same line or on separate lines, depending on the length of each. Use commas to separate categories within the same line, but not to conclude a line. Women may choose to include *Ms., Mrs.,* or *Miss* before their names. Parentheses are optional. Men do not use *Mr.* before their names.

Sincerely yours,

Jeremy M. Wood, Manager
Technical Sales and Services

Cordially yours,

Casandra Baker-Murillo
Executive Vice President

Some organizations include their names in the signature block. In such cases the organization name appears in all caps two lines below the complimentary close, as shown here.

Cordially,

LITTON COMPUTER SERVICES

Ms. Shelina A. Simpson
Executive Assistant

Reference Initials.   If used, the initials of the typist and writer are typed two lines below the writer's name and title. Generally, the writer's initials are capitalized and the typist's are lowercased, but this format varies.

Enclosure Notation.   When an enclosure or attachment accompanies a document, a notation to that effect appears two lines below the reference initials. This notation reminds the typist to insert the enclosure in the envelope, and it reminds the recipient to look for the enclosure or attachment. The notation may be spelled out *(Enclosure, Attachment),* or it may be abbreviated *(Enc., Att.).* It may indicate the number of enclosures or attachments, and it may also identify a specific enclosure *(Enclosure: Form 1099).*

Copy Notation.   If you make copies of correspondence for other individuals, you may use *cc* to indicate carbon copy, *pc* to indicate photocopy, or merely *c* for any kind of copy. A colon following the initial(s) is optional.

Second-page Heading.   When a letter extends beyond one page, use plain paper of the same quality and color as the first page. Identify the second and succeeding pages with a heading consisting of the name of the addressee, the page number, and the date. Use either of the following two formats:

Ms. Rachel Ruiz   2   May 3, 1995

Ms. Rachel Ruiz
Page 2
May 3, 1995

Both headings appear on line 7 followed by two blank lines to separate them from the continuing text. Avoid using a second page if you have only one line or the complimentary close and signature block to fill that page.

Plain-paper Return Address.   If you prepare a personal or business letter on plain paper, place your address immediately above the date, as shown in Figure A.3. Do not include your name; you will type (and sign) your name at the end of your letter. If your return address contains two lines, begin typing it on line 11 so that the date appears on line 13. Avoid abbreviations except for a two-letter state abbreviation.

FIGURE A.3   Letter on Plain Paper, Modified Block Style

Single-space return address; don't abbreviate street names or date

↓ line 11
580 East Leffels Street
Springfield, OH 45501
November 7, 199x

Ms. Ellen Rabkin
Retail Credit Department
Union National Bank
P.O. Box 2051
Little Rock, AR 72203

Dear Ms. Rabkin:

Optional subject line may be centered; use all caps or upper- and lowercase letters as shown here

SUBJECT: Charges to Credit Account; #4002-3422-8910-3299

Because of the wide acceptance of the Visa credit card and because of your bank's attractive interest rate, my wife and I were eager to become cardholders two years ago. Recently, however, we experienced a charge to our account that we would like to discuss with you.

1¼-inch margins for long letter

Between the period of August 7 and September 17, we made 12 small purchases. Ten of these purchases received telephone approval. When we received our October statement, a copy of which is enclosed, we were surprised to see that we were charged $10 for each of these purchases because our account was over our limit. The total charge was $120.

Of course, we should have been more aware of the limit and the number of charges that we were making against our account. We assumed, however, that if our purchases received telephone approval from your credit processors, we were still within our credit limit.

Paragraphs may be indented or flush left in modified-block style

Upon receipt of our October statement, we immediately called your headquarters and were referred to Mr. Jonathon Walker, who listened to our story patiently. However, he said he

---

Ms. Ellen Rabkin   2   ↓ line 7
                                                                  November 7, 199x
                                                                  ↓ 2 lines

Please examine our account, Ms. Rabkin, and reconsider this penalty. Since we have never exceeded our credit limit in the past and since we received telephone approval for most of the charges in question, we feel that the $120 charge should be removed. We appreciate the efforts of Mr. Walker, and we look forward to a speedy resolution of this problem.

Sincerely,

Phillip M. Stevenson

Enclosure

Two-page letters require second-page heading

Align closing lines with return address and date

For letters prepared in the block style, type the return address at the left margin. For modified block-style letters, start the return address at the center to align with the complimentary close.

LETTER STYLES

Business letters are generally prepared in one of three formats. The most popular is the block style, but the simplified style has much to recommend it.

Block Style. In the block style, shown in Figure A.1, all lines begin at the left margin. This style is a favorite because it is easy to format.

Modified Block Style. The modified block style differs from block style in that the date and closing lines appear in the center, as shown at the bottom of Figure A.1. The date may be (1) centered, (2) begun at the center of the page (to align with the closing lines), or (3) backspaced from the right margin. The signature block—including the complimentary close, writer's name and title, or organization identification—begins at the center. The first line of each paragraph may begin at the left margin or may be indented five or ten spaces. All other lines begin at the left margin.

Simplified Style. Introduced by the Administrative Management Society a number of years ago, the simplified letter style, shown in Figure A.4, requires little formatting. Like the block style, all lines begin at the left margin. A subject line appears in all caps three lines below the inside address and three lines above the first paragraph. The salutation and complimentary close are omitted. The signer's name and identification appear in all caps five lines below the last paragraph. This letter style is efficient and avoids the problem of appropriate salutations and courtesy titles.

LETTER PLACEMENT

Business letters should be typed so that they are framed by white space. By setting proper margins and by controlling the amount of space between the date and the inside address, you can balance a letter attractively on a page.

The following chart shows margins for short, medium, and long letters. To use the chart, first estimate the number of words in the body of your letter (excluding the inside address and closing lines). Then set the appropriate margins. Notice that a short letter (under 100 words) requires 2-inch margins while a long letter (over 200 words) uses margins of 1 to 1¼ inches. Your goal is to place your message in the middle of a page surrounded by a balanced frame of white space.

LETTER LENGTH	WORDS IN BODY	SIDE MARGINS	BLANK LINES AFTER DATE
Short	Under 100	2 inches	7 to 11 (12 pitch) 6 to 8 (10 pitch)
Medium	100 to 200	1½ inches	2 to 8 (12 pitch) 2 to 3 (10 pitch)
Long	Over 200	1 to 1¼ inches	2 to 8 (12 pitch) 2 to 3 (10 pitch)

FIGURE A.4   Simplified Letter Style

ABC ★ Automation Business Consultants
One Peachtree Plaza
Atlanta, GA 30312   (404) 369-1109

July 19, 199x

Identifies method
of delivery.

FAX TRANSMISSION

Ms. Sara Hendricks, Manager
American Land and Home Realty
P.O. Box 3392A
Atlanta, GA 30308

Replaces salutation
with subject line.

SIMPLIFIED LETTER STYLE

Leaves 2 blank
lines above and
below subject line.

You may be interested to learn, Ms. Hendricks, that some years ago the
Administrative Management Society recommended the simplified letter
format illustrated here. Notice the following efficient features:

1. All lines begin at the left margin.

2. The salutation and complimentary close are omitted.

3. A subject line in all caps appears 3 lines below the inside address and 3
   lines above the first paragraph.

4. The writer's name and identification appear 5 lines below the last
   paragraph.

In addition to its efficiency, this letter style is helpful in dealing with the problem of appropriate salutations. Since it has no salutation, your writers need
not worry about which to choose. For many reasons we recommend this
style to your staff.

Omits
complimentary
close.

Highlights
writer's name and
identification with
all caps.

HOLLY HIGGINS, MANAGER, OFFICE DIVISION

tib

Identifies copy.

c John Fox

Some companies prescribe standard margins, usually 1 to 1¼ inches. This practice improves efficiency because margins are never changed; however, standard margins often result in unbalanced documents, particularly for short messages. Adjusting the number of blank lines between the date and the inside address helps balance a letter on the page. Another aid, available in some word processing programs, is a command that automatically centers a document on the page. Word processing programs also improve efficiency by storing preset margins for different documents. Learning to use the special features of your word processing program can save time in the long run and improve the appearance of your documents.

PUNCTUATION STYLES

Two punctuation styles are commonly used for letters. *Open* punctuation, shown with the block-style letter in Figure A.1, contains no punctuation after the salutation or complimentary close. *Mixed* punctuation, shown with the modified block–style letter in Figure A.1, requires a colon after the salutation and a comma after the complimentary close. Many business organizations prefer mixed punctuation, even in a block-style letter.

If you choose mixed punctuation, be sure to use a colon—not a comma or semicolon—after the salutation. Even when the salutation is a first name, the colon is appropriate.

ENVELOPES

An envelope should be printed on the same quality and color of stationery as the letter it carries. Because the envelope introduces your message and makes the first impression, you need to be especially careful in addressing it. Moreover, how you fold the letter is important.

Return Address.   The return address is usually printed in the upper left corner of an envelope, as shown in Figure A.5. In large companies some form of identification (the writer's initials, name, or location) may be typed above the company name and return address. This identification helps return the letter to the sender in case of nondelivery.

On an envelope without a printed return address, single-space the return address in the upper left corner. Beginning on line 3 on the fourth space (½ inch) from the left edge, type the writer's name, title, company, and mailing address.

Mailing Address.   On legal-sized No. 10 envelopes (4⅛ by 9½ inches), begin the address on line 13 about 4¼ inches from the left edge, as shown in Figure A.5. For small envelopes (3⅝ by 6½ inches), begin typing on line 12 about 2½ inches from the left edge.

The U.S. Postal Service recommends that addresses be typed in all caps without any punctuation. This Postal Service style, shown in the small envelope in Figure A.5, was originally developed to facilitate scanning by optical character readers. Today's OCRs, however, are so sophisticated that they scan upper- and lowercase letters easily. Many companies today do not follow the Postal Service format because they prefer to use the same format for the envelope as for the inside address. If the same format is used, writers can take advantage of word processing programs to "copy" the inside address to the envelope, thus saving keystrokes and reducing errors. Having the same format on both the inside address

FIGURE A.5   Envelope Formats

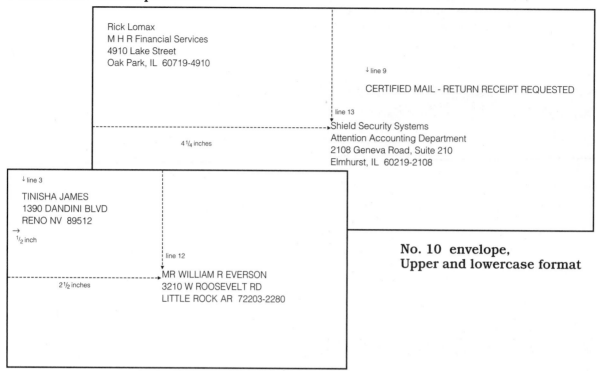

Rick Lomax
M H R Financial Services
4910 Lake Street
Oak Park, IL 60719-4910

↓ line 9

CERTIFIED MAIL - RETURN RECEIPT REQUESTED

line 13

Shield Security Systems
Attention Accounting Department
2108 Geneva Road, Suite 210
Elmhurst, IL 60219-2108

4 1/4 inches

**No. 10 envelope,
Upper and lowercase format**

↓ line 3

TINISHA JAMES
1390 DANDINI BLVD
RENO NV 89512

→
1/2 inch

line 12

MR WILLIAM R EVERSON
3210 W ROOSEVELT RD
LITTLE ROCK AR 72203-2280

2 1/2 inches

No. 6³⁄₄ envelope, Postal Service uppercase format

and the envelope also looks more professional and consistent. For these reasons you may choose to use the familiar upper- and lowercase combination format. But you will want to check with your organization to learn its preference.

In addressing your envelopes for delivery in this country or in Canada, use the two-letter state and province abbreviations shown in Figure A.6. Notice that these abbreviations are in capital letters without periods.

Folding.   The way a letter is folded and inserted into an envelope sends additional nonverbal messages about a writer's professionalism and carefulness. Most businesspeople follow the procedures shown here, which produce the least number of creases to distract readers.

For large No. 10 envelopes, begin with the letter face up. Fold slightly less than one third of the sheet toward the top, as shown below. Then fold

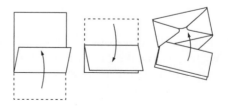

FIGURE A.6 Abbreviations of States, Territories, and Provinces

STATE OR TERRITORY	TWO-LETTER ABBREVIATION	STATE OR TERRITORY	TWO-LETTER ABBREVIATION
Alabama	AL	North Dakota	ND
Alaska	AK	Ohio	OH
Arizona	AZ	Oklahoma	OK
Arkansas	AR	Oregon	OR
California	CA	Pennsylvania	PA
Canal Zone	CZ	Puerto Rico	PR
Colorado	CO	Rhode Island	RI
Connecticut	CT	South Carolina	SC
Delaware	DE	South Dakota	SD
District of Columbia	DC	Tennessee	TN
Florida	FL	Texas	TX
Georgia	GA	Utah	UT
Guam	GU	Vermont	VT
Hawaii	HI	Virgin Islands	VI
Idaho	ID	Virginia	VA
Illinois	IL	Washington	WA
Indiana	IN	West Virginia	WV
Iowa	IA	Wisconsin	WI
Kansas	KS	Wyoming	WY
Kentucky	KY		
Louisiana	LA	CANADIAN PROVINCE	TWO-LETTER ABBREVIATION
Maine	ME		
Maryland	MD	Alberta	AB
Massachusetts	MA	British Columbia	BC
Michigan	MI	Labrador	LB
Minnesota	MN	Manitoba	MB
Mississippi	MS	New Brunswick	NB
Missouri	MO	Newfoundland	NF
Montana	MT	Northwest Territories	NT
Nebraska	NE	Nova Scotia	NS
Nevada	NV	Ontario	ON
New Hampshire	NH	Prince Edward Island	PE
New Jersey	NJ	Quebec	PQ
New Mexico	NM	Saskatchewan	SK
New York	NY	Yukon Territory	YT
North Carolina	NC		

down the top third to within ⅓ inch of the bottom fold. Insert the letter into the envelope with the last fold toward the bottom of the envelope.

For small No. 6¾ envelopes, begin by folding the bottom up to within ⅓ inch of the top edge. Then fold the right third over to the left. Fold the left third to within ⅓ inch of the last fold. Insert the last fold into the envelope first.

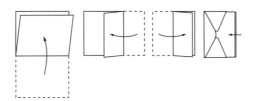

MEMORANDUMS

As discussed in Chapter 5, memorandums deliver messages within organizations. Many offices use memo forms imprinted with the organization name and, optionally, the department or division names, as shown in Figure A.7. Although the design and arrangement of memo forms vary, they usually include the basic elements of *TO, FROM, DATE,* and *SUBJECT.* Large organizations may include other identifying headings, such as *FILE NUMBER, FLOOR, EXTENSION, LOCATION,* and *DISTRIBUTION.*

Because of the difficulty of aligning computer printers with preprinted forms, many business writers store memo formats in their computers and call them up when preparing memos. The guide words are then printed with the message, thus eliminating alignment problems.

If no printed or stored computer forms are available, memos may be typed on company letterhead or on plain paper, as shown in Figure A.8. On a full sheet of paper, start on line 13; on a half sheet, start on line 7. Double-space and type in all caps the guide words: *TO:, FROM:, DATE:, SUBJECT:.* Align all the fill-in information two spaces after the longest guide word *(SUBJECT:).* Leave three lines after the last line of the heading and begin typing the body of the memo. Like business letters, memos are single-spaced.

FIGURE A.7   Printed Memo Forms

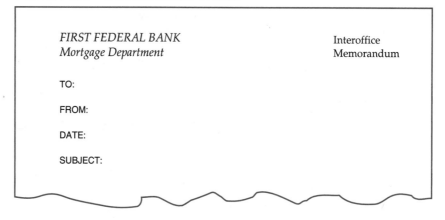

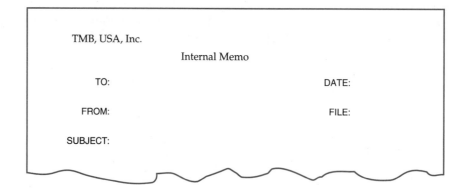

FIGURE A.8   Memo on Plain Paper

↓ line 13

MEMO

1¼ inches →

TO: Dawn Stewart, Manager   DATE: February 3, 1995
             Sales and Marketing

FROM: Jay Murray, Vice President *JM*
             Operations

SUBJECT: TELEPHONE SERVICE REQUEST FORMS

↓ 3 lines

To speed telephone installation and improve service within the Bremerton facility, we are starting a new application procedure.

Service request forms will be available at various locations within the three buildings. When you require telephone service, obtain a request form at one of the locations that is convenient for you. Fill in the pertinent facts, obtain approval from your division head, and send the form to Brent White. Request forms are available at the following locations:

FIGURE A.9   Fax Cover Sheet

FAX TRANSMISSION

DATE: _____

                                        FAX
TO: _____   NUMBER: _____
        _____
        _____

                                        FAX
FROM: _____   NUMBER: _____
        _____
        _____

NUMBER OF PAGES TRANSMITTED INCLUDING THIS COVER SHEET: _____

MESSAGE:

If any part of this fax transmission is missing or not clearly received, please call:

NAME: _____

PHONE: _____

Memos are generally formatted with side margins of 1¼ inches, or they may conform to the printed memo form. (For more information about memos, see Chapter 5.)

FAX COVER SHEET

Documents transmitted by fax are usually introduced by a cover sheet, such as that shown in Figure A.9. As with memos, the format varies considerably. Important items to include are (1) the name and fax number of the receiver, (2) the name and fax number of the sender, (3) the number of pages being sent, and (4) the name and telephone number of the person to notify in case of unsatisfactory transmission.

When the document being transmitted requires little explanation, you may prefer to attach an adhesive note (such as a Post-it™ fax transmitted form) instead of a full cover sheet. These notes carry essentially the same information as shown in our printed fax cover sheet. They are perfectly acceptable in most business organizations and can save considerable paper and transmission costs.

PROOFREADING MARKS

PROOFREADING MARK	DRAFT COPY	FINAL COPY
═ Align horizontally	TO: Rick Munoz	TO: Rick Munoz
‖ Align vertically	‖166.32 / 132.45	166.32 / 132.45
≞ Capitalize	Coca-cola / runs on ms–dos	Coca-Cola / runs on MS-DOS
◡ Close up space	meeting at 3 p. m.	meeting at 3 p.m.
⨼⊏ Center	⏋Recommendations⊏	Recommendations
⅋ Delete	in my final judgement	in my judgment
⌄ Insert apostrophe	our companys product	our company's product
⌃ Insert comma	you will of course	you will, of course,
⌃ Insert semicolon	value therefore, we feel	value; therefore, we feel
⹀ Insert hyphen	tax free income	tax-free income
⊙ Insert period	Ms Holly Hines	Ms. Holly Hines
⌄⌄ Insert quotation mark	shareholders receive a / bonus	shareholders receive a / "bonus"
# Insert space	wordprocessing program	word processing program
/ Lowercase (remove capitals)	the Vice President	the vice president
⊏ Move to left	HUMAN RESOURCES	Human Resources
⊐ Move to right	⊏I. Labor costs	I. Labor costs
⟲ Spell out	A. Findings of study ⊐ / aimed at 2 depts	A. Findings of study / aimed at two departments
¶ Start new paragraph	¶Keep the screen height / at eye level.	Keep the screen / height at eye level.
⋯ Stet (don't delete)	officials talked openly	officials talked openly
∿ Transpose	accounts recievable	accounts receivable
⌁ Use boldface	Conclusions	**Conclusions**
— Use italics	The Perfect Résumé	*The Perfect Résumé*
⌐ Start new line	Globex, 23 Acorn Lane	Globex / 23 Acorn Lane
⌇ Run lines together	Invoice No., / 122059	Invoice No. 122059

DOCUMENTATION FORMATS

Not many writers enjoy the task, but most take pains nevertheless to properly document report data—for many reasons. Citing sources strengthens a writer's argument. Acknowledging sources also shields writers from charges of plagiarism. Moreover, good references help your readers pursue further research. Fortunately, word processing programs have taken much of the pain out of documenting data, so the task is no longer so tedious.

The task is further eased by recognizing the difference between *source* notes and *content* notes. Source notes identify quotations, paraphrased passages, and author references. They lead readers to the sources of cited information, and they must follow a consistent format. Content notes, on the other hand, enable writers to add comments, explain information not directly related to the text, or refer readers to other sections of a report. Because content notes are generally infrequent, most writers identify them in the text with a raised asterisk (*). At the bottom of the page, the asterisk is repeated with the content note following. If two content notes appear on one page, a double asterisk identifies the second reference.

Your real concern will be with source notes. These identify quotations or paraphrased ideas in the text, and they direct readers to the complete list (bibliography) of references at the end of your report.

SOURCE NOTES

Source notes tell where ideas and information in the text originated. Researchers have struggled for years to develop the perfect documentation system, one that is efficient for the writer and crystal clear to the reader. As a result, many systems exist, each with its advantages. The important thing for you is to adopt one system and use it consistently. Naturally, you'll check with your organization to learn its preferences. To simplify matters in our discussion, we'll concentrate on the three most common source note formats: footnotes, endnotes, and parenthetic notes.

FOOTNOTES

A traditional method for citing sources is footnoting. As the name suggests, references appear at the foot or bottom of each page. Footnotes position the references where readers can see them easily. Although manual placement of notes at the bottom of pages is admittedly difficult, today's word processing software greatly simplifies the process. At a command your software inserts a superscript (raised) number in the text and allows you to key in the footnote information. The program then stores this information. At print time it automatically calculates the number of lines required to position the text and footnotes on each page. Best of all, it renumbers all footnotes after any additions or deletions so that the list is always consecutive and current.

Placement.   Generally, you'll try to place a source note reference, as shown in the following example, at the *end* of a sentence containing information to be acknowledged. If, however, the sentence is long and the reader might confuse the reference, place the reference number closer to the quoted or paraphrased information, as shown in the following example. Notice, too, that you need not repeat an author's name in the footnote if it is mentioned in the text.

> People who do well internationally are flexible, patient, and willing to invest in relationships. No one flies into Beijing or Cairo or Rome one day, works out a deal the next day, and returns home on the third day with the job complete.[1] Peters reports that it took Arco three and a half years to negotiate an off-shore drilling contract with China,[2] and other experts also stress the need to establish relationships before conducting business.
>
> ---
>
> [1]Leonard A. Cohen and Cordeleeza Love, "Investing in International Relationships," Forbes, 20 August 1993, 39.
>
> [2]Thriving on Chaos (New York: Alfred A. Knopf, 1991), 256.

Footnotes appear at the bottom of the page, separated from the text by a 1½-inch line. This separating line has a single blank line above and below it. Entries are single-spaced with a double space between them.

Format.   Because consistency is important in source note formatting, you'll want to study the sequence, capitalization, and punctuation of the model formats shown in the list on pages 358–359. If you aren't sure how much information to include in your notes, put yourself in the position of the reader trying to track down your citation. And remember, it's always better to include too much information than too little.

Our examples show small superscript figures with each note at the bottom of the page. Your word processing program, however, may print full-sized figures that are not raised—and that format is certainly acceptable.

ENDNOTES

A second alternative for documenting references is the endnote method. Like footnotes, endnotes use superscript numerals within the text to identify cited data. Instead of appearing at the bottom of each page, however, all source notes are located at the end of the report on a separate page, generally called *Notes.* This method is easier for the writer but not quite so convenient for the reader, who must flip to the end of a report to find its references. Most word processing programs offer a choice of footnote or endnote placement.

Endnotes are listed in the order cited in the text, and they are numbered consecutively, as shown in the brief sample here.

Notes

1. Laurie M. Grossman, "From Sharks to Hornets, Team Logos Help Sports Apparel Score," The Wall Street Journal, 3 January 1994, B1.

2. Dean Peebles and John Ryans, Management of International Advertising, 2nd ed. (Chicago: Intercultural Press, 1992), 304.

3. Katherine J. Klein, "The 100 Best Companies to Work For in America," Los Angeles Times, 12 February 1994, C1, C5.

To review a complete list of endnotes, see Figure 12.8. Because the formats for footnotes and endnotes are identical, the models shown in the list on pages 358–359 are appropriate for both.

PARENTHETIC NOTES

A third documentation method uses parenthetical data within the text to cite and identify references. The two best-known parenthetic methods are the MLA system and the APA system.

MLA System.   The Modern Language Association recommends that writers cite references with a brief note within the text, such as *(Peters 214).* This parenthetic comment usually consists of the author's last name and the page on which the reference is found. If no author name is available, as sometimes is the case in newspaper and magazine articles, an abbreviated title is used to identify the reference. The following excerpt illustrates the MLA documentation method:

> In many countries business card etiquette is no mere ritual. In places such as Japan, a business card is both a mini-résumé and a ticket to the game of business (Copeland and Griggs 161). In emphasizing the importance of business cards, experts say that the first rule is never to be without an ample supply ("Business Without Boundaries" 32). Author Roger Axtell notes that Americans must learn to treat business cards with reverence (158).

The main purpose of the parenthetical reference is to point the reader to a list of complete references in the Bibliography or Works Cited. For more information about the MLA referencing style, see the *MLA Handbook for Writers of Research Papers,* 3rd ed., by Joseph Gibaldi and Walter S. Achtert (New York: The Modern Language Association, 1988).

APA System.   Another referencing system that uses parenthetic citations is the APA style, recommended by the American Psychological Association, In this style the author's last name, the year of publication, and pertinent page number(s) appear in parentheses after the information cited, such as

(*Smith, 1990, p. 4*). For a more thorough discussion of the APA system, consult the *Publication Manual of the American Psychological Association*, 3rd ed. (Washington, DC: American Psychological Association, 1983).

BIBLIOGRAPHIES

A bibliography is a complete list of all references cited in a report. It may also include all references consulted by the researcher, particularly for more formal reports. For less formal reports and those with fewer than ten footnotes or endnotes, a bibliography may be omitted. For reports with many references, though, a bibliography is necessary because its alphabetical arrangement helps readers locate items quickly. If a bibliography has a great many entries, it may be divided into sections, such as books, periodicals, and professional journals.

Like source notes, bibliographies have different styles. For our purposes we'll show only two styles: the traditional bibliography and the MLA Works Cited style.

TRADITIONAL BIBLIOGRAPHY

In the traditional bibliography, entries are listed by the author's last name or by the first word of an entry. The format of each entry, as shown in the list on pages 359–360, is similar to that of a source note. The primary differences are in punctuation and indentations.

Notice that each segment of the entry ends with a period instead of a comma. The author's full name is followed by a period, the title is followed by a period, and so on. Note, too, that entries are typed in hanging indented form, with the second and succeeding lines indented five spaces from the first line. This placement highlights the first word of each entry, thus enabling readers to locate specific entries quickly. Entries are single-spaced with double-spacing between them. If the bibliography appears on a page by itself, the title is centered on line 13. To review an example of a complete bibliography, see the model report in Figure 12.8.

BIBLIOGRAPHY

Bonoma, Elizabeth. "Gone Are the Cash Cows of Yesteryear." U.S. News and World Report, 19 May 1993, 58–61.

Kaplan, Robert S. Relevance Lost: The Rise and Fall of Management Accounting. Paper presented at the annual meeting of the American Association of Accountancy, Boston, April 1992.

Peters, Tom. Thriving on Chaos. New York: Alfred A. Knopf, 1991.

WORKS CITED BIBLIOGRAPHY

Reports prepared according to the MLA (Modern Language Association) style include parenthetic source notes, discussed earlier, along with a Works Cited Bibliography. Writers are advised to prepare a complete list of all works planned as references for the report *before* composing the report. From this list, writers know what information to present in parenthetic source notes within the text. A citation such as *(Peters 59–61)*, for example, directs readers to the complete reference in the Works Cited.

Bibliographic entries in a Works Cited list are formatted similarly to those in traditional bibliographies. Notice in the following example that references are listed alphabetically in the hanging indented style. However, they are double-spaced. Moreover, in a reference for a newspaper, magazine, or other periodical, dates are separated from page numbers by colons. Months are abbreviated.

Works Cited

Chang, Alicia. "America's New-Wave Chip Firms." The Wall Street Journal 20 Jan.

1994: B1, B5.

Dreyfuss, Joel. The Leadership Challenge; Shaping and Managing Shared Values.

Homewood, Illinois: Dow Jones-Irwin, 1992.

Levitt, Theodore. "Marketing Success Through Differentiation—of Anything," Har-

vard Business Review 46 (Jan/Feb 1993): 324–331. ["46" refers to vol. 46.]

Walton, Mary A., and Steven M. Gilbert. "The Riches in Market Niches," Entrepre-

neur Feb 1992: 45.

If you prepare a research report using the parenthetic source note method, along with a Works Cited bibliography, you'll want to refer to the *MLA Handbook for Writers of Research Papers.*

SOURCE NOTE FORMATS FOR ENDNOTES AND FOOTNOTES*

BOOK, ONE AUTHOR

[1]Jane Bryant Quinn, Making the Most of Your Money (New York: Simon & Schuster), 359.

BOOK, TWO AUTHORS, EDITION

[2]Dean Peebles and John Ryans, Management of International Advertising, 2nd ed. (Chicago: Intercultural Press, 1992), 304.

BOOK, EDITED

[3]Glen Fisher, ed., International Negotiation: A Cross-Cultural Perspective (Rockleigh, NJ: Allyn and Bacon, 1993), 155.

BOOK, CHAPTER OR SECTION

[4]John L. Waltman, "Evaluating Technical Reports," in The Handbook of Executive Communication, ed. John Louis Digaetani (Homewood, Illinois: Dow Jones-Irwin, 1986), 436.

ANNUAL REPORT, PAMPHLET, OR OTHER PUBLICATION FROM PRIVATE ORGANIZATION

[5]Federal Express Corporation, 1993 Annual Report (Memphis: Federal Express, 1993), 2-3.

*The formats shown are based on traditional format alternatives contained in *The Chicago Manual of Style,* 14th ed. (Chicago and London: University of Chicago Press. 1993). pp. 487–635.

[6]Pinkerton Investigation Services, The Employers' Guide to Investigation Services (Atlanta: Pinkerton Information Center, 1994), 5, 15-16.

GOVERNMENT PUBLICATION

[7]U.S. Small Business Administration, Business Plan for Small Manufacturers (Washington: U.S. Government Printing Office, 1992), 11.

MAGAZINE ARTICLE, ONE AUTHOR

[8]Peter Coy, "Cheers for Corporate Collaboration," *Business Week,* 3 May 1994, 39. [Note that popular magazines do not require volume and part numbers.]

MAGAZINE ARTICLE, NO AUTHOR

[9]"Inc. 100: The Hottest Small Public Companies," Inc., May 1993, 42.

NEWSPAPER ARTICLE, ONE AUTHOR

[10]Laurie M. Grossman, "From Sharks to Hornets, Team Logos Help Sports Apparel Score," The Wall Street Journal, 3 January 1994, B1.

NEWSPAPER ARTICLE, NO AUTHOR

[11]"Executives, Take Your Risks," The New York Times, 27 March 1993, C1.

PROFESSIONAL JOURNAL WITH VOLUME AND PART NUMBERS

[12]Nancy M. Burson, John A. Walker, and Jill I. Wiley, "Tensions in Conflict Situations as Revealed by Metaphoric Analysis," Journal of Management Communication 6, no. 2 (November 1993): 116. [An alternate but acceptable form identifies the volume and part numbers more clearly: Journal of Management Communication, vol. 6, no. 2, November 1993, 116.]

INTERVIEWS AND UNPUBLISHED MATERIALS

[13]John F. Welch, Jr., interview with author, Fairfield, Connecticut, 2 April 1995.

[14]Dr. Marie Meir-Lansky, letter to Richard M. Law, 4 June 1992.

[15]Chan Su Park, "Estimation and Prediction of Brand Equities Through Survey Measurement of Consumer Preference Structures" (Ph.D. diss., Stanford University, 1993), 259.

ELECTRONIC DOCUMENTS

[16]Dale Winston, "How to Find the Perfect Job," in Businesswire [database online] (San Francisco: Business Wire, 1993 [updated 9 April 1994; cited 14 March 1995]), accession no. 000926; NO=BW430; 4 screens; available from DIALOG Information Services, Inc., Palo Alto, Calif.

SECOND REFERENCES

[17]Peebles and Ryans, 307. [Include only last names and page numbers.]

[18]Waltman, Handbook of Executive Communication, 483. [Add a shortened title if the author has more than one title listed.]

BIBLIOGRAPHIC FORMATS FOR ENDNOTES AND FOOTNOTES

BOOK, ONE AUTHOR

Peters, Tom. Thriving on Chaos. New York: Alfred A. Knopf, 1991.

BOOK, TWO AUTHORS, EDITION

Peebles, Dean, and John Ryans. Management of International Advertising. 2nd ed. Chicago: Intercultural Press, 1992.

BOOK, EDITED

Mendoza, Jeremy, ed. Quest for Quality. Minneapolis: Franklin Press, 1990.

BOOK, CHAPTER OR SECTION

Waltman, John L. "Evaluating Technical Reports." In The Handbook of Executive Communication, edited by John Louis Digaetani. Homewood, Illinois: Dow Jones-Irwin, 1986.

ANNUAL REPORT, PAMPHLET, OR OTHER PUBLICATION FROM PRIVATE ORGANIZATION

AMR Corporation, 1993 Annual Report. Fort Worth: American Airlines, 1993.

Pinkerton Investigation Services. The Employer's Guide to Investigation Services. Atlanta: Pinkerton Information Center, 1994.

GOVERNMENT PUBLICATION

Statistical Abstract of the United States. U.S. Bureau of the Census. Washington, DC: Government Printing Office, 1993.

MAGAZINE ARTICLE, ONE AUTHOR

Bonoma, Elizabeth, "Gone Are the Cash Cows of Yesteryear." U.S. News and World Report, 19 May 1993, 58-61.

MAGAZINE ARTICLE, NO AUTHOR

"America Must Compete on Value, Not Price," Industry Week, 29 June 1994, 34-37.

NEWSPAPER ARTICLE, ONE AUTHOR

Klein, Katherine J. "The 100 Best Companies to Work for in America," Los Angeles Times. 12 February 1995, C1, C5.

NEWSPAPER ARTICLE, NO AUTHOR

"The Winning Edge." Kansas City Star, 3 January 1994. Sports sec., 2.

PROFESSIONAL JOURNAL WITH VOLUME AND PART NUMBERS

Phillips, Ramon D., Jr. "Exploring Determinants of Success in Corporate Ventures." Journal of Business Venturing, 22, no. 3 (Winter 1993):254-73. [Alternate form: Journal of Business Venturing, vol. 22, no. 3 (Winter 1993), 254-73.

INTERVIEWS AND UNPUBLISHED MATERIALS

Tully, Susanne. Telephone interview with author. 14 March 1995.

Kaplan, Robert S. Relevance Lost: The Rise and Fall of Management Accounting. Paper presented at the annual meeting of the American Association of Accountancy, Boston, April 1993.

ELECTRONIC DOCUMENTS

Winston, Dale. "How to Find the Perfect Job." In Businesswire [database online]. San Francisco: Business Wire, 1993 [updated 9 April 1994; cited 14 March 1995]. Accession no. 000926; NO=BW430. 4 screens. Available from DIA-LOG Information Services, Inc., Palo Alto, Calif.

GRAMMAR/MECHANICS

HANDBOOK

The Grammar/Mechanics Handbook consists of three parts:

1. Grammar/Mechanics Diagnostic Test
   - To assess your strengths and weaknesses in eight areas of grammar and mechanics
2. Grammar/Mechanics Profile
   - To pinpoint specific areas in which you need remedial instruction or review
3. Grammar Review with Review and Editing Exercises
   - To review basic principles of grammar, punctuation, capitalization, and number style
   - To provide reinforcement and quiz exercises allowing you to interact with the principles of grammar and test your comprehension
   - To serve as a systematic reference to grammar and mechanics throughout the writing course
   - To be used for classroom-centered instruction or self-guided learning

GRAMMAR/MECHANICS DIAGNOSTIC TEST

Name _____

This diagnostic test is intended to reveal your strengths and weaknesses in using the following:

plural nouns	adjectives	punctuation
possessive nouns	adverbs	capitalization style
pronouns	prepositions	number style
verbs	conjunctions	

The test is organized into sections corresponding to these categories. In sections A–H, each sentence is either correct or has one error related to the category under which it is listed. If a sentence is correct, write *C*. If it has an error, underline the error and write the correct form in the space provided. Use ink to record your answers. When you finish, check your answers with your instructor and fill out the Grammar/Mechanics Profile on page 365.

A. PLURAL NOUNS

branches

Example: The newspaper named editors in chief for both branchs.

attorneys

1. Three of the attornies representing the defendants were from cities in other states.

freshmen

2. Four freshmans discussed the pros and cons of attending colleges or universities.

companies

3. Since the 1970s, most companys have begun to send bills of lading with shipments.

Morrises

4. Neither the Johnsons nor the Morris's knew about the changes in beneficiaries.

Saturdays

5. The manager asked all secretaries to work on the next four Saturday's.

B. POSSESSIVE NOUNS

jury's

6. We sincerely hope that the jurys judgment reflects the stories of all the witnesses.

months'

7. In a little over two months time, the secretaries had finished three reports for the president.

Franklin's

8. Mr. Franklins staff is responsible for all accounts receivable contracted by customers purchasing electronics parts.

stockholders'

9. At the next stockholders meeting, we will discuss benefits for employees and dividends for shareholders.

Smith's

10. Three months ago several employees in the sales department complained of Mrs. Smiths smoking.

C. PRONOUNS

me

Example: Whom did you ask to replace Tom and I?

I

11. My manager and myself were willing to send the copies to whoever needed them.

me
its
C
its

12. Some of the work for Mr. Benson and I had to be reassigned to Mark and him.
13. Although it's motor was damaged, the car started for the mechanic and me.
14. Just between you and me, only you and I know that she will be transferred.
15. My friend and I applied for employment at Reynolds, Inc., because of their excellent employee benefits.

D. VERB AGREEMENT

has

Example: The list of arrangements have to be approved by Tim and her.

cost
was

16. The keyboard, printer, and monitor costs less than I expected.
17. A description of the property, together with several other legal documents, were submitted by my attorney.

were
C
prefers

18. There was only two enclosures and the letter in the envelope.
19. Neither the manager nor the employees in the office think the solution is fair.
20. Because of the holiday, our committee prefer to delay its action.

E. VERB MOOD, VOICE, AND TENSE

were
omit you

21. If I was able to fill your order immediately, I certainly would.
22. To operate the machine, first open the disk drive door and then you insert the diskette.

choose
lain
gone

23. If I could chose any city, I would select Honolulu.
24. Those papers have laid on his desk for more than two weeks.
25. The auditors have went over these accounts carefully, and they have found no discrepancies.

F. ADJECTIVES AND ADVERBS

26. Until we have a <u>more</u> clearer picture of the entire episode, we shall proceed cautiously.   *omit* more

27. For about a week their newly repaired copier worked just <u>beautiful</u>.   *beautifully*

28. The recently elected official benefited from his <u>coast to coast</u> campaign.   *coast-to-coast*

29. Mr. Snyder <u>only has</u> two days before he must complete the end-of-the-year report.   *has only*

30. The architects submitted <u>there</u> drawings in a last-minute attempt to beat the deadline.   *their*

G. PREPOSITIONS AND CONJUNCTIONS

31. Can you tell me where the meeting is scheduled <u>at</u>?   *omit* at

32. It seems <u>like</u> we have been taking this test forever.   *as if; as though*

33. Our investigation shows that the distribution department is more efficient <u>then</u> the sales department.   *than*

34. My courses this semester are totally different <u>than</u> last semester's.   *from*

35. Do you know where this shipment is going <u>to</u>?   *to*

H. COMMAS

For each of the following sentences, insert any necessary commas. Count the number of commas that you added. Write that number in the space provided. All punctuation must be correct to receive credit for the sentence. If a sentence requires no punctuation, write *C*.

Example: However, because of developments in theory and computer applications, management is becoming more of a science.   *2*

36. For example, management determines how orders, assignments, and responsibilities are delegated to employees.   *3*

37. Your order, Mrs. Swift, will be sent from Memphis, Tennessee, on July 1.   *4*

38. When you need service on any of your pieces of equipment, we will be happy to help you, Mr. Lopez.   *2*

39. Kevin Long, who is the project manager at Techdata, suggested that I call you.   *2*

40. You have purchased from us often, and your payments in the past have always been prompt.   *1*

I. COMMAS AND SEMICOLONS

Add commas and semicolons to the following sentences. In the space provided, write the number of punctuation marks that you added.

41. The salesperson turned in his report; however, he did not indicate what time period it covered.   *2*

42. Interest payments on bonds are tax deductible; dividend payments are not.   *1*

43. We are opening a branch office in Kettering and hope to be able to serve all your needs from that office by the middle of January.   *C*

44. As suggested by the committee, we must first secure adequate funding; then we may consider expansion.   *2*

45. When you begin to conduct research for a report, consider the many library sources available; namely, books, periodicals, government publications, and databases.   *3*

J. COMMAS AND SEMICOLONS

46. After our office manager had the printer repaired, it jammed again within the first week, although we treated it carefully.   *2*

47. Our experienced, courteous staff has been trained to anticipate your every need.   *1*

_3_   48. In view of the new law that went into effect April 1, our current liability insurance must be increased; however, we cannot immediately afford it.

_1_   49. As stipulated in our contract, your agency will supervise our graphic arts and purchase our media time.

_3_   50. As you know, Mrs. Simpson, we aim for long-term business relationships, not quick profits.

K. OTHER PUNCTUATION

Each of the following sentences may require dashes, colons, question marks, quotation marks, periods, and underscores, as well as commas and semicolons. Add the appropriate punctuation to each sentence. Then, in the space provided, write the total number of marks that you added.

_3_   **Example:** Price, service, and reliability—these are our prime considerations.

_1_   51. The following members of the department volunteered to help on Saturday: Kim, Carlos, Dan, and Sylvia.

_4_   52. Mr. Danner, Miss Reed, and Mrs. Garcia usually arrived at the office by 8:30 a.m.

_2_   53. Three of our top managers—Tim, Marcy, and Thomas—received cash bonuses.

_3_   54. Did the vice president really say, "All employees may take Friday off"?

_4_   55. We are trying to locate an edition of <u>Newsweek</u> that carried an article entitled "Microcomputers Beat the Office Crunch."

L. CAPITALIZATION

For each of the following sentences, circle any letter that should be capitalized. In the space provided, write the number of circles that you marked.

_4_   **Example:** Ⓥice Ⓟresident Ⓓaniels devised a procedure for expediting purchase orders from Ⓐrea 4 warehouses.

_4_   56. Ⓐlthough Ⓔnglish was his native language, he also spoke Ⓢpanish and could read Ⓕrench.

_8_   57. Ⓞn a trip to the Ⓔast Ⓒoast, Ⓤncle Ⓗenry visited the Ⓔmpire Ⓢtate Ⓑuilding.

_2_   58. Ⓚaren enrolled in classes in history, Ⓖerman, and sociology.

_2_   59. Ⓣhe business manager and the vice president each received a new Ⓐpple computer.

_4_   60. Ⓙames Ⓛee, the president of Ⓚendrick, Ⓘnc., will speak to our conference in the spring.

M. NUMBER STYLE

Decide whether the numbers in the following sentences should be written as words or as figures. Each sentence either is correct or has one error. If it is correct, write C. If it has an error, underline it and write the correct form in the space provided.

five   **Example:** The bank had <u>5</u> branches in three suburbs.

2 million   61. More than <u>2,000,000</u> people have visited the White House in the past five years.

_3_   62. Of the 35 letters sent out, only <u>three</u> were returned.

_$40_   63. We set aside <u>forty dollars</u> for petty cash, but by December 1 our fund was depleted.

May 5   64. The meeting is scheduled for May <u>5th</u> at 3 p.m.

twenty   65. In the past <u>20</u> years, nearly 15 percent of the population changed residences at least once.

GRAMMAR/MECHANICS PROFILE

In the spaces at the right, place a check mark to indicate the number of correct answers you had in each category of the Grammar/Mechanics Diagnostic Test.

		NUMBER CORRECT*				
		5	4	3	2	1
1–5	Plural Nouns	_____	_____	_____	_____	_____
6–10	Possessive Nouns	_____	_____	_____	_____	_____
11–15	Pronouns	_____	_____	_____	_____	_____
16–20	Verb Agreement	_____	_____	_____	_____	_____
21–25	Verb Mood, Voice, and Tense	_____	_____	_____	_____	_____
26–30	Adjectives and Adverbs	_____	_____	_____	_____	_____
31–35	Prepositions and Conjunctions	_____	_____	_____	_____	_____
36–40	Commas	_____	_____	_____	_____	_____
41–45	Commas and Semicolons	_____	_____	_____	_____	_____
46–50	Commas and Semicolons	_____	_____	_____	_____	_____
51–55	Other Punctuation	_____	_____	_____	_____	_____
56–60	Capitalization	_____	_____	_____	_____	_____
61–65	Number Style	_____	_____	_____	_____	_____

Note: 5 = have excellent skills; 4 = need light review; 3 = need careful review; 2 = need to study rules; 1 = need serious study and follow-up reinforcement.

GRAMMAR REVIEW

PARTS OF SPEECH (1.01)

1.01 Functions

English has eight parts of speech. Knowing the functions of the parts of speech helps writers better understand how words are used and how sentences are formed.

a. **Nouns:** name persons, places, things, qualities, concepts, and activities (for example, *Kevin, Phoenix, computer, joy, work, banking*).
b. **Pronouns:** substitute for nouns (for example, *he, she, it, they*).
c. **Verbs:** show the action of a subject or join to the subject words that describe it (for example, *walk, heard, is, was jumping*).
d. **Adjectives:** describe or limit nouns and pronouns and often answer the questions *what kind? how many?* and *which one?* (for example, *fast* sale, *ten* items, *good* manager).
e. **Adverbs:** describe or limit verbs, adjectives, or other adverbs and frequently answer the questions *when? how? where?* or *to what extent?* (for example, *tomorrow, rapidly, here, very*).
f. **Prepositions:** join nouns or pronouns to other words in sentences (for example, desk *in* the office, ticket *for* me, letter *to* you).
g. **Conjunctions:** connect words or groups of words (for example, you *and* I, Mark *or* Jill).
h. **Interjections:** express strong feelings (for example, *Wow! Oh!*).

NOUNS (1.02–1.06)

Nouns name persons, places, things, qualities, concepts, and activities. Nouns may be classified into a number of categories.

1.02   Concrete and Abstract

Concrete nouns name specific objects that can be seen, heard, felt, tasted, or smelled. Examples of concrete nouns are *telephone, dollar, IBM,* and *apple.* Abstract nouns name generalized ideas such as qualities or concepts that are not easily pictured. *Emotion, power,* and *tension* are typical examples of abstract nouns.

Business writing is most effective when concrete words predominate. It's clearer to write *We need 16-pound bond paper* than to write *We need office supplies.* Chapter 2 provides practice in developing skill in the use of concrete words.

1.03   Proper and Common

Proper nouns name specific persons, places, or things and are always capitalized (*General Electric, Baltimore, Jennifer*). All other nouns are common nouns and begin with lowercase letters (*company, city, student*). Rules for capitalization are presented in Sections 3.01–3.16.

1.04   Singular and Plural

Singular nouns name one item; plural nouns name more than one. From a practical view, writers seldom have difficulty with singular nouns. They may need help, however, with the formation and spelling of plural nouns.

1.05   Guidelines for Forming Noun Plurals

a. Add *s* to most nouns (*chair, chairs; mortgage, mortgages; Monday, Mondays*).
b. Add *es* to nouns ending in *s, x, z, ch,* or *sh* (*bench, benches; boss, bosses; box, boxes; Lopez, Lopezes*).
c. Change the spelling in irregular noun plurals (*man, men; foot, feet; mouse, mice; child, children*).
d. Add *s* to nouns that end in *y* when *y* is preceded by a vowel (*attorney, attorneys; valley, valleys; journey, journeys*).
e. Drop the *y* and add *ies* to nouns ending in *y* when *y* is preceded by a consonant (*company, companies; city, cities; secretary, secretaries*).
f. Add *s* to the principal word in most compound expressions (*editors in chief, fathers-in-law, bills of lading, runners-up*).
g. Add *s* to most numerals, letters of the alphabet, words referred to as words, degrees, and abbreviations (*5s, 1990s, Bs, ands, CPAs, qts.*).
h. Add *'s* only to clarify letters of the alphabet that might be misread, such as *A's, I's, M's,* and *U's* and *i's, p's,* and *q's.* An expression like *c.o.d.s* requires no apostrophe because it would not easily be misread.

1.06   Collective Nouns

Nouns such as *staff, faculty, committee, group,* and *herd* refer to a collection of people, animals, or objects. Collective nouns may be considered singular or plural depending upon their action. See Section 1.10i for a discussion of collective nouns and their agreement with verbs.

REVIEW EXERCISE A—NOUNS

In the space provided for each item, write *a* or *b* to complete the following statements accurately. When you finish, compare your responses with those shown below. For each item on which you need review, consult the numbered principle shown in parentheses.

1. Nearly all (a) *editor in chiefs,* (b) *editors in chief* demand observance of standard punctuation.	*b*	*(1.05f)*
2. Several (a) *attorneys,* (b) *attornies* worked on the case together.	*a*	*(1.05d)*
3. Please write to the (a) *Davis's,* (b) *Davises* about the missing contract.	*b*	*(1.05b)*
4. The industrial complex has space for nine additional (a) *companys,* (b) *companies.*	*b*	*(1.05e)*
5. That accounting firm employs two (a) *secretaries,* (b) *secretarys* for five CPAs.	*a*	*(1.05e)*
6. Four of the wooden (a) *benches,* (b) *benchs* must be repaired.	*a*	*(1.05b)*
7. The home was constructed with numerous (a) *chimneys,* (b) *chimnies.*	*a*	*(1.05d)*
8. Tours of the production facility are made only on (a) *Tuesdays,* (b) *Tuesday's.*	*a*	*(1.05a)*
9. We asked the (a) *Lopez's,* (b) *Lopezes* to contribute to the fund-raising drive.	*b*	*(1.05b)*
10. Both my (a) *sister-in-laws,* (b) *sisters-in-law* agreed to the settlement.	*b*	*(1.05f)*
11. The stock market is experiencing abnormal (a) *ups and downs,* (b) *up's and down's.*	*a*	*(1.05g)*
12. Three (a) *mouses,* (b) *mice* were seen near the trash cans.	*b*	*(1.05c)*
13. This office is unusually quiet on (a) *Sundays,* (b) *Sunday's.*	*a*	*(1.05a)*
14. Several news (a) *dispatchs,* (b) *dispatches* were released during the strike.	*b*	*(1.05b)*
15. Two major (a) *countries,* (b) *countrys* will participate in arms negotiations.	*a*	*(1.05e)*
16. Some young children have difficulty writing their (a) *bs and ds,* (b) *b's and d's.*	*b*	*(1.05h)*
17. The (a) *board of directors,* (b) *boards of directors* of all the major companies participated in the surveys.	*b*	*(1.05f)*
18. In their letter the (a) *Metzes,* (b) *Metzs* said they intended to purchase the property.	*a*	*(1.05b)*
19. In shipping we are careful to include all (a) *bill of sales,* (b) *bills of sale.*	*b*	*(1.05f)*
20. Over the holidays many (a) *turkies,* (b) *turkeys* were consumed.	*b*	*(1.05d)*

---

1. b   3. b   5. a   7. a   9. b   11. a   13. a   15. a   17. b   19. b (Only odd-numbered answers are provided. Consult your instructor for the others.)

PRONOUNS (1.07–1.09)

Pronouns substitute for nouns. They are classified by case.

1.07 Case

Pronouns function in three cases, as shown in the following chart.

NOMINATIVE CASE (USED FOR SUBJECTS OF VERBS AND SUBJECT COMPLEMENTS)	OBJECTIVE CASE (USED FOR OBJECTS OF PREPOSITIONS AND OBJECTS OF VERBS)	POSSESSIVE CASE (USED TO SHOW POSSESSION)
I	me	my, mine
we	us	our, ours
you	you	your, yours
he	him	his
she	her	her, hers
it	it	its
they	them	their, theirs
who, whoever	whom, whomever	whose

1.08 Guidelines for Selecting Pronoun Case

a. Pronouns that serve as subjects of verbs must be in the nominative case:

He and *I* (not *Him* and *me*) decided to apply for the jobs.

b. Pronouns that follow linking verbs (such as *am, is, are, was, were, be, being, been*) and rename the words to which they refer must be in the nominative case:

It must have been *she* (not *her*) who placed the order. (The nominative-case pronoun *she* follows the linking verb *been* and renames *it*.)

If it was *he* (not *him*) who called, I have his number. (The nominative-case pronoun *he* follows the linking verb *was* and renames *it*.)

c. Pronouns that serve as objects of verbs or objects of prepositions must be in the objective case:

Mr. Andrews asked *them* to complete the proposal. (The pronoun *them* is the object of the verb *asked*.)

All computer printouts are sent to *him*. (The pronoun *him* is the object of the preposition *to*.)

Just between you and *me*, profits are falling. (The pronoun *me* is one of the objects of the preposition *between*.)

d. Pronouns that show ownership must be in the possessive case. Possessive pronouns (such as *hers, yours, ours, theirs,* and *its*) require no apostrophes:

We found my diskette, but *yours* (not *your's*) may be lost.

All parts of the machine, including *its* (not *it's*) motor, were examined.

The house and *its* (not *it's*) contents will be auctioned.

Don't confuse possessive pronouns and contractions. Contractions are shortened forms of subject-verb phrases (such as *it's* for *it is, there's* for *there is*, and *they're* for *they are*).

e. When a pronoun appears in combination with a noun or another pronoun, ignore the extra noun or pronoun and its conjunction. In this way pronoun case becomes more obvious:

The manager promoted Jeff and *me* (not *I*). (Ignore *Jeff and*.)

f. In statements of comparison, mentally finish the comparative by adding the implied missing words:

Next year I hope to earn as much as *she*. (The verb *earns* is implied here: . . . *as much as she earns*.)

g. Pronouns must be in the same case as the words they replace or rename. When pronouns are used with appositives, ignore the appositive:

A new contract was signed by *us* (not *we*) employees. (Temporarily ignore the appositive *employees* in selecting the pronoun.)

We (not *us*) citizens have formed our own organization. (Temporarily ignore the appositive *citizens* in selecting the pronoun.)

h. Pronouns ending in *self* should be used only when they refer to previously mentioned nouns or pronouns:

Robert and *I* (not *myself*) are in charge of the campaign.

i. Use objective-case pronouns as objects of the prepositions *between, but, like,* and *except*:

Everyone but John and *him* (not *he*) qualified for the bonus.

Employees like Miss Gillis and *her* (not *she*) are hard to replace.

j. Use *who* or *whoever* for nominative-case constructions and *whom* or *whomever* for objective-case constructions. In making the correct choice, it's sometimes helpful to substitute *he* or *who* or *whoever* and *him* for *whom* or *whomever*:

For *whom* was this book ordered? (*This book was ordered for him/whom?*)

Who did you say would drop by? (*Who/he . . . would drop by?*)

Deliver the package to *whoever* opens the door. (In this sentence the clause *whoever opens the door* functions as the object of the preposition *to*. Within the clause itself *whoever* is the subject of the verb *opens*. Again, substitution of *he* might be helpful: *He/Whoever opens the door.*)

1.09   Guidelines for Making Pronouns Agree with Their Antecedents

Pronouns must agree with the words to which they refer (their antecedents) in gender and in number.

a. Use masculine pronouns to refer to masculine antecedents, feminine pronouns to refer to feminine antecedents, and neuter pronouns to refer to antecedents without gender:

The man opened *his* office door. (Masculine gender applies.)

A woman sat at *her* desk. (Feminine gender applies.)

This computer and *its* programs fit our needs. (Neuter gender applies.)

b. Use singular pronouns to refer to singular antecedents:

Any customer who writes us should have *his* (not *their*) letter answered promptly. (The singular pronoun *his* refers to the singular subject *customer*.)

Common-gender (masculine) pronouns traditionally have been used when the gender of the antecedent is unknown. Sensitive writers today, however, prefer to recast such constructions to avoid the need for common-gender pronouns. Study these examples for alternatives to the use of common-gender pronouns:*

Customers' letters should be answered promptly.

Customers who write us should have their letters answered promptly.

Any customer who writes us should have *his* or *her* letter answered promptly. (This alternative is the least acceptable since it is wordy and calls attention to itself.)

c. Use singular pronouns to refer to singular indefinite subjects and plural pronouns for plural indefinite subjects. Words such as *anyone, something,* and *anybody* are considered indefinite because they refer to no specific person or object. Some indefinite pronouns are always singular; others are always plural.

ALWAYS SINGULAR		ALWAYS PLURAL
anybody	everything	both
anyone	neither	few
anything	nobody	many
each	no one	several
either	somebody	
everyone	someone	

Somebody in the group of touring women left *her* (not *their*) purse in the museum.

Either of the companies has the right to exercise *its* (not *their*) option to sell stock.

d. Use singular pronouns to refer to collective nouns and organization names:

The engineering staff is moving *its* (not *their*) facilities on Friday. (The singular pronoun *its* agrees with the collective noun *staff* because the members of *staff* function as a single unit.)

*See Chapter 3, page 45, for additional discussion of common-gender pronouns.

Jones, Cohen, & James, Inc., has (not *have*) canceled *its* (not *their*) contract with us. (The singular pronoun *its* agrees with *Jones, Cohen, & James, Inc.,* because the members of the organization are operating as a single unit.)

e. Use a plural pronoun to refer to two antecedents joined by *and*, whether the antecedents are singular or plural:

Our company president and our vice president will be submitting *their* expenses shortly.

f. Ignore intervening phrases—introduced by expressions like *together with, as well as,* and *in addition to*—that separate a pronoun from its antedecent:

One of our managers, along with several salespeople, is planning *his* retirement. (If you wish to emphasize both subjects equally, join them with *and*: One of our managers *and* several salespeople are planning *their* retirements.)

g. When antecedents are joined by *or* or *nor,* make the pronoun agree with the antecedent closest to it.

Neither Jackie nor Kim wanted *her* (not *their*) desk moved.

REVIEW EXERCISE B—PRONOUNS

In the space provided for each item, write *a, b,* or *c* to complete the statement accurately. When you finish, compare your responses with those shown below. For each item on which you need review, consult the numbered principle shown in parentheses.

a	(1.08h)	1. Mr. Behrens and (a) *I,* (b) *myself* will be visiting sales personnel in the Wilmington district next week.
b	(1.08b)	2. James promised that he would call; was it (a) *him,* (b) *he* who left the message?
b	(1.08c)	3. Much preparation for the seminar was made by Mrs. Washington and (a) *I,* (b) *me* before the brochures were sent out.
a	(1.09d)	4. The Employee Benefits Committee can be justly proud of (a) *its,* (b) *their* achievements.
b	(1.08c, 1.08e)	5. A number of inquiries were addressed to Jeff and (a) *I,* (b) *me,* (c) *myself.*
b	(1.08j)	6. (a) *Who,* (b) *Whom* did you say the letter was addressed to?
a	(1.09d)	7. When you visit Sears Savings Bank, inquire about (a) *its,* (b) *their* certificates.
b	(1.08c, 1.08e)	8. Copies of all reports are to be reviewed by Mr. Sanders and (a) *I,* (b) *me,* (c) *myself.*
a	(1.09b)	9. Apparently one of the female applicants forgot to sign (a) *her,* (b) *their* application.
b	(1.08d)	10. Both the printer and (a) *it's,* (b) *its* cover are missing.
b	(1.08f)	11. I've never known any man who could work as fast as (a) *him,* (b) *he.*
b	(1.08c, 1.08i)	12. Just between you and (a) *I,* (b) *me,* the stock price will fall by afternoon.
a	(1.08j)	13. Give the supplies to (a) *whoever,* (b) *whomever* ordered them.
b	(1.08g)	14. (a) *Us,* (b) *We* employees have been given an unusual voice in choosing benefits.
a	(1.09f)	15. On her return from Mexico, Mrs. Sanchez, along with many other passengers, had to open (a) *her,* (b) *their* luggage for inspection.
a	(1.09g)	16. Either James or Robert will have (a) *his,* (b) *their* work reviewed next week.
a	(1.09b)	17. Any woman who becomes a charter member of this organization will be able to have (a) *her,* (b) *their* name inscribed on a commemorative plaque.
b	(1.08d)	18. We are certain that (a) *our's,* (b) *ours* is the smallest wristwatch available.
b	(1.08i)	19. Everyone has completed the reports except Debbie and (a) *he,* (b) *him.*
b	(1.08f)	20. Lack of work disturbs Mr. Thomas as much as (a) *I,* (b) *me.*

1. a 3. b 5. b 7. a 9. a 11. b 13. a 15. a 17. a 19. b

CUMULATIVE EDITING QUIZ 1

Use proofreading marks (see Appendix B) to correct errors in the following sentences. All errors must be corrected to receive credit for the sentence. Check with your instructor for the answers.

Example: Nicholas and ~~him~~ *he* made all th~~ere~~ *ir* money in the 1980~~'~~s.

1. Just between you and I, whom do you think would make the best manager?
2. Either Stacy or me is responsible for correcting all errors in news dispatchs.
3. Several attornies asked that there cases be postponed.
4. One of the secretarys warned Bill and I to get the name of whomever answered the phone.
5. The committee sent there decision to the president and I last week.
6. Who should Susan or me call to verify the three bill of sales received today?
7. Several of we employees complained that it's keyboard made the new computer difficult to use.
8. All the CEO's agreed that the low interest rates of the early 1990's could not continue.
9. Every customer has a right to expect there inquirys to be treated courteously.
10. You may send you're contribution to Eric or myself or to whomever is listed as your representative.

VERBS (1.10–1.15)

Verbs show the action of a subject or join to the subject words that describe it.

1.10 Guidelines for Agreement with Subjects

One of the most troublesome areas in English is subject-verb agreement. Consider the following guidelines for making verbs agree with subjects.

a. A singular subject requires a singular verb:

The stock market *opens* at 10 a.m. (The singular verb *opens* agrees with the singular subject *market.*)
He *doesn't* (not *don't*) work on Saturday.

b. A plural subject requires a plural verb:

On the packing slip several items *seem* (not *seems*) to be missing.

c. A verb agrees with its subject regardless of prepositional phrases that may intervene:

This list of management objectives *is* extensive. (The singular verb *is* agrees with the singular subject *list.*)
Every one of the letters *shows* (not *show*) proper form.

d. A verb agrees with its subject regardless of intervening phrases introduced by *as well as, in addition to, such as, including, together with,* and similar expressions:

An important memo, together with several letters, *was* misplaced. (The singular verb *was* agrees with the singular subject *memo.*)
The president as well as several other top-level executives *approves* of our proposal. (The singular verb *approves* agrees with the subject *president.*)

e. A verb agrees with its subject regardless of the location of the subject:

Here *is* one of the letters about which you asked. (The verb *is* agrees with its subject *one*, even though it precedes *one*. The adverb *here* cannot function as a subject.)

There *are* many problems yet to be resolved. (The verb *are* agrees with the subject *problems*. The adverb *there* cannot function as a subject.)

In the next office *are* several word processing machines. (In this inverted sentence the verb *are* must agree with the subject *machines*.)

f. Subjects joined by *and* require a plural verb:

Analyzing the reader and organizing a strategy *are* the first steps in letter writing. (The plural verb *are* agrees with the two subjects, *analyzing* and *organizing*.)

The tone and the wording of the letter *were* persuasive. (The plural verb *were* agrees with the two subjects, *tone* and *wording*.)

g. Subjects joined by *or* or *nor* may require singular or plural verbs. Make the verb agree with the closer subject:

Neither the memo nor the report *is* ready. (The singular verb *is* agrees with *report*, the closer of the two subjects.)

h. The following indefinite pronouns are singular and require singular verbs: *anyone, anybody, anything, each, either, every, everyone, everybody, everything, many a, neither, nobody, nothing, someone, somebody*, and *something*:

Either of the alternatives that you present *is* acceptable. (The verb *is* agrees with the singular subject *either*.)

i. Collective nouns may take singular or plural verbs, depending on whether the members of the group are operating as a unit or individually:

Our management team *is* united in its goal.

The faculty *are* sharply *divided* on the tuition issue. (Although acceptable, this sentence sounds better recast: The faculty *members* are sharply divided on the tuition issue.)

j. Organization names and titles of publications, although they may appear to be plural, are singular and require singular verbs.

Clark, Anderson, and Horne, Inc., *has* (not *have*) hired an automation consultant.

Thousands of Investment Tips is (not *are*) again on the best-seller list.

1.11   Voice

Voice is that property of verbs that shows whether the subject of the verb acts or is acted upon. Active-voice verbs direct action from the subject toward the object of the verb. Passive-voice verbs direct action toward the subject.

ACTIVE VOICE: Our employees *write* excellent letters.
PASSIVE VOICE: Excellent letters *are written* by our employees.

Business writing that emphasizes active-voice verbs is generally preferred because it is specific and forceful. However, passive-voice constructions can help a writer be tactful. Strategies for effective use of active- and passive-voice verbs are presented in Chapter 4.

1.12   Mood

Three verb moods express the attitude or thought of the speaker or writer toward a subject: (1) the indicative mood expresses a fact; (2) the imperative mood expresses a command; and (3) the subjunctive mood expresses a doubt, a conjecture, or a suggestion.

INDICATIVE: I *am looking* for a job.
IMPERATIVE: *Begin* your job search with the want ads.
SUBJUNCTIVE: I wish I *were* working.

Only the subjunctive mood creates problems for most speakers and writers. The most common use of subjunctive mood occurs in clauses including *if* or *wish*. In such clauses substitute the subjunctive verb *were* for the indicative verb *was*:

If he *were* (not *was*) in my position, he would understand.

Mr. Simon acts as if he *were* (not *was*) the boss.

I wish I *were* (not *was*) able to ship your order.

The subjunctive mood may be used to maintain goodwill while conveying negative information. The sentence *I wish I* were *able to ship your order* sounds more pleasing to a customer than *I cannot ship your order,* although, for all practical purposes, both sentences convey the same negative message.

1.13   Tense

Verbs show the time of an action by their tense. Speakers and writers can use six tenses to show the time of sentence action; for example:

PRESENT TENSE: I *work*; he *works*.
PAST TENSE: I *worked*; she *worked*.
FUTURE TENSE: I *will work*; he *will work*.
PRESENT PERFECT TENSE: I *have worked*; he *has worked*.
PAST PERFECT TENSE: I *had worked*; she *had worked*.
FUTURE PERFECT TENSE: I *will have worked*; he *will have worked*.

1.14   Guidelines for Verb Tense

a. Use present tense for statements that, although they may be introduced by past-tense verbs, continue to be true:

What did you say his name *is*? (Use the present tense *is* if his name has not changed.)

b. Avoid unnecessary shifts in verb tenses:

The manager *saw* (not *sees*) a great deal of work yet to be completed and *remained* to do it herself.

Although unnecessary shifts in verb tense are to be avoided, not all the verbs within one sentence have to be in the same tense; for example:

She *said* (past tense) that she *likes* (present tense) to work late.

1.15   Irregular Verbs

Irregular verbs cause difficulty for some writers and speakers. Unlike regular verbs irregular verbs do not form the past tense and past participle by adding *-ed* to the present form. Here is a partial list of selected troublesome irregular verbs. Consult a dictionary if you are in doubt about a verb form.

TROUBLESOME IRREGULAR VERBS

PRESENT	PAST	PAST PARTICIPLE (ALWAYS USE HELPING VERBS)
begin	began	begun
break	broke	broken
choose	chose	chosen
come	came	come
drink	drank	drunk
go	went	gone
lay (to place)	laid	laid
lie (to rest)	lay	lain
ring	rang	rung
see	saw	seen
write	wrote	written

"No, Timmy, not 'I <u>sawed</u> the chair'. It's
'I <u>saw</u> the chair' or 'I <u>have seen</u> the chair'."

Reprinted with special permission of glenn Bernhardt.

a. **Use only past-tense verbs to express past tense. Notice that no helping verbs are used to indicate simple past tense:**

The auditors *went* (not *have went*) over our books carefully.
He *came* (not *come*) to see us yesterday.

b. **Use past participle forms for actions completed before the present time. Notice that past participle forms require helping verbs:**

Steve had *gone* (not *went*) before we called. (The past participle *gone* is used with the helping verb *had.*)

c. Avoid inconsistent shifts in subject, voice, and mood. Pay particular attention to this problem area, for undesirable shifts are often characteristic of student writing.

INCONSISTENT: When Mrs. Taswell read the report, the error was found. (The first clause is in the active voice; the second, passive.)

IMPROVED: When Mrs. Taswell read the report, she found the error. (Both clauses are in the active voice.)

INCONSISTENT: The clerk should first conduct an inventory. Then supplies should be requisitioned. (The first sentence is in the active voice; the second, passive.)

IMPROVED: The clerk should first conduct an inventory. Then he or she should requisition supplies. (Both sentences are in the active voice.)

INCONSISTENT: All workers must wear security badges, and you must also sign a daily time card. (This sentence contains an inconsistent shift in subject from *all workers* in first clause to *you* in second clause.)

IMPROVED: All workers must wear security badges, and they must also sign a daily time card.

INCONSISTENT: Begin the transaction by opening an account; then you enter the customer's name. (This sentence contains an inconsistent shift from the imperative mood in first clause to the indicative mood in second clause.)

IMPROVED: Begin the transaction by opening an account; then enter the customer's name. (Both clauses are now in the indicative mood.)

REVIEW EXERCISE C—VERBS

In the space provided for each item, write *a* or *b* to complete the statement accurately. When you finish, compare your responses with those shown below. For each item on which you need review, consult the numbered principle shown in parentheses.

1. A list of payroll deductions for our employees (a) *was*, (b) *were* sent to the personnel manager.   *a*   *(1.10c)*

2. There (a) *is*, (b) *are* a customer service engineer and two salespeople waiting to see you.   *b*   *(1.10e, 1.10f)*

3. Increased computer use and more complex automated systems (a) *is*, (b) *are* found in business today.   *b*   *(1.10f)*

4. Crews, Meliotes, and Bove, Inc., (a) *has*, (b) *have* opened an office in Boston.   *a*   *(1.10j)*

5. Yesterday Mrs. Phillips (a) *choose*, (b) *chose* a new office on the second floor.   *b*   *(1.15a)*

6. The man who called said that his name (a) *is*, (b) *was* Johnson.   *a*   *(1.14a)*

7. Modern Office Procedures (a) *is*, (b) *are* beginning a campaign to increase readership.   *a*   *(1.10j)*

8. Either of the flight times (a) *appears*, (b) *appear* to fit my proposed itinerary.   *a*   *(1.10h)*

9. If you had (a) *saw*, (b) *seen* the rough draft, you would better appreciate the final copy.   *b*   *(1.15b)*

10. Across from our office (a) *is*, (b) *are* the parking structure and the information office.   *b*   *(1.10e, 1.10f)*

11. Although we have (a) *began*, (b) *begun* to replace outmoded equipment, the pace is slow.   *b*   *(1.15b)*

12. Specific training as well as ample experience (a) *is*, (b) *are* important for that position.   *a*   *(1.10d)*

13. Inflation and increased job opportunities (a) *is*, (b) *are* resulting in increased numbers of working women.   *b*   *(1.10f)*

14. Neither the organizing nor the staffing of the program (a) *has been*, (b) *have been* completed.   *a*   *(1.10g)*

15. If I (a) *was*, (b) *were* you, I would ask for a raise.   *b*   *(1.12)*

b	*(1.15b)*	16. If you had (a) *wrote*, (b) *written* last week, we could have sent a brochure.
a	*(1.10a)*	17. The hydraulic equipment that you ordered (a) *is*, (b) *are* packed and will be shipped Friday.
a	*(1.10c)*	18. One of the reasons that sales have declined in recent years (a) *is*, (b) *are* lack of effective advertising.
a	*(1.10h)*	19. Either of the proposed laws (a) *is*, (b) *are* going to affect our business negatively.
b	*(1.10b)*	20. Merger statutes (a) *requires*, (b) *require* that a failing company accept bids from several companies before merging with one.

1. a 3. b 5. b 7. a 9. b 11. b 13. b 15. b 17. a 19. a

REVIEW EXERCISE D—VERBS

In the following sentence pairs, choose the one that illustrates consistency in use of subject, voice, and mood. Write *a* or *b* in the spaces provided. When you finish, compare your responses with those shown below. For each item on which you need review, consult the numbered principle shown in parentheses.

b	*(1.15c)*	1. (a) You need more than a knowledge of equipment; one also must be able to interact well with people.
		(b) You need more than a knowledge of equipment; you also must be able to interact well with people.
a	*(1.14b)*	2. (a) Tim and Jon were eager to continue, but Bob wanted to quit.
		(b) Tim and Jon were eager to continue, but Bob wants to quit.
b	*(1.15c)*	3. (a) The salesperson should consult the price list; then you can give an accurate quote to a customer.
		(b) The salesperson should consult the price list; then he or she can give an accurate quote to a customer.
b	*(1.15c)*	4. (a) Read all the instructions first; then you install the printer program.
		(b) Read all the instructions first, and then install the printer program.
a	*(1.14b)*	5. (a) She was an enthusiastic manager who always had a smile for everyone.
		(b) She was an enthusiastic manager who always has a smile for everyone.

1. b 3. b 5. a

CUMULATIVE EDITING QUIZ 2

Use proofreading marks (see Appendix B) to correct errors in the following sentences. All errors must be corrected to receive credit for the sentence. Check with your instructor for the answers.

1. Assets and liabilitys is what my partner and myself must investigate.
2. If I was you, I would ask whomever is in charge for their opinion.
3. The faculty agree that it's first concern is educating students.
4. The book and it's cover was printed in Japan.
5. Waiting to see you is a sales representative and a job applicant who you told to drop by.
6. Every employee could have picked up his ballot if he had went to the cafeteria.
7. Your choice of hospitals and physicians are reduced by this plan and it's restrictions.
8. My uncle and her come to visit my parents and myself last night.
9. According to both editor in chiefs, the tone and wording of all our letters needs revision.
10. The Davis'es, about who the article was written, said they were unconcerned with the up's and down's of the stock market.

ADJECTIVES AND ADVERBS (1.16–1.17)

Adjectives describe or limit nouns and pronouns. They often answer the questions *what kind? how many?* or *which one?* Adverbs describe or limit verbs, adjectives, or other adverbs. They often answer the questions *when? how? where?* or *to what extent?*

1.16 Forms

Most adjectives and adverbs have three forms, or degrees: positive, comparative, and superlative.

	POSITIVE	COMPARATIVE	SUPERLATIVE
ADJECTIVE:	clear	clearer	clearest
ADVERB:	clearly	more clearly	most clearly

Some adjectives and adverbs have irregular forms.

	POSITIVE	COMPARATIVE	SUPERLATIVE
ADJECTIVE:	good	better	best
	bad	worse	worst
ADVERB:	well	better	best

Adjectives and adverbs composed of two or more syllables are usually compared by the use of *more* and *most*; for example:

> The Payroll Department is *more efficient* than the Shipping Department.
> Payroll is the *most efficient* department in our organization.

1.17 Guidelines for Use

a. Use the comparative degree of the adjective or adverb to compare two persons or things; use the superlative degree to compare three or more:

> Of the two letters, which is *better* (not *best*)?
> Of all the plans, we like this one *best* (not *better*).

b. Do not create a double comparative or superlative by using *-er* with *more* or *-est* with *most*:

> His explanation couldn't have been *clearer* (not *more clearer*).

c. A linking verb (*is, are, look, seem, feel, sound, appear,* and so forth) may introduce a word that describes the verb's subject. In this case be certain to use an adjective, not an adverb:

> The characters on the monitor look *bright* (not *brightly*). (Use the adjective *bright* because it follows the linking verb *look* and modifies the noun *characters*. It answers the question *What kind of characters?*)
> The company's letter made the customer feel *bad* (not *badly*). (The adjective *bad* follows the linking verb *feel* and describes the noun *customer*.)

d. Use adverbs, not adjectives, to describe or limit the action of verbs:

> The business is running *smoothly* (not *smooth*). (Use the adverb *smoothly* to describe the action of the verb *is running*. *Smoothly* tells how the business is running.)
> Don't take his remark *personally* (not *personal*). (The adverb *personally* describes the action of the verb *take*.)

e. Two or more adjectives that are joined to create a compound modifier before a noun should be hyphenated:

The *four-year-old* child was tired.

Our agency is planning a *coast-to-coast* campaign.

Hyphenate a compound modifier following a noun only if your dictionary shows the hyphen(s):

Our speaker is very *well-known*. (Include the hyphen because most dictionaries do.)

The tired child was four years old. (Omit the hyphens because the expression follows the word it describes, *child*, and because dictionaries do not indicate hyphens.)

f. Keep adjectives and adverbs close to the words that they modify:

She asked for a cup of *hot* coffee (not a *hot cup of coffee*).

Patty had *only* two days of vacation left (not *Patty only had two days*).

Students may sit in the *first* five rows (not *in the five first rows*).

He has saved *almost* enough money for the trip (not *He has almost saved*).

g. Don't confuse the adverb *there* with the possessive pronoun *their* or the contraction *they're*:

Put the documents *there*. (The adverb *there* means "at that place or at that point.")

There are two reasons for the change. (The adverb *there* is used as an expletive or filler preceding a linking verb.)

We already have *their* specifications. (The possessive pronoun *their* shows ownership.)

They're coming to inspect today. (The contraction *they're* is a shortened form of *they are*.)

REVIEW EXERCISE E—ADJECTIVES AND ADVERBS

In the space provided for each item, write *a*, *b*, or *c* to complete the statement accurately. If two sentences are shown, select *a* or *b* to indicate the one expressed more effectively. When you finish, compare your responses with those shown below. For each item on which you need review, consult the numbered principle shown in parentheses.

a	*(1.17c)*	1. After the interview, Tim looked (a) *calm*, (b) *calmly*.
a	*(1.17b)*	2. If you had been more (a) *careful*, (b) *carefuler*, the box might not have broken.
b	*(1.17d)*	3. Because a new manager was appointed, the advertising campaign is running very (a) *smooth*, (b) *smoothly*.
b	*(1.17e)*	4. To avoid a (a) *face to face*, (b) *face-to-face* confrontation, she wrote a letter.
a	*(1.17d)*	5. Darren completed the employment test (a) *satisfactorily*, (b) *satisfactory*.
a	*(1.17c)*	6. I felt (a) *bad*, (b) *badly* that he was not promoted.
a	*(1.17a)*	7. Which is the (a) *more*, (b) *most* dependable of the two models?
b	*(1.17g)*	8. Can you determine exactly what (a) *there*, (b) *their*, (c) *they're* company wants us to do?
b	*(1.17a)*	9. Of all the copiers we tested, this one is the (a) *easier*, (b) *easiest* to operate.
b	*(1.17f)*	10. (a) Mr. Aldron almost was ready to accept the offer. (b) Mr. Aldron was almost ready to accept the offer.
b	*(1.17f)*	11. (a) We only thought that it would take two hours for the test. (b) We thought that it would take only two hours for the test.
a	*(1.17f)*	12. (a) Please bring me a glass of cold water. (b) Please bring me a cold glass of water.
a	*(1.17f)*	13. (a) The committee decided to retain the last ten tickets. (b) The committee decided to retain the ten last tickets.
a	*(1.17e)*	14. New owners will receive a (a) *60-day*, (b) *60 day* trial period.
b	*(1.17d)*	15. The time passed (a) *quicker*, (b) *more quickly* than we expected.
b	*(1.17e)*	16. We offer a (a) *money back*, (b) *money-back* guarantee.
a	*(1.17a)*	17. Today the financial news is (a) *worse*, (b) *worst* than yesterday.
b	*(1.17d)*	18. Please don't take his comments (a) *personal*, (b) *personally*.
a	*(1.17e)*	19. You must check the document (a) *page by page*, (b) *page-by-page*.

20. (a) We try to file only necessary paperwork.   *a*   *(1.17f)*
    (b) We only try to file necessary paperwork.

---

1. a   3. b   5. a   7. a   9. b   11. b   13. a   15. b   17. a   19. a

PREPOSITIONS (1.18)

Prepositions are connecting words that join nouns or pronouns to other words in a sentence. The words *about, at, from, in,* and *to* are examples of prepositions.

1.18 Guidelines for Use

a. Include necessary prepositions:

What type *of* software do you need (not *what type software*)?
I graduated *from* high school two years ago (not *I graduated high school*).

b. Omit unnecessary prepositions:

Where is the meeting? (Not *Where is the meeting at?*)
Both printers work well. (Not *Both of the printers.*)
Where are you going? (Not *Where are you going to?*)

c. Avoid the overuse of prepositional phrases.

WEAK: Your application for credit at our branch in the Fresno area is before me.
IMPROVED: Your Fresno credit application is before me.

d. Repeat the preposition before the second of two related elements:

Applicants use the résumé effectively *by* summarizing their most important experiences and *by* relating their education to the jobs sought.

e. Include the second preposition when two prepositions modify a single object:

George's appreciation *of* and aptitude *for* computers led to a promising career.

(The use of prepositions in idiomatic expressions is discussed in Chapter 2, page 31.)

CONJUNCTIONS (1.19)

Conjunctions connect words, phrases, and clauses. They act as signals, indicating when a thought is being added, contrasted, or altered. Coordinate conjunctions (such as *and, or, but*) and other words that act as connectors (such as *however, therefore, when, as*) tell the reader or listener in what direction a thought is heading. They're like road signs signaling what's ahead.

1.19 Guidelines for Use

a. Use coordinating conjunctions to connect only sentence elements that are parallel or balanced.

WEAK: His report was correct and written in a concise manner.
IMPROVED: His report was correct and concise.
WEAK: Management has the capacity to increase fraud, or reduction can be achieved through the policies it adopts.
IMPROVED: Management has the capacity to increase or reduce fraud through the policies it adopts.

b. Do not use the word *like* as a conjunction:

It seems *as if* (not *like*) this day will never end.

c. Avoid using *when* or *where* inappropriately. A common writing fault occurs in sentences with clauses introduced by *is when* and *is where*. Written English ordinarily requires a noun (or a group of words functioning as a noun) following the linking verb *is*. Instead of acting as conjunctions in these constructions, the words *where* and *when* function as adverbs, creating faulty grammatical equations (adverbs cannot complete equations set up by linking verbs). To avoid the problem, revise the sentence, eliminating *is when* or *is where*.

WEAK: A bullish market is when prices are rising in the stock market.
IMPROVED: A bullish market is created when prices are rising in the stock market.
WEAK: A flowchart is when you make a diagram showing the step-by-step progression of a procedure.
IMPROVED: A flowchart is a diagram showing the step-by-step progression of a procedure.
WEAK: Word processing is where you use a computer and software to write.
IMPROVED: Word processing involves the use of a computer and software to write.

A similar faulty construction occurs in the expression *I hate when*. English requires nouns, noun clauses, or pronouns to act as objects of verbs, not adverbs.

WEAK: I hate when we're asked to work overtime.
IMPROVED: I hate it when we're asked to work overtime.
IMPROVED: I hate being asked to work overtime.

d. Don't confuse the adverb *then* with the conjunction *than*. *Then* means "at that time"; *than* indicates the second element in a comparison:

We would rather remodel *than* (not *then*) move.

First, the equipment is turned on; *then* (not *than*) the program is loaded.

REVIEW EXERCISE F—PREPOSITIONS AND CONJUNCTIONS

In the space provided for each item, write *a* or *b* to indicate the sentence that is expressed more effectively. When you finish, compare your responses with those shown below. For each item on which you need review, consult the numbered principle shown in parentheses.

a *(1.18b)*	1. (a) Do you know where this shipment is being sent? (b) Do you know where this shipment is being sent to?
a *(1.18e)*	2. (a) She was not aware of nor interested in the company insurance plan. (b) She was not aware nor interested in the company insurance plan.
b *(1.18a)*	3. (a) Mr. Samuels graduated college last June. (b) Mr. Samuels graduated from college last June.
b *(1.19c)*	4. (a) "Flextime" is when employees arrive and depart at varying times. (b) "Flextime" is a method of scheduling worktime in which employees arrive and depart at varying times.
a *(1.18b)*	5. (a) Both employees enjoyed setting their own hours. (b) Both of the employees enjoyed setting their own hours.
b *(1.19c)*	6. (a) I hate when the tape sticks in my VCR. (b) I hate it when the tape sticks in my VCR.
a *(1.18a)*	7. (a) What style of typeface should we use? (b) What style typeface should we use?
b *(1.19a)*	8. (a) Business letters should be concise, correct, and written clearly. (b) Business letters should be concise, correct, and clear.

9. (a) Mediation in a labor dispute occurs when a neutral person helps union and management reach an agreement. *a*   *(1.19c)*
   (b) Mediation in a labor dispute is where a neutral person helps union and management reach an agreement.

10. (a) It looks as if the plant will open in early January. *a*   *(1.19b)*
    (b) It looks like the plant will open in early January.

11. (a) We expect to finish up the work soon. *b*   *(1.18b)*
    (b) We expect to finish the work soon.

12. (a) At the beginning of the program in the fall of the year at the central office, we experienced staffing difficulties. *b*   *(1.18c)*
    (b) When the program began last fall, the central office experienced staffing difficulties.

13. (a) Your client may respond by letter or a telephone call may be made. *b*   *(1.19a)*
    (b) Your client may respond by letter or by telephone.

14. (a) A résumé is when you make a written presentation of your education and experience for a prospective employer. *b*   *(1.19c)*
    (b) A résumé is a written presentation of your education and experience for a prospective employer.

15. (a) Stacy exhibited both an awareness of and talent for developing innovations. *a*   *(1.18e)*
    (b) Stacy exhibited both an awareness and talent for developing innovations.

16. (a) This course is harder then I expected. *b*   *(1.19d)*
    (b) This course is harder than I expected.

17. (a) An ombudsman is an individual hired by management to investigate and resolve employee complaints. *a*   *(1.19c)*
    (b) An ombudsman is when management hires an individual to investigate and resolve employee complaints.

18. (a) I'm uncertain where to take this document to. *b*   *(1.18b)*
    (b) I'm uncertain where to take this document.

19. (a) By including accurate data and by writing clearly, you will produce effective memos. *a*   *(1.18d)*
    (b) By including accurate data and writing clearly, you will produce effective memos.

20. (a) We need computer operators who can load software, monitor networks, and files must be duplicated. *b*   *(1.19a)*
    (b) We need computer operators who can load software, monitor networks, and duplicate files.

---

1. a 3. b 5. a 7. a 9. a 11. b 13. b 15. a 17. a 19. a

CUMULATIVE EDITING QUIZ 3

Use proofreading marks (see Appendix B) to correct errors in the following sentences. All errors must be corrected to receive credit for the sentence. Check with your instructor for the answers.

1. If Cindy types faster then her, shouldn't Cindy be hired?
2. We felt badly that his newly-redecorated home was not chose for the tour.
3. Neither the company nor the workers is pleased at how slow the talks seems to be progressing.
4. Just between you and I, it's better not to take his remarks personal.
5. After completing there floor by floor inventory, managers will deliver there reports to Mr. Quinn and I.
6. If the telephone was working, Jean and myself could have completed our calls.
7. Powerful software and new hardware allows us to send the newsletter to whomever is currently listed in our database.

8. The eighteen year old girl and her mother was given hot cups of tea after there ordeal.

9. We begun the work two years ago, but personnel and equipment has been especially difficult to obtain.

10. Today's weather is worst then yesterday'.

PUNCTUATION REVIEW

COMMAS 1 (2.01–2.04)

2.01 Series

Commas are used to separate three or more equal elements (words, phrases, or short clauses) in a series. To ensure separation of the last two elements, careful writers always use a comma before the conjunction in a series:

> Business letters usually contain a dateline, address, salutation, body, and closing. (This series contains words.)
>
> The job of an ombudsman is to examine employee complaints, resolve disagreements between management and employees, and ensure fair treatment. (This series contains phrases.)
>
> Trainees complete basic keyboarding tasks, technicians revise complex documents, and editors proofread completed projects. (This series contains short clauses.)

2.02 Direct Address

Commas are used to set off the names of individuals being addressed:

> Your inquiry, *Mrs. Johnson*, has been referred to me.
>
> We genuinely hope that we may serve you, *Mr. Lee*.

2.03 Parenthetical Expressions

Skilled writers use parenthetical words, phrases, and clauses to guide the reader from one thought to the next. When these expressions interrupt the flow of a sentence and are unnecessary for its grammatical completeness, they should be set off with commas. Examples of commonly used parenthetical expressions follow:

all things considered	however	needless to say
as a matter of fact	in addition	nevertheless
as a result	incidentally	no doubt
as a rule	in fact	of course
at the same time	in my opinion	on the contrary
consequently	in the first place	on the other hand
for example	in the meantime	therefore
furthermore	moreover	under the circumstances

> *As a matter of fact*, I wrote to you just yesterday. (Phrase used at the beginning of a sentence.)
>
> We will, *in the meantime*, send you a replacement order. (Phrase used in the middle of a sentence.)
>
> Your satisfaction is our first concern, *needless to say*. (Phrase used at the end of a sentence.)

Do not use commas if the expression is necessary for the completeness of the sentence:

> Kimberly had *no doubt* that she would finish the report. (Omit commas because the expression is necessary for the completeness of the sentence.)

2.04 Dates, Addresses, and Geographical Items

When dates, addresses, and geographical items contain more than one element, the second and succeeding elements are normally set off by commas.

a. Dates:

> The conference was held February 2 at our home office. (No comma is needed for one element.)
>
> The conference was held February 2, 1994, at our home office. (Two commas set off the second element.)
>
> The conference was held Tuesday, February 2, 1994, at our home office. (Commas set off the second and third elements.)
>
> In February 1994 the conference was held. (This alternate style omitting commas is acceptable if the month and year only are written.)

b. Addresses:

> The letter addressed to Mr. Jim W. Ellman, 600 Via Novella, Agoura, CA 91306, should be sent today. (Commas are used between all elements except the state and zip code, which in this special instance are considered a single unit.)

c. Geographical items:

> She moved from Toledo, Ohio, to Champaign, Illinois. (Commas set off the state unless it appears at the end of the sentence, in which case only one comma is used.)

In separating cities from states and days from years, many writers remember the initial comma but forget the final one, as in the examples that follow:

> The package from Austin, Texas {,} was lost.
> We opened June 1, 1985 {,} and have grown steadily since.

REVIEW EXERCISE G—COMMAS 1

Insert necessary commas in the following sentences. In the space provided write the number of commas that you add. Write *C* if no commas are needed. When you finish, compare your responses with those shown below. For each item on which you need review, consult the numbered principle shown in parentheses.

1. As a rule, we do not provide complimentary tickets.	1	(2.03)
2. You may be certain, Mr. Martinez, that your policy will be issued immediately.	2	(2.02)
3. I have no doubt that your calculations are correct.	C	(2.03)
4. The safety hazard, on the contrary, can be greatly reduced if workers wear rubber gloves.	2	(2.03)
5. Every accredited TV newscaster, radio broadcaster, and newspaper reporter had access to the media room.	2	(2.01)
6. Deltech's main offices are located in Boulder, Colorado, and Seattle, Washington.	3	(2.04c)
7. The employees who are eligible for promotions are Terry, Evelyn, Vicki, Rosanna, and Steve.	4	(2.01)
8. During the warranty period, of course, you are protected from any parts or service charges.	2	(2.03)
9. Many of our customers include architects, engineers, attorneys, and others who are interested in database management programs.	3	(2.01)
10. I wonder, Mrs. Stevens, if you would send my letter of recommendation as soon as possible.	2	(2.02)
11. The new book explains how to choose appropriate legal protection for ideas, trade secrets, copyrights, patents, and restrictive covenants.	4	(2.01)
12. The factory is scheduled to be moved to 2250 North Main Street, Ann Arbor, Michigan 48107, within two years.	3	(2.04b)

_2_	_(2.03)_	13. You may , however , prefer to correspond directly with the manufacturer in Hong Kong.
_C_	_(2.03)_	14. Are there any alternatives in addition to those that we have already considered?
_2_	_(2.04a)_	15. The rally has been scheduled for Monday , January 12 , in the football stadium.
_1_	_(2.02)_	16. A check for the full amount will be sent directly to your home , Mr. Jefferson.
_2_	_(2.03)_	17. Goodstone Tire & Rubber , for example , recalled 400,000 steelbelted radial tires because some tires failed their rigorous tests.
_2_	_(2.01)_	18. Kevin agreed to unlock the office , open the mail , and check all the equipment in my absence.
_1_	_(2.03)_	19. In the meantime , thank you for whatever assistance you are able to furnish.
_3_	_(2.04c)_	20. Research facilities were moved from Austin , Texas , to Santa Cruz , California.

1. rule,   3. C   5. newscaster, radio broadcaster,   7. Terry, Evelyn, Vicki, Rosanna, 9. architects, engineers, attorneys,   11. ideas, trade secrets, copyrights, patents,   13. may, however,   15. Monday, January 12,   17. Rubber, for example,   19. meantime,

COMMAS 2 (2.05–2.09)

2.05 Independent Clauses

An independent clause is a group of words that has a subject and a verb and that could stand as a complete sentence. When two such clauses are joined by *and, or, nor,* or *but,* use a comma before the conjunction:

> We can ship your merchandise July 12, *but* we must have your payment first.
>
> Net income before taxes is calculated, *and* this total is then combined with income from operations.

Notice that each independent clause in the preceding two examples could stand alone as a complete sentence. Do not use a comma unless each group of words is a complete thought (that is, has its own subject and verb).

> Net income before taxes is calculated *and* is then combined with income from operations. (No comma is needed because no subject follows *and*.)

2.06 Dependent Clauses

Dependent clauses do not make sense by themselves; for their meaning they depend on independent clauses.

a. **Introductory clauses.** When a dependent clause precedes an independent clause, it is followed by a comma. Such clauses are often introduced by *when, if,* and *as:*

> *When your request came*, we immediately responded.
>
> *As I mentioned earlier*, Mrs. James is the manager.

b. **Terminal clauses.** If a dependent clause falls at the end of a sentence, use a comma only if the dependent clause is an afterthought:

> The meeting has been rescheduled for October 23, *if this date meets with your approval*. (Comma used because dependent clause is an afterthought.)
>
> We responded immediately *when we received your request*. (No comma is needed.)

c. **Essential versus nonessential clauses.** If a dependent clause provides information that is unneeded for the grammatical completeness of a sentence, use commas to set it off. In determining whether such a clause is essential or nonessential, ask yourself whether the reader needs the information contained in the clause to identify the word it explains:

Our district sales manager, *who just returned from a trip to the Southwest District*, prepared this report. (This construction assumes that there is only one district sales manager. Since the sales manager is clearly identified, the dependent clause is not essential and requires commas.)

The salesperson *who just returned from a trip to the Southwest District* prepared this report. (The dependent clause in this sentence is necessary to identify *which* salesperson prepared the report. Therefore, use no commas.)

The position of assistant sales manager, *which we discussed with you last week*, is still open. (Careful writers use *which* to introduce nonessential clauses. Commas are also necessary.)

The position *that we discussed with you last week* is still open. (Careful writers use *that* to introduce essential clauses. No commas are used.)

2.07 Phrases

A phrase is a group of related words that lacks both a subject and a verb. A phrase that precedes a main clause is followed by a comma only if the phrase contains a verb form or has five or more words:

Beginning November 1, Worldwide Savings will offer two new combination checking/savings plans. (A comma follows this introductory phrase because the phrase contains the verb form *beginning*.)

To promote their plan, we will conduct an extensive direct-mail advertising campaign. (A comma follows this introductory phrase because the phrase contains the verb form *to promote*.)

In a period of only one year, we were able to improve our market share by 30 percent. (A comma follows the introductory phrase—actually two prepositional phrases—because its total length exceeds five words.)

In 1985 our organization installed a multiuser system that could transfer programs easily. (No comma needed after the short introductory phrase.)

2.08 Two or More Adjectives

Use a comma to separate two or more adjectives that equally describe a noun. A good way to test the need for a comma is this: mentally insert the word *and* between the adjectives. If the resulting phrase sounds natural, a comma is used to show the omission of *and*:

We're looking for a versatile, programmable calculator. (Use a comma to separate *versatile* and *programmable* because they independently describe *calculator*. *And* has been omitted.)

Our *experienced, courteous* staff is ready to serve you. (Use a comma to separate *experienced* and *courteous* because they independently describe *staff*. *And* has been omitted.)

It was difficult to refuse the *sincere young* telephone caller. (No commas are needed between *sincere* and *young* because *and* has not been omitted.)

2.09 Appositives

Words that rename or explain preceding nouns or pronouns are called *appositives*. An appositive that provides information not essential to the identification of the word it describes should be set off by commas:

James Wilson, *the project director for Sperling's,* worked with our architect. (The appositive, *the project director for Sperling's*, adds nonessential information. Commas set it off.)

REVIEW EXERCISE H—COMMAS 2

Insert only necessary commas in the following sentences. In the space provided, indicate the number of commas that you add for each sentence. If a sentence requires no commas, write *C*. When you finish, compare your responses with those shown below. For each item on which you need review, consult the numbered principle shown in parentheses.

_1_____ *(2.05)* 1. A corporation must be registered in the state in which it does business and it must operate within the laws of that state.

_C_____ *(2.05)* 2. The manager made a point-by-point explanation of the distribution dilemma and then presented his plan to solve the problem.

_1_____ *(2.06a)* 3. If you will study the cost analysis you will see that our company offers the best system at the lowest price.

_2_____ *(2.06c)* 4. Molly Epperson who amassed the greatest number of sales points was awarded the bonus trip to Hawaii.

_C_____ *(2.06c)* 5. The salesperson who amasses the greatest number of sales points will be awarded the bonus trip to Hawaii.

_1_____ *(2.07)* 6. To promote goodwill and to generate international trade we are opening offices in the Far East and in Europe.

_1_____ *(2.07)* 7. On the basis of these findings I recommend that we retain Jane Rada as our counsel.

_1_____ *(2.08)* 8. Mary Bantle is a dedicated hard-working employee for our company.

_C_____ *(2.08)* 9. The bright young student who worked for us last summer will be able to return this summer.

_1_____ *(2.06a)* 10. When you return the completed form we will be able to process your application.

_C_____ *(2.06b)* 11. We will be able to process your application when you return the completed form.

_C_____ *(2.06c)* 12. The employees who have been with us over ten years automatically receive additional insurance benefits.

_1_____ *(2.07)* 13. Knowing that you wanted this merchandise immediately I took the liberty of sending it by Express Parcel Services.

_C_____ *(2.05)* 14. The central processing unit requires no scheduled maintenance and has a self-test function for reliable performance.

_1_____ *(2.05)* 15. Foreign competition nearly ruined the American shoe industry but the textile industry remains strong.

_2_____ *(2.09)* 16. Stacy Wilson our newly promoted office manager has made a number of worthwhile suggestions.

_1_____ *(2.07)* 17. For the benefit of employees recently hired we are offering a two-hour seminar regarding employee benefit programs.

_C_____ *(2.06b)* 18. Please bring your suggestions and those of Mr. Mason when you attend our meeting next month.

_1_____ *(2.06b)* 19. The meeting has been rescheduled for September 30 if this date meets with your approval.

_C_____ *(2.06c)* 20. Some of the problems that you outline in your recent memo could be rectified through more stringent purchasing procedures.

1. business,   3. analysis,   5. C   7. findings,   9. C   11. C   13. immediately,   15. industry,   17. hired,   19. September 30,

COMMAS 3 (2.10–2.15)

2.10 Degrees and Abbreviations

Degrees following individuals' names are set off by commas. Abbreviations such as *Jr.* and *Sr.* are also set off by commas unless the individual referred to prefers to omit the commas:

Anne G. Turner, *M.B.A.,* joined the firm.

Michael Migliano, *Jr.,* and Michael Migliano, *Sr.,* work as a team.

Anthony A. Gensler *Jr.* wrote the report. (The individual referred to prefers to omit commas.)

The abbreviations *Inc.* and *Ltd.* are set off by commas only if a company's legal name has a comma just before this kind of abbreviation. To determine a company's practice, consult its stationery or a directory listing:

Firestone and Blythe, *Inc.,* is based in Canada. (Notice that two commas are used.)

Computers *Inc.* is extending its franchise system. (The company's legal name does not include a comma just before *Inc.*)

2.11 Omitted Words

A comma is used to show the omission of words that are understood:

On Monday we received 15 applications; on Friday, only 3. (Comma shows the omission of *we received.*)

2.12 Contrasting Statements

Commas are used to set off contrasting or opposing expressions. These expressions are often introduced by such words as *not, never, but,* and *yet*:

The consultant recommended dual-tape storage, *not* floppy-disk storage, for our operations.

Our budget for the year is reduced, *yet* adequate.

The greater the effort, the greater the reward.

If increased emphasis is desired, use dashes instead of commas, as in *Only the sum of $100—not $1,000—was paid on this account.*

2.13 Clarity

Commas are used to separate words repeated for emphasis. Commas are also used to separate words that may be misread if not separated:

The building is a long, long way from completion.

Whatever is, is right.

No matter what, you know we support you.

2.14 Quotations and Appended Questions

a. A comma is used to separate a short quotation from the rest of a sentence. If the quotation is divided into two parts, two commas are used:

The manager asked, "Shouldn't the managers control the specialists?"

"Not if the specialists," replied Tim, "have unique information."

b. A comma is used to separate a question appended (added) to a statement:

You will confirm the shipment, won't you?

2.15 Comma Overuse

Do not use commas needlessly. For example, commas should not be inserted merely because you might drop your voice if you were speaking the sentence:

One of the reasons for expanding our West Coast operations is {,} that we anticipate increased sales in that area. (Do not insert a needless comma before a clause.)

I am looking for an article entitled {,} "State-of-the-Art Communications." (Do not insert a needless comma after the word *entitled.*)

A number of food and nonfood items are carried in convenience stores such as {,} 7-Eleven and Stop-N-Go. (Do not insert a needless comma after *such as.*)

We have {,} at this time {,} an adequate supply of parts. (Do not insert needless commas

around prepositional phrases.)

REVIEW EXERCISE I—COMMAS 3

Insert only necessary commas in the following sentences. Remove unnecessary commas with the delete sign (✍). In the space provided, indicate the number of commas inserted or deleted in each sentence. If a sentence requires no changes, write *C*. When you finish, compare your responses with those shown below. For each item on which you need review, consult the numbered principle shown in parentheses.

2	(2.12)	1. We expected Charles Bedford, not Tiffany Richardson, to conduct the audit.
1	(2.14a)	2. Brian said, "We simply must have a bigger budget to start this project."
2	(2.14a)	3. "We simply must have," said Brian, "a bigger budget to start this project."
1	(2.11)	4. In August customers opened at least 50 new accounts; in September, only about 20.
1	(2.14b)	5. You returned the merchandise last month, didn't you?
1	(2.13)	6. In short, employees will now be expected to contribute more to their own retirement funds.
1	(2.12)	7. The better our advertising and recruiting, the stronger our personnel pool will be.
2	(2.12)	8. Mrs. Delgado investigated selling her stocks, not her real estate, to raise the necessary cash.
2	(2.14a)	9. "On the contrary," said Mrs. Mercer, "we will continue our present marketing strategies."
1	(2.15)	10. Our company will expand into surprising new areas such as, ✍ women's apparel and fast foods.
2	(2.12)	11. What we need is more, not fewer, suggestions for improvement.
4	(2.10)	12. Randall Clark, Esq., and Jonathon Georges, M.B.A., joined the firm.
2	(2.14a)	13. "America is now entering," said President Saunders, "the Age of Information."
1	(2.15)	14. One of the reasons that we are inquiring about the publisher of the software is ✍ that we are concerned about whether that publisher will be in the market five years from now.
2	(2.10)	15. The talk by D. A. Spindler, Ph.D., was particularly difficult to follow because of his technical and abstract vocabulary.
1	(2.13)	16. The month before, a similar disruption occurred in distribution.
2	(2.15)	17. We are very fortunate to have ✍ at our disposal ✍ the services of excellent professionals.
1	(2.13)	18. No matter what you can count on us for support.
1	(2.11)	19. Mrs. Sandoval was named legislative counsel; Mr. Freeman, executive adviser.
1	(2.15)	20. The data you are seeking can be found in an article entitled, ✍ "The Fastest Growing Game in Computers."

---

1. Bedford, Richardson,   3. have," said Brian,   5. month,   7. recruiting,   9. contrary," Mercer,   11. more, not fewer,   13. entering," Saunders,   15. Spindler, Ph.D.,   17. have at our disposal   19. Freeman,

CUMULATIVE EDITING QUIZ 4

Use proofreading marks (see Appendix B) to correct errors and omissions in the following sentences. All errors must be corrected to receive credit for the sentence. Check with your instructor for the answers.

1. Business documents must be written clear, to ensure that readers comprehend the message quick.
2. Needless to say the safety of our employees have always been most important to the president and I.
3. The Small Business Administration which provide disaster loans are setting up an office in Miami Florida.

4. Many entrepreneurs who want to expand there markets, have choosen to advertise heavy.

5. Our arbitration committee have unanimously agreed on a compromise package but management have been slow to respond.

6. Although the business was founded in the 1950's its real expansion took place in the 1980s.

7. According to the contract either the dealer or the distributor are responsible for repair of the product.

8. Next June, Lamont and Jones, Inc., are moving their headquarters to Denton Texas.

9. Our company is looking for intelligent, articulate, young, people who has a desire to grow with an expanding organization.

10. As you are aware each member of the jury were asked to avoid talking about the case.

SEMICOLONS (2.16)

2.16 Independent Clauses, Series, Introductory Expressions

a. **Independent clauses with conjunctive adverbs.** Use a semicolon before a conjunctive adverb that separates two independent clauses. Some of the most common conjunctive adverbs are *therefore, consequently, however,* and *moveover*:

Business letters should sound conversational; *therefore,* familiar words and contractions are often used.

The bank closes its doors at 3 p.m.; *however,* the ATM is open 24 hours a day.

Notice that the word following a semicolon is *not* capitalized (unless, of course, that word is a proper noun).

b. **Independent clauses without conjunctive adverbs.** Use a semicolon to separate closely related independent clauses when no conjunctive adverb is used:

Bond interest payments are tax deductible; dividend payments are not.

Ambient lighting fills the room; task lighting illuminates each workstation.

Use a semicolon in *compound* sentences, not in *complex* sentences:

After one week the paper feeder jammed; we tried different kinds of paper. (Use a semicolon in a compound sentence.)

After one week the paper feeder jammed, although we tried different kinds of paper. (Use a comma in a complex sentence. Do not use a semicolon after *jammed.*)

The semicolon is very effective for joining two closely related thoughts. Don't use it, however, unless the ideas are truly related.

c. **Independent clauses with other commas.** Normally, a comma precedes *and, or,* and *but* when those conjunctions join independent clauses. However, if either clause contains commas, change the comma preceding the conjunction to a semicolon to ensure correct reading:

If you arrive in time, you may be able to purchase a ticket; but ticket sales close promptly at 8 p.m.

Our primary concern is financing; and we have discovered, as you warned us, that money sources are quite scarce.

d. **Series with internal commas.** Use semicolons to separate items in a series when one or more of the items contain internal commas:

Delegates from Miami, Florida; Freeport, Mississippi; and Chatsworth, California, attended the conference.

The speakers were Kevin Lang, manager, Riko Enterprises; Henry Holtz, vice president, Trendex, Inc.; and Margaret Slater, personnel director, West Coast Productions.

e. **Introductory expressions.** Use a semicolon when an introductory expression such as *namely, for instance, that is,* or *for example* introduces a list following an independent clause:

Switching to computerized billing are several local companies; namely, Ryson Electronics, Miller Vending Services, and Black Advertising.

The author of a report should consider many sources; for example, books, periodicals, government publications, and newspapers.

COLONS (2.17–2.19)

2.17 Listed Items

a. **With colon.** Use a colon after a complete thought that introduces a formal list of items. A formal list is often preceded by such words and phrases as *these, thus, the following,* and *as follows.* A colon is also used when words and phrases like these are implied but not stated:

Additional costs in selling a house involve *the following*: title examination fee, title insurance costs, and closing fee. (Use a colon when a complete thought introduces formal list.)

Collective bargaining focuses on several key issues: cost-of-living adjustments, fringe benefits, job security, and hours of work. (The introduction of the list is implied in the preceding clause.)

b. **Without colons.** Do not use a colon when the list immediately follows a *to be* verb or a preposition:

The employees who should receive the preliminary plan are James Sears, Monica Spears, and Rose Lopez. (No colon is used after the verb *are*.)

We expect to consider equipment for Accounting, Legal Services, and Payroll. (No colon is used after the preposition *for*.)

2.18 Quotations

Use a colon to introduce long one-sentence quotations and quotations of two or more sentences:

Our consultant said: "This system can support up to 32 users. It can be used for decision support, computer-aided design, and software development operations at the same time."

2.19 Salutations

Use a colon after the salutation of a business letter:

Gentlemen: Dear Mrs. Seaman: Dear Jamie:

REVIEW EXERCISE J—SEMICOLONS, COLONS

In the following sentences, add semicolons, colons, and necessary commas. For each sentence indicate the number of punctuation marks that you add. If a sentence requires no punctuation, write *C*. When you finish, compare your responses with those shown below. For each item on which you need review, consult the numbered principle shown in parentheses.

_2_ _____ *(2.16a)*   1. A strike in Canada has delayed shipments of parts ;consequently ,our production has fallen behind schedule.

_1_ _____ *(2.16b)*   2. Our branch in Sherman Oaks specializes in industrial real estate ;our branch in Canoga Park concentrates on residential real estate.

3. The sedan version of the automobile is available in these colors:Olympic red, metallic silver,and Aztec gold.   *3*   *(2.01, 2.17a)*

4. If I can assist the new manager,please call me;however,I will be gone from June 10 through June 15.   *3*   *(2.06a, 2.16a)*

5. The individuals who should receive copies of this announcement are Henry Doogan, Alicia Green, and Kim Wong.   *2*   *(2.01, 2.17b)*

6. We would hope,of course,to send personal letters to all prospective buyers;but we have not yet decided just how to do this.   *3*   *(2.03, 2.16c)*

7. Many of our potential customers are in Southern California;therefore,our promotional effort will be strongest in that area.   *2*   *(2.16a)*

8. Since the first of the year,we have received inquiries from one attorney,two accountants,and one information systems analyst.   *3* *(2.01, 2.07, 2.17b)*

9. Three dates have been reserved for initial interviews:January 15,February 1, and February 12.   *3*   *(2.01, 2.17a)*

10. Several staff members are near the top of their salary ranges,and we must reclassify their jobs.   *1*   *(2.05)*

11. Several staff members are near the top of their salary ranges;we must reclassify their jobs.   *1*   *(2.16b)*

12. Several staff members are near the top of their salary ranges;therefore,we must reclassify their jobs.   *2*   *(2.16a)*

13. If you open an account within two weeks,you will receive a free cookbook; moreover, your first 500 checks will be imprinted at no cost to you.   *3*   *(2.16a)*

14. Monthly reports from the following departments are missing:Legal Department, Personnel Department, and Engineering Department.   *3*   *(2.01, 2.17a)*

15. Monthly reports are missing from the Legal Department,Personnel Department, and Engineering Department.   *2*   *(2.01, 2.17b)*

16. Since you became director of that division,sales have tripled;therefore,I am recommending you for a bonus.   *3*   *(2.06a, 2.16a)*

17. The convention committee is considering Portland, Oregon; New Orleans, Louisiana;and Phoenix,Arizona.   *5*   *(2.16d)*

18. Several large companies allow employees access to their personnel files; namely,General Electric,Eastman Kodak,and Infodata.   *4*   *(2.01, 2.16e)*

19. Sherry first asked about salary;next she inquired about benefits.   *1*   *(2.16b)*

20. Sherry first asked about the salary,and she next inquired about benefits.   *1*   *(2.05)*

---

1. parts; consequently,   3. colors: Olympic red, metallic silver,   5. Doogan, Alicia Green,
7. California; therefore,   9. interviews: January 15, February 1,   11. ranges;   13. weeks,
cookbook; moreover, 15. Department, Personnel Department,   17. Portland, Oregon;
New Orleans, Louisiana; Phoenix,   19. salary;

APOSTROPHES (2.20–2.22)

2.20 Basic Rule

The apostrophe is used to show ownership, origin, authorship, or measurement.

OWNERSHIP: We are looking for *Brian's keys.*
ORIGIN: At the *president's* suggestion, we doubled the order.
AUTHORSHIP: The *accountant's annual report* was questioned.
MEASUREMENT: In *two years' time* we expect to reach our goal.

a. **Ownership words not ending in *s*.** To place the apostrophe correctly, you must first determine whether the ownership word ends in an *s* sound. If it does not, add an apostrophe and an *s* to the ownership word. The following examples show ownership words that do not end in an *s* sound:

the employee's file   (the file of a single employee)
a member's address   (the address of a single member)
a year's time   (the time of a single year)

a month's notice   (notice of a single month)
the company's building   (the building of a single company)

b. **Ownership words ending in s.** If the ownership word does end in an *s* sound, usually add only an apostrophe:

several employees' files   (files of several employees)
ten members' addresses   (addresses of ten members)
five years' time   (time of five years)
several months' notice   (notice of several months)
many companies' buildings   (buildings of many companies)

A few singular nouns that end in *s* are pronounced with an extra syllable when they become possessive. To these words, add *'s*.

my boss's desk
the waitress's table
the actress's costume

Use no apostrophe if a noun is merely plural, not possessive:

All the sales representatives, as well as the secretaries and managers, had their names and telephone numbers listed in the directory.

2.21 Names

The writer may choose either traditional or popular style in making singular names that end in an *s* sound possessive. The traditional style uses the apostrophe plus an *s*, while the popular style uses just the apostrophe. Note that only with singular names ending in an *s* sound does this option exist.

TRADITIONAL STYLE	POPULAR STYLE
Russ's computer	Russ' computer
Mr. Jones's car	Mr. Jones' car
Mrs. Morris's desk	Mrs. Morris' desk
Ms. Horowitz's job	Ms. Horowitz' job

The possessive form of plural names is consistent: the Joneses' car, the Horowitzes' home, the Lopezes' daughter.

2.22 Gerunds

Use *'s* to make a noun possessive when it precedes a gerund, a verb form used as a noun:

Mr. Smith's smoking prompted a new office policy. (*Mr. Smith* is possessive because it modifies the gerund *smoking*.)
It was Betsy's careful proofreading that revealed the discrepancy.

REVIEW EXERCISE K—APOSTROPHES

Insert necessary apostrophes in the following sentences. In the space provided for each sentence, indicate the number of apostrophes that you added. If none were added, write *C*. When you finish, compare your responses with those shown below. For each item on which you need review, consult the numbered principle shown in parentheses.

1   *(2.20b)*   1. Your account should have been credited with six months' interest.
1   *(2.21)*   2. If you go to the third floor, you will find Mr. London's office.

3. All the employees'personnel folders must be updated.	*1*	*(2.20b)*
4. In a little over a year's time, that firm was able to double its sales.	*1*	*(2.20a)*
5. The Harrises'daughter lived in Florida for two years.	*1*	*(2.21)*
6. An inventor's patent protects his or her patent for seventeen years.	*1*	*(2.20a)*
7. Both companies'headquarters will be moved within the next six months.	*1*	*(2.20b)*
8. That position requires at least two years'experience.	*1*	*(2.20b)*
9. Some of their assets could be liquidated; therefore, a few of the creditors were satisfied.	*C*	*(2.20b)*
10. All secretaries'workstations were equipped with terminals.	*1*	*(2.20b)*
11. The package of electronics parts arrived safely despite two weeks'delay.	*1*	*(2.20b)*
12. Many nurses believe that nurses'notes are not admissable evidence.	*1*	*(2.20b)*
13. According to Mr. Cortez' [or Cortez's] latest proposal, all employees would receive an additional holiday.	*1*	*(2.21)*
14. Many of our members'names and addresses must be checked.	*1*	*(2.20b)*
15. His supervisor frequently had to correct Jack's financial reports.	*1*	*(2.21)*
16. We believe that this firm's service is much better than that firm's.	*2*	*(2.20a)*
17. Mr. Jackson estimated that he spent a year's profits in reorganizing his staff.	*1*	*(2.20a)*
18. After paying six months'rent, we were given a receipt.	*1*	*(2.20b)*
19. The contract is not valid without Mrs. Harris' [or Harris's] signature.	*1*	*(2.21)*
20. It was Mr. Smith's signing of the contract that made us happy.	*1*	*(2.22)*

---

1. months' 3. employees' 5. Harrises' 7. companies' 9. C 11. weeks'
13. Cortez' or Cortez's 15. Jack's 17. year's 19. Harris' or Harris's

CUMULATIVE EDITING QUIZ 5

Use proofreading marks (see Appendix B) to correct errors and omissions in the following sentences. All errors must be corrected to receive credit for the sentence. Check with your instructor for the answers.

1. The three C's of credit are the following character capacity and capital.
2. We hope that we will not have to sell the property however that may be our only option.
3. As soon as the supervisor and her can check this weeks sales they will place an order.
4. Any of the auditors are authorized to proceed with an independent action however only the CEO can alter the councils directives.
5. Although reluctant technicians sometimes must demonstrate there computer software skills.
6. On April 6 1994 we opened an innovative fully-equipped employee computer center.
7. A list of maintenance procedures and recommendations are in the owners manual.
8. The Morrises son lived in Flint Michigan however there daughter lived in Albany New York.
9. Employment interviews were held in Dallas Texas Miami Florida and Chicago Illinois.
10. Mr. Lees determination courage and sincerity could not be denied however his methods was often questioned.

OTHER PUNCTUATION (2.23–2.29)

2.23 Periods

a. **Ends of sentences.** Use a period at the end of a statement, command, indirect question, or polite request. Although a polite request may have the same structure as a question, it ends with a period:

Corporate legal departments demand precise skills from their workforce. (End a statement with a period.)

Get the latest data by reading current periodicals. (End a command with a period.)

Mr. Rand wondered if we had sent any follow-up literature. (End an indirect question with a period.)

Would you please reexamine my account and determine the current balance. (A polite request suggests an action rather than a verbal response.)

b. **Abbreviations and initials.** Use periods after initials and after many abbreviations.

R. M. Johnson	c.o.d.	Ms.
M.D.	a.m.	Mr.
Inc.	i.e.	Mrs.

Use just one period when an abbreviation falls at the end of a sentence:

Guests began arriving at 5:30 p.m.

2.24   Question Marks

Direct questions are followed by question marks:

Did you send your proposal to Datatronix, Inc.?

Statements with questions added are punctuated with question marks.

We have completed the proposal, haven't we?

2.25   Exclamation Points

Use an exclamation point after a word, phrase, or clause expressing strong emotion. In business writing, however, exclamation points should be used sparingly:

Incredible! Every terminal is down.

2.26   Dashes

The dash (constructed at a keyboard by striking the hyphen key twice in succession) is a legitimate and effective mark of punctuation when used according to accepted conventions. As an emphatic punctuation mark, however, the dash loses effectiveness when overused.

a. **Parenthetical elements.** Within a sentence a parenthetical element is usually set off by commas. If, however, the parenthetical element itself contains internal commas, use dashes (or parentheses) to set it off:

Three top salespeople—Tom Judkins, Tim Templeton, and Mary Yashimoto—received bonuses.

b. **Sentence interruptions.** Use a dash to show an interruption or abrupt change of thought:

News of the dramatic merger—no one believed it at first—shook the financial world.
Ship the materials Monday—no, we must have them sooner.

Sentences with abrupt changes of thought or with appended afterthoughts can usually be improved through rewriting.

c. **Summarizing statements.** Use a dash (not a colon) to separate an introductory list from a summarizing statement:

Sorting, merging, and computing—these are tasks that our data processing programs must perform.

2.27 Parentheses

One means of setting off nonessential sentence elements involves the use of parentheses. Nonessential sentence elements may be punctuated in one of three ways: (1) with commas, to make the lightest possible break in the normal flow of a sentence; (2) with dashes, to emphasize the enclosed material; and (3) with parentheses, to deemphasize the enclosed material. Parentheses are frequently used to punctuate sentences with interpolated directions, explanations, questions, and references:

> The cost analysis (which appears on page 8 of the report) indicates that the copy machine should be leased.
>
> Units are lightweight (approximately 13 oz.) and come with a leather case and operating instructions.
>
> The IBM laser printer (have you heard about it?) will be demonstrated for us next week.

A parenthetical sentence that is not imbedded within another sentence should be capitalized and punctuated with end punctuation:

> The Model 20 has stronger construction. (You may order a Model 20 brochure by circling 304 on the reader service card.)

2.28 Quotation Marks

a. **Direct quotations.** Use double quotation marks to enclose the exact words of a speaker or writer:

> "Keep in mind," Mrs. Frank said, "that you'll have to justify the cost of automating our office."
>
> The boss said that automation was inevitable. (No quotation marks are needed because the exact words are not quoted.)

b. **Quotations within quotations.** Use single quotation marks (apostrophes on the typewriter) to enclose quoted passages within quoted passages:

> In her speech Mrs. Deckman remarked, "I believe it was the poet Robert Frost who said, 'All the fun's in how you say a thing.' "

c. **Short expressions.** Slang, words used in a special sense, and words following *stamped* or *marked* are often enclosed within quotation marks:

> Jeffrey described the damaged shipment as "gross." (Quotation marks enclose slang.)
>
> Students often have trouble spelling the word "separate." (Quotation marks enclose words used in a special sense.)
>
> Jobs were divided into two categories: most stressful and least stressful. The jobs in the "most stressful" list involved high risk or responsibility. (Quotation marks enclose words used in a special sense.)
>
> The envelope marked "Confidential" was put aside. (Quotation marks enclose words following *marked*.)

In the four preceding sentences, the words enclosed within quotation marks can be set in italics, if italics are available.

d. **Definitions.** Double quotation marks are used to enclose definitions. The word or expression being defined should be underscored or set in italics:

> The term *penetration pricing* is defined as "the practice of introducing a product to the market at a low price."

e. **Titles.** Use double quotation marks to enclose titles of literary and artistic works, such as magazine and newspaper articles, chapters of books, movies, television shows, poems, lectures, and songs. Names of major publications—such as books, magazines, pamphlets, and newspapers—are set in italics (underscored) or typed in capital letters.

> Particularly helpful was the chapter in Smith's EFFECTIVE WRITING TECHNIQUES entitled "Right Brain, Write On!"

> In the Los Angeles Times appeared John's article, "Corporate Raiders"; however, we could not locate it in a local library.

f. **Additional considerations.** Periods and commas are always placed inside closing quotation marks. Semicolons and colons, on the other hand, are always placed outside quotation marks:

> Mrs. James said, "I could not find the article entitled 'Technology Update.'"

> The president asked for "absolute security": all written messages were to be destroyed.

Question marks and exclamation points may go inside or outside closing quotation marks, as determined by the form of the quotation:

> Sales Manager Martin said, "Who placed the order?" (The quotation is a question.)

> When did the sales manager say, "Who placed the order?" (Both the incorporating sentence and the quotation are questions.)

> Did the sales manager say, "Ryan placed the order"? (The incorporating sentence asks question; the quotation does not.)

> "In the future," shouted Bob, "ask me first!" (The quotation is an exclamation.)

2.29 Brackets

Within quotations, brackets are used by the quoting writer to enclose his or her own inserted remarks. Such remarks may be corrective, illustrative, or explanatory:

> Mrs. Cardillo said, "OSHA [Occupational Safety and Health Administration] has been one of the most widely criticized agencies of the federal government."

REVIEW EXERCISE L—OTHER PUNCTUATION

Insert necessary punctuation in the following sentences. In the space provided for each item, indicate the number of punctuation marks that you added. Count sets of parentheses and dashes as two marks. Emphasis or deemphasis will be indicated for some parenthetical elements. When you finish, compare your responses with those shown below. For each item on which you need review, consult the numbered principle shown in parentheses.

1	(2.23a)	1. Will you please stop payment on my Check No. 233.
2	(2.26b)	2. (Emphasize.) Your order of October 16 will be on its way—you have my word—by October 20.
3	(2.23a, 2.23b)	3. Mr. Sirakides, Mrs. Sylvester, and Miss Sanchez have not yet responded.
4	(2.23b)	4. Mrs. Franklin asked if the order had been sent cod.
6	(2.23b)	5. Interviews have been scheduled for 3:15 p.m., 4 p.m., and 4:45 p.m.
2	(2.27)	6. (Deemphasize.) Three knowledgeable individuals (the plant manager, the construction engineer, and the construction supervisor) all expressed concern about soil settlement.
2	(2.25)	7. Fantastic! The value of our stock just rose 10 points on the stock market exchange!
3	(2.28d)	8. The word de facto means "exercising power as if legally constituted."
2	(2.27)	9. (Deemphasize.) Although the appliance now comes in limited colors (brown, beige, and ivory) we expect to see new colors available in the next production run.

10. Was it the manager who said, "What can't be altered must be endured"?	*3*	*(2.28f)*
11. The stock market went "bonkers" over the news of the takeover.	*2*	*(2.28c)*
12. Because the envelope was marked "Personal," we did not open it.	*2*	*(2.28c)*
13. Price, service, and reliability—these are our prime considerations in equipment selection.	*1*	*(2.26c)*
14. The lettercarrier said, "Would you believe that this package was marked 'Fragile'?"	*6*	*(2.28b, 2.28f)*
15. (Emphasize.) Three branch managers—Carmen Lopez, Stan Meyers, and Ivan Sergo—will be promoted.	*2*	*(2.26a)*
16. (Deemphasize.) The difference between portable and transportable computers (see Figure 4 for weight comparisons) may be considerable.	*2*	*(2.27)*
17. All the folders marked "Current Files" should be sent to the Personnel Division.	*2*	*(2.28c)*
18. I am trying to find the edition of <u>Newsweek</u> that carried an article entitled "The Future Without Shock."	*3*	*(2.28e)*
19. Martin Simon, M.D., and Gail Nemire, R.N., were hired by Healthnet, Inc.	*9*	*(2.23b)*
20. The computer salesperson said, "This innovative, state-of-the-art laptop sells for a fraction of the cost of big-name computers."	*3*	*(2.28a)*

1. 233. 3. Mr. Mrs. responded. 5. p.m. p.m. p.m. 7. Fantastic! exchange!
9. (brown ivory) 11. "bonkers" 13. reliability— 15. managers— Sergo—
17. "Current Files" 19. Simon, M.D., Nemire, R.N., Inc.

CUMULATIVE EDITING QUIZ 6

Use proofreading marks (see Appendix B) to correct errors and omissions in the following sentences. All errors must be corrected to receive credit for the sentence. Check with your instructor for the answers.

1. Although the envelope was marked Confidential the vice presidents secretary thought it should be opened.
2. Would you please send my order c.o.d?
3. To be eligible for an apartment you must pay two months rent in advance.
4. We wanted to use Russ computer, but forgot to ask for permission.
5. Wasnt it Jeff Song not Eileen Lee who requested a 14 day leave.
6. Miss. Judith L. Beam is the employee who the employees council elected as their representative.
7. The Evening Post Dispatch our local newspaper featured an article entitled The Worlds Most Expensive Memo.
8. As soon as my manager or myself can verify Ricks totals we will call you, in the meantime you must continue to disburse funds.
9. Just inside the entrance, is the receptionists desk and a complete directory of all departments'.
10. Exports from small companys has increased thereby affecting this countrys trade balance positively.

STYLE AND USAGE

CAPITALIZATION (3.01–3.16)

Capitalization is used to distinguish important words. However, writers are not free to capitalize all words they consider important. Rules or guidelines governing capitalization style have been established through custom and use. Mastering these guidelines will make your writing more readable and more comprehensible.

3.01   Proper Nouns

Capitalize proper nouns, including the *specific* names of persons, places, schools, streets, parks, buildings, religions, holidays, months, agreements, programs, services, and so forth. Do *not* capitalize common nouns that make only *general* references.

PROPER NOUNS	COMMON NOUNS
Michael DeNiro	a salesperson in electronics
West Germany, Japan	two countries that trade with the United States
El Camino College	a community college
Sam Houston Park	a park in the city
Phoenix Room, Statler Inn	a meeting room in the hotel
Catholic, Presbyterian	two religions
Memorial Day, New Year's Day	two holidays in the year
Express Mail	a special package delivery service
George Washington Bridge	a bridge
Consumer Product Safety Act	a law to protect consumers
Greater Orlando Chamber of Commerce	a chamber of commerce
Will Rogers World Airport	a municipal airport

3.02   Proper Adjectives

Capitalize most adjectives that are derived from proper nouns:

Greek symbol	British thermal unit
Roman numeral	Norwegian ship
Xerox copy	Hispanic markets

Do not capitalize the few adjectives that, although originally derived from proper nouns, have become common adjectives through usage. Consult your dictionary when in doubt:

manila folder	diesel engine
india ink	china dishes

3.03   Geographic Locations

Capitalize the names of *specific* places such as cities, states, mountains, valleys, lakes, rivers, oceans, and geographic regions:

New York City	Great Salt Lake
Allegheny Mountains	Pacific Ocean
San Fernando Valley	Delaware Bay
the East Coast	the Pacific Northwest

3.04   Organization Names

Capitalize the principal words in the names of all business, civic, educational, governmental, labor, military, philanthropic, political, professional, religious, and social organizations:

Inland Steel Company	Board of Directors, Midwest Bank
*The Wall Street Journal**	San Antonio Museum of Art
New York Stock Exchange	Securities and Exchange Commission
United Way	National Association of Letter Carriers
Commission to Restore the Statue of Liberty	Association of Information Systems Professionals

*Note: Capitalize *the* only when it is part of the official name of an organization, as printed on the organization's stationery.

3.05   Academic Courses and Degrees

Capitalize particular academic degrees and course titles. Do not capitalize references to general academic degrees and subject areas:

> Professor Bernadette Ordian, *Ph.D.,* will teach *Accounting* 221 next fall.
> Mrs. Snyder, who holds *bachelor's* and *master's* degrees, teaches *marketing* classes.
> Jim enrolled in classes in *history, English,* and *management.*

3.06   Personal and Business Titles

a. Capitalize personal and business titles when they precede names:

> Vice President Ames   Uncle Edward
> Board Chairman Frazier   Councilman Herbert
> Governor G. W. Thurmond   Sales Manager Klein
> Professor McLean   Dr. Samuel Washington

b. Capitalize titles in addresses, salutations, and closing lines:

> Mr. Juan deSanto   Very Truly yours,
> Director of Purchasing
> Space Systems, Inc.
> Boxborough, MA 01719   Clara J. Smith
>   Supervisor, Marketing

c. Capitalize titles of high governmental rank or religious office, whether they precede a name, follow a name, or replace a name:

> The President of the United States   James Lee, Senator
> the Premier's palace   the Secretary of State
> the Governor of Ohio   an audience with the Pope
> J. W. Ross, Attorney General   the Chief Justice

d. Do not capitalize more common titles following names:

> The speech was delivered by Timothy J. McEwen, *president*, South-Western College Publishing.
> Lois Herndon, *chief executive officer*, signed the order.

e. Do not capitalize common titles appearing alone:

> Please speak to the *supervisor* or to the *office manager.*
> Neither the *president* nor the *vice president* was asked.

However, when the title of an official appears in that organization's minutes, bylaws, or other official document, it may be capitalized.

f. Do not capitalize titles when they are followed by appositives naming specific individuals:

> We must consult our *director of research*, Ronald E. West, before responding.

g. Do not capitalize family titles used with possessive pronouns:

> my mother   our aunt
> your father   his cousin

h. Capitalize titles of close relatives used without pronouns:

> Both *Mother* and *Father* must sign the contract.

3.07　Numbered and Lettered Items

Capitalize nouns followed by numbers or letters (except in page, paragraph, line, and verse references):

Flight 34, Gate 12　　　　　　　　Plan No. 2
Volume I, Part 3　　　　　　　　 Warehouse 33-A
Invoice No. 55489　　　　　　　　Figure 8.3
Model A5673　　　　　　　　　　Serial No. C22865404-2
State Highway 10　　　　　　　　 page 6, line 5

3.08　Points of the Compass

Capitalize *north, south, east, west,* and their derivatives when they represent *specific* geographical regions. Do not capitalize the points of the compass when they are used in directions or in general references.

SPECIFIC REGIONS	GENERAL REFERENCES
from the South	heading north on the highway
living in the Midwest	west of the city
Easterners, Southerners	western Nevada, southern Indiana
going to the Middle East	the northern part of the United States
from the East Coast	the east side of the street

3.09　Departments, Divisions, and Committees

Capitalize the names of departments, divisions, or committees within your own organization. Outside your organization capitalize only *specific* department, division, or committee names:

The inquiry was addressed to the *Legal Department* in our *Consumer Products Division.*
John was appointed to the *Employee Benefits Committee.*
Send your résumé to their *personnel division.*
A *planning committee* will be named shortly.

3.10　Governmental Terms

Do not capitalize the words *federal, government, nation,* or *state* unless they are part of a specific title:

Unless *federal* support can be secured, the *state* project will be abandoned.
The *Federal* Deposit Insurance Corporation protects depositors from bank failure.

3.11　Product Names

Capitalize product names only when they refer to trademarked items. Except in advertising, common names following manufacturers' names are not capitalized:

Magic Marker　　　　　　　　　Apple computer
Kleenex tissues　　　　　　　　 Swingline stapler
Q-tips　　　　　　　　　　　　 3M diskettes
Levi 501 jeans　　　　　　　　　Sony dictation machine
DuPont Teflon　　　　　　　　　Canon camera

3.12 Literary Titles

Capitalize the principal words in the titles of books, magazines, newspapers, articles, movies, plays, songs, poems, and reports. Do *not* capitalize articles (*a, an, the*), short conjunctions (*and, but, or, nor*), and prepositions of fewer than four letters (*in, to, by, for,* etc.) unless they begin or end the title:

Jackson's *What Job Is for You?* (Capitalize book titles.)
Gant's "Software for the Executive Suite" (Capitalize principal words in article titles.)
"Performance Standards to Go By" (Capitalize article titles.)
"The Improvement of Fuel Economy With Alternative Motors" (Capitalize report titles.)

3.13 Beginning Words

In addition to capitalizing the first word of a complete sentence, capitalize the first word in a quoted sentence, independent phrase, item in an enumerated list, and formal rule or principle following a colon:

The business manager said, "*All* purchases must have requisitions." (Capitalize first word in a quoted sentence.)
Yes, if you agree. (Capitalize an independent phrase.)
Some of the duties of the position are as follows:
  1. *Transcribing* dictation from recording equipment
  2. *Receiving* and routing telephone calls
  3. *Verifying* records, reports, and applications (Capitalize items in an enumerated list.)
One rule has been established through the company: *No* smoking is allowed in open offices. (Capitalize a rule following a colon.)

3.14 Celestial Bodies

Capitalize the names of celestial bodies such as *Mars, Saturn,* and *Neptune.* Do not capitalize the terms *earth, sun,* or *moon* unless they appear in a context with other celestial bodies:

Where on *earth* did you find that manual typewriter?
Venus and *Mars* are the closest planets to *Earth.*

3.15 Ethnic References

Capitalize terms that refer to a particular culture, language, or race:

Oriental	Hebrew
Caucasian	Indian
Latino	Japanese
Persian	Judeo-Christian

3.16 Seasons

Do not capitalize seasons:

In the *fall* it appeared that *winter* and *spring* sales would increase.

REVIEW EXERCISE M—CAPITALIZATION

In the following sentences correct any errors that you find in capitalization. Circle any lowercase letter that should be changed to a capital letter. Draw a slash (/)

through a capital letter that you wish to change to a lowercase letter. In the space provided, indicate the total number of changes you have made in each sentence. If you make no changes, write *0*. When you finish, compare your responses with those shown below. For each item on which you need review, consult the numbered principle shown in parentheses.

5   **Example:** Bill McAdams, currently Assistant Manager in our Personnel department, will be promoted to Manager of the Employee Services division.

3   (3.01)   1. The social security act, passed in 1935, established the present system of social security.

2   (3.03)   2. Our company will soon be moving its operations to the west coast.

5   (3.01, 3.05)   3. Marilyn Hunter, m.b.a., received her bachelor's degree from Ohio university in athens.

4   (3.06e, 3.12)   4. The President of Datatronics, Inc., delivered a speech entitled "Taking off into the future."

3   (3.06e, 3.06g)   5. Please ask your Aunt and your Uncle if they will come to the Attorney's office at 5 p.m.

4   (3.01, 3.07)   6. Your reservations are for flight 32 on american airlines leaving from gate 14 at 2:35 p.m.

2   (3.01)   7. Once we establish an organizing committee, arrangements can be made to rent holmby hall.

1   (3.05)   8. Bob was enrolled in history, spanish, business communications, and physical education courses.

4   (3.06e, 3.11)   9. Either the President or the Vice President of the company will make the decision about purchasing xerox copiers.

2   (3.01, 3.07)   10. Rules for hiring and firing Employees are given on page 7, line 24, of the Contract.

2   (3.02)   11. Some individuals feel that american companies do not have the sense of loyalty to their employees that japanese companies do.

2   (3.01, 3.14)   12. Where on Earth can we find better workers than Robots?

4   (3.06c 3.10, 3.13)   13. The secretary of state said, "we must protect our domestic economy from foreign competition."

4   (3.01, 3.08)   14. After crossing the sunshine skyway bridge, we drove to Southern Florida for our vacation.

6   (3.01)   15. All marketing representatives of our company will meet in the empire room of the red lion motor inn.

5   (3.01, 3.05, 3.06e)   16. Floyd Elkins, ph.d., has been named director of research for spaceage strategies, inc.

3   (3.01, 3.02, 3.11)   17. The special keyboard for the IBM Computer must contain greek symbols for Engineering equations.

3   (3.05, 3.09)   18. After she received a master's degree in electrical engineering, Joanne Dudley was hired to work in our product development department.

5   (3.01, 3.03, 3.16)   19. In the Fall our organization will move its corporate headquarters to the franklin building in downtown los angeles.

1   (3.13)   20. Dean Amador has one cardinal rule: always be punctual.

---

1. Social Security Act   3. M.B.A.   University   Athens   5. aunt   uncle   attorney's
7. Holmby Hall   9. president   vice president   Xerox   11. American   Japanese
13. Secretary   State   We   foreign   15. Empire Room   Red Lion Motor Inn
17. computer   Greek   engineering   19. fall   Franklin Building   Los Angeles

CUMULATIVE EDITING QUIZ 7

Use proofreading marks (see Appendix B) to correct errors and omissions in the following sentences. All errors must be corrected to receive credit for the sentence. Check with your instructor for the answers.

1. The Manager thinks that you attending the three day seminar is a good idea, however we must find a replacement.
2. We heard that professor watson invited edward peters, president of micropro, inc. to speak to our business law class.
3. Carla Jones a new systems programmer in our accounting department will start monday.
4. After year's of downsizing and restructuring the u.s. has now become one of the worlds most competitive producers.
5. When our company specialized in asian imports our main office was on the west coast.
6. Company's like amway discovered that there unique door to door selling methods was very successful in japan.
7. If you had given your sony camera to she or I before you got on the roller coaster it might have stayed dry.
8. Tracy recently finished a bachelors degree in accounting, consequently she is submitting many résumé's to companys across the country.
9. The Lopezs moved from San Antonio Texas to Urbana Illinois when mr lopez enrolled at the university of illinois.
10. When we open our office in montréal we will need employees whom are fluent in english and french.

NUMBER STYLE (4.01–4.13)

Usage and custom determine whether numbers are expressed in the form of figures (for example, *5, 9*) or in the form of words (for example, *five, nine*). Numbers expressed as figures are shorter and more easily understood, yet numbers expressed as words are necessary in certain instances. The following guidelines are observed in expressing numbers in written *sentences*. Numbers that appear on business forms—such as invoices, monthly statements, and purchase orders—are always expressed as figures.

4.01 General Rules

a. The numbers *one* through *ten* are generally written as words. Numbers above *ten* are written as figures:

The bank had a total of *nine* branch offices in *three* suburbs.
All *58* employees received benefits in the *three* categories shown.
A shipment of *45,000* light bulbs was sent from *two* warehouses.

b. Numbers that begin sentences are written as words. If that number involves more than two words, however, the sentence should be written so that the number does not fall at the beginning.

Fifteen different options were available in the annuity programs.
A total of *156* companies participated in the promotion (not *One hundred fifty-six companies* participated in the promotion).

4.02 Money

Sums of money $1 or greater are expressed as figures. If a sum is a whole dollar amount, omit the decimal and zeros (whether or not the amount appears in a sentence with additional fractional dollar amounts):

We budgeted *$30* for diskettes, but the actual cost was *$37.96*.
On the invoice were items for *$6.10, $8, $33.95*, and *$75*.

Sums less than $1 are written as figures that are followed by the word *cents*:

By shopping carefully, we can save *15 cents* per diskette.

4.03   Dates

In dates, numbers that appear after the name of the month are written as cardinal figures (*1, 2, 3*, etc.). Those that stand alone or appear before the name of a month are written as ordinal figures (*1st, 2d, 3d,** etc.):

The Personnel Practices Committee will meet *May 7.*

On the *5th* day of February and again on the *25th*, we placed orders.

In domestic business documents, dates generally take the following form: *January 4, 1995.* An alternative form, used primarily in military and foreign correspondence, begins with the day of the month and omits the comma: *4 January 1995.*

4.04   Clock Time

Figures are used when clock time is expressed with *a.m.* or *p.m.* Omit the colon and zeros in referring to whole hours. When exact clock time is expressed with the contraction *o'clock*, either figures or words may be used:

Mail deliveries are made at *11 a.m.* and *3:30 p.m.*

At *four* (or *4*) *o'clock* employees begin to leave.

4.05   Addresses and Telephone Numbers

a. Except for the number *one*, house numbers are expressed in figures:

540 Elm Street   17802 Washington Avenue

One Colorado Boulevard   2 Highland Street

b. Street names containing numbers *ten* or lower are written entirely as words. For street names involving numbers greater than *ten*, figures are used:

330 Third Street   3440 Seventh Avenue

6945 East 32 Avenue   4903 West 103 Street

If no compass direction (*North, South, East, West*) separates a house number from a street number, the street number is expressed in ordinal form (*-st, -d, -th*).

256 42d Street   1390 11th Avenue

c. Telephone numbers are expressed with figures. When used, the area code is placed in parentheses preceding the telephone number:

Please call us at *(818) 347-0551* to place an order.

Mr. Sims asked you to call *(619) 554-8923, Ext. 245*, after 10 a.m.

4.06   Related Numbers

Numbers are related when they refer to similar items in a category within the same reference. All related numbers should be expressed as the largest number is expressed. Thus if the largest number is greater than *ten*, all the numbers should be expressed in figures:

Only *5* of the original *25* applicants completed the processing. (Related numbers require figures.)

The *two* plans affected *34* employees working in *three* sites. (Unrelated numbers use figures and words.)

Getty Oil operated *86* rigs, of which *6* were rented. (Related numbers require figures.)

*Many writers today are using the more efficient *2d* and *3d* instead of *2nd* and *3rd.*

The company hired *three* accountants, *one* customer service representative, and *nine* sales representatives. (Related numbers under *ten* use words.)

4.07 Consecutive Numbers

When two numbers appear consecutively and both modify a following noun, readers may misread the numbers because of their closeness. The writer should (1) rewrite the expression or (2) express one number in word form and the other in figure form. Use word form for the number that may be expressed in the fewest number of words. If both numbers have an equal count, spell out the first number and place the second one in figures:

> We need *350 five-page* colored inserts. (Use word form for the number that may be expressed in the fewest words.)
>
> Please purchase *thirty 4-inch* galvanized nails for the job. (Use word form for the first number since both have an equal word count.)

4.08 Periods of Time

Periods of time are generally expressed in word form. However, figures may be used to emphasize business concepts such as discount rates, interest rates, warranty periods, credit terms, loan or contract periods, and payment terms:

> This business was incorporated over *fifty* years ago. (Use words for a period of time.)
>
> Any purchaser may cancel a contract within *72* hours. (Use figures to explain a business concept.)
>
> The warranty period is *5* years. (Use figures for a business concept.)
>
> Cash discounts are given for payment within *30* days. (Use figures for a business concept.)

4.09 Ages

Ages are generally expressed in word form unless the age appears immediately after a name or is expressed in exact years and months:

> At the age of *twenty-one*, Elizabeth inherited the business.
>
> Wanda Tharp, *37*, was named acting president.
>
> At the age of *4 years and 7 months*, the child was adopted.

4.10 Round Numbers

Round numbers are approximations. They may be expressed in word or figure form, although figure form is shorter and easier to comprehend:

> About *600* (or *six hundred*) stock options were sold.
>
> It is estimated that *1,000* (or *one thousand*) people will attend.

For ease of reading, round numbers in the millions or billions should be expressed with a combination of figures and words:

> At least *1.5 million* readers subscribe to the ten top magazines.
>
> Deposits in money market accounts totaled more than *$115 billion*.

4.11 Weights and Measurements

Weights and measurements are expressed with figures:

> The new deposit slip measures *2 by 6 inches*.
>
> Her new suitcase weighed only *2 pounds 4 ounces*.
>
> Toledo is *60 miles* from Detroit.

4.12 Fractions

Simple fractions are expressed as words. Complex fractions may be written either as figures or as a combination of figures and words:

Over *two-thirds* of the stockholders voted.

This microcomputer will execute the command in *1 millionth* of a second. (Combination of words and numbers is easier to comprehend.)

She purchased a *one-fifth* share in the business.*

4.13 Percentages and Decimals

Percentages are expressed with figures that are followed by the word *percent*. The percent sign (%) is used only on business forms or in statistical presentations:

We had hoped for a *7 percent* interest rate, but we received a loan at *8 percent*.

Over *50 percent* of the residents supported the plan.

Decimals are expressed with figures. If a decimal expression does not contain a whole number (an integer) and does not begin with a zero, a zero should be placed before the decimal point:

The actuarial charts show that *1.74* out of *1,000* people will die in any given year.

Inspector Norris found the setting to be *.005* inch off. (Decimal begins with a zero and does not require a zero before the decimal point.)

Considerable savings will accrue if the unit production cost is reduced *0.1 percent*. (A zero is placed before a decimal that neither contains a whole number nor begins with a zero).

QUICK CHART—EXPRESSION OF NUMBERS

USE WORDS	USE FIGURES
Numbers *ten* and under	Numbers *11* and over
Numbers at beginning of sentence	Money
Periods of time	Dates
Ages	Addresses and telephone numbers
Fractions	Weights and measurements
	Percentages and decimals

REVIEW EXERCISE N—NUMBER STYLE

Circle *a* or *b* to indicate the preferred number style. Assume that these numbers appear in business correspondence. When you finish, compare your responses with those shown below. For each item on which you need review, consult the numbered principle shown in parentheses.

b	*(4.01a)*	1. (a) 2 alternatives	(b) two alternatives	
a	*(4.05b)*	2. (a) Seventh Avenue	(b) 7th Avenue	
b	*(4.01a)*	3. (a) sixty sales reps	(b) 60 sales reps	
b	*(4.03)*	4. (a) November ninth	(b) November 9	
b	*(4.02)*	5. (a) forty dollars	(b) $40	
a	*(4.03)*	6. (a) on the 23d of May	(b) on the twenty-third of May	
b	*(4.04)*	7. (a) at 2:00 p.m.	(b) at 2 p.m.	
b	*(4.07)*	8. (a) 4 two-hundred-page books	(b) four 200-page books	
b	*(4.08)*	9. (a) at least 15 years ago	(b) at least fifteen years ago	
b	*(4.10)*	10. (a) 1,000,000 viewers	(b) 1 million viewers	
b	*(4.02)*	11. (a) twelve cents	(b) 12 cents	

Note: Fractions used as adjectives require hyphens.

12.	(a) a sixty-day warranty	(b) a 60-day warranty	*b*	*(4.08)*
13.	(a) ten percent interest rate	(b) 10 percent interest rate	*b*	*(4.13)*
14.	(a) 4/5 of the voters	(b) four-fifths of the voters	*b*	*(4.12)*
15.	(a) the rug measures four by six feet	(b) the rug measures 4 by 6 feet	*b*	*(4.11)*
16.	(a) about five hundred people attended	(b) about 500 people attended	*a or b*	*(4.10)*
17.	(a) at eight o'clock	(b) at 8 o'clock	*a or b*	*(4.04)*
18.	(a) located at 1 Wilshire Boulevard	(b) located at One Wilshire Boulevard	*b*	*(4.05a)*
19.	(a) three computers for twelve people	(b) three computers for 12 people	*b*	*(4.06)*
20.	(a) 4 out of every 100 licenses	(b) four out of every 100 licenses	*a*	*(4.06)*

1. b   3. b   5. b   7. b   9. b   11. b   13. b   15. b   17. a or b   19. b

CUMULATIVE EDITING QUIZ 8

Use proofreading marks (see Appendix B) to correct errors and omissions in the following sentences. All errors must be corrected to receive credit for the sentence. Check with your instructor for the answers.

1. The president spoke for over 1/2 hour before a joint session of congress.

2. Please meet at my attorneys office at four p.m. on May 10th to sign our papers of incorporation.

3. A Retail Store at 405 7th avenue had sales of over one million dollars last year.

4. Every new employee must receive their permit to park in lot 5-A or there car will be cited.

5. Mr thompson left three million dollars to be divided among his 4 children rachel, timothy, rebecca and kevin.

6. Most companys can boost profits almost one hundred percent by retaining only 5% more of there current customers.

7. Although the bill for coffee and doughnuts were only three dollars and forty cents Phillip and myself had trouble paying it.

8. Only six of the 19 employees, who filled out survey forms, would have went to hawaii as their vacation choice.

9. Danielles report is more easier to read then david because her's was better organized and had good headings.

10. At mcdonald's we devoured 4 big macs 3 orders of french fries and 5 coca colas for lunch.

Chapter 1

1. Mona Casady and F. Stanford Wayne, "Communication Skills in Employment Ads of Major United States Newspapers," *The Delta Pi Epsilon Journal*, Spring 1993, 86–99.

2. Robert Mehaffy and Constance Warloe, "Corporate Communications: Next Step for the Community Colleges," *The Technical College Teacher*, Winter 1989, 1.

3. Julie Amparano Lopez, "Firms Force Job Seekers to Jump Through Hoops," *The Wall Street Journal*, 6 October 1993, B1.

4. James C. Bennett and Robert J. Olney, "Executive Priorities for Effective Communication in an Information Society," *The Journal of Business Communication*, Spring 1986, 15.

5. J. Douglas Andrews and Normal B. Sigband, "How Effectively Does the 'New' Accountant Communicate" Perceptions by Practitioners and Academics," *The Journal of Business Communication*, Spring 1984, 20.

6. Portions of this section are adapted from Mary Ellen Guffey, *Business Communication: Process and Product* (Belmont, CA: Wadsworth, 1994), Chapter 2.

7. Endel-Jakob Kolde, *Environment of International Business*, 2nd ed. (Boston: PWS-KENT, 1985), 420–424.

8. Kathleen K. Reardon, *Where Minds Meet* (Belmont, CA: Wadsworth, 1987), 199.

9. Vivienne Luk, Mumtaz Patel, and Kathryn White, "Personal Attributes of American and Chinese Business Associates," *The Bulletin of the Association for Business Communication*, December 1990, 67.

10. Susan S. Jarvis, "Preparing Employees to Work South of the Border," *Personnel*, June 1990, 63.

11. Jane Applegate, "Don't Let a Global Deal Get Yanked," *Los Angeles Times*, 2 April 1993, D3.

12. Lennie Copeland and Lewis Griggs, *Going International* (New York: Penguin Books, 1985), 12.

13. Copeland and Griggs, *Going International*, 108.

14. Shari Caudron, "Training Ensures Success Overseas," *Personnel Journal*, December 1991, 29.

15. Robert McGarvey, "Foreign Exchange," *USAir Magazine*, June 1992, 61.

16. Jeff Copeland, "Stare Less, Listen More," *American Way*, American Air Lines, 15 December 1990, 61.

17. Nancy Rivera Brooks, "Exports Boom Softens Blow of Recession," *Los Angeles Times*, 29 May 1991, D1.

18. Roger Axtell, *Do's and Taboos Around the World*, 2nd ed. (New York: Wiley, 1990), 7.

19. Bob Weinstein, "When in Rome," *Entrepreneur*, March 1991, 70.

20. McGarvey, "Foreign Exchange," 64.

Chapter 2

1. Based on Michele L. Simpson, Sherrie L. Nist, and Kate Kirby, "Ideas in Practice: Vocabulary Strategies Designed for College Students," *Journal of Developmental Education*, November 1987, 20.

Chapter 3

1. Portions of this section are adapted from Mary Ellen Guffey, *Business Communication: Process and Product* (Belmont, CA: Wadsworth, 1994), Chapter 3.
2. Robert McGarvey, "Do the Right Thing," *Entrepreneur*, October 1992, 140.
3. Robert C. Solomon and Kristine Hanson, *It's Good Business* (New York: Atheneum, 1985).
4. Mary E. Guy, *Ethical Decision Making in Everyday Work Situations* (New York: Quorum Books, 1990), 3.
5. *Ethical Decision Making*, 3.
6. Joanne Lipman, "FTC Puts Advertisers on Notice of Crackdown on Misleading Ads," *The Wall Street Journal*, 4 February 1991, B6.
7. Jane Applegate, "Women Starting Small Businesses Twice as Fast as Men," *The Washington Post*, 2 September 1991, WB10.
8. Based on Michael Josephson's remarks reported in Alison Bell, "What Price Ethics?" *Entrepreneurial Woman*, January–February 1991, 68.
9. Diane Cole, "Ethics: Companies Crack Down on Dishonesty," *The Wall Street Journal*, Spring 1991, Managing Your Career, sec. 8.

Chapter 5

1. See, for example, Mary K. Kirtz and Diana C. Reep, "A Survey of the Frequency, Types, and Importance of Writing Tasks in Four Career Areas," *The Bulletin of the Association for Business Communication*, December 1990, 3; and Anita S. Bednar and Robert J. Olney, "Communication Needs of Recent Graduates," *The Bulletin of the Association for Business Communication*, December 1987, 22.
2. Robert Half International, as quoted in Cynthia A. Barnes, *Model Memos* (Englewood Cliffs, NJ: Prentice-Hall, 1990), 4.
3. "Your E-mail?" *PC Magazine*, August 1993, 167.

Chapter 6

1. William Safire, *New York Times Magazine*, 25 June 1989, 10–12.

Chapter 8

1. Michael Granberry, "Lingerie Chain fined $100,000 for Gift Certificates," *Los Angeles Times*, 14 November 1992, D3.

Chapter 10

1. Lauren Picker, "Job References: To Give or Not to Give," *Working Woman*, February 1991, 22.

Chapter 12

1. Portions of this section are adapted from Mary Ellen Guffey, *Business Communication: Process and Product* (Belmont, CA: Wadsworth, 1994), Chapters 11 and 12.
2. Based on Karen S. Sterkel, "Integrating Intercultural Communication and Report Writing in the Communication Class," *The Bulletin of the Association of Business Communication*, September 1988, 14–16.

Chapter 13

1. Portions of this chapter are adapted from Mary Ellen Guffey, *Business Communication: Process and Product* (Belmont, CA: Wadsworth, 1994); Chapter 16.

2. Dan Moreau, "Write a Resume That Works," *Changing Times*, June 1990, 91.

3. Quoted in Jacqueline Trace, "Teaching Resume Writing the Functional Way," *The Bulletin of the Association for Business Communication*, June 1985, 41.

4. James Bates, "Pitfalls of the Resume," *Los Angeles Times*, 16 September 1991, 18–19.

5. Marc Silver, "Selling the Perfect You," *U.S. News & World Report*, 5 February 1990, 70–72.

6. Harriet M. Augustin, "The Written Job Search: A Comparison of the Traditional and a Nontraditional Approach," *The Bulletin of the Association for Business Communication*, September 1991, 13.

7. J. Kenneth Horn, "Personnel Administrators' Reactions to Job Application Follow-up Letters Regarding Extending Interviews and Offering Jobs," The Bulletin of the Association for Business Communication, September 1991, 24.

8. Julia Lawlor, "Networking Opens More Doors to Jobs," *USA Today*, 19 November 1990, B7.

9. J. Michael Farr, *The Very Quick Job Search* (Indianapolis, IN: JIST Works, 1991), 24.

INDEX